A

BOOK

The Philip E. Lilienthal imprint
honors special books
in commemoration of a man whose work
at University of California Press from 1954 to 1979
was marked by dedication to young authors
and to high standards in the field of Asian Studies.
Friends, family, authors, and foundations have together
endowed the Lilienthal Fund, which enables UC Press
to publish under this imprint selected books
in a way that reflects the taste and judgment
of a great and beloved editor.

T0385499

The publisher gratefully acknowledges the generous support of the Asian Studies Endowment Fund of the University of California Press Foundation.

The publisher also gratefully acknowledges the generous contribution to this book provided by the Massachusetts Institute of Technology.

Eurasian

Children of Yung Kwai and Mary Burnham Yung (a–e) with children of Tong Shao-yi, in the Tong residence, Tianjin, September 1908.

Yung Kwai Papers (MS1795), Manuscripts and Archives, Yale University Library. Courtesy of Dana B. Young.

Eurasian

Mixed Identities in the United States,
China, and Hong Kong, 1842–1943

Emma Jinhua Teng

UNIVERSITY OF CALIFORNIA PRESS
Berkeley · Los Angeles · London

University of California Press, one of the most
distinguished university presses in the United States,
enriches lives around the world by advancing scholarship
in the humanities, social sciences, and natural sciences. Its
activities are supported by the UC Press Foundation and
by philanthropic contributions from individuals and
institutions. For more information, visit www.ucpress.edu.

University of California Press
Berkeley and Los Angeles, California

University of California Press, Ltd.
London, England

Library of Congress Cataloging-in-Publication Data

Eurasian : mixed identities in the United States, China,
and Hong Kong, 1842–1943 / Emma Jinhua Teng.
    pages   cm.
Includes bibliographical references and index.
ISBN 978-0-520-27626-0 (cloth : alk. paper)
ISBN 978-0-520-27627-7 (pbk. : alk. paper)
    1. Chinese Americans—Ethnic identity—History.
2. Chinese American families—Social conditions.
3. Interracial marriage—United States. 4. Chinese
Americans—China—Ethnic identity—History.
5. Chinese American families—China—Social
conditions. 6. Interracial marriage—China. 7. Chinese
Americans—China—Hong Kong—Ethnic identity—
History. 8. Chinese American families—China—Hong
Kong—Social conditions. 9. Interracial marriage—
China—Hong Kong. I. Title.
    E184.C5T46   2013
    305.8'5951013—dc23
                                    2012049224

22   21   20   19   18   17   16   15   14   13
10   9   8   7   6   5   4   3   2   1

This book is dedicated to my parents.

Contents

Illustrations

A Note on Romanization

Most Chinese words in this book have been transliterated into pinyin romanization, with the following important exceptions: personal names of individuals who commonly used Cantonese, Hokkien, or other non-Mandarin names, or are well known by names based on other romanization systems; names of businesses or associations; well-known place names, such as Hong Kong and Macao. A Chinese glossary at the back of the book provides all modern Mandarin pinyin equivalents and Chinese characters, except in the case of well-known place names. Chinese surnames precede given names, and I follow this practice except in cases where individuals adopted Western-style names.

Acknowledgments

In the long years it has taken to research and write this book, I have
accumulated many debts, large and small. I thank the following men-
tors, colleagues, and friends: Adam McKeown, Allen Chun, Alyce
Johnson, Andrea Louie, Andrew Jones, Anne McCants, Antoinette
Burton, Bob Lee, Bruno Perreau, Bryna Goodman, Caroline Fache,
Chris Gilmartin, Christina Klein, Christopher Capozzola, Christopher
Leighton, Craig Wilder, Daisy Ng, David Der-wei Wang, David
Palumbo-Liu, David Schaberg, Deborah Fitzgerald, Diana Henderson,
Donald Sutton, Dorothy Ko, Dru Gladney, Edmund Bertschinger,
Edward Baron Turk, Elizabeth Alexander, Elizabeth Garrels, Elizabeth
Sinn, Elizabeth Wood, Ellen Widmer, Evelyn Hu-DeHart, Fa-ti Fan,
Frank Dikötter, Franziska Seraphim, Gary Okihiro, Harriet Ritvo,
Heather Lee, Hilde Heynan, Hiromu Nagahara, Huang Ying-kuei, Ian
Condry, Isabelle de Courtivron, James Leibold, Jane Dunphy, Jean
Jackson, Jeff Ravel, Jeffrey Pearlin, Jia Jianfei, Jing Tsu, Jing Wang,
Joanna Levin, John Carroll, John Dower, John Kuo Wei Tchen, Jona-
than Lipman, Joshua Fogel, Judith Vichniac, Judith Zeitlin, Julian
Wheatley, Juliette Yuehtsen Chung, K. Scott Wong, Ke Ren, Kiara
Kharpertian, Kimberly DaCosta, Kornel Chang, Kristin Collins, Kym
Ragusa, Leo Ching, Leo Lee, Leo Shin, Lerna Ekmekcioglu, Leti Volpp,
Li Wai-yee, Lin Man-houng, Ling-chi Wang, Lisa See, Liu Ching-cheng,
Liu Wenpeng, Mae Ngai, Malick Ghachem, Margery Resnick, Mark
Elliott, Mary Fuller, Mary Lui, Matthew Mosca, Melissa Brown,

Melissa Dale, Melissa Nobles, Min Song, Min-Min Liang, Nayan Shah, Nicholas Tapp, Nicole Newendorp, Pamela Kyle Crossley, Pat Giersch, Patrick Hanan, Pauline Yu, Peter Bol, Peter Perdue, Peter Zarrow, Philip Khoury, Rania Huntington, Rey Chow, Robert Weller, Ronald Richardson, Sally Haslanger, Sarah Song, Sau-ling Wong, Shao Qin, Shigeru Miyagawa, Shih Shu-mei, Shirley Geok-lin Lim, Sophie Volpp, Stephanie Fan, Stephen Owen, Stephen Murphy-Shigematsu, Stevan Harrell, Steve Kaplan, Steven Masami Ropp, Tani Barlow, Thomas Levenson, Thomas Mullaney, Tim Rood, Tobie Meyer-Fong, Tong Chen, Tu Wei-ming, Tuli Banerjee, Victor Jew, Victor Mair, Vivek Bald, Wang Ayling, Wen-hui Tang, Wesley Harris, William Rowe, William Uricchio, Xiao-huang Yin, Zhang Jin, my colleagues in the Borders Research Initiative at MIT, my colleagues and friends at the Radcliffe Institute for Advanced Study, the Departments of History and Foreign Languages and Literatures at MIT, the MIT School of Humanities, Arts, and Social Sciences Dean's office, and many others. The following student research assistants helped at various stages of the project: Joa Alexander, Charles Broderick, Catherine Cheng, Amy Chou, Rebecca Deng, Em Ho, Charles Huang, Kuan-chi Lai, Jacky Lau, Yi-hang Ma, Sarah Sheppard, Katherine Tan, and Betty Zhang.

I owe a special debt of gratitude to those who shared with me their knowledge of Eurasian communities, genealogical expertise, family histories, rare sources, or images: Terese Tse Bartholomew, Dr. Bruce Chan, Geoffrey Chan, "Lily," Peter Hall, Lord Tim Clement-Jones, Frances Tse Liu, Andrew Tse, Christopher N. Wu, William F. Wu, George Yip, Dana Bruce Young, and the staff at the Eurasian Association, Singapore.

I am also especially grateful to the wonderful editors and editorial staff at the University of California Press who helped to shepherd this project through to completion—Niels Hooper, Kim Hogeland, Francisco Reinking, Jack Young, and others. Thanks also to Pam Suwinsky for her meticulous work on the manuscript and Susan Stone for her thorough work on the index.

All errors and shortcomings in this book remain my own.

I am grateful for generous assistance from the following libraries and archives: Avon Historical Society; Bancroft Library, University of California, Berkeley; Beinecke Rare Book and Manuscript Library, Yale University; Boston Public Library; the British Library; C.V. Starr East Asian Library, Columbia University; C.V. Starr East Asian Library, University of California, Berkeley; Connecticut Historical Society;

County of Los Angeles Public Library; Harvard Archives; Harvard College Library; Harvard-Yenching Library; Manuscripts and Archives, Yale University; MASC, Washington State University Libraries; Massachusetts Institute of Technology Archives; Massachusetts Institute of Technology Libraries; National Portrait Gallery, London; the National Archives, Kew, Richmond, Surrey; the National Library of China; National Central Library, Taiwan; New York Public Library; Rare Book and Manuscript Library, Columbia University in the City of New York; University of Chicago Library; Wayland Free Public Library; Weston Public Library; Wellesley College Library; Wellesley Free Library, and others. A special thanks to Michelle Baildon and Raymond Lum, and Beverly Lucas, director, Cedar Hill Cemetery Foundation.

This work was supported in part by the T.T. and Wei Fong Chao Professorship at MIT; a Frederick Burkhardt Fellowship from the American Council of Learned Societies; and by the Radcliffe Institute for Advanced Study at Harvard University. My sincere gratitude for providing me with the time, resources, and inspiration to carry out this project.

My deepest debt of appreciation is owed to my family for inspiring and supporting me through this long process. A special thanks is owed to my mother, who cared for my children while I attended conferences and traveled for research. Most of all I must thank my husband and my two loving and energetic sons.

Portions of this book were previously published as the following journal articles and are reprinted here with permission: "Eurasian Hybridity in Chinese Utopian Visions: From 'One World' to 'A Society Based on Beauty' and Beyond," in *positions: east asia cultures critiques*, Vol. 14, issue. 1, pp. 131–64. Copyright, 2006, Duke University Press. All rights reserved. Reprinted by permission; "'A Problem for Which There Is No Solution': Eurasians and the Specter of Degeneration in *New York's Chinatown,*" *Journal of Asian American Studies*, Vol. 15, Number 3 (October 2012), pp. 271–98. Copyright, 2012, The Johns Hopkins University Press. Reprinted by permission; and "On Not Looking Chinese: Does 'Mixed Race' Decenter the Han from Chineseness?" in Thomas S. Mullaney et al., eds., *Critical Han Studies: The History, Representation, and Identity of China's Majority* (Berkeley: University of California Press, 2012), 45–72. Copyright, 2012, University of California Press.

Prelude

At one point in the early 1990s, I gathered with some Taiwanese friends in a Boston coffeehouse to catch up on the latest gossip, listening with interest to a particularly titillating morsel about a successful thirty-something career woman in Taipei who had decided to become a single mother. She had flown to Los Angeles for the in vitro fertilization (IVF) procedure. While the others debated the stigma of single motherhood, I was preoccupied with this last detail. "Why fly all the way to California?" I asked in surprise. "There are excellent IVF clinics in Taipei." The group of Taiwanese women laughed at my naïveté. The reason she wanted the procedure done in the United States, they informed me, was that she wanted a "Caucasian" sperm donor. Contrary to my assumption, then, what this Chinese woman sought was not American medical science, but American genetic material. Even more surprised, I asked what had compelled her to make this unusual request. Again, the group laughed at my persistent naïveté. Because, of course, they explained, "everyone knows" Eurasian mixed bloods (hunxue'er) are beautiful and intelligent. Although I have never ascertained whether the child was born, the story has continued to haunt me.

Having spent my formative years in the United States, with its long history of anti-miscegenation laws (which were only repealed in 1967), I found that my friends' commonsense understanding of the desirability of Eurasian admixture called into question some of my fundamental presumptions concerning the racial order of things.[1] I had to wonder:

How widespread was this attitude—which I found at once liberating and disturbing—among contemporary ethnic Chinese, and what were its historical roots? How did this desire for intermixing coexist with Han Chinese chauvinism, which continues to be a powerful force in the contemporary era, even in the so-called Chinese diaspora? Being myself a child of Chinese–English intermarriage, I had long been aware of the Chinese stereotype that Eurasians are the "most beautiful" and of the popularity of the Eurasian look in the Chinese modeling and entertainment industries.[2] But could this fetishization be so powerful as to prompt people to seek out interracial genetic engineering?

I was forced to revisit the incident in the coffeehouse years later when I came across an article in the weekly magazine *Duowei zhoukan* with the provocative title, "Can Mongrelized Mixed-Bloods Really Improve the Chinese Race?"[3] Written by online pundit Shangguan Tianyi, the article was a commentary on the trend of ethnic Chinese seeking intermarriage with white Americans in order to produce genetically "superior" offspring. My reaction this time around, some ten years later, was shaped by the marked change in climate toward "hybridity" that was palpable both at home in the United States and abroad. By the turn of the new millennium, hybridity had gained cachet—as a theoretical concept, a marketing strategy, and a political issue.[4] No longer taboo: hybridity was now in vogue.

One does not have to look very far in contemporary discourse to find celebratory statements about hybridity, many focusing on "mixed-race" peoples of Asian descent. Suggesting a "Eurasian Invasion," as declared by *Time* magazine in 2001, glamorized images of mixed celebrities from L'Oreal's Asia cover girl Li Jiaxin to champion golfer Tiger Woods and singer Dennis O are ubiquitous in the media.[5] In the United States, college campuses from University of California Berkeley to MIT have established student groups for Asians of mixed heritage, while online forums dedicated to Eurasian issues have targeted virtual communities across the globe. Census 2000 for the first time allowed people to check off multiple race boxes on the census, signaling the official end of the "one-drop rule."[6] The current multiracial buzz is generally attended by much feel-good rhetoric, but it has also generated a great deal of controversy and backlash both in the West and in Asia, with some of the fiercest criticisms coming not only from racial conservatives but also from traditional civil rights organizations.[7] What is it about hybridity that has aroused such intense interest at this historical juncture?

In contemporary cultural politics, the figure of the hybrid subject operates as a metaphor for the simultaneous euphoria and anxiety surrounding the increasing cross-fertilization of cultures, languages, and capital in an age of globalization. Hybridity has even been identified by some critics as *the* characteristic condition of the postcolonial world, a world, as Ien Ang writes, "in which we no longer have the secure capacity to draw the line between us and them, between the different and the same, here and there, and indeed, between Asia and the West."[8]

Yet, as the anecdote with which I began this piece suggests, if hybridity and multiracial chic are being packaged as a new trend in the West, in Greater China this trend taps into a longstanding fetishization of Eurasians, pointing to important cultural differences in constructions of racial "mixedness" despite the global dimensions of the current buzz. Cross-cultural perspectives, however, are rarely reflected in the U.S. media, where intermarriage is currently touted as a cure-all for American racial tensions, a rhetoric memorably exemplified in a Fall 1993 special issue of *Time* that triumphantly declared on its cover—under the visage of a "mixed-race" woman—"The New Face of America: How Immigrants Are Shaping the World's First Multicultural Society."[9]

. . .

These are some of the issues that are at stake in this book, which examines mixed race in an earlier era of globalization.

Introduction

Fate brought me face to face with a remarkable woman. She had skeletons in the closet, she told me. Born in China, as a teenager Lily had come to the United States via Hong Kong. On paper she was a recent immigrant, yet in fact she had deep ancestral links to this country: like so many other Cantonese, her great-grandfather had been among the "Railroad Chinese," as she called them, who had helped to build the great American transcontinental railroad before returning to his village with tales of Gold Mountain. As a child, Lily thought often of her great-grandfather's adventures among the "foreign devils," especially when village children teased her for her freckles and her chestnut tresses that curled wildly in the summer heat.

Lily always knew that she looked different from the other village children, but she never understood why. Nor could she understand why, in the years after the family had moved to Hong Kong, Mother began to speak of her longing to return "home" to North America. Searching for answers, Lily came up against a wall of silence in her family. Finally, before his death, Lily's father opened up: her mother's grandfather, he told her, had returned from Gold Mountain with more than just stories of riches; he had brought back with him a "foreign devil" wife and a young son—Lily's grandfather.

Here at last was the answer to the unidentifiable difference that Lily had always noticed when she looked over childhood photographs and saw herself as the odd one out among her Chinese classmates. But her mother, an ardent defender of family secrets, continued to deny that the family was anything but "pure Chinese," even after their eventual move "back" to the United States. Today, Lily wonders how many other Chinese like herself are living with the hidden secrets of the past that once linked China and the West across oceans and across generations.[1]

And what of families on the other side of the Pacific? As Diana Birchall has written, her great-aunt May, the daughter of Edward Eaton and his Chinese wife, Lotus Blossom, concealed her "Chinese blood" so completely that "the knowledge was not even passed down to her own grandchildren."[2] How many others have kept their secrets by Anglicizing their names and rewriting their genealogies?

Until their stories are told, we will never know.

. . .

In the second half of the nineteenth century, trade, imperial expansion, missionary movements, global labor migration, and overseas study brought China and the United States in closer contact than ever before. Out of the cross-cultural encounters engendered by these intersecting transnational movements emerged mixed families—giving lie to the hackneyed adage that "East is East and West is West, and ne'er the twain shall meet." Some of these families formed in the United States, some in China, and countless others in the British colony of Hong Kong, a vital *entrepôt* for the China trade and a key hub in the migrant corridor between China and the United States. Yet their stories remain largely unknown. How did mixed families negotiate their identities within these diverse contexts, in societies in which monoracial identity was the norm and interracial marriage regarded with suspicion, if not outright hostility?

For years, untold numbers of interracial families hid their origins out of shame and a desire to belong. In the words of one Hong Kong Eurasian, "We were told solemnly not to disclose these family secrets to anyone."[3] As a result, their histories have been obscured. It has been only in the past decade or so, with changing attitudes toward intermixing, that such families have been able to come to terms with their origins; and some have even undertaken genealogical research to trace their unknown ancestors. Their journeys have taken them across the oceans that their forebears traversed so long ago.

This book retraces numerous journeys like these as it sets out to examine the ideas concerning racial and cultural intermixing that shaped Eurasian lived experiences in China, Hong Kong, and the United

States during an earlier age of globalization. These ideas can be grouped into two sets: the belief that amalgamation was detrimental gave rise to ideas of hybrid degeneracy and abnormality; in contrast, the belief that racial crossing was eugenic gave rise to ideas of hybrid vigor and racial improvement. The chapters of this book track the interplay of these ideas across a variety of texts on both sides of the Pacific.

Identities, as Melissa Brown has written, are "the negotiated outcome of what people claim for themselves and what people in their social environment allow them to enact."[4] Negotiated identity is the conceptual framework of my study, which examines *both* the range of determinative ideas concerning race, culture, gender, family, and nation that shaped the formation of Eurasian identities, *and* the claims set forth by individual Eurasians concerning their own identities within the contexts of their environment. To this end, while the heart of this book is a comparative examination of ideas about mixed race, I also foreground life narratives and other forms of self-representation that offer a unique window into individual perspectives on this process of negotiation. In this manner, the framework of negotiated identity moves us beyond the one-sided study of "images" or stereotypes to get at the dynamic and situational nature of social identities. Juxtaposing Eurasian lives on both sides of the Pacific, I demonstrate that mixed race is not simply an "Asian American issue," as might be supposed, but also an important topic for understanding China's "encounter with the West."

Two important dates frame this book's narrative: 1842 and 1943. The signing of the Treaty of Nanjing at the conclusion of the First Opium War (1839–42) marked the opening of China to the Western powers and the beginning of the Treaty Port era, a time of increasing foreign influence and dominance in China. With this treaty, China was forced to cede Hong Kong to Britain and to open five treaty ports to foreign trade and residence: Guangzhou (Canton), Xiamen (Amoy), Fuzhou, Ningbo, and Shanghai. In its wake followed treaties with America, France, and others demanding the same privileges of extraterritoriality as the British. Thus, the Treaty Port era is also known as the era of "unequal treaties," as treaty after treaty was forced upon China by various imperialist powers.

This was a time of American imperial expansionism, and also a time when the United States, and other settler societies like Canada and Australia, began to see an influx of Chinese immigrants. Indeed, the opening of China had a profound impact on patterns of Chinese migration, which for centuries had largely been limited to Southeast Asia. The opium trade and subsequent Opium Wars severely disrupted China's economy and society, driving many to emigrate in search of new livelihoods. With the treaty ports providing a secure base, foreigners recruited these uprooted workers to fill the growing demand for labor generated by Western imperialism and industrialism, shipping millions to far-flung destinations across the globe.[5] The onset of Chinese mass migration was thus a direct result of Western imperialism. Whether lured by the California Gold Rush (1848–55), or the promises of labor contractors seeking workers for the transcontinental railroad (1865–69), many chose America as their destination.

On ships like the *Huntress* and the *Mandarin*, in search of riches, adventure, and opportunity, Americans went East and Chinese went West. These contrapuntal movements can be viewed as interrelated migrations, both set in motion by the economic and ideological impetuses that drove American imperialism. Yet we must bear in mind that the forces of globalization that propelled these intersecting diasporas touched these two sets of travelers in very different ways.[6] The "global unevenness" of this era, as Rebecca Karl calls it, meant that the foreign communities in China became increasingly privileged and powerful after the Treaty of Nanjing, while Chinese migrants to the United States conversely experienced increasing discrimination as the century wore on.[7]

The imbalance of power was starkly evidenced by the passage of the Chinese Exclusion Act in 1882. Enacted by the U.S. Congress in response to labor agitation, Chinese exclusion barred the entry of Chinese laborers into the country for a period of ten years and prohibited the naturalization of Chinese. Although the act permitted the so-called exempt classes ("officials, teachers, students, merchants and travelers for curiosity or pleasure") to enter the United States, the insult was nonetheless felt keenly by all Chinese. After this act a series of ever-harsher laws was passed until Chinese exclusion was made permanent in 1902. Thus, the United States attempted to exclude Chinese from its shores even as it projected its economic and cultural power into China.

The increasing cultural contact between China and the West during this era generated new fears and hopes surrounding transcultural flows and interracial encounters. Against this backdrop, East–West intermarriage and so-called amalgamation became vital issues for both Chinese and Americans. Despite their locations within very different national contexts, commentators on both sides of the Pacific took up the subject of Euro-Asian interracialism and used the figure of the Eurasian in various ways as a metaphor to condense the cultural anxieties and desires produced by East–West encounters. At times, Eurasians were portrayed as a "problem," portending racial extinction, the decline of civilization, or social unrest. At other times, Eurasians were hailed as the embodiment of the *best of both worlds*, as harbingers of international peace or a cosmopolitan future. The different contexts that shaped diverse representations of Eurasians as "problem" or "promise" are examined in the chapters of this work. What we learn is that negotiating Eurasian identities meant navigating a minefield of contradictions between prejudice and privilege.

1943 marked the end of the era of unequal treaties and also saw the repeal of the Chinese Exclusion Act, as China became an important ally to the United States in World War II.[8] It is this doubly symbolic date that I have chosen as the endpoint of my narrative, the closure of this particular chapter of Chinese–Western interracialism. World War II, which ushered in new racial ideologies across the globe, and further gave rise to new patterns of interracialism and a new generation of "Amerasians," began a new chapter with dramatically different outlines than the one told in this book.[9] Thus, 1842 and 1943 bookend this study.

Framing Eurasian interracialism within the contrapuntal movements of American imperialism and Chinese migration, I focus on the three sites of China, Hong Kong, and the United States.[10] I include the British colony of Hong Kong because of its historical importance as a hub of East–West contact, and also because of the significant population of Eurasians who resided in the colony prior to World War II. Hong Kong enables us to ask how, and under what circumstances, Eurasians were able to define themselves as a distinct communal group. I argue that particular features of its colonial society promoted the institutionalization of a Eurasian identity, separate from Chinese and European, in ways that were not available in the United States, nor, to the same degree, in China. I thus compare the very different meanings of being Eurasian in these three sites, which varied across time and place, and also according to gender and class status.

INVISIBLE FROM HISTORY: EURASIANS IN CHINA, HONG KONG, AND AMERICA

I should make clear from the start that some of the individuals described in this book did not consider themselves Eurasian, and some actively disliked the name. Nonetheless, among the various choices available, I have selected "Eurasian" as the best (though not perfect) umbrella term for my comparative purposes. *Eurasian* was coined in British colonial India in the early nineteenth century as a euphemistic phrase to replace derogatory labels such as "half-caste." In India, the term designated only the children of European fathers and Asian mothers. The label soon spread to other parts of the British Empire and beyond, including to North America and China. As the word moved, its meaning changed. Hence, in China and North America, *Eurasian* might refer to children of European mothers and Asian fathers. Moreover, whereas *Eurasian* acquired disparaging overtones in India, elsewhere it continued to be used by some Eurasians themselves as an acceptable label.[11] Indeed, dictionary definitions are perhaps less useful than a more concrete understanding of the historical circumstances in which mixed families came into being.

. . .

> When James Bridges Endicott (1814–70) went out to China in 1842 as an officer of the American ship the *Mandarin*, one of the first things the opium trader did was to purchase for himself in Canton a young woman named Ng Akew (ca. 1820–1914). In time, she would bear him five children. When Endicott later married Miss Ann Russell of London in 1852, he took James Jr., Henry, and Sarah away to America, leaving a son and daughter behind with their mother.[12] Akew never saw the three children again.

Such were the beginnings of many Eurasians on the China Coast. Of course the existence of a "mixed" population of European and Chinese ancestry certainly predated the Treaty Port era, dating back at least to the arrival of the Portuguese in China in the sixteenth century.[13] As ever greater numbers of Europeans and Americans went out to China and Hong Kong during the Treaty Port era, so the numbers of mixed children grew.[14] Their origins can be traced to several distinct phenomena. First, there were the children born to Chinese mothers and foreign merchants, consuls, sailors, and other male sojourners on the China Coast. Many of these children were born from "temporary alliances" like Endicott's.[15] Second were the children of Western missionaries (male or female) who married Chinese Christian converts. A third phenomenon was that of Chinese migrants (students, diplomats, merchants, and laborers) who married Western women overseas and brought their families back to China. Sometimes, Chinese migrants stayed abroad but sent their Eurasian sons back to China for education. Finally, there were the mixed populations on the borders with Russia. The flood of White Russian refugees into China after the Russian Revolution led to dramatic increases in the population of Sino-Russian children in places like Harbin. Eurasians could also be located across the spectrum of class privilege, as we will see, with many abandoned to poverty and misery but others rising up the ladder to become fabulously wealthy and prominent.

By the late Qing, interracial families were increasingly common in Shanghai, Canton, Hankou, Tianjin, Beijing, and other large cities.[16] Although more numerous in the cities, such families could also be found in the villages of emigrant-sending communities in South China, as return migrants brought overseas families home with them. Eurasians were particularly visible in the British colony of Hong Kong. Unfortunately, they were never well documented in censuses, and we lack reliable figures concerning their numbers (see chapter 8).[17] Nonetheless, by 1860, growing concern over the "Eurasian problem" in Hong Kong led to the founding of the Diocesan Native Female Training School as an institution for educating Eurasian pupils, many of whom were orphaned. Similar worries over the expanding population of mixed-race children drove the Anglo-American expatriate community in Shanghai to found a Eurasian School in 1870.

. . .

When pioneering Chinese American journalist Wong Chin Foo (b. 1851) toured New York's Chinatown in 1888 he estimated that there were over one hundred "half-breed" children, as he called them, "born of white mothers and Mongolian fathers," mostly Chinese merchants. These children, he thought, represented a new generation that was Chinese by descent, but American in their ways and customs.

In the United States, Sino-American mixed families mainly arose from two distinct phenomena: Chinese migration to the United States (predominantly male), and the return migration of American men who married Chinese or Eurasian women in Asia. American men who established interracial families overseas tended not to bring their "protected women" home, although some sent their children back to the United States. Thus, in a reversal of the situation on the China Coast, in North America most Eurasians were born to Chinese fathers—sailors, laborers, merchants, students, and others—and not Chinese mothers, a significant difference in an era when personal status and citizenship laws gave different weight to maternal and paternal inheritance, as we will see in the chapters to come.[18]

Historians have demonstrated that mixed families formed virtually from the first arrival of Chinese sailors on American shores. In New

York, where Chinese began to arrive decades before the California Gold Rush, many Chinese men married Irish and other European immigrant women.[19] By 1900, an astonishing 60 percent of all marriages in New York's Chinatown were between Chinese men and European or Euro-American women.[20] Such partnering was not confined to New York, and mixed families existed across the nation, wherever Chinese settled, from Boston, to Chicago, San Francisco, and Los Angeles. Intermarriage was most common in Hawaii (annexed by the United States in 1898), where attitudes toward racial intermixing were considerably more tolerant.[21]

Indeed, owing to the fact that Chinese female immigration to the United States was tightly restricted between 1875 and 1945, Chinese male migrants who wished to form American families often had little choice but to look beyond their own ethnic group, especially during the early years. Even Tom Lee, the infamous "mayor" of New York's Chinatown between the 1870s and 1890s, had a German American wife.[22] As a result, the first generation of children born into the emergent Chinese immigrant communities was largely mixed.[23]

Yet, these mixed-race individuals have often been rendered invisible in the master narratives of history, whether national histories (Chinese, American) or ethnic histories (Chinese American). The reasons for this erasure are multifaceted. First, Eurasians have always constituted a very small numerical minority—with Macao being a notable exception. Second, Eurasians disrupt boundaries of colonizer and colonized, white and nonwhite, rendering them problematic figures in accepted paradigms of nationalist and ethnic histories. In Asian American historiography, for instance, normative presumptions of monoracial identity have, until very recently, contributed to their invisibility. Such presumptions are evident, for example, in an authoritative textbook account of the development of a second generation of Asian Americans: "Though second generation Asian Americans date back to the early 1850s, they composed a very small subpopulation until the 1920s. Children were few in number because very few Asian women came."[24] The premise of this statement is that Asian American children are produced by Asian fathers and Asian mothers: the "normal" family is single race. Finally, the histories of mixed families have been obscured through shame and silencing. As Anglo-Indian writer Peter Moss has lamented in a parallel context: "Why was it so hard to trace our descent or track down our history? Why was so much of who we were, what we had done, vanished beyond recall? Because we had been taught to live with shame."[25]

BEYOND THE "TRAGIC MULATTO": PREJUDICE AND PRIVILEGE

If Eurasians have been subjected to historical erasure, it is a central premise of this book that these so-called mixed-race figures, in disrupting the taken-for-granted boundaries between white and yellow, West and East, call attention to the instability of these very categories themselves. That such categories have always been in flux, shaped by historical and geographic context, makes evident that race is fundamentally a social identity and not simply a matter of biological descent. Taking stock of the long history of mixed race thus offers us a new way to imagine the politics of race beyond the essentialist and static models promoted by ethnic nationalism.

This book further seeks to complicate the commonplace understanding of "half-castes" as tragic figures who were "despised by both sides." I challenge this colonial-era truism by demonstrating that *privilege*, in addition to *prejudice*—depending on time and place, on class status, and cultural capital—shaped Eurasian lived experiences on both sides of the Pacific. Eurasian social experiences did not conform to a single pattern but were deeply inflected by geographic location, by gender, and by class.[26] Thus, I examine a range of Eurasian lives, from Hong Kong's rags-to-riches millionaire Sir Robert Ho Tung to New York's infamous pickpocket George Appo, and many in between. I demonstrate how Eurasians were detested but also admired, marginalized but also indispensable. Unfortunately, due to the limitations of sources, this book gives more space to the stories of literate, and necessarily more privileged, Eurasians, while lamenting the fact that the stories of the Eurasian underclass have for the most part been lost forever.

Eurasians were despised and feared, for in blurring the color line they radically destabilized the racial hierarchies of the era, threatening the social and political orders. In colonial contexts, mixed-race peoples jeopardized what Emmanuelle Saada has called "efforts by the colonizers to maintain the 'proper distance' from the colonized."[27] As Ann Stoler has written of race mixing in colonial Southeast Asia: "Conceived as a dangerous source of subversion, [racial mixing] was seen as a threat to white prestige, an embodiment of European degeneration and moral decay."[28]

Yet, Eurasians were not only viewed as a threat, for they also served to *stabilize* imperialist interests by *bridging* the distance and serving vital intermediary functions: as compradores in Hong Kong and the treaty ports; as officials of the Chinese Imperial Customs Service; and as interpreters for the U.S. Customs Bureau (the body charged with enforcing Chinese exclusion). The contradictions between prejudice and privilege are starkly evident in the fact that Western firms in Hong Kong and China paid Eurasian employees higher wages than Chinese, thus reinforcing imperial prestige by signaling that whiteness (even partial whiteness) elevated one above native status, though never to the level of "pure" Europeans. With such connections to white privilege, Eurasians were envied, but also resented and despised by Chinese as colonial collaborators.[29]

Thus, an important framework that structures my analysis derives from theoretical insights developed by Ann Stoler in her work on race mixing in colonial Southeast Asia.[30] As Stoler argues, one of the key "tensions of empire" manifested in various colonial contexts was the tension between discourses of inclusion, on one hand, and exclusionary, discriminatory practices on the other. "Nowhere," Stoler asserts, was the "relationship between inclusionary impulses and exclusionary practices more evident" than in the legal handling of mixed race, which she examined in French Indochina and the Dutch East Indies.[31] Although my study deals with very different contexts, analogous tensions arose as Chinese Eurasians were alternately subjected to discourses of exclusion and discourses of inclusion, depending on time and place. The chapters of this book seek to elucidate how Chinese Eurasians negotiated their identities between prejudice and privilege, inclusion and exclusion, moving us beyond the stereotype of the "tragic mulatto" or "hostage to the East."

STUDYING "MIXED RACE"

In using negotiated identity as a framework for studying mixed race, my approach both builds on and departs from the long history of the study of racial intermixing, which has shifted its focus and approach significantly over time. In the second half of the nineteenth century, racial hybridity became a major preoccupation of Western racial theorists.[32] Predominantly working in anthropology and natural sciences, scholars focused attention on the physical and mental characteristics of so-called human hybrids.[33] Based on various claims, they advanced a range of theories, generally propounding the detrimental effects of racial amalgamation. A vocal minority supported the thesis of hybrid vigor, with some suggesting that racial crossing in the colonies could produce new races more suitably acclimatized to the tropics than Europeans. Hence, race mixing was alternately constituted as a "problem" or as a "solution."

In the early twentieth century, sociological approaches to race relations, which eschewed biological explanations and treated mixed race as a social phenomenon, came into importance, though research efforts in physical anthropology, genetics, and tropical medicine continued. The influence of sociological models of mixed race was heightened through the connections of sociologists with American and British policymakers during the interwar years.[34] Sociology was similarly influential in Republican-era China (1912–49). The sociological literature was again split, with one camp emphasizing hybrid pathology, and the other propagating notions of so-called mulatto superiority.

A third significant approach emerged in the 1990s, connected to "multiracial" or "mixed-race" social movements. The new mixed-race studies aims to interrogate dominant constructs of race and monoracialism, while also reclaiming the histories of mixed-race peoples. One feature distinguishing the new mixed-race studies is that the majority of practitioners are scholars who self-identify as mixed themselves. In addition, whereas scientists and sociologists of the earlier eras frequently emphasized the dangers of miscegenation, mixed-race studies tends to adopt a celebratory approach, often portraying hybridity as the key to a postracial future.

While similarly celebrating the changes in racial ideology and public opinion that have allowed mixed families and their descendants to break down the wall of silence and openly acknowledge their multiple heritages, this book also cautions against an oversimplified understanding of the past upon which much of the current discourse is founded. In Routledge's popular *"Mixed-Race" Studies: A Reader*, for example, editor Jayne Ifekwunigwe lays out three "ages" in the study of mixed race: the age of pathology (nineteenth century through the 1980s), the age of celebration (1990s), and the age of critique (turn of the twenty-first century).[35] One of my aims is to complicate this intellectual genealogy by offering an alternate picture of discourses on mixed race.[36] I contend that the span of time from 1800 through the 1980s cannot simply be dismissed as an "age of pathology," for there was active debate concerning the outcome of racial and cultural hybridity. The diversity of opinion is especially apparent when we turn our attention away from Anglo-American discourses and consider a broader spectrum of ideas, from Latin America, for example, or East Asia, as in this case. Cross-cultural comparison reveals that discourses from the past were not only concerned with safeguarding racial purity, but also with considering hybridity's potential for racial improvement or regeneration.

Thus, this book takes up the question of how Chinese intellectuals of the late nineteenth and early twentieth centuries came to view Sino–Western intermixing as a eugenic vehicle for improving the Chinese race. I argue that the selective idealization of the Eurasian as a particular type of "mix" reveals an important facet of the construction of "Chineseness." As Prasenjit Duara has demonstrated, the notion of an East–West binary is integral to the master narrative of modern Chinese nationalism, a narrative founded in large part on the idea of resistance to Western imperialism. In terms of this binary, Chinese racial identity is defined by its difference from the West, which is portrayed as aggressive, materialistic, and devoid of true cultural values.[37] My reading of discourses of Eurasian hybridity elucidates a lesser-known part of the story: how the modern Chinese construction of the "Chinese race" depends not only on a binary opposition between Chinese and Western, but also on the notion of racial proximity between the two relative to the so-called darker races.[38] I thus argue that modern Chinese identity formation is structured at once around the notion of "not-white," and the notion of "like-white," an ambivalent condition embodied in the figure of the Eurasian.

In tracing this genealogy of the idealization of Eurasians, I do not wish to reinforce the idea of Eurasian exceptionalism but rather to problematize what I regard as overly general constructs of hybridity that are often invoked in postcolonial and multiracial discourses. I thus argue that we must attend to how *particular* forms of hybridity are constructed within specific cultural and/or historical contexts, rather than constituting hybridity as a universal or undifferentiated condition.

"MIXED RACE" IN CROSS-CULTURAL CONTEXTS

My work builds directly on the pioneering research of John Kuo Wei Tchen on Chinese–Irish intermarriage in New York, as well as the more recent work of Mary Lui and Henry Yu on Chinese–white interracialism in the United States. I have also been inspired by Nayan Shah to treat interracial intimacy beyond the nuclear family households and the "setting down roots" narrative privileged in immigration and national histories, and by many others.[39] The literature in Asian American studies is part of a broader development in the study of interracial relations beyond black and white, the predominant focus for many decades. A recent work that has been widely recognized in this regard is Peggy

Pascoe's *What Comes Naturally: Miscegenation Law and the Making of Race in America,* a history of American anti-miscegenation law from the Reconstruction era through the landmark *Loving v. Virginia* case of 1967.[40] This book expands the scope of our understanding of miscegenation laws in the United States by tracing the history of such laws in regions beyond the South, and their impact on multiple racial groups, including Asians, Native Americans, and Hispanics in addition to African Americans and whites. In doing so, Pascoe shows us the wider web of interracial relations implicated in the making of race in American history.

Building on this scholarship, I seek to expand the scope of comparative inquiry beyond North America by examining Chinese–Western interracialism on both sides of the Pacific. Through a multisited account of mixed families I call into question contemporary presumptions concerning the United States as a privileged, or exceptional, site of hybrid identities.

This book also differs from Pascoe's study in two crucial respects. Pascoe makes an important contribution to the ethnic studies literature that has drawn our attention to the important role of anti-miscegenation laws historically in racializing Asian immigrants as nonwhites and enforcing their segregation and subordination. While similarly emphasizing this history, I argue that there is another story to tell as well: a story that includes such exclusionary practices, but also inclusive discourses and assimilationist impulses that complicated the picture. How did the claims that miscegenation was "unnatural" coexist in tension with suggestions that racial crossing might have eugenic effects? In addition, I differ from Pascoe in expanding beyond anti-miscegenation laws and interracial unions to consider the implications for the next generation: that is, for mixed-race people themselves.

Recent years have also witnessed a surge in historical scholarship on European–Asian intermixing in the context of colonialism. Whereas the bulk of this literature has focused on South and Southeast Asia, my work contributes to the study of mixed race in the rather different contexts of China and Hong Kong. While drawing inspiration from the colonial studies literature, for example, Ann Stoler's work as cited previously, my work differs in that my central focus is not an analysis of the colonizer–colonized relationship, per se. Rather, this study attempts to broaden the analytical focus of mixed-race studies by examining Chinese–Western interracialism across geographic spaces that are delimited neither by national nor by imperial boundaries. In further contrast to colonial studies, which has primarily analyzed European and/or American racial concepts and categories, my study also examines Chinese racial thought. Tracking the movement, circulation, and reception of ideas concerning mixed race on two sides of the Pacific, I demonstrate how such ideas served competing interests within different national and/or imperialist projects. In short, this book is written neither as part of a national history (U.S. or Chinese), nor as part of a national colonial history.

Another point of difference derives from perspective: whereas colonial studies has predominantly focused on the perspectives of colonizers and on colonial anxieties concerning the boundary between rulers and ruled, this book also considers the voices and perspectives of Eurasians themselves. In this regard, my work is in dialogue with recent scholarship by Emmanuelle Saada on the "métis question" in the French Empire, and by Durba Ghosh on mixed families in colonial India, even as I further foreground Eurasian perspectives through the use of memoirs and other works of self-representation.[41] Moreover, I consider mixed identities not only in relation to whiteness, but I also examine how Eurasians attempted to assert claims to Chineseness. Thus, *passing* in this book does not simply mean "passing for white"; as we saw from the story of Lily that opened this chapter, it may also mean "passing for Chinese."

Studying race comparatively can yield insights by denaturalizing our everyday assumptions concerning the nature of race and racial classification. Until recent years, many Americans have taken for granted the notion of a "one-drop rule," which meant that mixed-race peoples with even a small fraction of nonwhite "blood" could not be considered white.[42] Based on the convention of hypodescent (the classification of mixed-race individuals following the racial identity of the parent with lower racial status), the one-drop rule was an extreme extension of blood quantum rules used to determine white and nonwhite status. Although not in fact widely codified until the 1910s and 1920s, as Daniel Sharfstein argues, many have presumed the one-drop rule has been "the American regime of race."[43] The continuing legacy of this idea today is evident in that President Barack Obama is commonly referred to as "black," or "biracial," but rarely as "white."

Like Sharfstein, I demonstrate that the history of the color line was in reality more complex than presumed, and I further highlight the arbitrary nature of the one-drop rule by juxtaposition with Chinese principles of classification, which ignored blood quantum and assigned identity based on paternal descent. When China promulgated its first nationality law in 1909, it institutionalized the privileging of paternal descent by granting Chinese nationality to children born to Chinese fathers and foreign mothers, but not (marital) children born to Chinese mothers and foreign fathers.[44] The reliance on paternal descent meant that Chinese conceptions of we-group identity, especially prior to the 1911 revolution, did not give much weight to the notion of blood "purity" or blood quantum. As Patricia Ebrey has argued for earlier eras of Chinese history, "The issue was origins, not purity; emphasis was not on keeping others out, but on knowing who you were and how you were connected to others."[45]

In contrast, as Ian Haney López and others have demonstrated, from the late nineteenth century through the first half of the twentieth, American courts defined the parameters of whiteness through a process of negation, by systematically defining the groups who were "nonwhite": in short, by "keeping others out."[46] Whiteness thereby came to be predicated on a notional purity evidenced through the *absence* of nonwhite blood, leading to a proliferation of blood quantum rulings and racial prerequisite cases between 1878 and 1952.

The desire to keep others out also informed British colonial practices in Hong Kong, though blood quantum was never codified in the American way (some colonial officials suggested it *ought* to be).[47] Thus, while the British followed the English common law tradition of assigning children the status of the father, they nonetheless systematically distinguished Eurasians from those of "pure European descent" through World War II and its immediate aftermath.[48] This led to numerous contradictions that are explored further in chapter 8.

A related question that I take up is the role of phenotype. Whereas a "touch of the tar brush" constrained Eurasians in claiming whiteness in Anglo-American society (pushing some Eurasians to extreme measures to pass), especially after the ascendancy of the one-drop rule, I contend that in the Chinese case phenotype was relatively less important than claims of patrilineal descent, the possession of Chinese "blood" (again, without reference to blood quantum), and cultural practices in asserting one's Chineseness. Based on my reading of Eurasian life narratives and other sources, I argue that race as phenotype was outweighed by the notion of race as lineage, or, during the revolutionary era, by race as nation—though phenotype does retain some importance.[49] In other words, although individuals with a visibly mixed phenotype undoubtedly experienced prejudice among Chinese, in comparison to contemporaneous

Anglo-American conceptions of race, the body was of less importance as a primary site for demarcating group membership.[50]

TRAVELING BETWEEN CHINA STUDIES AND CHINESE AMERICAN STUDIES

Bridging China studies and Chinese American studies is not always an easy task, because these fields differ dramatically in their histories and perspectives. Let us take Yung Wing (1828–1912) as an example: the first Chinese student to graduate from an American university, Yung Wing is celebrated in China today as the "Father of Overseas Students," a loyal patriot who never forgot his homeland. In sharp contrast, Yung Wing is hailed in Chinese American studies as a pioneer, an early immigrant who took U.S. nationality, married an American woman, and made Connecticut his home. Sojourner or settler, which?

Analyzing this conflict of paradigms, Adam McKeown has demonstrated the advantages of a transnational perspective over nation-based approaches for the study of migration.[51] A transnational approach proves particularly fruitful for this study since many of the figures whom I discuss lived and worked between China and America. Their writings, furthermore, were published in both countries. Labels such as "Chinese," "Chinese American," and "Hong Kong Chinese" do not adequately describe the geographic mobility and fluid identities of many of those whose lives I analyze.[52]

By traveling between Chinese and Chinese American studies, examining lives that were produced in the intersections of diasporas, I seek to contribute to the dialogue concerning the changing meanings of "Chineseness" in a globalizing world. I argue that by analyzing the borders of Chineseness, in this case through mixed race, we can learn much about the ever-evolving meanings of "being Chinese."[53]

THE DISPUTED MEANINGS OF BEING CHINESE

"What do you mean you feel Chinese in your heart? You don't look Chinese."

Lisa See, "The Funeral Banquet," 1998

In an essay on biracial and bicultural identity, best-selling author Lisa See (b. 1955) recounts this reaction from readers of her epic, *On Gold Mountain: The One-Hundred-Year Odyssey of My Chinese-American Family*.[54] With her red hair and freckles, it is perhaps not surprising that

See frequently encounters this reaction from both Chinese and non-Chinese observers alike. Yet, such a charge—"You don't look Chinese"—deserves to be interrogated, for it can only be understood given an a priori assumption of who is Chinese and who is not. What does it mean to be Chinese? And who defines it?[55]

A great deal has been said on the issue of defining Chineseness in the years since the publication of Tu Wei-ming's seminal edited collection, *The Living Tree: The Changing Meaning of Being Chinese Today,* and yet the question of what constitutes Chinese identity still remains a vital field of contention.[56] In conferences, classrooms, and on the Internet, people continue to ponder the question of whether Chineseness is primarily a matter of race (biology) or of culture (behavior), and whether one can be authentically Chinese if one lives overseas.

One approach to defining group membership is exemplified in the mission statement of the global web-based organization Huaren.org: "Huaren [ethnic Chinese] are people of Chinese origin by birth, descent and heritage inside and outside China."[57] This is a notably primordialist vision of Chinese identity—one that emphasizes origins, descent, and putative shared ancestry. These primordialist ties serve to produce an imagined global community of ethnic Chinese, linked by little else except "blood," and displaying remarkable cultural diversity. Huaren outside of China, it is explained, may not use Chinese names, may not know the Chinese language, and may be citizens of other nations. "Furthermore, ethnic Chinese do not share a common religion, we do not practice a prescribed set of customs or culture, and we certainly do not subscribe to any given set of political ideology."[58] In the absence of common culture, language, territory, political loyalty, and even names, the belief in common descent assumes primary importance here in defining Chinese identity.

A somewhat different perspective is offered by Lisa See's meditations on her own experiences grappling with Chinese identity. As See wrote in *On Gold Mountain,* the story of her great-grandfather Fong See and the generations of his Eurasian descendants: "Though I don't physically look Chinese . . . I am Chinese in my heart."[59] The complex implications of this statement are further explored by See in "The Funeral Banquet," an essay on the Chinatown funeral banquet of her grandmother Stella, a Euro-American woman who had "become Chinese" by marrying into the See family. In these works, See explains that she considers herself Chinese not by phenotype, but by cultural heritage, and in her "being."[60] For See, this sense of identity has been constructed "from the outside in," just as it was for Stella, shaped through her experiences growing up in a large, old-time Los Angeles Chinatown family, by years of eating the food, learning the traditions, hearing the stories of her forebears, attending weddings and funerals, practicing respect and honor for her elders, and by mastering the complex rules of Chinese kinship relations.[61] Chineseness, then, is not a given of inheritance; it is not defined by genetics and phenotype, but by everyday practice. It is a matter of "heart" and not "blood."[62]

One might well ask if we can we really reduce Chineseness to a matter of either biological descent or of culture alone, as these examples might have us believe. And if it is a matter of descent, does blood quantum matter? (one-half? one-quarter? one-eighth? one drop?) Was Princess Der Ling, the daughter of Qing diplomat Yu Geng and his Eurasian wife Louisa Pierson, "more Chinese" than her "half-Chinese" mother? Or was she "less Chinese" because of the Parisian influences she embraced as a young girl in France, where she scandalously studied dance with Isadora Duncan?[63] And what do we make of Lisa See, "one-eighth Chinese" by blood quantum, who proclaims herself Chinese in her heart? The question of so-called mixed-blood Chinese brings these issues to the fore as it challenges the boundaries of what we consider Chineseness. Mixed race further forces us to consider whether the dichotomy between "descent" and "consent"—to borrow from Werner Sollors—is even a productive way of thinking about identities.[64]

This is a particularly important moment for thinking about Chinese diasporic identities in relation to mixed race. Current demographic developments and the growth of mixed-race social movements have made the subject of Eurasian interracialism especially germane. According to a report issued by the Pew Research Center in 2012, American public attitudes toward intermarriage have changed dramatically since the landmark case of *Loving v. Virginia* in 1967, which struck down the last of the anti-miscegenation laws. The Pew survey found that 43 percent of Americans agree that the increase in interracial marriage has been a change for the better. The report further shows that rates of intermarriage have more than doubled since 1980 (from 6.7 percent to 15 percent).[65] U.S. population data for 2010 indicate that the intermarriage rate is significantly higher for Asians (approximately 28 percent of newlyweds), when compared against both whites (9 percent) and blacks (17 percent).[66] Already the numbers of Asian Americans who identify as more than one race have dramatically increased: between 2000 and 2010, this figure grew from 1,655,830 to 2,646,604. According to the

2010 census, 15.3 percent of Asians (or 2.6 million) in the United States identify as multiracial, constituting nearly one-third of the self-identified multiracial population (9 million total).[67] In China, as well, interracial relationships have grown increasingly common since the country's liberalization and opening in the 1980s, giving rise to contentious debates over Chinese identity and multiracialism.[68]

STRUCTURE OF THE BOOK

The chapters of this book are divided into three parts. Part I examines debates concerning Chinese–Western intermarriage in the United States and China. Aiming to debunk the truism that intermarriage was "never accepted by either side," I analyze competing voices, arguing *for* as well as *against* Chinese–Western intermarriage, and the tensions between inclusive and exclusionary discourses within each society. Chapter 1 provides a thematic overview of discourses and counter-discourses on Chinese–Western intermarriage as they evolved in both countries between the 1850s and 1910s. Probing how the dynamics of Sino-American intermarriage changed after 1907, when the U.S. Congress passed the Marital Expatriation Act, chapter 2 considers the problematic of gender and dependent citizenship through the case of an American woman who married a Chinese student and followed him to China, a form of marital migration that touched off debate on both sides of the Pacific.

The three chapters of part II analyze diverse discourses—scientific and nonscientific—regarding the offspring of such unions, showing how the figure of the Eurasian was treated at times as a social or national "problem," and at other times as a "promise," heralding a utopian future of international and interracial harmony. Chapter 3 examines nineteenth-century American discourses on hybrid degeneracy and journalistic representations of the "half-breed" in relation to the Chinese Question. Chapter 4 shifts from theories of hybrid degeneracy to hybrid vigor, analyzing the idealization of the Eurasian in the eugenic theories of late nineteenth- and early twentieth-century Chinese thinkers. Chapter 5 considers the early twentieth-century turn from biological to sociological discourses on mixed race, comparing the work of Chinese and American sociologists who researched the transnational phenomenon of Sino-American miscegenation. Together these three chapters question whether the era from the nineteenth century to the 1990s can truly be considered a monolithic "age of pathology," or whether competing notions of mixed race, evolving over time, should also factor in our understandings of the past.

Part III turns from considering the Eurasian as an *object* of discourse to considering Eurasians as *producers* of life narrative and other works of self-representation. Through an examination of works produced by Eurasians born during this era, I demonstrate how individuals attempted to negotiate their own identities in the face of dominant understandings of mixed race and competing discourses of exclusion and inclusion. Each chapter of part 3 takes up a central question that has been posed in the fields of Asian American studies, China studies, and mixed-race studies, respectively. Chapter 6 uses the works of Edith Eaton (a.k.a. Sui Sin Far) and others to examine specific examples of how individual Chinese Eurasians in North America navigated the color line and the strictures of Chinese Exclusion. Whereas the analysis of majority–minority dynamics has been central to Asian American studies, this chapter asks how mixed race destabilizes this binary, and further questions whether the monoracialist impulses of both the majority and minority communities left Chinese Eurasians during this era, as Paul Spickard contends, "with no place to be."[69] Chapter 7 uses mixed race to gain a new perspective on ongoing debates in China studies concerning Chinese identity and the tension between culturalist and racialist conceptions of Chineseness. Focusing on Irene Cheng and Han Suyin, this chapter considers the life narratives of Chinese-identified Eurasians in Hong Kong and China, examining the varied grounds—through descent and consent—on which they claimed Chineseness. Chapter 8 takes up the question of whether mixed-race subjects really challenge or deconstruct race, or simply reconfigure racial formations along different lines through the constitution of new "mixed" identities.[70] Through a reading of Charles Graham Anderson's manifesto for Eurasian unity, this chapter uses the founding of a Eurasian Welfare League in interwar Hong Kong to demonstrate how an ethnic shift among the colony's mixed-race population enabled the emergence of a distinct Eurasian communal identity that was neither Chinese nor European.

The coda picks up the story of descendants of the early mixed marriages discussed in this book. I end by considering how changing attitudes toward mixed race have allowed the descendants of these pioneering mixed families to reclaim their dual heritages and to pursue various projects of collective memory.

Finally, the epilogue briefly considers how the stories and ideas examined in this book help us to reflect upon the present moment.

I argue that the contemporary fascination with mixed-race icons as the best of both worlds, who can bridge racial and cultural divides, represents not simply a disavowal of a racist past in which miscegenation was taboo, but also in some respects replicates, whether consciously or unconsciously, earlier discourses of hybrid vigor and exceptionalism. Hence, despite the dramatic changes discussed in the coda, I contend that it is nonetheless worth paying attention to the historical stemma of these contemporary images, and the continuing entanglements of biology and culture.

PART ONE

Debating Intermarriage

Prologue to Chapter 1

THE REVEREND BROWN TAKES ELIZABETH
BARTLETT ABOARD THE *MORRISON*

The Reverend Samuel Robbins Brown (1810–80) was in a hurry to set sail. Seven days after his marriage to Elizabeth Goodwin Bartlett, the Yale graduate and newly ordained missionary took his bride aboard the *Morrison*, ready to voyage halfway across the globe. The Reverend Brown was to take up a calling at the Morrison School in China, and the newlyweds had been sent off with fanfare from their hometown of East Windsor, Connecticut. They were set to sail with free passage on the *Morrison*, for the ship belonged to the Olyphant brothers, prominent figures in the tea trade and leading backers of the Morrison Educational Society.

It was October 17, 1838, when the Browns sailed from New York, and with favorable winds and Providence on their side they rounded the Cape of Good Hope and reached Macao on February 18, 1839. Brown had to smuggle his wife secretly into the country, because foreign women were banned from landing in China.[1] Once settled in Macao, Brown was placed in charge of the Morrison Memorial School, named in honor of the Reverend Robert Morrison (1782–1834), the first Protestant missionary to China. Brown viewed his mission as the training of Chinese Christians who would be enlightened through Western education but ultimately "return to their own people" and "still be Chinese."[2] The energetic educator was so successful that by 1842 the school moved to larger quarters in Hong Kong. Despite the occasional stonings they had to endure from Chinese villagers, the Browns earned the devotion of their young pupils.[3]

When Elizabeth's failing health necessitated the family's return to the United States in 1846, the Reverend Brown announced he would bring three students with him to further their studies. The first to stand up and volunteer was a Cantonese village boy named Yung Wing. With free passage on the Olyphant merchant ship *Huntress*, which was destined for New York with a full cargo of tea, he set sail on January 4, 1847.[4]

A Canton Mandarin Weds a Connecticut Yankee

Chinese–Western Intermarriage Becomes a "Problem"

As a pupil at the Morrison School, Yung Wing (fig. 1) had once written an English composition on the subject of "An Imaginary Voyage to New York and up the Hudson." At the time, he little dreamed that he would ever have the chance to see New York in person. Yet a mere two years later, in 1847, the imagined voyage became a reality as Yung Wing set sail for the great metropolis. In his memoir, *My Life in China and America* (1909), Yung pondered, "This incident leads me to the reflection that sometimes our imagination foreshadows what lies uppermost in our minds and brings possibilities within the sphere of realities."[5] Such was also true, the aging Yung mused, in the case of another daydream that he had cherished during his student years—that of one day marrying an American wife.

Yung Wing had journeyed far from his humble roots by the time that he married Mary Louise Kellogg (1851–86) on an icy day in February, 1875.[6] As the *New York Times* reported:

YUNG WING MARRIES A CONNECTICUT LADY

Mr. Yung Wing, of Canton, China, chief of the Chinese Educational Commission now at Hartford, was married on Wednesday to Miss Mary L. Kellogg, at the residence of her father, [Bela Crocker] Kellogg, in Avon, the ceremony being performed by Rev. J.H. Twichell, of the Asylum Hill Congregational Church in Hartford, a very particular friend of the bridegroom . . . . The bride wore a dress of white crape [sic], imported expressly for this occasion from China, and elaborately trimmed with floss

FIGURE 1. Yung Wing, Yale College class of 1854.
Class album, Manuscripts and Archives, Yale University.

silk embroidery . . . . After the ceremony, a collation was served, in which Chinese delicacies were mingled with more substantial dishes of American style. [Chinese officials] were present in national costume, but the groom, who long since adopted our style, appeared in full evening dress . . . .[7]

This highly publicized union between a Chinese official and the daughter of a prominent New England family was like nothing ever seen before in quiet Avon, a picturesque suburb of Hartford, Connecticut. One imagines that the cross-cultural spectacle of the nuptial celebrations, presided over by a local notable like Joseph Twichell (Mark

FIGURE 2. Mary Louise Kellogg, at the time of her marriage to
Yung Wing, 1875.

Courtesy of Thomas LaFargue Papers, 1873–1946 (#5983),
MASC, Washington State University Libraries.

Twain's confidant) and attended by Manchu-robed Mandarins from
far-off Cathay, must have caused quite a sensation. As Twichell recorded
in his diary, "The presence of these Chinese gentlemen in their strange
dress at a solemn religious service and social festival in a Puritan home
in a Connecticut country town was a striking and to me exceedingly
impressive feature of the occasion."[8] The guests must have marveled at
the lavish collation of Chinese delicacies and the bride's elaborately
embroidered gown of imported Chinese silk (fig. 2). No doubt they
approved also of the groom's elegant American evening dress, his
refined English, and his decision to dispose of his queue. The bridal
presents, as the *Times* duly noted, "were numerous and costly." The

story of this exotic and sumptuous wedding, virtually the first of its kind, was picked up by American newspapers across the country and would soon travel across the oceans to China.

If the wedding caused a stir in Avon, when news of the marriage reached China it lit sparks of indignation that would slowly grow into a heated debate among Chinese elites as growing numbers of Chinese overseas students would follow Yung Wing's suit and take foreign brides. In the end, this unconventional marriage would prove to be a source of bitter controversy for the Chinese Educational Mission (CEM) in Hartford, and a contributing factor to its closing in 1881. The fulfillment of Yung Wing's youthful daydream would thus have repercussions on both sides of the Pacific.

Yung Wing has been counted among the most important figures of modern Chinese and Chinese American history, celebrated in the United States and China alike as the first Chinese student to graduate from an American university (Yale, 1854), and as a founder of the Chinese Educational Mission, which sent 120 young Chinese students to the United States between 1872 and 1881.[9] Schools in both countries have been named in Yung Wing's honor, and matching statues memorializing the great man stand in his native place of Zhuhai, China, and on the Yale campus.[10] Overlooked in many of these tributes, however, is that as the first Chinese official to marry an American woman, Yung Wing was a trailblazer on another front. The only monument testifying to this lesser-known aspect of his remarkable story is a joint tombstone in Hartford's bucolic Cedar Hill Cemetery.

Using the story of Yung Wing's marriage to Mary Louise Kellogg as a focal point, this chapter presents a brief overview of American and Chinese discourses on Chinese–Western intermarriage as they evolved between 1850 and 1910. The aim of this chapter is simple: to refute the commonplace assumption that "intermarriage was never accepted by either side" by showing that there were, in fact, diverse opinions on Chinese–Western intermarriage in both societies: discourses of inclusion as well as exclusion. At the same time, I demonstrate that the *terms* in which intermarriage was debated differed significantly between the United States and China. In the United States, objections to intermarriage were generally framed in terms of the taboo nature of miscegenation, which was cast as a violation of natural or divine law.[11] Those who supported East–West intermarriage in contrast framed it as a vehicle for assimilating immigrants (and converting them to Christianity). Chinese discourses, on the other hand, did not invoke nature or religious authority but instead framed

East–West intermarriage in Confucian terms, weighing the costs and benefits of the effects on state and society. Within such a framework, East–West intermarriage was alternatively cast as a symptom of cultural deracination and national betrayal, or as a mechanism for strengthening international relations and promoting interracial harmony.

The backdrop for these debates, as noted in the introduction, was the increasing cross-cultural contact between the United States and China spurred by trade, imperial expansion, missionary activity, labor migration, and other transnational exchanges. Within such a context, would Chinese–Western intermarriage become a problem or a solution? I demonstrate that whereas there was a relative openness to such unions at the time of the Kellogg–Yung wedding in the 1870s, this tolerance would later give way to a hardening of attitudes and a tide of governmental restrictions on both sides of the Pacific.

BEFORE EXCLUSION

Yung Wing's marriage to Mary Kellogg represented the culmination of a long journey that began with his voyage on the *Huntress* in 1847. Arriving in New York, Yung proceeded to the Monson Academy in Massachusetts, where he studied before entering Yale. While at Yale, he was naturalized as a U.S. citizen by a New Haven judge in 1852. Entering deeply into his new American life, Yung remained concerned about China's future, and he returned to his native land after graduating Yale, pursuing a number of successful business ventures while attempting to promote schemes for China's modernization. When his proposal for a government-sponsored program to send students to the United States was at last accepted, Yung Wing was appointed co-commissioner of the Chinese Educational Mission, establishing its headquarters in Hartford in 1872.

Although the Yung–Kellogg wedding made headlines, the couple did not initially encounter any serious obstacles or ostracism. Mary's parents, Mary Golden Bartlett and Bela Crocker Kellogg, welcomed Yung into the Kellogg family, and the pair became established members of Hartford society—helped, no doubt, by Yung's status as a "Mandarin" and the fortune he had amassed in China. Eleven months after the wedding, the Chinese government appointed Yung as associate minister from China to the United States, Spain, and Peru, and Mary accompanied him to Washington, D.C.[12]

This was the 1870s, an era when attitudes toward East–West marriage were still evolving. The Chinese Exclusion Act had not yet been passed, and

Patrician Orientalism, as John Kuo Wei Tchen has termed it, still influenced American understandings of the "Celestials," especially on the East Coast, even as a mounting tide of anti-Chinese sentiment was rising from the West.[13] State legislatures were just beginning to extend anti-miscegenation laws to the Chinese, a process that did not gain full momentum until the 1880s.[14] On the other side of the Pacific, Chinese modernizers were looking to Western learning as a means to strengthen China's position in the modern world, and anti-foreignism and anti-Christian sentiment had yet to reach the fever pitch of the Boxer Uprising of 1900. China had entrusted some of its brightest sons to schooling in far-off America, and in return many of the "best families" in New England had opened their homes to the boys. Signifying the hopefulness of this educational exchange, the marriage between the CEM founder and a Connecticut woman with *Mayflower* roots perhaps seemed symbolically fitting.

Even at this early hour, however, controversy was brewing. As Joseph Twichell, Yung Wing's pastor and close friend, confided to his diary after the wedding, "The match was a good deal commented on. Some people feel doubtful about it; some disapproved it utterly; some (like me) gloried in it."[15] Twichell's remark is revealing, because it suggests the wide range of reactions to Chinese–Western intermarriage that were still possible in American society during the 1870s—with each rooted in a particular way of thinking about race, nation, and family, and reflecting the tension between inclusive and exclusionary discourses that animated debates concerning Chinese immigration during this era. This tension emerged as defenders of the Chinese drew on discourses of equal rights, fair play, and Christian universalism to argue that Chinese immigrants, like any others, could be effectively assimilated into American society, while the anti-Chinese camp conversely argued that the "heathen Chinese" were inherently unassimilable—both culturally and biologically—and therefore must be excluded from the nation. As we will see later, conflicting discourses concerning intermarriage were informed by this fundamental tension.

INTERMARRIAGE AND THE CHINESE QUESTION IN NINETEENTH-CENTURY AMERICA

It is not surprising that the Kellogg–Yung union would have met with disapproval; the taboo against interracial marriage ran deep in American culture, a legacy of slavery. As Peggy Pascoe has demonstrated in her history of miscegenation law and the making of race in America, the notion that interracial marriage was "unnatural" became so taken for granted in the post–Civil War era that "between the 1860s and the 1960s, [majority] Americans saw their opposition to interracial marriage as a product of nature rather than a product of politics."[16] Yet, as suggested in the introduction, this understanding of interracialism, as important as it is, does not tell the whole story, because such exclusionary practices existed in tension with inclusive discourses that complicated the picture.

Early in the formation of the American republic there emerged a compelling vision of the nation as a place where a new "American race" was being formed from the mixing of various immigrant nationalities. Answering the question "What is an American?" in 1782, J. Hector St. John de Crèvecoeur famously wrote, "They are a mixture of English, Scotch, Irish, French, Dutch, Germans, and Swedes. From this promiscuous breed, that race now called Americans have arisen."[17] In this idea of Americanness, intermarriage was a vehicle for immigrant assimilation and the production of a new American race.[18]

With the arrival of the Chinese in the mid-nineteenth century, the American public was faced with the question: Could these newest immigrants, like the Dutch and the Swedes, be assimilated into American society, or were they, like the "Negroes," yet another "unamalgamable" racial group whose cultural and physical differences disrupted the homogeneity of the nation? There was in fact some initial uncertainty on this matter, which had much to do with the ambiguity, in the years before Chinese exclusion, concerning whether Chinese should be classed as "whites" or "nonwhites." The lack of clarity on this issue meant that a few early Chinese immigrants, including Yung Wing and Wong Chin Foo, were able to naturalize as U.S. citizens, even in the years when this right was limited to "free whites."[19] Gradually, however, the Chinese were increasingly seen as "nonwhites," a status definitively confirmed when the Chinese Exclusion Act of 1882 barred Chinese categorically from naturalization.[20] The uncertain racial status of Chinese during the pre–exclusion era helps to explain why discourses concerning Chinese–white intermarriage were not always uniformly negative and displayed both inclusive and exclusionary impulses.

"Some Disapproved It Utterly"

By the time that Yung Wing married Mary Kellogg, the issue of miscegenation had already been linked to the public debate over Chinese

FIGURE 3. "The Result of the Immigration from China," *Yankee Notions*, March 1858.

Courtesy of Harvard University Widener Library P432.1; March 1858, Vol. VII, no. 3: The Result of the Immigration from China.

immigration—the so-called Chinese Question. As early as 1858, for example, a satirical cartoon on the cover of *Yankee Notions* magazine (fig. 3) warned that amalgamation would be "The Result of the Immigration from China."[21] The cartoon portrays an Irishwoman speaking with her Chinese husband and their three children in a mixed-up dialogue interspersed with pidgin: the "result" of immigration, it is implied, is the corruption or mongrelization of American culture—a notion that was at once comic and threatening. As the Chinese immigrant population expanded during the next few decades, the anxiety concerning the mixing of races became increasingly pronounced, generating much public discourse on the issue.

Drawing on prevailing fears concerning racial amalgamation, anti-Chinese agitators used the issue to mobilize support for the call to stem Chinese immigration. Demagogues linked the fear of economic competition to the notion of a sexual threat posed by Chinese men to white women. Chinese cheap labor, the argument went, undermined the white man's ability to support his family, leaving white women and girls no choice but to prostitute themselves, or perhaps to cast their lot with the Chinese. The threat of miscegenation was also a threat to the imagined racial homogeneity of the nation. David Croly and George Wakeman, who infamously coined the term "miscegenation" in an inflammatory pamphlet of 1863, warned that "the opening of California to the teeming millions of east Asia" would lead to the amalgamation of Chinese and Japanese into a "composite race" that would one day supplant the Anglo-Saxon majority.[22] Cautioning against racial amalgamation as a source of pollution, chaos, and degradation, anti-Chinese propagandists invoked the threat of miscegenation as a compelling reason to curtail Chinese immigration. Sharing these fears with readers in Shanghai, in 1870 a San Francisco correspondent to the English-language *North China Herald* wrote of his worries, "peering into the future," that the "masses of Eurasians, or Amerasians, that are beginning to spring" from Chinese immigrants, a "mongrel breed," would become the dominant class.[23]

One of the most extreme expressions of these overlapping fears was a short story, "The Battle of the Wabash," published in the *Californian* in 1880. Set in the future year of 2080, the story presents a nightmarish vision of a dystopian future in which Chinese immigration and miscegenation have reduced the white population to a minority, subjected to the tyrannical rule of a new Chinese and Eurasian majority.[24] As William Franking Wu has demonstrated, a cluster of short stories and novels on this "Yellow Peril" miscegenation theme were published between the 1880s and the 1910s.[25]

Although the anti-Chinese movement was initially strongest on the West Coast, by 1882 it had gained enough national momentum for Congress to pass the Chinese Exclusion Act. In tandem with the rise of anti-Chinese sentiment, the discourse on Chinese–white miscegenation grew increasingly negative and sensationalistic. As early as 1861,

Nevada had passed a law prohibiting miscegenation between whites and Chinese, and by 1910, six other states in the West and South had followed suit.[26]

Even after the passage of the Exclusion Act, anti-Chinese propagandists continued to link the miscegenation and immigration issues. The Asiatic Exclusion League, for example, defined its core issues as the restriction of Asian immigration, naturalization, land ownership, and intermarriage, all deemed necessary to ensure the separation of the races and prevent "the pollution of our blood by intermarriage."[27] The unnatural and abhorrent character of racial intermarriage was again used to justify exclusion: "The Asiatic in America is unassimilable. He must either remain a wholly unassimilable population among us, or we must absorb him into the breed of the American people. Now this crossing of the races produces a bad hybrid."[28] The separation of "Caucasians" and "Asiatics" was "required by the decree of the Father, and their amalgamation a violation of that decree."[29]

"SOME FEEL DOUBTFUL ABOUT IT"

Yet despite the prevalence of such anti-miscegenation rhetoric, which was particularly pronounced on the West Coast, depictions of Chinese–white unions were not necessarily always menacing and negative (fig. 4). Tchen has demonstrated, for example, that prior to the Exclusion era, New York popular culture produced a specific discourse on Chinese–Irish intermarriage, which was recognized as a growing phenomenon in the city.[30] From the 1850s to the 1870s, images of these unions were common in the New York press, burlesque theater, and other media—transformed into commercialized images that were marketed nationwide. Most of these representations were satirical or comical, poking fun at the "mixed-up" culture of New York's lower wards.

In fact, various newspaper reports of this era even represented Chinese husbands as fine, if "unnatural," partners for Irish and other immigrant women who occupied a low status in New York culture, claiming that the Chinese men were "good fellows" and "devoted to their wives."[31] Journalists often emphasized the class hypergamy entailed for working-class women who married Chinese merchants or laundry proprietors. Although they did not go so far as to endorse miscegenation, these reports at least took a fairly neutral stance. An article from the *New York Daily Tribune* of January 1869, for example, noted, "These Chinamen have a peculiar fancy for wives of Celtic origin; we do not recollect seeing one woman

PACIFIC RAILROAD COMPLETE.

FIGURE 4. "Pacific Railroad Complete," *Harper's Weekly*, June 12, 1869.

Courtesy of Massachusetts Institute of Technology Libraries.

among these many families that belonged to any other nationality. The great marvel is that these little domestic arrangements seldom give rise to disturbances."[32] For this reporter, the interracial couple remained more a curiosity than a "problem."

In reporting on the Chinese husbands' purported devotion to their Irish or German wives, such accounts of mixed marriages additionally tended to portray intermarriage as a vehicle for the assimilation and conversion of Chinese immigrants. Indeed, the presumption that assimilation entailed taking a "native" wife was so strong that a reporter for the *New York Times* blasted Chinese immigrants for their failure to take the step. An article on the "Chinese in New York" published in 1873, two years before the Yung–Kellogg wedding, accused them of a singular unwillingness to "marry American wives" like immigrants of other nationalities.[33] This claim was, of course, patently false, as we have seen, but it reveals how Chinese were stuck in a "damned if you do, damned if you don't" situation: while demagogues used the threat of miscegenation as a reason to exclude the Chinese, others used their purported refusal to intermarry as evidence of Chinese clannishness. Either way, they were unassimilable and therefore unfit to be members of the nation.

Well aware of such accusations of Chinese clannishness, decades earlier Chinese American leaders had in fact already attempted to defend the Chinese by invoking the notion of intermarriage as assimilation. In 1852, two Chinese merchant leaders from San Francisco, Hab Wa and Tong A-chick, wrote an open letter on behalf of "the Chinamen in California," protesting California Governor John Bigler's proposal to exclude Chinese contract laborers. Arguing that Chinese immigrants would become good citizens if the full privileges of American law were open to them, Hab and Tong charged that the Governor was "mistaken in supposing no Chinaman has ever yet applied to be naturalized," and informed him that there "is a Chinaman now in San Francisco who is said to be a naturalized citizen, and to have a free white American wife. He wears the American dress, and is considered a man of respectability."[34] Hab and Tong thus linked intermarriage with assimilation and the desire for citizenship.

Pioneering Chinese American journalist Wong Chin Foo used a similar tactic in an article he wrote on the New York Chinese for the *Cosmopolitan* in 1888. Reporting that many Chinese had married Irish, German, or Italian immigrant wives, Wong explained that "most of these women are poor working girls, who through necessity married well-to-do Chinamen. The Chinamen often make them better husbands than men of their own nation, as quite a number of them who ran away from their former husbands to marry Chinamen have openly declared. The Chinaman never beats his wife, gives her plenty to eat and wear, and generally adopts her mode of life."[35] A naturalized American citizen himself, and an active advocate of equal rights for the Chinese in America, Wong Chin Foo similarly appropriated the discourse of intermarriage as assimilation to defend the Chinese immigrant's place in American society. Class hypergamy, we will note, was key to Wong's argument that Chinese men made "better husbands." Such examples indicate that even into the 1880s, opposition to Chinese–white intermarriage (especially in cases involving European immigrant women) was not so widespread as to trump the rhetorical power of intermarriage as a vehicle for immigrant assimilation.

"SOME GLORY IN IT"

The presumption that intermarriage was a vehicle for assimilation informed the thinking of those rare individuals who went beyond skeptical tolerance of Chinese–white intermarriage to argue that good would come of it. Joseph Twichell and his wife were among the notable minority who supported this position. Having long urged Yung Wing to take an American wife, the Twichells were overjoyed when he decided to take this novel step. As Twichell noted in his diary, "I shall await the result of the step with great interest, he with much confidence that only good will come of it."[36] Twichell "gloried in" this marriage as a sign of Yung Wing's transformation into an Americanized Oriental and his dedication to Christian life.

Religious liberals like Twichell acknowledged the racial difference of the Chinese but firmly espoused the ideals of equal rights and Christian brotherhood. While no more accepting of the "heathen Chinese" than the anti-Chinese agitators, the liberals fervently believed that the Chinese could be assimilated through missionary efforts. They argued that the drive to exclude the Chinese violated both republican and Christian ideals, much as had slavery, and furthermore damaged missionary efforts in China. Contrary to those who argued that God had intended to separate the races by placing them on separate continents, missionaries argued that Chinese immigrants had been brought to American shores as part of a divine plan for their conversion and enlightenment.

Although the mainstream press on the whole stopped short of "glorying in" Yung Wing's marriage to Mary Kellogg, reports of the wedding, such as the *New York Times* announcement presented earlier, certainly steered clear of negative sensationalism and the overt racism of Croly and Wakeman. The mainstream press instead framed this union in terms of the time-honored paradigm of intermarriage as assimilation. This is perhaps not surprising given that Yung Wing very much stood apart from most Chinese immigrants of his generation: he was a Western-educated, Christian convert, and a naturalized citizen who had discarded his queue and adopted American dress. No doubt these factors contributed to the acceptance of Yung's unconventional marriage among the Connecticut circle that included respected families like the

Kelloggs, Bartletts, Twichells, and Clemenses (Mark Twain) among others. Yung was no "heathen Chinee" or "washee washee man": as newspaper reports of the time frequently emphasized, he was a "Yale man" who had "long adopted our ways."[37]

If Yung Wing was clearly exceptional, he was not the only one. When former CEM student Yan Phou Lee (1861–1938?, Yale class of 1887) married Elizabeth Maude Jerome in July 1887—another wedding presided over by Twichell—the press once again used the angle of intermarriage as assimilation.[38] *Hartford Daily Courant* headlines in no uncertain words proclaimed, "Yan Phou Lee Assimilates."[39] The *Courant* thereby portrayed this marriage not as an unnatural act that violated sanctified racial boundaries, but in terms of the inclusive discourse—and the *New York Times* adopted a similar storyline.[40] Like Yung, Lee enjoyed elite status as a "distinguished Chinaman," one who was highly educated and versed in the genteel manners of New England patricians—and this fact colored representations of his marriage in the East Coast press.

These wedding announcements can be read as examples of Patrician Orientalism, as described by John Kuo Wei Tchen. As Tchen has demonstrated, prior to the Exclusion era, Patrician Orientalism generated an abiding fascination among the American elite with Chinese luxury goods, cultural refinement, and even political ideals.[41] Tchen further shows how Patrician Orientalism informed representations of Chinese immigrants in New York, producing a compelling image of the "exemplary Chinaman," as embodied by astute, literate, and hard-working merchants. Patrician Orientalism thus supported a certain positive, though class-bound, stereotype of Chinese immigrants.

Patrician Orientalism similarly helps explain why the marriages of men like Yung Wing and Yan Phou Lee were eminently acceptable in some circles, suggesting the pivotal role of class status in shaping understandings of Chinese–Western intermarriage. Certainly, Yung Wing and Mary Kellogg present to us a very different image of the interracial couple than the *Yankee Notions* magazine cover of 1858: Yung was no Chinese peddler, but a Yale-educated Mandarin, and Kellogg was no Irish washerwoman, but a granddaughter of Avon's founding Puritan elite and a Daughter of the American Revolution.

A snapshot that brings us closer to the privileged milieu in which educated Chinese immigrants like Yung and Lee were ensconced can be found in the reminiscences of Yale Professor William Lyon Phelps (1865–1943). Phelps was an acquaintance of Yung Wing and the Yale classmate of Yan Phou Lee and had also attended Hartford High School with several of the CEM students. Recalling his school days, Phelps wrote of the Chinese students' prowess in sports and also on the dance floor, "When the Chinese youth entered the social arena, none of us had any chance at all. Their manner to the girls had a deferential elegance far beyond our possibilities. Whether it was the exotic pleasure of dancing with Orientals, or, what is more probable, the real charm of the manners and talk of our Eastern rivals, I do not know; certain it is that at all dances and receptions, the fairest and most sought-out belles invariably gave the swains from the Orient the preference."[42] Phelps presents here a highly romanticized vision of Oriental manners and charm, of the "exotic pleasure" of dancing with Chinese "patricians," which had a potent appeal to the "fairest belles" of Connecticut society. This was not the "mixed-up" port culture of Manhattan's lower wards or San Francisco's Barbary Coast; it was the elegant rivalry among New England gentlemen on the ballroom floor, where interracial competition was neutralized by class privilege and the rose-colored glasses of Orientalism.

Although the influence of Patrician Orientalism in American culture was limited, offset by the increasing demonization of the Chinese surrounding the passage of Chinese exclusion, it clearly supported a positive image of the Kellogg–Yung marriage as an "exceptional case." When press accounts continually emphasized the sumptuousness of their wedding—the luxurious bridal gown of imported Chinese silk crêpe, and the numerous expensive and exotic bridal gifts—they invoked Patrician Orientalism, casting a glow of romance and respectability over a possibly problematic union.

Patrician Orientalism even enabled some in Avon to regard this marriage connection as a point of pride. Avon's local history, included in the 1886 *Memorial History of Hartford County, Connecticut*, noted the famous marriage between the "distinguished Chinaman," with all his various credentials, and a "native of Avon," with her eminent pedigree.[43] The compiler of this history treated the union not as a shameful secret, but as a distinct local honor. Similarly, a Kellogg family genealogy, published in 1903 and 1906, recorded the multiple accomplishments of Yung Wing, husband to Mary Louise.[44] A feather in the cap of the Kellogg clan, this Chinese marital connection was no skeleton in the family closet, but conversely was given pride of place in the annals of family history.

Yet the limitations of Patrician Orientalist discourse are clearly indicated by the fact that even as some "gloried in" this match, there were others in Avon society who "disapproved utterly," Yung Wing's status notwithstanding. With race thus trumping class, it is evident that the miscegenation taboo had a strong grip on American society.

This taboo was less entrenched in Hawaii, where Yung Wing's Macao friend, Chen Fang (a.k.a. Afong), had established himself. A scholar turned merchant, Chen Fang (1825–1906) migrated to Honolulu in 1849 and soon made his fortune. In 1857, he married Julia Hope Fayerweather (1840–1919), the daughter of American merchant Abram Henry Fayerweather (1812–50) and a descendant of Hawaiian Chiefess Ahia (1792–1854). Although their marriage was frowned upon by some among Hawaii's white planter elite, it caused no public outcry, for intermarriage was relatively tolerated in Hawaii.[45] With Afong's money and Julia's beauty and royal connections, it was not long before the pair became a leading couple in Honolulu society. The "Afongs," as they were known, had sixteen children, including twelve daughters who would grow up to become the belles of the ball. Chen Fang sent two of his sons, Alung and Toney, to study in Hartford under Yung Wing's guardianship, and then at Yale. Another son attended Harvard.[46]

Intermarriage was quite a different phenomenon in Hawaii, for even before annexation (1898) it had been viewed as a strategy for white settlers to lay claim to native lands and to gain entry into local society, especially through unions with native Hawaiian elites.[47] After annexation, intermarriage between Euro-Americans and native Hawaiians was lauded by some as a symbol for the union between the United States and its new colonial territory. Others viewed amalgamation not in metaphorical terms, but as a means for cultural and biological assimilation. Missionaries like James McKinney Alexander, for example, represented interracial union as a means for the physical, intellectual, and moral improvement of the native Hawaiian race through what he called "an infusion of the best blood of the human race."[48] Although such eugenic imaginings focused on the native Hawaiian population, the Chinese— seen as an indispensable source of labor for Hawaii's growing plantation economy—were also included in visions of the vigorous new "composite race" of Hawaii.[49]

As these examples demonstrate, American discourses on Chinese– white intermarriage were not always uniformly negative. Rather, there was a diversity of opinion—especially in the years before Chinese exclusion—shaped by factors of class, geographic location, and gender. This diversity of opinion is significant, for despite the fact that mounting anti-Chinese demagoguery spread the idea that Chinese–white intermarriage was unnatural, the paradigm of intermarriage as assimilation would return to importance in the 1920s through the work of American sociologists, as we will see in chapter 5.

If some of Mary Kellogg's Avon neighbors had sharply disapproved of her marriage, while others considered it a distinguishing mark of the town's local heritage, what were the reactions to this unconventional union in Yung Wing's homeland? Yung Wing would find out soon enough, for in 1881 he was abruptly recalled to China, forced to leave behind his young wife and their two small sons—Morrison Brown Yung, born June 10, 1876, in Avon, Connecticut, and Bartlett Golden Yung, born January 22, 1879, in Washington, D.C.

• • •

In fact, the dark clouds of suspicion had been gathering over Yung Wing in the years following his wedding, a time when he served both as co-commissioner of the CEM in Hartford and associate minister in Washington. Serving in this dual capacity, Yung Wing found himself caught up in a series of mounting disagreements with his conservative colleagues, Chen Lanpin and Wu Zideng, who sent a stream of correspondence back to Beijing criticizing Yung.[50] In their eyes, everything that had made Yung Wing so acceptable in American society—his conversion to Christianity, his naturalization as an American citizen, his fluent English (at the cost of his Chinese), his decision to adopt Western clothing and cut off his queue—were symptoms of his waning loyalty to China. Arousing suspicion against Yung among conservatives at home, Chen and Wu railed against Yung's lenient treatment of the Chinese students, which was leading the boys, they claimed, to become Westernized, to neglect their Chinese studies, and, worst of all, to forget their love of the homeland. When Wu observed some of the Chinese boys walking home from church in the company of American women he sent an outraged report back to Viceroy Li Hongzhang calling for the immediate disbanding of the CEM. Matters were not helped when Yung Wing's own kinsman, Yung Kwai (1861–1943, Yale class of 1884), refused to return to China when ordered home in 1880.

In the midst of these escalating conflicts, the U.S. government refused permission for the CEM students to enter West Point and Annapolis, bringing matters to a head. In 1881, the mission was abruptly shuttered and the boys recalled to China. Yung Wing followed shortly in their wake, returning to report to the government in the autumn of 1881.

Mary did not accompany him on this journey but retired to the family home in Connecticut, a prudent move considering both her poor health and the risks raised by the antagonism toward Yung among conservatives in China.[51]

Although the close friendships and burgeoning romances between some of the Chinese students and American women were not the primary reason for the disbanding of the CEM, they were certainly an aggravating factor, as recorded in the famous elegy composed in 1881 by the Chinese statesman and poet Huang Zunxian (1845–1905), to commemorate the recall:

> [The students] dwell in a fantasy realm,
> Where fairest belles bestow fragrant blossoms upon them.
> They have found the land of perfect bliss,
> And are too happy to remember Home.[52]

In a typical poetic move, Huang blames the fair sex for enticing the students away, leading them to forget their duties and their homeland: later events would show that the idea of such a threat was not simply a literary trope, but a deeply held anxiety that would drive government policy.

In his memoir, Yung Wing studiously avoids any mention of his marriage in connection with the CEM recall, leaving us only to speculate on the impact of his private life on his career. To what degree did his American wife prove an issue for Yung Wing? To what degree was this only a pretext for taking down a man whose aggressive reformist stance had made him many enemies among conservatives at court? What was it that prompted Chinese conservatives to react with such hostility to marriages like that of Yung and those who would follow in his footsteps?

The Chinese concept of "national identity" (*guojia rentong*) helps us understand why international marriages like Yung's became an issue of contention during the late Qing and into the early Republican era. As the renowned "Father of Chinese Overseas Students," Yung Wing is remembered in China today as a great patriot who never forgot his love for homeland despite long years of residence abroad.[53] Yet, during the late Qing, Yung Wing was conversely suspected of the unpardonable sin of "forgetting the nation" (*wangguo*). This transgression, more than a taboo against racial amalgamation, shaped the era's condemnation of men like Yung. The debates on Chinese–Western intermarriage were thus not simply focused on race and blood purity, but were more fundamentally concerned with "national identity" and the fears of deracination that were magnified by the rising Western dominance of the era.[54]

ALLIANCE, ASSIMILATION, OR TREASON? CHINESE DISCOURSES ON INTERMARRIAGE

As in the United States, the emerging discourses on Chinese–Western unions took shape against the backdrop of deep-rooted cultural understandings of intermarriage.[55] Although some disparaged marriages between Chinese and supposedly culturally inferior "barbarians," such prejudices ebbed and flowed with the rise and fall of xenophobia in different periods of Chinese history, and intermarriage was never taboo or considered "unnatural." Indeed, intermarriage could also be perceived as having productive, and not threatening, effects for society at large. First, intermarriage had historically been used as a means of contracting political alliances. One of the most beloved stories in the Chinese historiographic tradition tells of Wang Zhaojun, a Han Dynasty palace woman sent by the Chinese emperor to marry a Xiongnu chief.[56] In cosmopolitan periods of Chinese history, the story of Wang Zhaojun served to exemplify the possibilities of Chinese–non-Chinese alliances; in xenophobic periods, Wang Zhaojun's exile exemplified the principle of loyalty to China. Second, there was a long-standing view of intermarriage as a mechanism for assimilating non-Chinese frontier peoples who lived on the borderlands of the ever-expanding Chinese empire. Proponents of such a view believed that intermarriage between Han Chinese men and local women would produce a second generation of Chinese subjects who followed Han cultural practices and were loyal to imperial authority. Some conversely feared, however, that intermarriage as assimilation might work in the opposite direction: that Han Chinese migrants to the frontiers who intermarried with indigenous women might "go native" and refuse allegiance to the Chinese state. During the Manchu-ruled Qing Dynasty, the court viewed intermarriage through the lens of frontier management and ethnic politics, and in cases where intermarriage aroused conflict among communal groups, especially on strategic frontiers, the government would intervene by issuing edicts against intermarriage. These edicts were generally aimed not at protecting the racial integrity of the majority Han Chinese, but conversely at protecting minority groups.

Given such long-standing views of intermarriage, what was to be made of intermarriage with the "barbarians" from the Far West, whose presence in China was growing during the course of the nineteenth century? In a history of marriage and the family in China, Li Mo has argued that Chinese social opinion was relatively tolerant of Chinese–Western intermarriages during the late Qing due to the fact that such unions were rare and generally involved elite Chinese men—diplomats and scholars like Yung Wing.[57] With the rise of Chinese nationalism in the first decade of the twentieth century, however, hostility toward Chinese–Western intermarriage, which was perceived as a form of racial and national betrayal, increased. In particular, when Chinese female students began to go abroad, racial nationalists issued heated statements against these women marrying foreign men.[58]

Yet, there were also circumstances in which unions between Chinese women and Western men were acceptable, particularly when such marital alliances were seen as beneficial to family or nation. The marriage of American Frederick Townsend Ward to Yang Zhangmei—a wedding that was every bit as exceptional as Yung Wing's marriage to Mary Kellogg—provides an excellent example of how a Chinese–Western union could be understood within the dual paradigms of intermarriage as alliance and intermarriage as assimilation (that is, as a step to becoming Chinese).

INTERMARRIAGE AS ALLIANCE: SECURING THE FOREIGNER TO CHINA

Frederick Townsend Ward (1831–62) of Salem, Massachusetts, was an American adventurer who became the first commander of the Ever-Victorious Army, the Western forces who joined the Qing in fighting the Taiping rebels between 1860 and 1864. In reward for his services, the Qing granted Ward the honored position of fourth-rank Mandarin. Ward became a Chinese subject, and in 1862, married Yang Zhangmei, the daughter of the powerful banker Yang Fang.[59] Yang Fang was a loyal backer of Ward and saw the marriage as a means of securing his alliance with this powerful foreigner. The marriage also appeared consistent with Ward's sworn declaration that in becoming a Chinese subject he had chosen to "submit to the Chinese way of life."[60] Whatever Ward's own motives, by external appearances the marriage solidified his alliance with the Yang family and confirmed his loyalty as a Chinese subject.[61]

Sir Robert Hart (1835–1911), the Irishman who served as China's first inspector general of the Imperial Maritime Customs Service, provides another illustrative example of the Chinese trust in marital alliances. In 1864, when Hart was in Beijing and expecting to receive Chinese rank, a Chinese minister at the Zongli Yamen (bureau in charge of foreign affairs) suggested that he ought to marry a Chinese wife as befitting his official Qing post: the presumption being that a Chinese wife and family would strengthen the foreigner's ties to China.[62] But Hart did not share Ward's unconventional streak, and when a Chinese associate offered his own daughter's hand in marriage, he steadfastly refused.[63] Hart contented himself instead, in true colonial fashion, with a series of discrete Chinese mistresses, one of whom bore him three children.[64]

As unusual as these famous cases were, involving high-ranking men in service to the Qing court, they nonetheless serve to illustrate a mode of thinking about intermarriage as alliance that would largely be displaced by the racialized discourse of the early twentieth century, as we will see in chapter 4. These cases also demonstrate that the Qing government was not opposed outright to Chinese–Western intermarriage, especially if such alliances could serve to secure their foreign servants' allegiance. The court would gradually be persuaded, however, to take a negative view of intermarriage when it involved overseas students like Yung Wing.

THE NEW FASHION FOR "INTERNATIONAL MARRIAGE": FEARS AND DESIRES

The early scandal touched off by the Yung–Kellogg wedding in 1875 gave rise to a controversy concerning international marriage (*guoji hunyin*) that would intensify in China as growing numbers of overseas students and diplomatic officials married foreign wives.[65] As Xing Long notes in his history of the Chinese family, in major cities like Shanghai, Canton, Hankou, Tianjin, and Beijing, mixed marriages between Chinese and foreigners grew increasingly common in the late Qing, especially among the "returned students" who had studied overseas and come home to China.[66] Although the absolute numbers of such marriages remained small, by the early twentieth century there were enough to draw the attention of Qing elites and to be labeled a "trend." As one writer declared, "Europeanization is gradually taking hold of the East. People vie with one another in pursuit of it. The phrase 'international marriage' is especially admired by young students who have studied abroad. Observing the fashion and following suit, one after another, people have spread the practice throughout the country."[67]

The author of this anonymous anecdote, composed circa 1909, not only suggests the emergence of a new fashion among young students, but furthermore connects this trend to the Europeanization of Chinese culture, whether as cause or effect. What is at stake here is cultural, and not blood, purity.

INTERMARRIAGE AND "FORGETTING THE NATION"

Indeed, conservatives who opposed the "new trend" of international marriages perceived these unions as a symptom of a larger pattern of Westernization among the overseas students, a pattern that included the pursuit of unscholarly activities like sports and dancing, not to mention the worst sin of all—embracing Christianity. Conservatives viewed the Westernization of the students as a dangerous erosion of their Chinese identities. Articulating many of the suspicions against the CEM, an article published by the Shanghai newspaper, *Shenbao*, at the time of the recall in 1881, denounced, "Some [of the boys] have cut off their queues and wear their hair unbound like barbarians; some wear the clothing of Westerners; all have abandoned their original Chinese appearance, and are becoming Americans. . . . When they return to China, their speech, laughter, and movements are exactly the same as those of foreigners. Even when they are reunited with their families, they have forgotten them; and even if their parents are still alive, they act as though they were dead to them."[68] In this passage we see fears that the "American" behavior of the CEM students would lead to deracination and unfilial conduct, a clear betrayal of the cornerstone values of Confucianism.

Hence, the emergent conservative discourse against Chinese–Western intermarriage linked the phenomenon to the broader process of deracination and the attendant threat of "forgetting the homeland," invoking the paradigm of intermarriage as treason. Such fears would have been confirmed when many of the overseas students who married foreign wives did indeed settle abroad. When the famous Chinese reformer Liang Qichao (1873–1929) traveled to the United States in 1903, he met with Yung Wing and ten former CEM students who had settled in America. Noting their talents in diverse fields from engineering to translation and banking, Liang lamented that were not put to service for China. As he wrote in his travelogue, "Every single one of them has a Western wife. This is one reason why their hearts [cherish sentiments] incompatible with patriotism. Alas."[69]

In fact, as Chinese sociologist Wu Jingchao demonstrated in the 1920s, intermarriage with local women had long been an accepted practice among Chinese male migrants, virtually wherever immigrant communities were to be found.[70] The practice was facilitated by the Chinese custom of polygamy, for migrants would often marry one wife in the home village and take a second wife overseas. In Southeast Asia, for example, intermarriage with local women had given rise to established creole communities by the mid-eighteenth century.[71] By the late nineteenth century, as mass migration effected the global spread of Chinese migrants, intermarriage could be observed in overseas communities everywhere from the Americas, to the Caribbean, Hawaii, and Australasia. Polygamy meant that intermarriage did not threaten the traditional family structure and represented instead a form of accommodation to migrant life.[72]

But what if migrants rejected polygamy or settled permanently abroad? In such situations, intermarriage was no longer a form of accommodation but signaled a break with established custom. Anxieties concerning such issues would in time erupt into a heated debate concerning international marriage, specifically targeting overseas students, as is explored in the next chapter.

INTERRACIALISM AS FOREIGN PENETRATION

The idea of intermarriage as cultural treason came to the fore with the rise of Chinese nationalism at the end of the nineteenth century. Anti-foreignism in China had been mounting since the Treaty of Nanjing and became increasingly linked to anti-Christian sentiment after the Peking Treaty of 1860 opened the Chinese interior to missionary work.[73] Anti-Christian riots and spontaneous attacks on missionaries gradually gained momentum, culminating in the infamous Boxer Uprising of 1900. As in the United States, the perceived cultural threat from outsiders was often expressed in sexual logic. In anti-Christian rhetoric, for example, we find accusations of rape, child molestation, and sexual perversions practiced by the "foreign devil" missionaries.

Similar rhetoric is evident in the famous polemical tract *Alarm Bells* (*Jingshizhong*), composed in the wake of the Boxers. Warning against Western imperialism and denouncing the Qing failure to deal with this threat, the revolutionary pamphlet stridently declared, "Our wealth and possessions, the fruits of our bitter toil—all will be seized by the

Westerner; our countrymen's cherished wives and children. . . . None will be spared his sword or his lust."[74] Mirroring in some regards the tactics of the anti-Chinese movement in the United States, the tract invokes a threat to the nation's women to mobilize the public against foreign encroachment.

Although the anxieties on both sides of the Pacific demonstrate a certain degree of parallelism, they must be understood within the context of the "global unevenness" of the era. In other words, in China, fears of Western cultural and economic encroachment were confirmed by the gun boats, unequal treaties, and other concrete evidences of Western imperialism.

INTERMARRIAGE AS INTERNATIONAL RELATIONS

While polemical tracts like *Alarm Bells* sought to mobilize radicals by appealing to a visceral xenophobia, anti-foreignism was not the only response to the crisis provoked by Western imperialism in China. In fact, certain forward-looking intellectuals who sought harmonious, cooperative relations with the West advocated Chinese–Western unions as a means to improve mutual understanding and international relations.[75] Such was the position taken by the celebrated diplomat, Wu Tingfang (1842–1922), for example, as we will see in the next chapter. Similarly, the radical Yi Nai published an article in the reformist newspaper *Hunan News* in 1898, proposing intermarriage as a long-term strategy to ensure peace between China and the West. Yi Nai argued that intermarriage would promote international relations through the establishment of kinship ties, and even proposed that an imperial order be sent down encouraging the populace to marry their sons and daughters to Westerners. With marital alliances forged between China and Western nations, he argued, China could recruit talented foreigners to serve as advisers and officials, with the assurance that they would work for China's benefit. In this manner, interracial unions could ultimately save China from Western imperialism and the Chinese race from extinction.[76] Yi thus proposed a strategy of "employing racial amalgamation as a means of extending the noble race."[77]

Anticipating resistance from those who held sacred the notions of racial and lineage purity, Yi conceded many feared that "if the people of this ancient empire, the noble descendants of the Yellow Emperor, marry with those who are not of our race, then it will lead to the decline of the pure descendants of the noble race and the flourishing of the stinking races."[78] This type of xenophobic and racialist thinking was known to take hold during historical moments when China faced foreign invasion. Indeed, the notion of intermarriage as treason, or a pollution of the sacred race and lineage, assumed heightened importance during the anti-Manchu revolutionary movement of the early twentieth century, leading to the emergence of a new racialized discourse on intermarriage, as we will see in chapter 4.

In sum, as in the United States, a range of discourses existed in China during this era. In response to a perceived imperative for national survival in the face of Western imperial aggression, Chinese intellectuals represented Chinese–Western intermarriage alternately as problem or solution: as a threat to the nation or the very means of its salvation. If the American rhetoric had become increasingly negative during the era of Chinese exclusion, in China hostility to Chinese–Western intermarriage rose with the surging tide of anti-foreignism in the years leading up to the Revolution of 1911, as we will see in the next chapter.

• • •

Casting about in China after the recall, Yung Wing received word that his wife's health had taken a turn for the worse. He immediately set sail for America, reaching home in 1883. Her spirits lifted by this reunion, Mary appeared to recover, but the respite was only temporary. Mary Kellogg Yung died in 1886, at the tender age of thirty-five, leaving behind a grief-stricken husband and her two young sons. Yung Wing found his "devoted sons" his only solace in the "great void" that he faced after burying his beloved wife, described in her obituary as a "New England woman of the true type," at Cedar Hill.[79] As Yung wrote in his memoir, "She did not leave me hopelessly deserted and alone; she left me two sons who are constant reminders of her beautiful life and character. They have proved to be my greatest comfort and solace in my declining years. They are most faithful, thoughtful and affectionate sons, and I am proud of their manly and earnest Christian character. My gratitude to God for blessing me with two such sons will forever rise to heaven, an endless incense."[80]

Prologue to Chapter 2

THE MERCHANT WITH TWO WIVES

A decade after Yung Wing was recalled to China, the Chinese minister to France returned from Paris and settled in Shanghai. After a fifteen-year sojourn abroad, he must have taken pleasure in the romantic stories and gossipy anecdotes featuring Western women published in the popular illustrated newspaper, *Dianshizhai Pictorial* (*Dianshizhai huabao*). One item published in 1892, shortly after his return, however, may have struck him as less than amusing (fig. 5):

THE BLOSSOMING OF SATISFACTION AND HAPPINESS

Since the opening of commerce with the West, there have been many cases of Westerners taking Chinese women as their mates, but few cases of Chinese marrying Western women. Yet, there are some Chinese men who have managed to marry not just one, but two Western beauties.

For example, there is a certain Mr. X from Jinling, who had not achieved much in his youth, but who was proficient in Western languages and made a substantial profit in foreign trade. Thus he gained the admiration of many Western beauties, marrying two in succession. . . . In this fashion, Mr. X lived harmoniously with his two wives for ten years, almost forgetting the loneliness of exile.

Recently, he became homesick and so returned East with his wives. He rented a place for them [in Shanghai]. . . . As soon as the locals got wind of this, they eagerly vied to be first to see the women. All who have seen them say that both are gentle and affable. . . . Truly, it can be said that Mr. X is enjoying the worldly pleasures of romance to the fullest.[1]

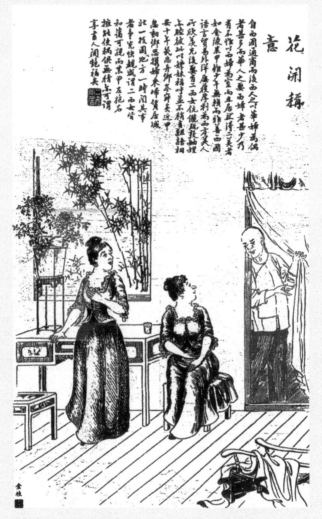

FIGURE 5. "Blossoming of Satisfaction and Happiness,"
Dianshizhai huabao, 1892.

Readers in the know might have recognized this humorous anecdote as
a sly dig at Chen Jitong (1851–1907), the Fujian native and erstwhile
diplomat who had returned to China with a French wife and an English
mistress. The infamous quarrels between the two women provided fod-
der for local gossip and satire.[2]

We can read in this anecdote more than an elaborate joke on Chen
Jitong, for it also makes issue of the gender imbalance of interracial

sexuality in the Treaty Port era, expressing an anxiety that more Western men were partnering with Chinese women than vice versa. But as the anecdote also suggests, the growth of Chinese migration was dramatically increasing the numbers of Chinese men marrying Western women abroad, and while such women were still a novelty in China, audiences could take satisfaction in the imagining of this exotic spectacle.

Against the Shanghai newspaper's playful fantasy, let us compare the experiences of two real merchants, plying the trade routes between East and West.

THE STORY OF EDWARD EATON AND LOTUS BLOSSOM

In the spring of 1863, ships belonging to an "Edward Eaton & Co." began to appear in the harbor of Shanghai. It must have been shortly after his arrival from England that Edward Eaton (1839–1915) met Lotus Blossom (1846–1922), a Chinese-born woman who had been raised in England by missionaries and recently returned to Shanghai to train for local mission work. The couple was married by the British consul in Shanghai and welcomed their first son, Edward Charles, in 1864, returning to England in the following year. There, in Eaton's ancestral hometown, the English silk center of Macclesfield, daughter Edith Maude was born in 1865. A row with Edward's parents set the family on the move again, and their next child was born in America in 1867. A business failure sent the family back to England in 1869, where three more children would be born before the family migrated to North America for a second time, living first in Hudson City, New York, before finally settling in Montréal, Canada. Chinese women were a rare sight in Montréal when the family arrived in 1873, and when the Eatons were taken by sleigh from the train station curious onlookers murmured, "Les pauvres enfants ... Chinoise, Chinoise." In Montréal, more children came one after the other, fourteen in all.[3]

THE STORY OF FONG SEE AND LETTICIE PRUETT

The son of a Chinese herbalist who was in Gold Mountain as early as 1866, Fong See (1857–1957) arrived by clipper ship in San Francisco harbor in 1871. As was typical for the time, Fong See was already married to a village girl before he set sail to make his fortune abroad. In California, the young adventurer went on to become a successful merchant, with stores in Sacramento and Los Angeles. It was at his

Sacramento store that Fong See first met Letticie Pruett (1876–1943), an American woman of Pennsylvania Dutch origins whose family were pioneers on the Oregon Trail. In search of work, eighteen-year-old Ticie had entered the Suie On Company to offer her services as a seamstress. Reluctantly, Fong See hired the "foreign devil" girl to deal with the American customers, and soon Ticie was helping the boss to run the store.

Two migrants in search of a better life, two savvy business people, Fong See and Ticie Pruett were married on January 15, 1897. Their union was sanctioned by no consulate, no town hall, no church. Instead, they had a contract drawn up in a lawyer's office, because "miscegenation" between white persons and "Mongolians, Negroes, mulattoes and persons of mixed blood" had been outlawed in California in 1880. Ticie was disowned by her family. Persuading her husband to move permanently to Los Angeles, the plucky redhead helped Fong See establish a successful Chinese antique shop, the F. Suie One Company, an enormous mercantile museum that would later supply Oriental props for Hollywood film productions. Five children were born on Californian soil—Milton, Ray, Bennie, Eddy, and Florence, known affectionately as "Sissie."[4]

CHAPTER 2

Mae Watkins Becomes a "Real Chinese Wife"

Marital Expatriation, Migration, and Transracial Hybridity

Fong See was known for his habit of reading the *Chung Sai Yat Po*, San Francisco's *Chinese Daily Paper*, taking particular notice of stories of interracial couples.[5] If Fong See had been reading the paper on December 13, 1913, one item would surely have caught his attention. The paper advertised a special lecture on law to be delivered that evening at the Chinese YMCA by a graduate of Detroit College of Law, Huang Tianfu (ca. 1889–1919), who was passing through San Francisco en route home to China. Accompanying the announcement was a striking photograph of Huang in his graduation regalia, standing beside his wife and son (fig. 6). As the *Chinese Daily Paper* informed readers, the Fujian native had the double distinction of having earned an American law degree and married an American coed.[6]

If curious readers hoped to catch a glimpse of this American wife, they must have been disappointed, for Huang Tianfu—or Tiam Hock Frank-ing, as he was known in America—did not bring Mae on this return voyage.[7] Instead, Mae had agreed to wait with baby Nelson at her parents' home in Ann Arbor, Michigan, while Tiam settled into his new job and found a suitable home for them in Shanghai. When Mae finally set forth for China in June 1914, she and Nelson made the long journey alone, without Tiam to guide them. Yet, Mae crossed the Pacific aboard a mail steamer, in accommodations reserved for "Asiatic travelers only."[8] Mae traveled thus, much to the ticket agent's surprise, for in marrying Tiam Hock she had lost her U.S. citizenship and become a Chinese national.[9]

FIGURE 6. Tiam Hock Franking with wife Mae and son Nelson, Michigan, 1913.

Courtesy of Christopher N. Wu and William F. Wu.

Why did marriage to a foreign national entail the loss of citizenship for American women at the time? What did it mean for a Euro-American woman like Mae to become Chinese through marriage, especially during the era of Chinese exclusion? The story of Mae Watkins (ca. 1890–1926) and Tiam Hock Franking, who married in Michigan in 1912, provides a window onto important legal and social changes that had taken place in the intervening decades since the Kellogg–Yung wedding in 1875 (see chapter 1) and also shifts our view to interracial families who made their homes in China. Their story, while unique in many respects, is representative of a trend that emerged gradually from 1900 onward, one that sociologist Herbert Lamson called the "distinctly modern phenomenon of Chinese highly educated returned students who bring back with them to China European or American wives."[10] This trend aroused reactions on both sides of the Pacific but caused particular anxiety in China.

Focusing on the figure of Mae Franking, whose experiences were related in a memoir, *My Chinese Marriage*, this chapter examines the discourses concerning white women's marital migration to China that emerged on both sides of the Pacific in the early twentieth century. I argue that the debates concerning this phenomenon, coupled with the legal principle of dependent citizenship, reveal the complex intersection of gender with nationality, race, and citizenship during this era. Mae's case serves as a sharp reminder that citizenship has been defined historically not only on the bases of *jus sanguinis* (right of blood) and/or *jus soli* (right of the soil), but also as an extension of the patriarchal institution of the family. Thus, whereas the previous chapter called for greater attention to class in analyses of intermarriage, this chapter highlights the centrality of gender in analyzing particular forms of hybridity.

Although contemporaneous commentators on both sides frequently condemned such marital migration as a doomed experiment, a reading of *My Chinese Marriage* in conjunction with other sources, such as the Franking family correspondence, census records, and immigration and naturalization statutes, provides a different view of the lived experiences of one such family and a challenge to the ideologies of race and gender underlying the dire predictions of naysayers. Written against the dominant presumption that a white woman in China was destined for a life of bitterness, *My Chinese Marriage* demonstrates how an American who suffered marital expatriation claimed a new transcultural identity as a "Chinese wife" and built a life for herself and her children in the face of legal and social constraints.

I further take *My Chinese Marriage*, the remarkable story of a woman whose life straddled the boundaries of race and nation, as a starting point for critiquing some of our contemporary assumptions concerning hybridity and "Chineseness." I contend that hybrid figures such as Mae, a Euro-American woman who "became Chinese" both legally (through marital naturalization) and culturally (through transculturation), prompt us to reconsider the racial boundaries of Chineseness, with far-reaching implications for current understandings of hybridity and identity. Juxtaposing Mae Franking against more conventional icons of cultural hybridity like Yung Wing enables us to treat Sinicization as a counterpart to Westernization and serves as a powerful reminder that migration and assimilation can be a two-way street, an issue that I take up in the coda.

INTERMARRIAGE IN THE NEW CENTURY: SOCIAL AND LEGAL CHANGES

By the time of Mae's marriage to Tiam on September 12, 1912, the climate toward Chinese–Western intermarriage on both sides of the Pacific had changed quite dramatically from the age of the Kellogg–Yung wedding. Mae had first met Tiam in 1907 when he enrolled at Ann Arbor High School. Although Mae's initial reaction to this "alien" was a "sense of his complete remoteness, an utter failure to regard him as a human being like the rest of us," this handsome young scion of a Fujian merchant family gradually won her over, and as students at the University of Michigan the couple decided to wed.[11] Mae's parents expressed concerns, but they were liberal minded and warm hearted and soon welcomed the young Chinese Christian into the family. The couple was married by the Episcopal minister at the Watkins's home. This time there was no fanfare in the *New York Times*. Instead, local papers published inflammatory articles with titles like "A Concrete Reason for the Race Prejudice at Ann Arbor," "American Girl Becomes Bride of Chinaman Who Formerly Lived in Grand Rapids; Friends Peeved."[12]

Although Michigan never joined the flurry of states that passed anti-miscegenation laws against the Chinese between 1910 and 1935 (bringing the overall total to fifteen), the Michigan House had considered such a bill in 1911, and would do so again in 1913 after a controversy surrounding a Chinese restaurant owner's marriage to a white woman in Detroit.[13] Following the Franking marriage, the local outcry was so intense that Tiam wrote a letter defending their union to the *Ann Arbor Times*. As Tiam wrote, "Don't the marriage confirmed with laws of both holy gospel and the land, and with the consent of the parents, as well as the parties . . . after all a private matter? [*sic*]."[14] The pairing of a Chinese man and white woman made their union especially controversial. As the *Ann Arbor Times* pointed out, "The marriage of an American man and a Japanese or Chinese or Hindoo girl creates little or no such furore, and is rather accounted a pleasurable social sensation, the bride, if she is pretty and attractive, being petted and feted."[15] As this chapter shows, this gendered double standard regarding intermarriage also found expression in the realm of law.

Public pressure compelled the Frankings to withdraw from the University of Michigan, cutting short Mae's dream of a college degree in foreign languages. Tiam enrolled at the Detroit College of Law, leaving Mae to weather the storm at home. In Detroit, Tiam was elected president of the Chinese Students' Alliance and soon became a favorite of his professors. But he was continually reminded that without citizenship he could not practice law in the United States.[16] Tiam thus began to make plans to return to China, where he hoped to play a role in China's modernization.[17]

But there were obstacles in that path too. Tiam had faced strong opposition from his parents in China, who were dismayed that their son's marriage would cause a grave breach of obligation to his Chinese fiancée, a match arranged in his infancy. Tiam's family lived on the small island of Kulangsu (Gulangyu), just off the treaty port of Amoy. Their impression of Westerners was thus shaped by the power dynamic that governed contact between Chinese and expatriates within the foreign concessions, and Tiam's mother was none too eager to have a haughty American—as she imagined Mae—as a daughter-in-law. On the eve of the wedding, Tiam's father cabled him a stern command: "Must not marry."[18] Having disobeyed his father and disgraced his family, Tiam was promptly disowned.

As Tiam would later find upon his return to China, the opposition was not only familial. The mounting debate concerning overseas student intermarriage, introduced in the previous chapter, had reached the highest levels, prompting the Qing court to issue a prohibition against such unions in 1910. Thus, whereas Yung Wing and Mary Kellogg had married in an era when sentiment was still evolving, Mae Watkins and Tiam Hock Franking took their vows in the face of intensified opposition from both sides.

Indeed, to say that times were different is perhaps an understatement. By 1902, the U.S. Congress had extended Chinese exclusion indefinitely. Even more dramatically, a revolution had taken place in China. Ending the centuries-old system of dynastic rule, the 1911 revolution established the Republic of China and ushered in a new era of modernization. It had also ushered in a period of heightened nationalism, with the revolutionary rallying cries of "Oust the Manchus" and "China for the Chinese" still ringing strong. These two events prompted overseas students to flock back to their homeland: some returned because they were eager to contribute to the "new China"; others because of the racial discrimination they faced in the United States and the barriers to professional mobility. The Frankings fervently believed that their life-work lay in China: Tiam as a lawyer or diplomat, and Mae as a language teacher and faithful helpmeet. Hence, Mae decided to follow her husband to China, despite warnings from friends and relatives.

MARITAL EXPATRIATION AND NATURALIZATION

When Mae married Tiam in September 1912, she faced not only ostracism from friends and relatives but legal consequences as well. Legal changes that had taken place since the Kellogg–Yung wedding affected both Tiam and Mae. Tiam was affected by the Chinese Exclusion Act of 1882, which barred Chinese from naturalization, and Mae by the Marital Expatriation Act of 1907, which stripped U.S. citizenship from all female citizens who married aliens.[19]

The act of 1907 was based on the gendered logic of dependent citizenship, which granted married women the status of their husbands and minor (marital) children that of their fathers.[20] Already in 1855, Congress had passed a statute granting U.S. citizenship to any foreign-born woman (eligible for naturalization) who married a U.S. citizen husband. The same, however, was not true in reverse for noncitizen men who married U.S. citizen wives. The 1855 act also granted U.S. citizenship to marital children born abroad to U.S. citizen fathers, but not to U.S. citizen mothers.[21] This gendered double standard was consistent with the legal principle of coverture, which subsumed a married woman's legal identity under that of her husband.

As Leti Volpp's analysis of dependent citizenship shows, thousands of American women like Mae Franking lost their citizenship by marrying foreign nationals. Although the Cable Act of 1922 partially overturned the act of 1907, Congress did not eliminate marital expatriation for American women who married "aliens ineligible to naturalize"—a category that primarily referred to Asians—until 1931.[22] Marital expatriation had far-reaching consequences for the rights of American women who married Chinese men during the Exclusion era. Dependent citizenship meant that these women would share the subordinate racial status of their husbands, at least in legal terms, and face the same restrictions regarding travel and entry into the United States.

When Ticie Pruett See traveled to her husband's home village in Canton, China for the first time in 1901, it was with no papers: the manifest of the steamer *Korea* listed her simply as "Mrs. Fong See, age 24, American." On her second voyage in 1919, however, she was required to obtain Form 431, the legal paperwork documenting her status as the wife of a lawfully domiciled Chinese merchant.[23] As Lisa See recounts, her great-grandmother Ticie presented a conundrum to the immigration officers: How could a white woman be Chinese? She submitted all the required paperwork, including a letter from the consulate general of the Republic of China claiming Mrs. Fong See as "a citizen of the Republic of China," yet by all appearances she was "American." Immigration Inspector W. G. Becktell wrote to his superiors, "There appears to be some conflict of opinion as to whether an American-born white woman married to a domiciled Chinese merchant should be given Form 431." Unable to comprehend the apparent contradiction of a "white" Chinese, Becktell suggested that "it might be assumed that in the opinion of the examining officers she is at least part Chinese."[24] After much internal discussion in the Immigration Service, Ticie was finally issued the form—her only guarantee of reentry to the country of her birth. Such cases demonstrate the implications of Chinese exclusion and dependent citizenship for white women who "crossed the line" to marry Chinese men.

Indeed, census evidence suggests that in crossing the line white American women not only risked losing their citizenship but also risked a change in their racial status. In the 1910 census of New York, for example, enumerators returned the Dutch American wife of the Reverend Huie Kin (1854–1934) as "Chinese."[25] Interestingly, Ticie See remained "Chinese" long after her divorce from Fong See in 1924. In the 1930 census of Los Angeles, Ticie (who was living with her son Eddy's family at the time) was still enumerated as Chinese in the "color or race" column.[26] This evidence suggests that the logic of dependent citizenship extended to racial classification. Such cases furthermore remind us that race has always been about much more than phenotype and demonstrate the conceptual slippage between "nationality" as citizenship and "nationality" as race, a slippage that was particularly pronounced in the nineteenth and early twentieth centuries but that still pertains today.

The census tells a different story about Mae Franking, however, revealing at the same time the confusion and ambiguity surrounding figures like Mae and Ticie: the paradox aroused perhaps in the eyes of census enumerators and immigration inspectors between the categories of "white" and "Chinese." In the 1920 census, taken when Mae was living with her parents in Ann Arbor, Mae was returned as white, despite the fact that her (deceased) husband was recorded as Chinese.[27]

The flip side of dependent citizenship was that women like Ticie and Mae were conferred Chinese nationality through their husbands. Provisions for marital naturalization were written into Chinese nationality law, which was first promulgated by the Qing in 1909.[28] As Lin Man-houng has demonstrated, Qing nationality law was crafted within the conventions of international law and hence was highly influenced by Western legal discourse.[29] As in the United States, the statutes concerning marriage and nationality were governed by the legal principle of coverture, which subsumed a wife's identity under her husband's.[30] Hence, Chinese nationality law decreed that foreign women who married Chinese men would become Chinese nationals, whereas Chinese women who married foreigners would be expatriated. Again, these nationality laws promoted a strongly patriarchal notion of national identity and citizenship.[31]

The legal principle of coverture corresponded perfectly with Confucian gender ideology. As codified in various Confucian texts throughout the ages, the idealized form of marriage in Chinese society involved the exogamous exchange of women. Hence, a bride was "given out" (jia) by her natal family and "taken in" (qu) by the groom's family. Since a woman belonged to her husband's family after marriage, becoming one of "his people," her identity and status were largely determined by his. This expectation was articulated in the pithy popular aphorism: "Marry the rooster, follow the rooster. Marry the dog, follow the dog" (jiaji suiji, jiagou suigou). Both legal convention and social custom thus perpetuated gender asymmetry in terms of identity. This had the effect of promoting the Sinicization of mixed families in which the father was Chinese. Indeed, as Patricia Ebrey has noted, "Patrilineal kinship as the key metaphor for connection allows rapid expansion [of the Chinese we-group] through intermarriage."[32] In other words, when Chinese men married non-Chinese women, intermarriage served as a means to incorporate Others into the lineage and into the larger Chinese we-group.

Within the context of this gender ideology, Mae voyaged to China, traveling as a Chinese national, to begin a new life in her adopted country. Tiam had rented a home for his family at 39 Fude Li in the city's International Settlement. Assisted by two servants and an amah for baby Nelson, Mae entered into an active social life formed around Shanghai's cosmopolitan society, which encompassed the families of returned students and Western expatriates. Teaching English and history at a Chinese girls' high school, Mae also helped an ambitious husband with his work as a teacher, textbook author, and lawyer. After Tiam was admitted to the Mixed Court in 1915, the family would move to a larger house in the French Concession. Tiam opened his own law office while Mae stayed home to await the delivery of her second son, born on January 5, 1916. In 1917, finally reconciled with Tiam's parents, the young family moved again—this time to the ancestral home of the Huang family in Kulangsu. Here at last, with two boys and a new baby girl, Mae would be fully ensconced within a Chinese family. Although life in China was not without its hardships, for Mae marital migration resulted in upward class mobility, exotic adventure, and a chance to "leave the west with its great unrest," as she rejoiced in an unpublished poem.[33]

A WOMAN'S PLACE IS IN THE HOME[LAND]
"Don't!": Discourses on Western Women Going East

As noted at the outset of this chapter, Mae was not the first Western woman to accompany her Chinese husband home. We have already seen how Chen Jitong brought his wives back to China, and Fong See had taken Ticie and their two young boys back to China in 1901 for a year (a trip they would repeat with five children in 1919). The See family sojourns were part of a larger pattern documented by Mary Ting Yi Lui, who found interracial families traveling from the United States to China—for both short-term and long-term stays—from the late nineteenth century on.[34] As Lui demonstrates, by 1908 this phenomenon had reached such alarming proportions that the U.S. consul general Amos P. Wilder felt compelled to order an investigation of "the condition of American women who are living in South China as the wives of Chinese."[35]

Gradually during the first decades of the twentieth century, small international communities of Chinese returned students and their Western wives grew up in the major cities and treaty ports of China, places like Beijing, Shanghai, Tianjin, Hankow, and Amoy. By the 1930s, Herbert Lamson would document the existence of "small groups for several of the leading European nations,—England, France, Germany, as well as the United States."[36] Arriving in China in 1914, the Frankings were not pioneers, but they were certainly among the early cohort of the new "modern phenomenon" of mixed families. Also in this cohort, engineer Zhou Yingtong (1883–1958), the father of Eurasian author Han Suyin, brought his Belgian wife back to China in January 1913.[37]

This emerging phenomenon produced new anxieties. Whereas Croly and Wakeman had warned of the impending invasion of Chinese immigrants and the proliferation of a miscegenated population on American shores (see chapter 1), the early twentieth century saw the emergence of a new discourse warning against the loss of (white) American women to China through intermarriage.

The fear of loss to the nation was reflected in the confidential report Wilder filed to Washington concerning his investigations of "American–Chinese marriages." Wilder did not oppose such marriages outright, but he expressed acute concern over the issues raised by marital migration to China.[38] As he wrote, "There are in the United States instances of happy homes thus constituted, but these are generally of persons of refinement, and their home, it will be noted, is not in China but in the country of the wife."[39] Wilder warned of the social and economic conditions that awaited American women in China—placing particular emphasis on the difficulties caused by polygamy and notoriously tyrannical Chinese mothers-in-law. He further warned that life was especially difficult in rural China, where a wife would likely find herself the only white person in the village.[40] In Wilder's view, "American wives of Chinese should stay in America."[41] According to Mary Lui, "Wilder was particularly appalled by what he viewed as these women's automatic assimilation into the Chinese husband's culture and society, that led them to accept non-Western practices such as foot binding or arranged marriages [for their daughters] and the lowering of their social status and autonomy as women."[42] In short, Wilder was dismayed that such women had "gone native." Cautioning his countrywomen against this fate, the consul wrote of the "sorry lot of American women who married Chinese and come with them to China to live." As he concluded, "The advice of these women would be an unqualified 'Don't.'"[43]

"Don't." This admonition to white women regarding marriage to "Orientals" was conveyed in much Anglo-American writing of the early twentieth century, including travel writing, newspapers, and fiction. Stories of white women who had married Asian husbands and subsequently suffered bitterly when they returned to their husbands' homelands—only to find their charmingly Westernized "Oriental swain" showing his true colors as an Oriental despot—served as warnings to any white woman who might dare to cross the color line. Popular travel writer Mary Gaunt, for example, wrote of her encounter with an Englishwoman who had been stranded in a railway town with her "half-caste" baby, trying to make her way from the Chinese interior to Beijing in the spring of 1914. Gaunt presented this woman, who had married a Chinese man in England, as a cautionary tale, warning that a life of bitterness was the inevitable lot for a "woman who had committed the unpardonable sin of the East, the sin against her race, the sin for which there is no atoning."[44] Marital migrants were further warned that they might discover—as Ticie did in 1901—that they were not in fact the first wife after all, but merely a second wife or concubine. Drawing on the biological discourse of acclimatization, others cautioned that white women were not suited to life in the East and would become physically "broken down."

Loss to the nation was certainly a theme in local newspaper accounts of the Franking wedding in Michigan. While the newspapers decried the mixed marriage, they comforted readers with assurances that at least the bride would never be forced to live in her husband's homeland. When friends and relatives later learned that Mae would in fact follow Tiam to China, they warned her against taking such a radical step, leaving behind her mother and forsaking her country for life in a heathen land. Their dire predictions weighed heavily on Mae's mind when she began her new life in China, choosing husband over nation.

"Don't": Discourses on Chinese Students Abroad

If "Don't" was the counsel to Western women, it was equally the imperative issued by the Chinese government to students abroad. Interestingly, the late Qing–early Republican debate on student intermarriage was explicitly gendered—but targeting men, reflecting the fact that virtually all the early overseas students were male. As discussed in chapter 1, there was mounting opposition among the official class to the "international marriages" of Chinese overseas students. This opposition was directly related to fears of what we would today call a "brain drain": Chinese overseas students had been sent abroad to acquire Western learning and were expected to return home to lead China's modernization. Critics of international marriages argued that unions with foreign women would derail this agenda.[45] Such anxieties were expressed in a memorial sent to the Qing Court in 1910 calling for the prohibition of intermarriage among overseas students. The memorial established three grounds of opposition: that marriage was a distraction from studies; that foreign women were known to be extravagant and therefore beyond the means of the student's allowance; and that students who married foreign wives developed the desire to settle abroad and would consequently turn their backs on the ancestral land. Thus, they would not put their talents to the service of China.[46]

The notion that a foreign wife would induce her husband to settle abroad would seemingly have been confirmed by the cases of men like Yung Wing, and Chinese Educational Mission alumni Yung Kwai and Yan Phou Lee, who did, in fact, settle in the United States after marrying American women.[47] One Chinese newspaper even published a story as early as 1899 warning that foreign wives were known to drug their husbands before they returned home to visit China. The only way to avoid illness or even death was for the Chinese man to go back to the side of his foreign wife to receive an antidote.[48] The cautionary tales thus went both ways.

In response to the 1910 petition, the Qing Court issued a prohibition against students marrying foreign women. Reflecting the particular concerns regarding a brain drain, the edict specifically stated that the ban would not apply to "ordinary overseas Chinese": that is, merchants and laborers.[49] The prohibition was unsuccessful, however, for the punishments were light and difficult to enforce, and the Republic of China would find it necessary to pass its own measures, which it did repeatedly in 1913, 1918, and 1936.[50] The fact that successive bans were passed suggests that they did not carry much force and that international marriage continued to be an ongoing issue.

Anxieties concerning loss to the nation played a central role in these debates. The 1918 prohibitions, passed in February and July of that year, once more emphasized the damage to both individual and nation caused by intermarriage, but clearly it was the nation that trumped the individual. Viewed by some as a deeply unpatriotic act, intermarriage represented the crime of "forgetting the nation" or "abandoning the ancestral land" (yanqi zuguo) (see chapter 1).[51] Indeed, I argue that the prohibitions against student intermarriage were not anti-miscegenation laws per se, because their true concern was not racial mixing (after all, "ordinary" overseas Chinese were exempted from the ban), but the loss of patriotic sentiment among the scholarly elite.

Moreover, intermarriage could potentially be viewed as an unfilial (and hence un-Confucian) act, since many Sino–Western marriages— as in Franking's case—were conducted without parental authority, flagrantly violating the traditional practice of arranged marriage that was still commonplace in this era. Similarly, many worried that a Western wife would not be willing to assume the proper duties of a daughter-in-law, who was expected to care for her husband's parents. Tiam's own cousin had appealed to this reasoning in a letter he wrote counseling against the match, warning Tiam of "the sorrows a foreign daughter-in-law would bring into his house—the bitterness of having in the family an alien and stubborn woman, who would be unwilling to give his parents the honor due to them or to render them the service they would expect of their son's wife."[52]

This cousin's letter articulates a particular anxiety concerning the place of a Western wife in the Chinese family and also raises questions of acculturation. By the time that Tiam's cousin composed this letter, the image of the Western woman as an independent-minded and dominant figure who defied Confucian gender norms was already a prevalent stereotype in China.[53] The presumption that a Western woman could not make a proper Chinese wife was expressed in an entry from the *Collected Compendium of Qing Anecdotes (Qingbai leichao)*. As we saw in chapter 1, "Li Fang Divorces Pauline" (*Li Fang yu Paierli lihun*, ca. 1909) begins with a description of international marriage as part of the new fashion for "Europeanization." The anecdote relates the story of Li Fang, who married an Englishwoman while studying in England. Having accompanied her husband to China in 1905, Pauline grew increasingly discontented and decided after three years to return on her own to England. Li Fang thereupon sought a divorce on the grounds that Pauline did not "conform to the rules of wifely conduct" (*bushou fudao*). Although the anecdote never explicitly condemns intermarriage, the author implies that the Western woman's inability (or refusal) to conform to Confucian norms of wifely conduct is an impediment to successful unions.[54]

Having arrived in China in 1913–14, the Frankings found themselves in the midst of these debates. On a spring morning in 1918, Tiam opened his newspaper and discovered that a petition had been sent to the government calling for (yet another) prohibition against overseas students marrying foreign wives. As chance would have it, Tiam was staying in Beijing at the time, making the rounds in official circles in the hope of securing a government post. One can only imagine the anxiety with which he must have greeted such news. With the issue in the public eye, Tiam even found himself consulted on the subject: the secretary of the Beijing YMCA, for example, questioned whether he was happy in his marriage. Tiam reported on these events in a letter to Mae, who had stayed behind in Kulangsu with Tiam's mother and the three children, Nelson, Alason, and Cecile. As Tiam assured Mae, "I said—'I couldn't get a better and happier wife.' Shut his mouth."[55] Tiam also informed Mae that there were more than a dozen Chinese among the elite circle who had brought home foreign wives. Perhaps attempting to reassure Mae (and himself) that a foreign wife would not damage his career prospects, Tiam wrote that even the minister of foreign affairs had an English wife. In the end, Tiam received an appointment at the consulate general's office in San Francisco, resulting in the family's unexpected departure in the winter of 1918.[56]

Counter-discourse: "The Best Path" for Intercultural Understanding

Despite the air of controversy, as we saw in the previous chapter there were also voices supporting, and even advocating, international marriage as a progressive phenomenon. The Frankings certainly found no obstacles to entering the elite circles of "advanced" Chinese and cosmopolitan expatriates in Shanghai.[57] In 1917, Mae boasted to her family that they had hosted a dinner at the Astor House—"THE hotel in Shanghai." As Mae wrote to her mother, the Frankings entertained the commissioner for foreign affairs, the judge of the U.S. Supreme Court for China, and others. "Oh, we have entertained Ex-ambassadors, railway and College Presidents, and all varieties of large-dimension ones, too," Mae reported.[58]

It must have been at this Astor House party that Mae first met Wu Tingfang, who, as noted in the previous chapter, was one of the most famous Chinese advocates of international marriage during this era. Wu was a British-educated barrister who served as minister to the United States, Spain, and Peru (1896–1902, 1907–09), and in various other posts, including acting premier of the Republic of China in 1917. Among the various subjects he took up in his writings and public lectures on race relations was East–West intermarriage. In 1911, Wu articulated his vision for the new China and asserted that "Westerners and Easterners should intermarry, for this is the best path for spreading knowledge, establishing kinship relations and ties of friendship."[59] Similarly, in America, Through the Spectacles of an Oriental Diplomat (1914), which was written for American audiences, Wu portrayed international marriage as a means of promoting permanent world peace, as well as a eugenic measure, a notion that is discussed further in chapter 4.[60] Like other Western-educated intellectuals of his age, Wu was keenly aware that anti-miscegenation laws, like immigration restrictions, served as foundations for the larger racial projects of Western supremacy, and he was anxious to challenge their premises. Wu's positive assessment of the outcome of interracial marriage was based on his own firsthand observations of mixed families like the Yung Wing family of Connecticut, the Yung Kwai family of Washington, D.C., the Huie Kin family of New York, the Ho Tung family and other leading Eurasian families of Hong Kong.[61] Now the Frankings were added to his acquaintance.

When Wu Tingfang dined with the Frankings in 1917 he was especially attentive to the question of Mae's cultural adjustment, and he was pleasantly surprised to see her dressed for the occasion in Chinese attire. With an accompanying illustration, this encounter was related in *My Chinese Marriage*:

> He looked at me very keenly for a moment, as if he meant to ask a serious question. Then he said, in his abrupt manner, "You are happy in that dress?"
> "Indeed I am," I answered.
> "You like it better than you like American clothes?" he persisted.
> I nodded firmly, smiling and catching my husband's eye.
> "Then wear it always," said the Doctor, with a pontifical lifting of his fingers.[62]

Wu Tingfang's approval, underscored by his serious demeanor, was directed toward the young bride's symbolic gesture of adopting Chinese dress. This symbolism was similarly appreciated by her husband, who was deeply moved on the first occasion when she donned Chinese costume: "I think the sight of me in the dress of his country confirmed in his mind my declaration that I loved China—that I wanted to be a real Chinese wife."[63] Dress, an issue to which I return in chapter 8, was a crucial signifier of ethnic identification during this era.

The notion of becoming a "real Chinese wife" is a thread that runs throughout *My Chinese Marriage*, which narrates the young bride's attempts to adjust to a new life in China and to express her devotion to her husband and adopted country. What does it mean for a white American woman to declare herself a *real Chinese* wife, a *real Chinese* daughter-in-law? How does this (apparently) simple claim set "whiteness" and "Chineseness" in tension? In the next section of the chapter, I turn to the claims set forth in *My Chinese Marriage* concerning Mae's attempts to fashion a new identity for herself after her migration to China.

MARITAL MIGRATION AND TRANSCULTURATION
M.T.F.'s My Chinese Marriage: *For "Lovers of the Orient"*

"Only American Co-ed who ever lived as the wife of a Chinese
aristocrat under the roof of her Chinese mother-in-law."

An ad placed in the *Chicago Daily Tribune* in May 1921 promised the
"authentic" story of M.T.F., to begin with the June issue of *Asia:
The American Magazine on the Orient*.[64] Divided into four installments,
the story enticed readers with the exotic experiences and titillating
details of an "American girl's" romance and marriage to a Chinese student. The narrative tells of their courtship, marriage, and subsequent
life with three children in China, including the ultimate challenge of
adjusting to domestic life in the bosom of a Chinese clan. It ends in
1918, when the family returns to the United States, where Tiam is to
take up a new posting in the consular service. Tragically, shortly after
their arrival in San Francisco, Tiam died of influenza. The final message
of the story is that true love, imbued with Christian spirituality, tri-
umphs over racial prejudice and the gulf of cultural difference.

Mae had drafted her memoir in the long months after her husband's
death, while she and the three children stayed with her parents in Ann
Arbor. New York's *Asia* magazine then hired budding author Katherine
Anne Porter as a ghostwriter to take dictation from Mae and rewrite the
manuscript.[65] When *Asia* finally published the story, the author's name
was given simply as "M.T.F." and the names of family members
changed to protect their privacy: Mae became "Margaret," and Tiam
Hock Franking "Chan King Liang."

To American readers of the time, the story of this mixed marriage
would have been quite radical. Indeed, even as *Asia* magazine used
tabloid-style advertisements to attract readers, editor John Foord was
compelled to defend its publication. Mae herself (as M.T.F.) also wrote
a disclaimer, stating that hers was a purely personal story, meant neither as an endorsement nor as a condemnation of intermarriage.[66]

Yet, in many respects it is not surprising that such a work would
have appeared in the pages of John Foord's *Asia*. Representing business
interests as the secretary for the American Asiatic Association, which
was dedicated to promoting Asian trade, Foord was well known as an
outspoken critic of Chinese exclusion, which he viewed as damaging to
American commerce. Marketed to "Lovers of the Orient," *Asia* magazine supported the association's stated purpose of promoting intercultural understanding and "the dissipation of ignorant prejudices," while

stimulating interest in travel and Oriental goods.[67] The story of the Frankings' successful marriage demonstrated the possibilities of shared values between "conservative West" and "very liberal East."[68] Skillfully balancing exotic Orientalist fantasy with an appeal to the Christian notion of the "brotherhood of man," *My Chinese Marriage* fit squarely the agenda of the association and its missionary allies.

In fact, despite the outcry from conservative readers—including a particularly vehement letter from a West Coast subscriber who found the depiction of interracial children to be "positively nauseating"— Foord also received letters expressing "pleasure and interest" in this unusual story.[69] Reader response was so positive (surely owing in part to Porter's literary skill) that the narrative was republished in book form by Duffield within a matter of months, with three reprints appearing between 1921 and 1928.[70] Mary Kellogg's hometown paper, the *Hartford Courant*, serialized the popular work in daily installments in May 1922, advertising to readers a "Thrilling Story," representing "a triumph of human sympathy over race prejudice."[71] The public interest in such "real-life stories" is further indicated by the *San Francisco Bulletin*'s publication in 1922 of Emma Fong Kuno's "My Oriental Husbands"—the narrative of a white woman who first married a Chinese pastor, and then (after his death) a Japanese professor.[72]

As Henry Yu has demonstrated, much of the public interest in such narratives was prurient in nature, representing a curiosity about interracial sexuality and a voyeuristic desire to peer into these women's lives.[73] At the same time, Mae's narrative also appealed to readers as a Cinderella-like story of an "ordinary girl" marrying a "Chinese aristocrat," and of true love in the face of obstacles. The underlying message of a common humanity united in Christ must also have increased the narrative's acceptability. The memoir received many favorable reviews from across the nation. The *Boston Globe*, for example, praised this "charming love story" as "the most ideal love story ever written," and lauded the "dignity and courage" shown by an "American girl who did marry, did go to China, and did, so far as one can, change her nationality."[74] Interest in the text was thus multifaceted.

My Chinese Marriage was also extremely popular among Chinese students in the United States, with one recalling that "almost every Chinese student in the US at that time owned a copy."[75] The work received two positive reviews in the *Chinese Students' Monthly* (*Zhongguo liumei xuesheng yuebao*).[76] Returning students brought copies of the book back to China, and it was translated into Chinese at least twice, once by a former student of Huang Tianfu, the famous Chinese journalist and publisher Zou Taofen (1895–1944).[77] As a tribute to his beloved "teacher's wife" (*shimu*), Zou published a serialized translation of the text in his popular Shanghai-based periodical, *Life Weekly*, between February and December 1927, with each installation followed by a brief translator's commentary.[78] In his commentary, Zou lauded the couple's true love and praised them as a model of intercultural understanding. Using his translation as a platform for advocating family reform and women's rights in China, Zou further extolled them as exemplars of the modern nuclear family. His translation received praise from readers, whose letters to the editor expressed deep enjoyment of the story, both on a literary level and as a vehicle for thinking through issues of cultural difference and reform.[79] The story proved so popular that it was soon published as an independent volume.

Putting on China: Intersections of Antifeminism with Antiracism

If Zou presented Mae's memoir as a portrait of a modern marriage, a case study in the need for reform of women's roles in China, I argue that the narrative itself does not necessarily support such an interpretation. Instead, in essentially embracing the gender ideology of dependent citizenship, *My Chinese Marriage* serves as an example of what I would call "Orientalist antifeminism," a mode seen in other writings of the period. Gender ideology is indeed central to the text, for even as it traces the narrator's changing attitude toward China and Chinese people, it simultaneously traces a transformation in her understanding of Chinese women's roles, which she initially views as degraded and subservient and later comes to respect. The intercultural story cannot be separated from the narrator's stance on gender roles: that is, her firm conviction, as "conservative West," that her highest calling is to be a "genuinely old-fashioned wife," thus resisting the burgeoning American feminist ideology of the age.[80] Ethnicity and gender are hence inextricably intertwined in her self-fashioning as a Chinese wife, producing a complex intersection of antifeminism with antiracism in the text. Interestingly, while Zou affirmed the narrative's antiracist message, he used the text to promote a feminist message that Mae herself did not embrace.

As related in *My Chinese Marriage*, "Margaret" attempts in numerous ways to fulfill the role of a "real Chinese wife." Her first test comes in Shanghai, when she is invited to *tiffin* at the home of a Chinese family. When the thoughtful hostess offers Margaret a fork, Chan-King declares that his wife is perfectly adept with chopsticks. Margaret recalls, "So my social conformity as a Chinese wife began there."[81] When her husband later worries over the difficulties of adapting to Chinese society, she declares, "You will see whether you haven't married a true Oriental."[82] In this idea of a "true Oriental" is suggested the existence of an internal "Oriental" essence that transcends the differences of what Franz Fanon called the "epidermal schema" of race: in this case, Mae's whiteness.[83]

Determined to become as Chinese as possible, Margaret studies Chinese, learns to manage a household of servants, masters Chinese etiquette, takes up elaborate needlework, and becomes a connoisseur of Chinese opera and exotic delicacies such as duck's feet. The children are raised as Chinese, speaking Chinese with their *amahs*, wearing Chinese clothing, and attending Chinese schools. When the family moves to Fujian, Margaret learns the local dialect. She even develops a respect for Chinese ancestor worship, although she stops short of renouncing Christianity. These gradual changes demonstrate the young wife's growing identification with China as her adopted country. Although *My Chinese Marriage* is the story of only a single individual's life in China, these attempts at acculturation are consistent with Wilder's findings in his investigation of American wives in South China. As Wilder wrote, "All learn the language and, if living in the country, don the native dress."[84]

As noted previously, *My Chinese Marriage* represents the act of donning native dress as a highly symbolic gesture. As the narrator declares after the encounter with Wu Tingfang, "I had put on China, to wear it always, in my heart and mind, and thought only of my husband, his work and his people."[85] In the context of Mae's time, when clothing was much more closely tied to ethnic identity than it is in our own age of multicultural fashion, to adopt the national dress of another culture was a self-conscious act that allowed one to assume the guise of the Other, even if only temporarily.[86] As Lamson documented in his research on the American community in Shanghai during the 1920s and 1930s, few Westerners, aside from the occasional missionary, adopted local dress in China.[87] Margaret's cultural cross-dressing is central to her self-fashioning as a real Chinese wife: dress becomes a way to outwardly mark her espousal of a new cultural identity through marriage, to articulate her affiliation with her adopted country. Wilder had similarly viewed the assumption of native dress as confirmation that Euro-American wives in China had "absolutely no social station . . . save among the Chinese."[88]

Margaret was particularly thankful that she was wearing Chinese dress at the moment when her mother-in-law unexpectedly visited the family in Shanghai, a moment that serves as Margaret's second major test. After some initial awkwardness, the two women gradually develop a warm bond, to the degree that "Madame Liang" is proud to publically acknowledge Margaret as her daughter-in-law. At the end of her stay she tells her son, "This is a Chinese house, with a Chinese wife in it. Everything is Chinese. I could never have believed it without seeing, for I thought your wife was a western woman. I am happy."[89]

The final test occurs when Margaret moves in with her mother-in-law and assumes the traditional role of "first daughter-in-law." This test she must pass to silence the doubters who predicted her marriage would founder on this point. When her husband is called to duty in Beijing, Margaret is left behind to assume the position of household manager and caretaker for her mother-in-law. Entering this role with some trepidation, she proclaimed, "My life as a real Chinese daughter-in-law had begun." In the end, this hurdle too is cleared, and the narrator declares herself "more deeply absorbed into the clan—a Chinese woman, dedicated anew, heart and spirit, to my adopted people."[90]

Margaret's identification with China can also be read through her redefinition of "home." When the time comes for the family to return to America, Margaret is heartbroken, crying, "A surging love of the very soil under my feet, a clinging to the earth of China, overwhelmed me . . . . 'This is home! I wish we were not leaving, even for a day!'"[91] At the close of the memoir, after the swift narration of Tiam's tragic death in San Francisco, Margaret reaffirms this commitment to her adopted land: "I have my children and my memories and my home in China, which waits with the gentle healing of sight and sound and place."[92] Sadly, Mae would never return to this waiting home, for she died of tuberculosis in Ann Arbor in 1926.

The redefinition of home enables the narrator to adopt an "insider's perspective" in depicting Chinese customs. This insider status is produced in the text through the narrator's repeated self-representation as a real Chinese wife or a Chinese woman, as well as through references to "my adopted people" or "our dialect." These linguistic markers continually highlight the narrator's new identity and her allegiance to China. This insider's perspective was valued by numerous reviewers of the work, including Chinese reviewers. The *Chinese Students' Monthly* praised the book for depicting a "true and inside story" of Chinese customs. *My Chinese Marriage* was different from other foreigners' accounts of China, the *Monthly* argued, because the author (presumed to be M.T.F.) was "living amongst the people and being considered as one of them."[93] In fact, the ethnographic authority of the text, which was used as a source for sociological analyses of women's roles and marriage in China, depended on the narrator's dual status as an insider (one of them), with privileged access to the private details of upper-class women's lives, and an outsider (one of us) who could report objectively on what she observed. Through this dual perspective, the text challenges the prevailing Western stereotype that traditional Chinese women were submissive and downtrodden chattel. Instead, *My Chinese Marriage* portrays Chinese women as strong, dignified, and intelligent individuals who recognize their centrality to the family. The narrative even defends customs like arranged marriage and foot-binding, customs that Christian missionaries had long held up as evidence to justify the need for Western missionary presence in China and for cultural interventions in the name of civilization and women's rights. This shift in perspective would have confirmed Wilder's worst fears concerning women like Mae Franking.[94]

If we read Mae Franking's correspondence alongside *My Chinese Marriage*, we see another example of Mae's growing identification with her adopted country that was omitted from the text: her position on the war. In letter after letter Mae wrote home of her indignation against England, especially for aiding the Japanese violation of China's neutrality.[95] Keeping her family apprised of the situation in China, Mae made clear her intense loyalty to her new nation and her willingness to break with popular American opinion on the war.

Transracial Nationality in the Age of Chinese Exclusion

Since firsthand accounts of marital migrants' lives in China are few and far between, there is no way of knowing how typical Mae's experiences were for women of her era. According to early twentieth-century sociologists, the Western wives of Chinese returned students generally found a comfortable niche for themselves in cities like Shanghai, Beijing, and Tianjin, where they enjoyed active social lives among foreign-educated Chinese, missionaries, and other mixed families.[96] Yet, Han Suyin's narrative of her Belgian mother's migration to China provides a drastically different portrait: that of a woman who fiercely resisted acculturation and who more than once packed her bags to return to Belgium.[97] Other accounts convey a range of experiences that were shaped by factors of class, location, personality, and the vicissitudes of life in twentieth-century China.[98]

Such limitations notwithstanding, *My Chinese Marriage*, with its particular claims to textual authority as a "real-life story," challenged the prevailing Western presumption that marital migration to China spelled inevitable ruin for the Western woman. In doing so, the text undermines the unspoken conviction of Western cultural superiority upon which such presumptions rested. Mae's case furthermore provides a compelling counterexample to the dominant discourse linking international marriage to national betrayal that shaped Chinese state policy in the 1910s through the 1930s. Whereas cultural conservatives argued that Chinese–Western intermarriage signaled the deracination of overseas students, Mae's example demonstrates that intermarriage could conversely serve to Sinicize the Western wife, ultimately resulting in the transfer of her loyalty to her adopted country.

Yet we might well ask if a white woman, a "foreign devil," could truly become a "real Chinese wife" as her text claimed. How do we understand this American woman's Sinicization? And what did she give up in the process? As Melissa Brown has argued in her study of processes of cultural change among Chinese minorities, identity construction depends not only on culture and ancestry, but also (more powerfully, Brown contends) on social experience.[99] We can identify elements of social experience that powerfully shaped Mae's individual identity construction from the time that she became Mrs. Tiam Hock Franking. The first is Mae's marital expatriation, which removed her from the American polity and transferred her to the Chinese. A second powerful influence was her migration to China, which thrust her into a new social domain with the expectation of conformity to Chinese gender roles. Instead of holding herself aloof from this expectation, as Han Suyin's mother did, Mae chose to embrace transculturation. Mae's correspondence indicates that the social group with whom she most closely identified shared experiences was not the American expatriate community, but the families of Chinese returned students, who lived after "semi-foreign ways."[100] Finally, the Chinese kinship system, which subsumed a woman's identity under her husband and the lineage, worked in tandem with Mae's own personal (avowedly antifeminist) understanding of marriage as a state of gendered dependency to shape her identity as a Chinese woman: a member of a Chinese family, a member of a Chinese lineage, and a member of the Chinese citizenry.

Although such an identity might seem anomalous, it was valued by *Life Weekly* readers in China. Responding to the translation of Mae's memoir, subscribers idealized the heroine precisely for her hybridity as an exotic Western woman who was educated and modern but yet willing to become a "real Chinese wife."[101] Similarly, overseas students of this era, as Zou Taofen recalled, "virtually all dreamed of getting a foreign wife as virtuous (xianhui) as Margaret."[102]

But what of the children? In part II, we turn to ideas of "mixedness" that Eurasians, in different times and different places, were thought to embody.

PART TWO

Debating Hybridity

Prologue to Chapter 3

QUIMBO APPO'S PATRIOTIC GESTURE

In the same year that Yung Wing sailed across the Atlantic trade route aboard the *Huntress*, bound for New York with its cargo of tea, an aspiring tea merchant from Ningbo sailed the Pacific route for San Francisco. Years later, their paths failed to cross once again—for Yung Wing graduated from Yale and returned to China in 1854, too early to see Quimbo Appo's tea shop listed in the New Haven city directory of 1855. With his hopes for a prosperous future, Quimbo Appo (1825–1912) must have been overjoyed when his wife gave birth to a son in New Haven, Connecticut, on July 4, 1856, and he chose a name that would reflect his growing allegiance to his new homeland. As the *New York Times* proclaimed, "The little fellow was born in New Haven on the Fourth of July last, and they have given him the name of GEORGE WASHINGTON."[1] A more American entry into the world is hard to imagine.

The name "Appo" too was purely American in its invention. As George would later testify, his father's "right name was Lee Ah Bow," and he "was born in the City of Ning Poo [Ningbo], China, and came to this country in the year of 1847 and settled down in San Francisco, Cal. in the tea business until 1849, when the gold excitement broke out in that section of the country [*sic*]."[2] Located in Zhejiang province, Ningbo was a center of the tea trade, as well as a profitable market for the sale of American manufactured goods.[3] Foreigners also were increasingly a common sight after Ningbo became a treaty port.

One of these foreigners was the Reverend Walter M. Lowrie (1819–47), yet another missionary who had sailed forth from New York aboard the *Huntress* destined for a "life among the heathen." Looking back from the perspective of his later experiences, one wonders whether Quimbo Appo would have agreed with an observation that Lowrie made in a letter to his father on May 30, 1845: "We are better treated here, by far, than a Chinaman would be in New York or London; though it does occasionally ruffle one's temper to hear himself called a pah-kwei, or *white devil*, with some other such choice epithets."[4]

After his adventures in the California Gold Rush, Appo came East, marrying Catherine Fitzpatrick at some point along the way. Following George's birth in New Haven, the family moved to New York City, where Appo found work as a tea dealer. In New York, Quimbo Appo met other men like himself, recent immigrants from China who had married Irish immigrant women, a pattern that was becoming widespread in New York, Boston, and other East Coast cities as the intersecting diasporas of Chinese and Irish migration brought couples into contact in working-class neighborhoods such as the lower wards of Manhattan.[5]

Quimbo Appo must have been proud to read about himself in the papers during these days, when he was rapidly becoming the most famous Chinese immigrant in 1850s New York.[6] Fluent in English, an enterprising businessman with a connoisseur's knowledge of tea, and a dashing figure in the latest American fashions, Quimbo Appo was embraced by the New York press as an "exemplary Chinaman."[7] The *New York Times* reporter who announced George's birth in 1856 heralded Quimbo Appo as a role model for other Chinese immigrants, who declared their intentions to likewise learn to read and write the English language, become American citizens, and marry "American girls."[8]

But the mood in the press would change during the next two decades as the "exemplary Chinaman" became prone to outbursts of violent temper, finding himself charged with a series of assaults and murders, and in and out of prison—earning the new moniker, "the Chinese devil man." The press that had once celebrated the Chinese immigrant's marriage to a European woman as confirming his willingness to assimilate now fixed on domestic strife in the Appo household as signaling the dark side of the mingling of races. One evening, Appo launched into a violent struggle with his wife, whom he suspected of drunkenness, and accidentally knifed his landlady, Mary Fletcher. Condemned to be hanged for her murder, Appo managed to get his sentence reduced to ten years for manslaughter.

Still, Appo could never climb out of his downward spiral into violence and delusions. Reading the writing on the wall, his wife left him, taking their young daughter with her. Appo's earlier fame as a model immigrant was now eclipsed by his notoriety as a violent criminal and a madman, a symbol of the dangers of the Other among us.[9] In the end, Quimbo Appo was incarcerated in the Matteawan State Hospital for the Criminal Insane, where he lived until his death in 1912. George, the Fourth of July baby, would have to make his own way in the world.

"A Problem for Which There Is No Solution"

The New Hybrid Brood and the Specter of Degeneration in New York's Chinatown

The most famous Eurasian in America during the 1890s was a criminal. A notorious pickpocket and "green-goods man," George Washington Appo (1856–1930) (fig. 7) regularly appeared in newspaper stories of the time. After he testified in the sensational Lexow Committee investigation of New York police corruption, the *New York Times* dubbed George "one of the country's most picturesque criminals," while Yung Wing's local paper, the *Hartford Courant*, unfailingly chronicled the "half-breed's" trials and testimony.[10] George Appo even turned up on the stage, playing himself in George Lederer's theatrical melodrama, *In the Tenderloin*, to national acclaim.[11] To cap it all off, the *World* voted him among "the People Who Made the History of 1894."[12]

Journalist Louis J. Beck devoted a chapter to this colorful character, son of Quimbo Appo, the infamous Chinese tea merchant turned murderer, in his *New York's Chinatown: An Historical Presentation of Its People and Places* (1898). Part tourist guidebook, part amateur ethnography, part muckraking exposé, Beck's volume was the first full-length book on New York's Chinese Quarter and would in time become a frequently quoted source for Chinatown history. Beck promised his audience that his book would shed light on the vexed Chinese Question by presenting the city's Chinese residents through the unbiased lens of the reporter.[13] At the heart of the Chinese Question was this: Could the Chinese in time become assimilated, and patriotic, American citizens, or did their "racial traits" render this impossible, warranting their

FIGURE 7. George Appo as pictured in *New York's Chinatown*, 1898.

Louis J. Beck, *New York's Chinatown*, 1898, p. 251.

exclusion from the nation? Beck offered George Appo's biography as food for thought: "George Appo was born in New York City, July 4, 1858 [*sic*], and is therefore an American citizen, and should be a patriotic one, but he is not. His father was a full-blooded Chinaman and his mother an Irishwoman. He was an exceedingly bright child, beautiful to look upon, sharp-witted and quick of comprehension. For ten years he was the pet of the neighborhood where his parents dwelt. . . . At the age of ten he became a pickpocket."[14]

Beck's decision to dedicate an entire chapter to the celebrity criminal can be explained not only by sensationalism (Appo Sr. was arguably more notorious), but also by the special significance he saw in George Appo's life story. Beck considered this "noted Chinese character" a valuable case study in "heredity and racial traits and tendencies," one well worth investigating, he claimed, for he was only the first of the emerging "new hybrid brood" to come to popular notice. As such, Beck argued, "The question which naturally presents itself to the thinker is, 'What part will the rest of his tribe take in our national development?'"[15]

It was a question that was on the minds of many journalists, social reformers, travelers, and others as they toured America's Chinatowns and saw growing numbers of "half-castes" on the streets and in doorways. Indeed, by the late nineteenth century, such "mixed" children could be found in virtually every Chinese American community, from Boston to Chicago and San Francisco (see introduction). When pioneering Chinese American journalist Wong Chin Foo reported on the New York Chinese for the *Cosmopolitan* in 1888, he asserted that there were more than a hundred "half-breed" Chinese children in that city alone.[16] Although their absolute numbers were small, their anomalous looks drew attention and aroused curiosity. Observers attached a special significance to these children that went beyond their numbers. For many, they represented the future shape of the Chinese American population, for better or worse. Some regarded these "hybrids" as living specimens who offered a chance to see firsthand the biological consequences of race mixing, a subject of intense scientific debate and social concern.

This chapter examines discourses on Chinese Eurasians as a "problem" in late nineteenth-century American society. Using Louis Beck's account of George Appo as a starting point, I explore the ways in which racial theories regarding the consequences of racial amalgamation (which were overwhelming dominated by discussions of white–black miscegenation) informed perceptions of Eurasians as a potential threat to the nation's development.[17] George Appo's case reveals that while the figure of the "half-caste" was frequently connected to dystopian visions of the future—the threat of the Yellow Peril or the specter of mongrelization—representations of Eurasians from this era were not always uniformly derisive, as has often been assumed. Rather, as we will see from a closer reading of Louis Beck's account of Appo, such representations often reveal an underlying ambivalence toward this "half-white/half-Chinese" figure. This ambivalence made the Eurasian a locus of anxiety and desire in age of increasing global interpenetration and migration.

In calling attention to the ambivalence directed toward hybrid figures such as George Appo, I suggest the need to reassess the contemporary periodization of mixed-race studies, with implications for the question of how we construct intellectual genealogies. This ambivalence, I argue, can be productively analyzed in terms analogous to the "tension of empire" theorized by Stoler (see introduction). We have already seen, in chapter 1, how the tension between inclusionary and exclusionary discourses was at the heart of debates concerning the Chinese Question and informed competing conceptions of intermarriage as either a vehicle for assimilation or a threat to the racial homogeneity of the nation. This chapter demonstrates how such a tension similarly animated debates concerning the offspring of intermarriage. Would the "half-breed" children develop into patriotic citizens as Chinese American writers like Wong Chin Foo promised? Or would they prove to be biologically and morally unfit, monsters like George Appo, a man whom Beck declared better off dead?

THE EURASIAN AS PROBLEM

As we saw in chapter 1, from the very beginning of Chinese immigration to the United States, nativists warned against miscegenation as an inevitable outcome of the Chinese presence in American society. A cartoon published on the cover of *Yankee Notions* in March 1858 (see fig. 3 in chapter 1), for example, portrayed an Irish–Chinese couple and their three children as "The Result of the Immigration from China."[18] The warnings were not far off. John Kuo Wei Tchen's study of the Chinese in pre–Exclusion era New York reveals that intermarriage between Chinese men and Irish women—as exemplified by Quimbo Appo and Catherine Fitzpatrick—was prevalent in the early years of Chinese immigration.[19] By 1900, Chinese immigrants in New York were marrying women of diverse backgrounds, but intermarriages still greatly outnumbered Chinese–Chinese marriages, 82 to 51.[20] Indeed, owing in large part to the strictures on the migration of Chinese women to the United States during this era, interracial marriage would remain the predominant marriage pattern for Chinese in New York City until 1925.[21] George Appo was an early example of this phenomenon.

The children of mixed couples increasingly drew the attention of journalists and reformers.[22] In 1890, a *Harper's Weekly* feature on New York's "Chinese Colony" included a description of Chinese–Irish intermarriages, as evidenced by the sight of mixed-race children: "Around the gutters, playing on terms of equality with the other gamins, may be seen a few boys whose features betray their mingled blood." The writer pondered the fact that "it is only about 12 or 15 years since these marriages began, so that the children are all yet young. What kind of people the hybrids will prove to be is yet an unsolved problem."[23] When Harry Wilson reported on the "Children of Chinatown" for the *New York Times* in 1896, he similarly represented mixed children as a "problem." Such children, he wrote, present "a view that is at once bewildering—a

problem for which there is no solution. . . . They were the result of marriage between a Chinaman and an American woman."[24] For those who
perceived these "hybrids" as a problem, Beck's account must surely
have been alarming. According to Beck, there were only thirty-two "full
blooded Chinese children" in Chinatown, compared to forty-seven
mixed children. This was the "new hybrid brood" that Beck warned the
public would "hear more from . . . as time rolls on."[25]

Why was the Eurasian a problem for American society? A problem
for which there was no solution? In Wong Chin Foo's eyes, the "half-
breed children" were successful examples of Chinese assimilation into
American society.[26] As he wrote, "[They] speak the English language,
adopt the American ways and dress."[27] In sharp contrast, the two journalists cited displayed particular anxiety concerning racial mixing as
an unknown. Although the *Harper's* writer confidently described the
"Chinaman" and "Hibernians" as racial types, it remained for him an
open question "what kind of people the hybrids will prove to be."
What would be the effects, biological and cultural, of "mingled blood"?
Building on long-standing American concerns over white–black and
white–Native American interracialism that dated back to the colonial
era (see introduction), such were the questions that the Eurasian "half-
breed" frequently raised in the minds of curious observers.

Despite the long history of Euro-Asian interracialism in Asia, the New
York press generally tended to look close at hand for answers, portraying Eurasian hybridity as a "new" phenomenon and an unknown, a
rhetorical move that had the effect of sensationalizing this offshoot of
the Chinese Question. The visual scrutiny of Eurasian faces and bodies
was part of the anxious search for clues. The *Harper's Weekly* article of
1890, for example, was accompanied by a full-page illustration of a
scene on Mott Street: the focal point is an Irishwoman standing next to
her Chinese husband, holding a baby in her arms, two older mixed-race
children playing beside them. Vividly visualizing the mixed character of
Chinatown life, the illustration prompted readers to consider the yet
"unsolved problem" of what such hybrids would become as they
matured. Similarly, Wilson's *New York Times* article was illustrated
with photographs of "Chinese Half-Castes." Wilson found one girl, a
"Red-Headed Chinese-American Girl," to be a particular curiosity, and
she was featured in several of the photographs.[28] The "half-caste" as
visual spectacle thus emerged as a feature of this time period.

With a naturalist's eye for hereditary patterns, Wilson ventured some
curious rules as to the effects of this "Chinese–American" intermixing.

"Half-caste" boys, he claimed, invariably looked Chinese, but the girls might "incline in resemblance toward their mothers." Mentally, he asserted, the children inherited "the qualities of both nations." Hence Wilson depicted these interracial households as "mixed up" and eclectic. In one family, the younger son wears American dress while the older son wears Chinese. Bilingualism is similarly presented as a strange curiosity of the "mixed" family. As a reporter for the *New York Daily Tribune* had written in 1869, "It is very curious to hear the little half-bred children running about the rooms and alternately talking Irish to their mothers and Chinese to their fathers."[29] For some, the bilingualism/biculturalism displayed by the interracial family was more than a simple curiosity, for it represented a threat to the idealized homogeneity of American society.

Eurasians thus presented a problem in part because of their indeterminacy and liminal status. At once Chinese and European, Sinophone and Anglophone, what place could they be assigned in the American hierarchy of race and ethnicity that was evolving at the turn of the twentieth century? Straddling the boundary between white and non-white, Eurasians were troublesome for, like others of "mixed race," they disrupted the notion of a clearly delineated color line. The ambiguity of Eurasian identity during this era is suggested in the story of one child encountered by a reporter for the *World* in 1877: "'Joe is his name,' said the proud [Irish] mother. 'He don't look like a Chinaboy, does he, when he's asleep! His eyes show it, though, when he's awake.'"[30]

One can only imagine the confusion faced by census enumerators confronted with a child like Joe: Should such a child be classed as "white"? Or "Chinese"? It is perhaps no wonder that the New York census displayed the inconsistencies that John Kuo Wei Tchen first identified regarding the classification of Eurasian children, who were sometime categorized as "Chinese," sometimes as "white," and sometimes as "mulatto."[31] These inconsistencies would persist well into the twentieth century despite the Census Bureau's attempt to formulate rules regarding persons of "mixed-race" (see chapter 6). If Eurasians could manage to fool census enumerators into classifying them as "white," was there a danger that such racially indeterminate peoples would attempt "racial migration" ("crossing the color line")?[32] Or, even worse, "play both sides"?

Within this context of ever-evolving understandings of race and racial hierarchy in late nineteenth-century New York City, Louis Beck produced his biographical sketch of George Appo.

"BORN CRIMINAL": MISCEGENATION AND CONGENITAL DEGENERACY

"GEORGE APPO—BORN TO CRIME." This was the title Louis Beck gave to his account of the notorious pickpocket and con artist. Representing George Appo as a criminal by birth, one who began life as a bright and beautiful child but ended it in violence, "wickedness," and insanity like his father, Beck intimates that Appo's criminality was essentially hereditary rather than a product of his environment, deleterious though it was. On this point, Beck differed radically from Appo's attorney, reformer Frank Moss, who blamed environmental factors for producing New York's habitual criminals.[33] In portraying Appo as a "born criminal," Beck invoked notions of biological determinism that were current at the time, linking ideas of heredity, race, criminality, and other forms of pathology. Such ideas were central to the scientific and social movement of eugenics, a term coined in 1883 by British scientist Francis Galton. Dedicated to promoting "better breeding," as defined by Charles B. Davenport in 1911, when American eugenics became institutionalized in the 1910s and 1920s it took up precisely the issues posed by Beck concerning the effects of immigration, miscegenation, and urban poverty on the nation's development.[34]

Indeed, while Beck intimates that George Appo's criminal tendencies (and his later insanity) were inherited from his father, he also suggests a connection between these traits and the fact of his "unfortunate birth" as the product of miscegenation—the ill-fated union between Quimbo Appo and his Irish wife.[35] As we saw, the history of George's parents is a story in and of itself—colorful, sensational, and in many respects illustrative, as John Kuo Wei Tchen, Tyler Anbinder, and others have demonstrated.[36] Tchen argues that the story of Quimbo Appo's fall from grace "embodied the profound shift in the attitude of New Yorkers toward the Chinese" over the span of three decades, a shift from the earlier period of Patrician Orientalism (see chapter 1) to a post–Reconstruction era of "criminalization, ghettoization, and political exclusion."[37] The story also reflects changing attitudes toward the Irish, who traversed a reverse path from demonization to respectability, exclusion to inclusion, over the same time period. Indeed, Beck evinces anti-Irish sentiment in his account, portraying Catherine Fitzpatrick as an alcoholic and thief who drove her husband to his violent outbursts.[38]

George Washington Appo began his life in the New York press as the son of this famous father, and his media image followed the same trajectory. Initially, the boy's birth was heralded by papers such as the

New York Times as an illustrative instance of the exemplary China-man's Americanization, with reporters lauding Appo's patriotic naming of his Fourth of July baby. The *Times* article furthermore represented the Eurasian baby as a veritable "Yankee boy" who embodied an imag-ined racial assimilation (becoming "like us") of the Chinese through intermarriage. Exemplifying the inclusionary discourse that was some-times extended to the "half-breed," the *Times* declared that George was "a handsome, healthy boy, very sprightly, as white as his mother—a Yankee boy to all appearances, with only the Chinaman's breadth between his eyes."[39] Hence, while Quimbo Appo was still portrayed as "the exemplary Chinaman," George was likewise represented as an exemplary Eurasian—virtually white, an embodiment of the promise and hope of Chinese assimilability, biological and cultural.

But the early promise of George's auspicious birth and his status as the son of the exemplary Chinaman and neighborhood pet soon gave way as the family's circumstances declined. After his father was sent to prison and his mother and sister disappeared from the scene, George was effectively orphaned. He was taken in by the family of a longshore-man named Allen, who lived on Donovan's Lane in the notorious slum of Five Points.[40] In this place, renowned as a breeding ground for phys-ical and moral pollution, wretchedness, and vice, young George began the criminal career that would later catapult him into national fame. As Appo *père* was transformed into "the Chinese devil man" over the years, so too was Appo *fils* transformed into a criminal monster by the media. Even as George gained his own notoriety as a pickpocket and confidence man, the press continually referred to him as the son of Quimbo Appo, a label that not only enhanced the sensationalism of his case but also served to racialize George as Chinese, with all the associ-ated vices and defects. This racial Othering can also be seen in various newspaper cartoons depicting George Appo, as documented in Timothy Gilfoyle's study of the pickpocket's criminal career.[41] In case after case, Appo is depicted in the visual iconography of the "Heathen Chinee," with slanted eyes, buck teeth, and black hair—images that contrast sharply with photographs from the time. Having begun his life in the press as a near-white "Yankee boy to all appearances," George Appo was increasingly represented in terms of his phenotypical Chineseness, moved along the spectrum from inclusion to exclusion.

When Beck placed George Appo at the center of his book on New York's Chinatown, he furthermore indelibly linked the man with the racialized associations of that physical space, a place of darkness, mystery, inscrutability, and the "peculiar" habits and vices of the Chinaman. Beck drew this association despite the fact that George was raised in the racially diverse neighborhood of Five Points, which was populated by Irish, Germans, Eastern European Jews, Italians, and African Americans among others—long before the term "China Town" was even coined in 1880.[42] As George himself would later recall of this neighborhood, "There lived in this Donavan's lane [sic] poor people of all nationalities."[43] While Beck and other contemporaries firmly associated Appo with Chinatown and its racialized connotations of Chinese-ness, the press also simultaneously continued to label him a "half-breed" or "half-caste." Such labels reinforced the notion that the son of the "Chinese devil man" not only came from "bad stock," but, even worse, "mixed stock." The exemplary Eurasian now became a virtual poster child for hybrid degeneracy.

As numerous scholars have demonstrated, degeneration, conceptualized as the "dark side" of progress, was one of the most powerful ideas of nineteenth-century Western thought. Degeneration, in the words of Gilman and Chamberlin, was "for the nineteenth century the most frightening of prospects, as well as at times the most enthralling."[44] A host of social ills and pathologies were associated with degeneracy: urban poverty, alcoholism, drug addiction, prostitution, miscegenation, criminality, insanity, and idiocy.[45] For journalists like Louis Beck, many of these social ills came together in the person of George Appo. Degeneration embodied, George Appo at once frightened and enthralled.

Degeneration theory served as a foundation for the idea of the born criminal, popularized by Cesare Lombroso, the Italian criminologist who pioneered a new pseudoscience of criminal anthropology in the second half of the nineteenth century. Lombroso argued that criminal behavior was hereditary and that physiognomy could be used to identify those with a propensity for crime.[46] The born criminal thus became a set "type." Lombroso's theories were immediately popular in the United States. Interestingly, as Gilfoyle has demonstrated, Quimbo Appo was one of the first prisoners to be subjected to Lombrosian medical evaluations and anthropometric measurements.[47] When Beck labeled George Appo "born to crime," he suggested that his fall from grace was predetermined by heredity, both familial and racial.

Race and eugenics were inextricably intertwined in Lombrosian criminal anthropology. Lombroso argued that criminality represented a form of atavism, a reversion to a primitive evolutionary type. Comparing the traits of criminals to those of "savages," Lombroso posited race as one biological determinant of atavistic behavior and linked the born criminal with the racial Other. Those of "mixed race" stood to inherit a propensity for crime and violence through their nonwhite blood.[48] The new criminal anthropology thereby reinforced established ideas concerning racial amalgamation as a cause of degeneration, a notion that Nancy Stepan calls "one of the most enduring ideas in Western scientific thought."[49]

THE "HUMAN HYBRID": AMALGAMATION IN WESTERN RACIAL THEORY

Even before the advent of "human hybridity" as a scientific concept in the mid-nineteenth century, racial intermixing was long associated with anomalies, abnormalities, and monstrosity. In 1799, for example, British surgeon Charles White reported numerous instances of "irregularities" in the offspring of white–black unions, including piebald children, twins of opposite racial phenotype, and children who were quite literally half-black and half-white—one white on the right side of his body and black on the left, another white from the navel upward and black on his lower body.[50] While such associations with monstrosity or physical abnormalities did not disappear, the nineteenth century ushered in a new body of scientific racial theory on the question of amalgamation and related discourses on the historical effects of "race mixing" on civilizations. As demonstrated by George Stocking and Robert Young, the issue of so-called human hybridity was at the center of nineteenth-century debates over race, pitting monogenists against polygenists, abolitionists against slaveholders—positions that again can be seen as inclusionary versus exclusionary discourses. Young identifies five possible positions that emerged from these debates: (1) the polygenist denial that productive crossing could occur between human races; (2) the amalgamation thesis that racial intermixing produces a new mixed race; (3) the decomposition thesis that mixed-race progeny inevitably revert to parental type; (4) the variable hybridity thesis that unions between "proximate" races are fertile, whereas unions between "distant" races are infertile or degenerate; and (5) the mongrelization thesis that miscegenation produces "raceless chaos."[51]

I add to this list a sixth thesis: that of hybrid vigor. As Nancy Stepan has demonstrated, although this position was a minority one, it nonetheless remained a constant in debates on racial amalgamation throughout the nineteenth century, playing a central role in Quatrefages's discussions of racial hybridity, for example, and even surfacing in Darwin's *The Descent of Man* (1871) among other texts. Indeed, the notion of what Stepan calls "constructive miscegenation" assumes greater historical importance when we extend our attention beyond the Anglo-American sphere to French colonial debates concerning acclimatization; to Latin American eugenics as studied by Stepan; and to Chinese racial theorists, as the next chapter will show. Among Anglo-American theorists, the idea that racial amalgamation was dysgenic remained the dominant view between the 1850s and the 1930s. Nonetheless, it is important to take stock of hybrid vigor as an alternative thesis, as we will see following, for the continuing (if submerged) influence of this viewpoint—which was made plausible through commonplace experiences with plant and animal breeding—helps to explain the deep-seated ambivalence toward the miscegen as a symbol alternatively of mongrelization or of assimilation.

One of the most prominent early proponents of hybrid degeneracy was American polygenist Josiah Nott, who warned of the "Probable Extermination of the Two Races If the Whites and Blacks Are Allowed to Intermarry" in the *American Journal of the Medical Sciences* in 1843. Theorizing the "laws" of human hybridity, Nott declared that "the Mulatto or Hybrid is a degenerate, unnatural offspring, doomed by nature to work out its own destruction."[52] Edinburgh anatomist, Robert Knox, a polygenist like Nott, elaborated the laws of human hybridity in his influential book *The Races of Men*, declaring that "the hybrid was a degradation of humanity and was rejected by nature."[53] Asserting that hybridity was unviable, Knox argued that miscegens either were infertile or reverted to one of the parental types after a few generations. From New York, the polygenist physician John H. van Evrie asserted in 1864 that the "facts" proved "the crossing of distinct races produces a mongrel population, which . . . has less powers of virility, greater tendency to disease, and hence is shorter lived . . . that the condition is an abnormalism, and one of unspeakable wrong and suffering."[54] If unchecked, van Evrie warned, miscegenation would lead to the inevitable downfall of American civilization.

Demonstrating its staying power, Stepan writes, the theory of hybrid degeneracy even survived the revolution of evolutionary biology. The opinion that "crossed races of men are singularly savage and degraded" found support in no less a man than Darwin himself, who speculated that the "degraded state of so many half-castes is in part due to reversion to a primitive and savage condition, induced by the act of crossing, even if mainly due to the unfavorable moral conditions under which they are generally reared."[55] Although Darwin explained "half-caste" degradation in terms of *both* environmental *and* biological factors, it was the latter notion that found most traction during his time.

Nativists in California and elsewhere invoked pseudoscientific ideas of the horrors of biological degeneracy to justify segregating, and ultimately excluding, Chinese immigrants, as we saw from chapter 1.[56] At the Constitutional Convention of the State of California in 1878 delegates warned that "the result of the amalgamation [of Chinese and white] would be a hybrid of the most despicable, a mongrel of the most detestable that has ever afflicted the earth."[57] Decades later the authors of a pamphlet *For the Re-enactment of the Chinese Exclusion Law* (1901) would similarly declare that "the offspring [of intermarriages] has been invariably degenerate. It is well-established that the issue of the Caucasian and the Mongolian do not possess the virtues of either, but develop the vices of both. So physical assimilation is out of the question."[58] Hybrid degeneracy was thus taken as final proof of the unassimilability (biological and cultural) of the Chinese. Even scientific authorities like Herbert Spencer expressed approval for Chinese exclusion in light of the question of amalgamation. Spencer saw only two possible outcomes of Chinese immigration to the United States: either the Chinese would "remain unmixed" and thereby constitute a separate and slave-like class, "or if they mix they must form a bad hybrid." Either scenario would be damaging for American national development.[59]

Given the prevalence of such ideas, it is not surprising that Beck represents Appo in terms of familiar images of half-caste degeneracy and degradation, stereotypes that circulated not only in scientific, medical, and political discourses but also in literature and popular culture. Physically, the "half-caste" was said to be weak, indolent, lacking vitality, short lived, infertile, and susceptible to disease. Mentally and morally they were purportedly prone to alcoholism, promiscuity, criminality, hysteria, insanity, and suicide. Beck's portrait of George Appo confirmed many of these notions: "constituted" for wickedness, given to vice and dissipation, Beck's Appo was an opium addict and born criminal who turned suicidal and insane, finally ending up a "hopeless wreck."

THE WORST OF BOTH WORLDS: THE DUAL NATURE OF THE HYBRID

By far the most popular expression of a belief in hybrid degeneracy was the pithy saying, "The half-caste inherits the vices of both parents, and the virtues of neither." Although its origins are obscure, this cliché had become well worn by the time *New York's Chinatown* was published—and even given the stamp of scientific authority by men like van Evrie.[60] Beck certainly resorts to this chestnut in his portrait of George Appo, identifying specific traits and vices that the "half-breed" inherited from his Chinese father and Irish mother, respectively. From his father, Beck asserted, George inherited "mental cunning and duplicity" and a "cynicism which is particular to the Eastern character"; from his mother, a general "flyness," which also served him well as a professional thief. Combining the worst of (stereotypical) Chinese and Irish vices, Appo was set from birth to become a larger-than-life criminal.

One particular threat embodied by "half-castes" like George Appo was their putative ability to play both sides. Beck asserts that the "young halfbreed" carved out a role for himself as a go-between or interpreter between "Americans" and Irish, on one hand, and Chinese on the other. He worked for a time as a Chinatown guide, catering to sightseers eager to taste the exotic vices of the Quarter, but under the safety of an escort. Beck claimed that Appo's racial inheritance enabled him to function as the perfect inside guide to this mysterious and inscrutable world: "Appo had always, by virtue of his blood on his father's side, enjoyed to a certain extent the confidence of the Chinese—a confidence which the strange, secretive people seldom give to any one not of their own race."[61] If Appo served as a cultural interpreter, in Beck's eyes he was also an agent of transmission of Chinese vices to the non-Chinese community. Indeed, Beck blamed Appo, with his specialized "Chinese" knowledge of the art of cooking opium and his familiarity with the Chinatown "joints," for introducing a taste for the drug to the "New York roughs and crooks" who soon came to frequent Chinatown's opium dens, bringing other white patrons in their wake. Hence the "half-caste" represents not only a corruption of white racial purity, but also a corrupting moral influence. Racial pollution, moral contamination, vice unbalanced by virtue—such were the associations of "half-caste" status. In fact, Timothy Gilfoyle's detailed study of George Appo's criminal career demonstrates that he did have connections, and even financial backing, from criminal establishments both within Chinatown and beyond. According to Gilfoyle, however, it was the latter that played the major role in Appo's life.

The idea of the Eurasian's dual nature had earlier served as the premise for T. S. Denison's comedic drama, *Patsy O'Wang: An Irish Farce with a Chinese Mix-up* (1895).[62] The play centers on the character of

Patsy O'Wang, a.k.a. Chin Sum, a Eurasian of Chinese–Irish descent. As the playwright directed, "The key to this capital farce is the remarkable transformation of which Chin Sum is capable. Born of Irish father and Chinese mother and brought up in barracks in Hong Kong he has a remarkable dual nature."[63] The transformation is effected when Chin Sum imbibes whiskey, "the drink of his father," and undergoes a metamorphosis into a "true Irishman." Strong tea, "the drink of his mother," restores Patsy's "Chinese character," which is that of a sober and industrious Chinese cook. The ideas of hybrid reversion and latent racial traits (blood will tell) are thus enacted in this farce through the bifurcated character of Patsy/Chin Sum, who reverts to parental type based on the drink he consumes.

Hybridity may be farcical, but it is also a cause of chaos, confusion, and disorder—a case for the police and a psychiatrist. In the final act, Patsy/Chin Sum's frustrated employer crossly asks him, "What are you now? Irish or Chinese?"[64] When Patsy declares his choice to be Irish, he is immediately dismissed, roundly castigated for his "ambition" by the doctor's Irish assistant. The ultimate message of this ludicrous comedy is that the races should stay in their place.[65]

"THE NEW HYBRID BROOD": RACE FORMERS IN AMERICA

Whereas the notion of reversion to parental type was linked to the polygenist denial of viable human hybridity, there were others who argued that racial "crossing" would produce a new third race, a new form of humanity hitherto unknown. We see this idea reflected in Beck's identification of George Appo as representative of a "new hybrid brood" or "tribe." Still open for debate was what characteristics this new hybrid tribe would display.

Again, racial theorists were divided on such questions.[66] British ethnologist J. C. Pritchard, a staunch monogenist, argued that racial intermixture would lead to the production of "entirely new and intermediate stock," "mixed human races" that were fertile and prolific, with intermediate physical and mental characteristics.[67] In contrast, German anatomist Carl Vogt argued that amalgamation would produce a new mongrel group representing "raceless chaos," a corruption and degradation of the original, pure races.[68]

The idea of hybrids as "races in the making" also found expression in American literature and popular culture, where the new racial specimens were sometimes depicted as intermediary or composite and sometimes as virtually chimerical. Frank Norris, for example, writing for the San Francisco magazine, the *Wave*, in 1897, gave an account of what he viewed as new races in the making. "Among Cliff-Dwellers: A Peculiar Mixture of Races from the Four Corners of the Earth" depicts the multiracial inhabitants of Telegraph Hill, a place that Norris declares strange, curious, and foreign. Isolated from the rest of San Francisco, the "Cliff Dwellers" are a "queer, extraordinary mingling of peoples," who are losing their "national" characteristics through intermarriage and developing into a new race. Describing various multiracial combinations, each one "queerer" than the last, Norris marvels at the endless possibilities of human genetic combinations: "I have seen . . . a child who is half Jew, half Chinese, and its hair was red. . . . Imagine the Mongolian and African types merged into one. He should have the flat nose, and yet the almond eye, the thick lip and yet the high cheekbone; but how as to his hair? Should it be short and crinkly, or long and straight, or merely wavy? But the ideas of the man, his bias, his prejudices, his conception of things, his thoughts—what a jumble, what an amorphous, formless mist!"[69]

Calling the denizens of Telegraph Hill "race formers," Norris predicted that they would eventually merge into a single type: "And a curious type it will be," he declared.[70] The specter of mongrelization evident here echoes that raised earlier by the *Yankee Notions* cartoon (fig. 3, chapter 1), with the hybridized sons, Chang-Mike, Pat-Chow, and Rooney-Sing, physically embodying racial "mixing."[71] The illustration is accompanied by a short dialogue in hybridized language that soon degenerates into sheer nonsense. Although intended to be comedic, this depiction of a Chinese–Irish family also conjured up images of racial degradation and cultural mongrelization, the crossing of racial and linguistic boundaries producing a "neither/nor," "mixed-up" combination that amounts to nothing more than raceless chaos and pidgin.[72]

These questions of "race forming" are central to Beck's account of Chinatown, which he frames as an aid to the "vexed problem" of the "Chinese Question." As did so many other journalists and commentators of his time, Beck paints interracialism as a growing trend in Chinatown's development, a fact with implications for the future of the whole nation. Although Beck never directly states that Chinese immigration will lead to raceless chaos, he portrays the children of the neighborhood in terms of such imagery of bedlam and disorder: "The houses [on Pell Street] are old and dilapidated, veritable rookeries, swarming in the daytime with Mongol-American children."[73] Beck is certainly pessimistic about the possible place of a "new hybrid brood" in the future of the nation. As we saw at the beginning of this chapter, this is the framework in which Beck asks us to ponder George Appo's story. Appo may have been a celebrity criminal, but Beck prompts readers to consider him first and foremost as a "half-breed." From the opening of his chapter, Beck informs readers, "To-day there are scores of little half breeds playing about the streets and doorways of the Chinese quarter."[74] Appo becomes a type, a representative of a larger half-caste problem for the city and nation. Raising the question of what this tribe will bode for the "national development," Beck warned that "many of the half-breeds" would in time prove the same as Appo.[75] George Appo's story thus takes on a larger racial significance beyond a simple biographical sketch of a singular "picturesque criminal."

The significance of Appo's story is also portrayed in highly gendered terms as Beck emphasizes the proliferation of "young men of the George Appo type," expressing anxieties about a distinct sort of masculinity— urban, poor, often immigrant—that middle-class observers so frequently associated with New York's slums and the underworld of crime, violence, drugs, and other illicit activities that was at once a source of popular fascination and fear.

Class dynamics are also evident in Beck's selection of Appo as his case study. Beck glosses over the life of the Eurasian daughter of Dr. Jin Fuey Moy, who married an "American lady," as Beck tells us, and resided on West 134th Street.[76] He similarly remains silent on the Eurasian children of Yan Phou Lee even while featuring the Yale graduate as the paradigmatic example of "an educated Chinaman."[77] Beck assumes reader familiarity with Toney Afong, the Eurasian son of the famously wealthy Honolulu merchant Chen Fang (see chapter 1), but he also rejects him as a potential figure to shed light on the "problem."[78] It is not surprising that Beck might have viewed elite Chinese New Yorkers and their families as exceptional rather than representative, especially given the predominant tendency to associate the Chinese Question with labor. In addition, Beck's cursory treatment of uptown Chinese is symptomatic of the New York media's hyper-focus on the downtown neighborhoods of Five Points and Chinatown, spaces that had become sites of critical evaluation by the press, targets of reformist concern, domains of police surveillance, and settings for lurid literary imagination. Place thus looms large in Beck's perception of Appo.

Yet Beck also bypasses the two sons of sailor Lou Hoy Sing and his Irish wife as potential case studies. West 134th Street may have been a

world apart from the lower wards where George Appo spent his childhood, but the Lou family home on Cherry Street was well within the
vicinity of the riverfront neighborhood roamed by the young pickpocket.[79] Celebrating Lou, like Appo Sr., as one of the pioneering
Chinese residents of New York, Beck tells us simply that one of his sons
became a policeman and the other "an industrious truckman," with no
reflection on the implications for the issue of race mixing.[80] In the only
chapter of his book dedicated to a single individual, Beck raises George
Washington Appo to iconic status—as a symbol of hybrid degeneracy
personified.

DEGENERATE BUT BEAUTIFUL? HYBRID VIGOR
AND STRAINS OF AMBIVALENCE

Given that his work is a case study in "heredity and racial traits and
tendencies," Beck may have intended the lesson of George Appo as a
warning. Yet, even as he portrayed Appo as the embodiment of hybrid
degeneracy, degradation, and monstrosity, Beck also expressed a grudg-
ing respect for the man—a man who was, in fact, as Gilfoyle demonstrates, an inside informant who assisted the journalist in the compilation of *New York's Chinatown*.[81] In particular, Beck lauds Appo's
intelligence and cleverness, even if these traits were not put to good
uses. As evident in the opening of Beck's biographical sketch, one of the
first things he tells us is that George "was an exceedingly bright child,
beautiful to look upon, sharp-witted and quick of comprehension."[82]
While Beck goes on to narrate Appo's fall from grace, he nonetheless
repeatedly insists on the man's physical beauty (see fig. 7 previous).
Seemingly unable to let go of this point, Beck returns to Appo's unusual
attractiveness again paragraphs later: "The reference to his beauty is no
exaggeration. Throughout his long and varied career of crime he
retained the handsome features and charming manners which characterized him as a boy, and were it not for the scars of knife and bullet
wounds that are visible on his face he would now be a handsome man
of striking appearance."[83]

This assertion of Appo's particular beauty, as one whose face showed
the "characteristics of both his parents," confirmed yet another stereotype of the racial hybrid, one that paradoxically coexisted with that of
racial degeneracy. As Robert Young points out, at the same time "as
being instanced as degenerate, and literally, degraded (that is, lowered
by racial mixture from pure whiteness, the highest grade), those of

mixed race were often invoked as the most beautiful human beings of all."[84] French racial theorist Quatrefages, for example, praised the beauty of "women of colour, mulattoes and quadroons," who exercised a peculiar charm on European travelers.[85] For Quatrefages, this beauty was compelling evidence that mixed races were not inferior to the "pure" in all respects and actually exhibited a degree of hybrid vigor.

While Beck's offhand references to Appo's beauty strike a chord of dissonance with his dominant theme of hybrid degeneracy, this very dissonance calls our attention to a motif that figures in Beck's text as an instance of what we might regard as the "return of the repressed." What is repressed in Beck's sketch is the attraction exerted by the figure of the hybrid—an allure epitomized by the lovely Afong girls, daughters of the "Chinese Merchant Prince of Honolulu."

As we saw in chapter 1, in the second half of the nineteenth century, boosters were promoting Hawaii's image as a paradise of harmonious intermixing, which some extended even to the notion of constructive miscegenation.[86] This idea would become so compelling that by the first decades of the twentieth century American sociologists were treating the islands as a virtual "living laboratory" of racial fusion (see chapter 5).[87] Already in the 1880s, the American press were lauding the Afong girls, widely said to be "beautiful and intelligent," as testaments to the success of constructive miscegenation as a vehicle for assimilation—cultural and biological.[88] As the *New York Times* described the girls in 1885: "The mother and the daughters maintain a rigid adherence to the rules of fashion, and appear in the dress of white ladies and girls. When occasion demands, the lady and her older daughters are clad in as elegant raiment as the wealthiest lady on the islands . . . as the family is received cordially into the best society in Honolulu. . . . A close observer of the merry quintet on their afternoon drive could not tell that they were not the offspring of some wealthy Caucasian."[89]

Wealthy, beautiful, cultured, and by this account virtually "Caucasian" to the eye (echoing early depictions of George Appo as a veritable Yankee boy), the Afong girls were frequently depicted by mainland media as "very much sought after," several distinguished for having married "prominent men."[90] When Henrietta, the "belle of the islands," was wed to Naval Commander William Henry Whiting in 1893, the marriage shook Honolulu naval society but was acclaimed by Sanford Dole, head of Hawaii's provisional government, as a symbol for the potential union of Hawaii and the United States.[91] Indeed, the beauty and eligibility of the Afong girls loomed so large in American press coverage of the family that when the "merchant prince" died in 1906, the *New York Times* gave his obituary the following title: "AFONG DIES IN CHINA; FATHER OF 13 [*sic*] BEAUTIES—Chinese Merchant Made Millions in Honolulu. DAUGHTERS MARRIED WELL."[92]

The juxtaposition of the Afongs in Hawaii and the Appos in New York demonstrates the complex intersections of class, gender, and place in representations of Eurasian mixed race. If we consider place, in particular, the difference between Honolulu and the world of Manhattan's lower wards is striking. By comparison to New York's Five Points in particular, where anxieties surrounding social and sexual intercourse across racial, religious, and linguistic lines ran high during Appo's age, the discourse of constructive miscegenation came much more readily to the fore in Hawaii, where intermarriage was connected to U.S. imperial aspirations, as noted in chapter 1.

Hawaii was clearly a different context from New York, and yet we find that the discourse of constructive miscegenation is not entirely absent from representations of Chinese–white intermixing in the great metropolis, especially in the era before Chinese exclusion. Indeed, as we have seen, Beck was not alone in his portrayal of Appo's physical attractiveness, a trait commonly taken by racial theorists as evidence of hybrid vigor.[93] As mentioned previously, the *New York Times* reporter who chronicled George's birth described him as a handsome boy, as white as his mother.[94] Journalists also described other New York–born Eurasians in a similar fashion. An article in the *New York Daily Tribune*, for example, asserted, "As a rule the children [of Chinese fathers and Irish mothers] are decidedly well looking, which is more than one can say for their fathers."[95] When a reporter for the *World* investigated that city's "Celestial colony" in 1877, he expressed surprise at finding a number of young Irish women married to Chinese. Unnerved by the phenomenon, the reporter nonetheless gave a favorable physical description of one of the babies: "It was sleeping in a tidy crib, and was certainly a beautiful child, being fair and chubby and healthy in appearance."[96] Noticeably, all these descriptions associate the Eurasians' beauty with their partial whiteness: their fair skin, their fashionable "white" dress, their maternal inheritance. It is an "infusion of whiteness" that produces the good looks of Eurasian children, an infusion that overcomes the homeliness of Chinese fathers and their racial Otherness, transforming their offspring toward Sameness. In contrast to Quatrefages, who clearly valued the exotic and dusky beauty of the mulatto, these press accounts indicate that the notion of exceptional mixed-race beauty also contains within itself a privileging of whiteness. The mysterious charm exerted by mixed-race figures thus stems from their not-white/like-white physiognomy.

Here is where ambivalence rises to the surface in Beck's account: where the journalist cannot let go of Appo's beauty, despite his monstrous wickedness. Beck may regard Appo "better off dead," but he remains enthralled by his "striking appearance," unable to write him off entirely. In the end, George Washington Appo was a paradigmatic example of the contradiction Robert Young identifies in nineteenth-century Western racial theory: that is, the degenerate racial hybrid who is simultaneously invoked as a creature of great beauty. It is this doubleness that rendered the hybrid a figure of fascination and horror, of desire and anxiety.

Without a doubt, hybrid degeneracy is the dominant theme in Beck's biographical sketch of Appo, as it was among Anglo-American scientific discourses of the time. Yet I have emphasized the notion of underlying ambivalence even within this demonizing portrait in order to draw attention to alternate discourses of hybrid vigor that also circulated during this era. The notion of "constructive miscegenation" may have been a minority position, but hybrid vigor was taken seriously as an issue of scientific *debate* by men of no less stature than Gobineau, Quatrefages, and Darwin and continued to inform lay representations like Beck's even if only as an undercurrent of ambivalence. Hence, this counter-discourse should not be dismissed too readily from our readings of the period, as, I argue, is the case in Jayne O. Ifekwunigwe's characterization of the nineteenth century as the Age of Pathology in mixed-race studies.[97] As noted in the introduction, Harriet Ritvo has compellingly cautioned against monodimensional understandings of the past, which highlight dominant opinions of the age while obscuring alternative opinions and intense disagreement among experts, and in doing so force us to lose sight of the true variety of thought from the time.[98] Such would be the danger for the intellectual genealogy of "mixed race" if we were to see in Beck's sketch of Appo nothing more than a case study of hybrid degeneracy without its complicating ambivalence.

This point is further developed in the following chapters of part II, which will turn to counter-discourses on "racial amalgamation" on both sides of the Pacific. In the next chapter, we will see how ideas of hybrid vigor, which played only a secondary role in representations of George Appo, were mobilized by advocates of eugenics in China.

Prologue to Chapter 4

MADAM SZE: MATRIARCH OF A EURASIAN DYNASTY

At some point between 1855 and 1858, roughly around the time that George Appo was born in New Haven, a family of silk growers near Shanghai met with hard times and were forced to sell their daughter "down the river."[1] The daughter, Sze Tai, would turn up later in Hong Kong, where she became the "protected woman" of a Dutchman, Charles Henri Maurice Bosman (1839–92). Bosman worked for the firm of Cornelius Koopmanschap, which shipped goods and laborers between China and San Francisco, and he soon rose to partner.[2] Unlike Edward Eaton (see chapter 2), Bosman upheld the colonial taboo against interracial marriage, following instead the accepted custom of taking a local companion to provide him with the comforts of home.

Sze Tai gave birth to her first son—the second of her nine children—on December 22, 1862. She gave him the surname "Ho," possibly since his father was a "Ho-lan-yan"—a Dutchman—and the given name of "Tung." Like many other Eurasians of their era, Ho Tung and his brothers were educated at the Government Central School, where they excelled in both English and classical Chinese. Ho Tung's younger brother, known as Walter Bosman (1867–1946), became the first student to win a scholarship to pursue higher education in engineering in England. Ho Tung, Ho Fook (1863–1926), and Ho Kom-Tong (1866–1950) took positions as compradores (see chapter 8) in foreign trading companies and went on to become enormously successful and prominent in Hong Kong society.[3]

FIGURE 8. Sir Robert Ho Tung, by Elliott & Fry, ca. 1932.
© National Portrait Gallery, London.

Ho Tung (fig. 8) began his career after graduation in 1878, when he passed a competitive entrance examination and joined the Chinese Imperial Maritime Customs in Canton.[4] In 1880, Ho Tung returned to Hong Kong to work at Jardine, Matheson & Co. and within three years rose to chief compradore.[5] By 1900, he had resigned from Jardine's and established his own business and real estate empire. He soon became one of the wealthiest and most influential men in Hong Kong, in no small part through his generous philanthropic activities, which included the founding of the King George V School in 1900. In 1915, he was honored with the Knight Bachelor by King George V, and in 1955 he would be knighted as Knight Commander of the Order of the British Empire by Queen Elizabeth II. (Ho Kom-Tong was honored as a Commander of the Order of the British Empire in 1941.)

FIGURE 9. Wedding of Victoria Ho to M. K. Lo, Hong Kong, April 4, 1918.
Front row: Margaret, Lady Ho Tung; Grace Ho; M. K. Lo; Victoria Ho; Lady Clara Ho
Tung; Irene Ho; Jean Ho. Ho Fook is directly behind Lady Ho Tung.

From *Ho Kom-Tong: A Man for All Seasons.* Courtesy of Compradore House Ltd.

If business success came early, family came late. A year after joining
Jardine's, Ho Tung married Margaret Maclean/Mak Sau-Ying (1865–
1944), the Eurasian daughter of Hector Coll Maclean, Jardine's insurance agent in Tianjin. Margaret remained childless, and in 1895 she
arranged for her husband to marry her cousin, Clara Cheung Ching-
Yung (1875–1938), the daughter of Eurasian Cheung Tak Fai, who had
worked for the Chinese Customs Service in Jiujiang.[6] Margaret respect-
fully asked for Clara to be made an "equal wife," and thus the two
women became co-mothers to the children: Victoria, Henry, Daisy,
Edward, Eva, Irene, Robert, Jean, Grace, and Florence.[7] In 1906, the
Ho family became the first "Chinese" family to be granted special government permission to reside in the racially exclusive Peak area. Despite
their wealth, however, the children were refused entry to the Peak
School on the grounds that other parents had threatened a boycott.[8]

The women of the family (Lady Clara, in particular) were renowned
for their beauty—and several of the daughters for their brains as well.[9]
When Victoria Jubilee (Ho Kam-chee) married Man Kam Lo in April
1918, the elaborate wedding was considered the social event of the year
(fig. 9). Victoria was only the first of her siblings to marry the scion of

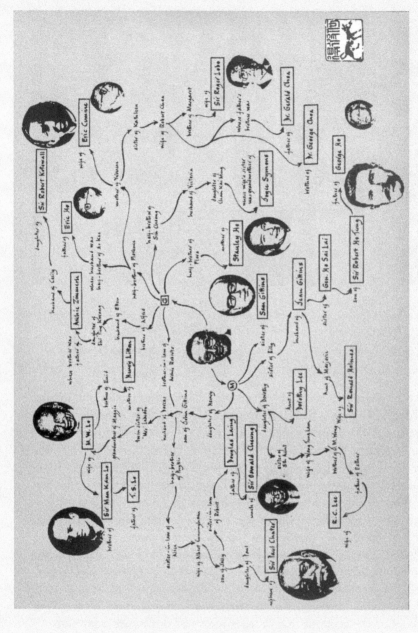

FIGURE 10. Book jacket for Peter Hall's *In the Web* (1992), illustrating connections among Eurasian families.
Courtesy of Peter Hall.

a prominent Eurasian family, and a catchy rhyme soon began to circulate among Eurasian mothers: "The daughters of the Ho, Lo, Shi [Zimmern], Sin [Hall] and Choa families need not worry about being married outside [their network]."[10] Such endogamous marriages helped to spin what Eurasian genealogist Peter Hall (b. 1935) calls "the web," a complex network of kinship ties that bound together elite Eurasian families in Hong Kong, and extended even into China (fig. 10).[11]

When Madam Sze passed away in 1896, her filial sons buried her at Mount Davis Cemetery in Hong Kong.[12] No husband lay by her side: Bosman had been buried at Brompton Cemetery in London four years earlier. But Madam Sze became an ancestor in her own right, with her grave serving as the focal point for the Ho lineage. An imperial title purchased from an obliging official in Canton, making Bosman posthumously a Qing official, allowed for Madam Sze to be recognized as a Lady of the Second Rank on her tombstone.[13] Twice a year on the festivals for paying homage to the deceased, the extended Ho family would gather at the cemetery, paying tribute to the honored matriarch of a Eurasian dynasty that still wields influence today.[14]

CHAPTER 4

"Productive of Good to Both Sides"

The Eurasian as Solution in Chinese Utopian Visions of Racial Harmony

September 21, 1898. Yung Wing and Kang Youwei were wanted men. Yung Wing had buried his beloved wife Mary in 1886, and now he was in China once again, hoping to promote the cause of reform and modernization—his boys left to the care of "Uncle Joe" Twichell. In the heady Hundred Days of Reform, launched by the young Guangxu Emperor under the urgings of leading reformer Kang Youwei (1858–1927), Yung had allowed his Beijing headquarters to be used as a rendezvous.[15] Now, the empress dowager had staged a reactionary coup d'état, and both Kang and Yung had a price on their heads. While Yung sought protection from the U.S. consulate in Shanghai (only to be told that the Chinese Exclusion Act of 1882 had rendered his U.S. citizenship invalid), Kang escaped to Hong Kong.[16]

Arriving by ship in the British colony on September 29, Kang was met at the docks by a welcoming party led by Ho Tung, who invited the great reformer and Confucian philosopher to stay with his family at their grand mansion, Idlewild.[17] The two men formed a close bond, and when Kang decided to embark on a global tour to seek support for the restoration of the emperor, Ho Tung generously supplied travel funds.[18] Recalling his family's rescue, and expressing gratitude for his host's largesse, Kang Youwei composed a calligraphic scroll praising Ho Tung for his chivalry and patriotism to China. Kang further praised the exceptional talent and intelligence of Ho Tung and his wives, their loyalty and attention to etiquette.[19]

This remarkable family undoubtedly must have served as an inspiration for Kang when he later wrote of the superior physical attractiveness and intelligence produced by the union of the yellow and white races in his famous utopian political tract, *One World Treatise* (*Datong shu*), a work completed during the years of his exilic travels. The *One World Treatise* is perhaps the most famous late Imperial reinterpretation of the Chinese Confucian tradition, a tract written in what the author perceived to be the final stages of the Age of Disorder. Central to Kang's program for moving the world into a utopian era of Great Peace and Great Unity were certain (rather unorthodox) ideas for eliminating national and racial boundaries, including the notion of unifying the human races through intermarriage. In this chapter, I read Kang Youwei's *One World Treatise* alongside a number of other pieces by well-known Chinese intellectuals from the late Qing—early Republican period who advocated racial amalgamation as a response to the crisis of Western imperialism. Focusing in particular on the utopian visions propounded by Kang Youwei and Zhang Jingsheng, I demonstrate how a particular interpretation of Social Darwinism led a range of thinkers to appropriate the notion of hybrid vigor and eugenic amalgamation for various political ends. Far from viewing Chinese–Western interracialism as a *problem* for China's national development, these men envisioned it as a potential *solution* for the global racial conflict they saw emerging between white and yellow and advanced proposals for placing yellow–white amalgamation in service to the nation.

THE IMPORTATION OF WESTERN RACIAL THEORY

Before turning to Kang's treatise, let us first examine the context of developing racial thought within which his ideas emerged. The evolution of Chinese ideas concerning racial hybridity during this time owed much to the Western scientific discourses examined in the previous chapter yet took place within a dramatically different setting. If the specter of degeneration and the prospect of racial decline was a source of cultural anxiety in the United States, particularly among opponents of immigration, Chinese intellectuals of this era were preoccupied with the threat that Western imperialism posed to China's future and the survival of the Chinese race. The first Opium War had given rise to a mounting sense of nationalism, which became especially acute after the disastrous Sino–Japanese War of 1895, leading Chinese intellectuals to become consumed with China's fate in the modern world and increasingly discontented with the failures of the Manchu rulers of the Qing. This moment of crisis was a crucial period in the formation of modern Chinese identity, when new ideas of race, nation, and culture were debated.[20] Modern Chinese racial theory was formulated within this context, drawing on both a long history of thought on racial and ethnic difference as well as new ideas derived from the West.

From the second half of the nineteenth century on, leading Chinese intellectuals began to engage deeply with "Western learning," including scientific racial theory, as a means of confronting the crises of the age. Predating Yung Wing's Chinese Educational Mission, in 1862 the court had established a translation bureau to promote foreign language training and translate key scientific, technical, political, and other texts.[21] Through this and other translation projects, the ideas of Darwin, Lamarck, and Spencer were beginning to circulate in China as early as the 1870s.[22] One basic idea that modern Chinese intellectuals adopted through these influences was the classification of humankind into color-based races such as white, yellow, black, brown, and red. As in the West, these broad anthropological categories coexisted with more specific ethnonational categories such as the "Chinese race," or the "German race," and writings of the time often vacillate between talking about the "yellow race" more generally and the "Chinese race" specifically.

Of the various ideas received from Western racial theory, perhaps none was more influential than the paradigm of Social Darwinism, which had been used to assert the superiority of the white race over the yellow based on the superior progress of Western civilization and technology. In reaction to this discourse, and the mounting pressure of Western imperialism, Chinese intellectuals of the late nineteenth century became consumed with the idea of an international struggle for the survival of the fittest, which they predominantly conceived in terms of a global conflict between whites and yellows.[23]

As important as these influences were, as we shall see later in the chapter, Western racial theory was fundamentally altered in its transmission and reception, which took place through multiple layers of translation (often first into Japanese), and ultimately adapted to suit Chinese needs.[24] In addition, Chinese intellectuals did not accept Western theories wholesale but synthesized these ideas with other strands of thought: Confucian, Buddhist, and Taoist. Modern Chinese racial theory is thus neither wholly "Westernized," nor "indigenous," but a hybrid discourse.

THE INVENTION OF THE "HAN" CHINESE RACE: RACIAL PURITY AND CLEANSING THE NATION

Within this context arose diverse responses to the question of Chinese identity, especially in relation to the concepts of race and nation. Probably the most important construct to emerge from this history was the modern, racialized construct of the "Hanzu"—Han lineage or Han nationality. As Kai-wing Chow and others have demonstrated, the modern formation of this construct took shape under the influence of two sets of historical forces: the experiences of European (and later Japanese) imperialism; and the ideological battle between moderate reformists and revolutionaries who sought to overthrow the Manchus—a battle that pit Kang Youwei against radical revolutionaries like Zhang Binglin (1868–1936).[25] Up until the first years of the twentieth century, Chinese intellectuals were consumed with the urgent need to defend China against Western imperialism, a battle that appeared in the framework of Social Darwinism as a global racial struggle of the white against yellow. Reformers like Kang Youwei and his disciple Liang Qichao conceptualized the Chinese as members of a larger yellow race and defined the nation primarily against the dominant Other of the white race. They sought to maintain the Chinese Imperial system in modified form and did not challenge the Manchu right to rule China per se, even as they urged change and modernization. Beginning around 1900, however, radical revolutionaries broke with the reformers and adopted increasingly anti-Manchu rhetoric. Calling for the ouster of the Manchus, they were compelled to formulate a new language to articulate the distinction between Chinese and Manchus and establish a new identity for the Chinese nation. As Zhang Binglin, Wang Jingwei (1883–1944), Zou Rong (1885–1905), and other revolutionary intellectuals shifted their discourse away from the global "race war" to the domestic power struggle against the Qing, the Manchus replaced the white race as the Other against which they defined Chinese identity. This discursive shift was indicated by the emergence of terms like *Hanzhong* ("Han race") and *Hanzu* ("Han nationality") to denote the "Chinese race" in revolutionary writings, replacing the concept of the "yellow race" (which included Manchus).[26]

The use of the term *Hanzu* was not only critical to marking an absolute distinction between Han Chinese and Manchu, but also to making the claim that China, as a territory and nation, belonged to the "Chinese race" and not the Manchu outsiders. The revolutionaries thus conceived of the nation in very different, racialized terms than the reformers. They further sought to mobilize unity by calling for "ousting the Manchus," a slogan that was extended to a general call to "oust the outsiders." As Jing Tsu writes, "Equated with one's loyalty to the nation, xenophobia was an essential testimony to loving the nation."[27] In the process, cleansing and purity became integral features of Chinese racial nationalism in its most visceral form.

This extreme version of Han Chinese nationalism was staunchly rejected by reformers like Kang Youwei and Liang Qichao, who viewed it as an ideological threat to the territorial integrity of the Qing Empire, which encompassed vast non-Han lands. As Peter Perdue writes of this ideological opposition, "Kang [Youwei] and Zhang [Binglin] displayed a clear opposition of culturalist and racialist ideologies, each invoked as a means of strengthening national unity."[28] Although the notion of the racial purification of China served as a potent rallying cry for the anti-Manchu cause leading up to the Revolution of 1911, ultimately the new republic adopted a broader, inclusive nationalism that encompassed the Manchus, Mongols, and others as members of the pluralistic "Chinese nationalities" (*Zhonghua minzu*).

THEORIZING HYBRIDITY

Through their engagement with Western racial theory, Chinese intellectuals were inevitably exposed to the debates on racial hybridity that were so central to European and American debates on race from the 1840s on, debates that took place against the backdrop of colonialism, slavery, and abolitionism. Although the particular stakes of these debates did not directly translate into the Chinese context, the subject of intermixing itself drew interest, and several prominent writers took up the issue, addressing it in their own terms: rather than deliberating the question of white–black amalgamation, they focused on yellow–white amalgamation or on the crossing of Han and non-Han internally within China. As in the West, then, the discourse on hybridity was produced within a specific material and cultural context and grew out of particular national anxieties: at stake was the question of how to unify and strengthen the Chinese race in the face of external threats.

As discussed in the previous chapter, numerous different positions on human hybridity emerged from the debates between monogenists and polygenists: hybridity has thus been invoked, as Robert Young notes, "to imply contrafusion and disjunction (or even separate development) as well as fusion and assimilation."[29] Young argues that the idea of hybrid degeneracy dominated Western racial theory from the 1850s to the 1930s.[30] Yet, as Nancy Stepan has demonstrated in her work on Latin American eugenics during the 1920s and 1930s, in other cultural contexts the notion of "constructive miscegenation" has played a more central role.[31] The notion of hybrid vigor similarly figured centrally in American accounts of racial mixing in Hawaii from the nineteenth century on, reaching a peak in the 1920s and 1930s when missionaries and sociologists fixed on Hawaii as the consummate melting pot (see chapter 5). Stepan notes that the idea of constructive miscegenation had in fact long been part of European racial science, especially in France, but had become "increasingly narrowly construed as European thought became more racist."[32] That is, constructive miscegenation was construed as possible between the Celtic and the Saxon, for example, but not between white and black. Geographer Griffith Taylor (1880–1963) was one of the few prominent voices in Anglo-American scientific circles to explicitly argue for the eugenic effects of "Anglo-Mongolian" amalgamation, based on his observations of Chinese–white intermarriage in Australia.[33]

If *hybridity* had this range of meanings, the concept was translated variously in Chinese, some translations connoting fusion and unity, others crossing, exchange, or communication, and yet others chaos or confusion. Hybridity could thus take on either positive or negative meanings. Whereas those who opposed intermixing used terms that emphasized mongrelity and chaos, those like Kang Youwei who advocated hybridity invoked union, assimilation, and incorporation, concepts with positive value within the Chinese philosophical tradition.

Indeed, the concept of hybridity coexisted with purity in modern formulations of Chinese national identity.[34] The notion of hybrid vigor in particular played a crucial role in certain articulations of the Hanzu construct. Liang Qichao, for example, regarded hybridity as a long historical process that had produced modern races from the amalgamation of various ancient peoples. Similarly, several early Republican intellectuals, including the eminent historian Gu Jiegang, argued that the Hanzu had originally been formed through the historical intermixing of various smaller ethnic groups—an argument that continues to be influential in China today. Instead of the fictive "purity" of the Han race, then, these thinkers emphasized the already hybrid nature of the so-called Han as a conglomerate race, incorporating and containing difference within itself. Some further called for future intermarriages between

Han and non-Han frontier peoples in order to revitalize the Chinese race through hybrid vigor. Such discourses on constructive miscegenation filtered over to debates concerning yellow–white amalgamation.

EURASIANS AS THE PERFECTED RACE OF THE FUTURE

The idealization of the Eurasian as an example of constructive miscegenation was vitally articulated by Kang Youwei, a man who has often been called late Imperial China's greatest Confucian philosopher. Like many other reformers of his time, Kang was concerned with China's fate in the modern world, but he was also invested in a universal philosophy that would ensure world peace. Kang expounded a vision of a utopian future in his philosophical tract the *One World Treatise* (*Datong shu*), a work that took shape over several decades but that was largely completed in 1902 while he was in exile.[35] The basic premise of the treatise is that the world's suffering arises from human-imposed boundaries—boundaries of nation, class, race, gender, family, occupation, law, and species: by eliminating these boundaries, humankind could eliminate suffering and enter the utopian age of "One World" (*Datong*), an era of peace, prosperity, and equality.

Kang's tract was informed by his experiences traveling overseas, including his sojourn in Hong Kong and some early trips to North America. Travel served as a crucial stimulus, exposing Kang to new ideas and enabling him to witness firsthand a range of foreign countries and Chinese communities abroad. Whether through travel or through his close associations with men like Ho Tung and Yung Wing, Kang Youwei had opportunity to see the effects of interracialism for himself, and he came to perceive this phenomenon as a wave of the future. Hence the ideas concerning racial amalgamation articulated in the *One World Treatise* were not mere abstractions, but were grounded in part in Kang's own personal experiences and observations, as well as inquiries he put to Chinese migrants who had intermarried. In contrast to the New York media I analyzed in the previous chapter, which tended to treat Chinese–white amalgamation as a local phenomenon, Kang viewed it as a product of both Western penetration into China and Chinese migration overseas.

With a view of racism as a global problem, Kang devoted the fourth chapter of his treatise to "Eliminating Racial Boundaries and Amalgamating the Races." Kang argues that the only way to institute racial equality is to eliminate distinctions by unifying the human race (*he renlei*). Kang divides the world into four races—the whites of Europe, the yellows of Asia, the blacks of Africa, and the browns of the Pacific and South Sea Islands—and asserts that distinctions among these groups gave rise historically to inequality and hence to suffering. As a resolution, Kang proposes to unify the human race through a three-step program of racial transformation.

In fact, Kang's scheme for racial unification is essentially a scheme for racial improvement (in his terms)—and one that involves some extreme measures. Kang denigrates the brown and black as inferior races and proposes a plan for racial improvement based on their gradual elimination and the eventual amalgamation (*tongzhong*) of the yellow and white races. Kang thus envisions his utopian One World populated by a eugenically perfected Eurasian race.

Migration constitutes the first stage of unifying the races. Theorizing that environment and climate have the power to transform race, particularly in successive generations, Kang proposes to transform the darker races by moving them away from the tropical into the temperate zones.[36] As evidence of such transformation, he writes, "Chinese children born in Europe and America are all rosy white (*hongbai*)."[37] Thus, Kang imagines Chinese migrants to the West to be the vanguard of racial change for the yellow race. Kang's advocacy of emigration was not purely theoretical: as early as 1897 he had taken an active role in sponsoring a plan to develop Chinese emigration to Brazil.[38] In Kang's model, diaspora thus becomes an important historical stage in the eugenic improvement of the Chinese race.

Intermarriage is the method for the second stage. Kang envisions blacks and browns gradually transformed into yellows through intermarriage with yellows and whites, and then yellows amalgamating with whites to produce the Eurasian race of the future. This hybrid race would possess what he imagined as the superior physical strength, beauty, and fair skin of the white race, combined with the superior intelligence, moral character, and fertility of the yellow race.

The third method entails *dietary change*, again with the goal of transforming the darker races toward whiteness. Hypothesizing that the types of food eaten and the various cooking methods (broiling, roasting, and so on) influence skin color, facial appearance, physical constitution, and body odor, Kong urges the colored races to adopt the same diet of cooked foods as the whites and yellows, thereby gradually undergoing transformation over several generations. Yellows, he proposes, should imitate the whites by consuming more roast meats.

In summarizing his proposal for eliminating racial boundaries, Kang provides a timeline for the various stages of racial transformation. In the final historical stage, gender inequality and the distinctions "between noble and base races" have been eradicated, and intermarriage has served to "equalize" all. As he wrote, "The yellows and the whites will be amalgamated and transformed into a single race. . . . Everyone will be tall; everyone will be strong; everyone will be beautiful; all will be equal."[39] It is this ultimate amalgamation that will usher in the One World age of racial equality and a unified human race.

In Kang's formulation, hybridization essentially serves as a mechanism for eugenic improvement and revitalization. Embracing the notion of hybrid vigor, Kang postulates that the crossing of white and yellow will produce a new breed exhibiting merged characteristics—but miraculously only the best characteristics—of the parent races. His position thus stands in sharp contrast to the American fixation on hybrid degeneracy examined in the previous chapter. Indeed, Kang specifically refutes the hypothesis that racial amalgamation will lead to degeneration or reversion, arguing that the yellow and white races will absorb the darker races in the long term.[40] He thus conceptualizes amalgamation as a means of elevating the so-called inferior races, rather than as a threat to the purity of the "superior." At the same time, however, it is evident that there is ultimately no place for the black and brown races in Kang's vision of One World.

The thesis of variable hybridity thus plays a pivotal role in Kang's theorization of racial amalgamation. Like French anthropologist Paul Broca, one of the most famous theorists of human hybridity, Kang argues that amalgamation is viable between proximate, or closely allied races, but difficult between distant races: "In order to unify the races for the racial equality of One World, it is necessary to start with those races that are similar in appearance and physique. If appearance and physique are dissimilar, then customs and rites, occupation and love cannot be unified."[41] Kang asserts that amalgamation between whites and yellows is readily achieved because the two races are similar in ability, intelligence, and appearance. As proximate races, white and yellow are naturally attracted to each other and will therefore rapidly amalgamate through intermarriage. Blacks and browns, however, are distant from white and yellow, he argues, and therefore not readily amalgamated or "equalized."[42] As a result, Kang largely rejects the method of amalgamation through sexual union in the case of the distant races. Thus, the concept of racial proximity between whites and yellows is a vital cornerstone of Kang's theorization of eugenic racial amalgamation.

It is difficult to pinpoint exactly what sources influenced Kang's racial thinking, but whatever his inspiration, Kang adapted these ideas to his own ends. Nineteenth-century Western racial theorists for the most part classified the yellow race as distant from the white or as an intermediate race between black and white. Kang, however, constructed yellow and white as proximate races, based on his criteria of ability, intelligence, and appearance, and thereby asserted the equivalent status of the two as "superior races"—a move notably dependent upon his distancing of the "darker races" as inferiors.

Thus, although the transformation of dark into light is the ultimate goal of Kang's program for "uniting and transforming" (*hehua*) the races, we should not mistake his idealization of whiteness for an uncritical acceptance of white racial supremacy. Kang clearly regards the white race as physically superior—admiring their fair skin, tall stature, plumpness, vigor, and strength (while detesting their hirsuteness). However, he also states that the white race will not be perfected until it has been ameliorated through amalgamation with the yellow, absorbing the positive traits of the latter. Moreover, there is also an ambiguity regarding the notion of whiteness in Kang's work: the term "white" (*bai*) refers both to the "white race of Europe" and to fair skin, long prized by Chinese as a sign of beauty and class status.[43] This ambiguity allows Kang to contest whiteness as a fixed racial category, arguing that southern Chinese who migrate north become white (fair), while northern Chinese who migrate to Singapore turn dark, as do Englishmen who live long in the tropics. Among Europeans, he asserts, the Italians, Spanish, and Portuguese are just as yellow as the Chinese. This decoupling of color and race means that Kang allows for the possibility for other races to obtain whiteness— through migration, intermarriage, diet, and exercise.

Indeed, from his own experiences in Chinese treaty ports, in the British colony of Hong Kong, and in North America, Kang saw the increasing interpenetration of the white and yellow races resulting from migration. Based on the mounting demands of the Western powers for territorial concessions in China, Kang predicted that in the near future China would be inhabited by yellows and whites living "mixed together," with intermarriage common. Across the world, he similarly forecast that the two races would live side by side in the Americas. Perhaps drawing from Darwin's theories of sexual selection, Kang argued that as proximate races, whites and yellow are naturally attracted to one another and would therefore rapidly amalgamate through intermarriage.

Thus, in the end, Kang's utopian vision of racial equality and unity is limited to what he considers the two proximate (and superior) races of yellow and white. He does not extend this vision to the black and brown races, both of which are effectively excluded from his program of eugenic racial amalgamation. The great reformer's idealization of Eurasians as the super-race of the future is scripted on the basis of this yellow/white exceptionalism.

STRENGTHENING YELLOW THROUGH THE INFUSION OF WHITENESS

Kang Youwei was not alone in advocating yellow–white amalgamation: during the time that he was shaping his treatise, other key intellectual figures in the Chinese reform movement also promoted similar proposals. One of these was the Hunanese reformer Tang Caichang (1867–1900), the leader of a failed uprising in 1900 that involved not only Kang Youwei but also his archrival Sun Yat-sen (1867–1925) and Yung Wing as well. Between November 1897 and February 1898, Tang Caichang published an extensive account of the world races in the major reformist newspaper, the *Hunanese Study Magazine* (*Xiangxue xinbao*).[44] Appended was an essay, "A Discourse on Racial Intermixing" (*Tongzhong shuo*), in which Tang argued for racial amalgamation as the best means of entering the utopian era of Great Peace (*Taiping*) and Great Unity (*Datong*). Synthesizing the new Western learning with classical erudition, Tang supports his essay with ten points of evidence based on botany, zoology, Confucian and Buddhist philosophy, historical examples, and contemporary observations—all of which support the thesis of hybrid vigor. Inbreeding poses a danger of decline and eventual extinction, he argues, and therefore hybridity, as a mechanism for infusing new vitality into populations, is vital for the very survival of the race. Tang thus frames racial amalgamation within Social Darwinism's paradigm of the "survival of the fittest." Invoking intermarriage as alliance, Tang further claims that racial intermixing will promote international relations and eventual world peace by joining the nations in ties of kinship. Racial intermixing, he argues, should be part of the general flow of political, artistic, military, and economic exchanges among the five continents of the world.

Beyond these general principles in favor of hybridity, Tang endorses a *particular* form of racial amalgamation—that between yellows and whites. Emphasizing the notion of eugenic amalgamation, he argues that the "weaker" Asiatic race can be improved through an infusion of stronger European blood. This notion of strengthening the Asiatic race through an infusion of European vitality reflects the influence of Social Darwinist thinking with its implicit privileging of the white race. That Tang had to a degree internalized Chinese racial inferiority to Western- ers is further evident in his assertion that "I have heard that intermixing of the Chinese and Western races is not limited to the treaty ports and foreign concessions, but that several high [Chinese] officials have taken Western wives. These Westerners did not reject them or feel ashamed to marry them because of China's weakness or the stupidity of the Chinese people."[45]

Tang here links China's weakness as a nation to the notional weak- ness of the Chinese race—a common theme of the time. Intermarriage with Westerners figures for him as an index of China's acceptability as a "worthy partner" in the eyes of the West: it thus functions to compen- sate for China's national weakness and holds the potential to elevate China's standing on the global stage. Tang further grants miscegenation an air of respectability by emphasizing that the phenomenon is "*not limited* to the treaty ports and foreign concessions" [my italics], but is also practiced by the scholar-official class, including high officials. He thereby urges readers not to equate "intermixing" exclusively with unsanctioned "treaty port alliances." Rather, intermixing has also entered the legitimate realm of marriage, even among the elite.

Building on his various arguments, Tang specifically identifies the Eurasian as his ideal model of eugenic hybridity. Describing Hong Kong, Singapore, and the Pacific Islands as crossroads for intercourse between Chinese and Westerners, he noted the existence of Eurasians in these various locations, writing that "they far surpass the rest of their generation in intelligence and ability, and they have great resolve. They are the first class of humans in the five continents. . . . From this we know that the yellow-white racial amalgamate (*huangbai hezhong*) will certainly be outstandingly intelligent and strong."[46] As with Kang Youwei, then, the idea of a Eurasian super-race is central to Tang's vision of utopian racial amalgamation. Whereas Kang's One World emphasized the unification of the human race, however, Tang's true focus is the improvement of the yellow race. Employing Social Darwin- ist discourse, Tang advocates yellow–white amalgamation for the sake of strengthening the yellow race, and even goes so far as to argue that such interbreeding is a matter of survival or extinction. Although Tang does not explicitly reject intermixing with the darker races, like Kang he posits the yellow and white as proximate (and superior) races, while denigrating the red and black.

Tang further establishes a basis for yellow–white amalgamation within Confucian and Mencian philosophy. First grounding the principle of exchange or intermixing in Confucian and Mencian thought, Tang extends the positive values of this principle to racial intermixing. Next Tang sets this phenomenon within the framework of the ideal of *Datong,* the Great Unity or One World. In this utopian stage, Tang argues, racial amalgamation would follow upon other forms of exchange and communication—among nations, schools of learning, religions, and so forth. He also argues that racial amalgamation will *lead* the world into the age of Great Unity: racial amalgamation is the starting point for racial improvement, and racial improvement will lead to the Great Unity of Confucius and Mencius. Tang thereby constructs the Eurasian as both the perfected racial specimen and the embodiment of Great Unity.

Like Kang Youwei, Tang conceptualizes racial amalgamation as a process of transformation and unification or synthesis, concepts with deep foundations in the Chinese philosophical tradition. This conceptualization contrasts sharply with contemporaneous Western understandings of amalgamation, as examined in chapter 3, which tended to emphasize the notions of crossing and mixing, with their attendant connotations of pollution, mongrelism, and disorder. The Chinese philosophical tradition thus provided a language within which utopian visions of racial hybridization could be articulated in familiar terms.

PRESERVING THE RACE THROUGH RACIAL AMALGAMATION

Following closely upon Tang's heels, his associate, Yi Nai (fl. 1898), published an essay in another leading reformist newspaper, the *Hunan News (Xiangbao)*. In "China Should Take Its Weakness for Strength" (1898),[47] Yi argued that racial amalgamation was a means of preserving the Chinese race and saving China from the impending crisis it faced from Western imperialism.[48] Although Yi did not formulate a full-fledged utopian vision, his ideas concerning the place of Eurasians in an idealized future are an interesting counterpart to those of Kang and Tang.

Yi very explicitly sets the parameters of beneficial amalgamation. In simple terms, he writes, "What is meant by 'racial amalgamation'?: the intermarriage of yellows and whites."[49] The blacks of Africa and the reds of America he dismisses as "base and ignoble races" with whom intermarriage is unfeasible. Yi constructs yellow and white as complementary opposites, aligning the yellow race with the feminine principle, and the white with the masculine—a move that reflects his cognizance of China's weakened international position during his age. In order to prevent the yellow race from falling into slavery and decline as had the blacks and reds, Yi argues, they must intermarry with the strong (and masculinized) whites.

On this basis, Yi proposes a policy of "extending the noble race through racial amalgamation."[50] Like Kang Youwei, Yi Nai specifically refuted the claim that degradation of Chinese racial purity would lead to the destruction of the Chinese race, arguing instead that it is precisely *mixing,* and *not* purity, that will allow the "noble race" to flourish. In making this argument, Yi Nai associates the notion of bloodline or racial purity with dysgenic inbreeding, racial degeneration, and the incest taboo. In contrast, he invokes hybrid vigor to argue that the crossing of yellow and white will produce strong, fit, refined, and intelligent offspring.

THE EURASIAN AS SOLUTION TO "INTERRACIAL PROBLEMS"

These visions of eugenic intermixing were produced in a particular moment of historical crisis in China, and before the full-fledged emergence of Han Chinese racial nationalism. With the rise of this nationalism, particularly after the Revolution of 1911, public sentiment turned against the "mixed blood," as I elaborate in chapters 7 and 8. Yet well past the revolution, Eurasians like Ho Tung continued to serve as inspirational examples to progressive Chinese writers who associated the Eurasian with both eugenic and cosmopolitan ideals. As we saw from chapter 2, the famous diplomat and statesman, Wu Tingfang, was one of the most outspoken advocates of interracialism from the era, bridging the late Qing and early Republic. In July 1911—just months before the revolution—Wu represented China at the First Universal Races Congress in London. Addressing the global inequities caused by Western imperialism and by exclusionary immigration policies, Wu declared, "With regard to the question of inter-racial marriage, in my opinion the principle is excellent, though I fear it is not easy to carry out. Broadly speaking, it is proper that Occidentals and Orientals should inter-marry, as this would be the best means of diffusing knowledge and creating ties of relationship and friendship. . . . I am inclined to the opinion that when a nation has a large number of its people who marry with foreigners, it is a sign of progress."[51]

Citing cases of happy mixed marriages, Wu argued for intermarriage both as a means of bridging cultural differences and of promoting constructive miscegenation. As he declared, "It has been proved that children inherit the traits of their parents, and, as the Chinese are noted for their patience, perseverance, honesty, and industry, these characters will naturally be imparted to the Eurasian children, who will have the good points from both sides."[52] It is notable here that Wu emphasized the Eurasian's inheritance of positive "racial characteristics" from the Chinese side, a sharp contrast to Tang Caichang's vision of eugenically improving the Chinese race through an infusion of whiteness.

Wu's address contributed to the wide-ranging debates among the international delegates concerning the "advantages and disadvantages" of racial mixture. Several other delegates, including Professor Earl Finch (United States), Dr. Jean Baptiste Lacerda (Brazil), Sir Sydney Olivier (Great Britain), and Sir Harry Johnston (Great Britain), similarly delivered remarks on the beneficial effects of race crossing, both social and biological, *under certain conditions*. Johnston, for example, rejected the crossing of black and white but endorsed the mixing of white and "any type of Mongol or Amerindian" as a means of biologically assimilating the latter into "the Caucasian group."[53] On this point, Johnston differed fundamentally from Wu, who claimed that yellow–white amalgamation was beneficial "to both sides."

Wu developed this theme further in *America, Through the Spectacles of an Oriental Diplomat*, first published in 1914. Arguing again that the offspring of East–West mixed marriages inherit the "good points of both sides," Wu specifically identified Hong Kong Eurasians as evidence. Citing the headmaster of Queen's College (formerly Government Central School), Wu asserted that Eurasians had been the top students ever since the school had admitted them—likely referring to prize-winning Eurasians like Sin Tak-fan (1856–1924) and the Ho and Hung brothers (see chapter 8). Wu further declared that "not only in school but in business also they have turned out well. It is well known that the richest man in Hong Kong is a Eurasian"—a clear reference to Ho Tung.[54] Wu concluded, "There is no doubt that mixed marriages of the white with the yellow races will be productive of good to both sides."[55]

Similarly, Zou Taofen, the journalist and publisher who translated Mae Franking's *My Chinese Marriage*, supported Chinese–Western intermarriage both as a eugenic mechanism and to promote intercultural understanding (see chapter 2). So too the *China Critic* in 1930, as we will see in chapter 5. Thus, despite the fact that the incipient nationalism of the late Qing had emerged as the dominant ideology of the early Republican era, cosmopolitan voices continued to support Chinese–Western intermarriage. Indeed, during the so-called New Culture movement initiated in the late 1910s, students and urban intellectuals who combined patriotism with a desire to modernize China often looked to the West for inspiration for reforming the family and women's roles even as they decried Western imperialism. Within this context, public intellectuals like Zou viewed Chinese–Western intermarriage (especially between educated Western women and Chinese men) as emblematic of modernity.

THE EURASIAN IN THE "SOCIETY BASED ON BEAUTY"

During the widespread iconoclasm of the New Culture era, the philosopher Zhang Jingsheng (1888–1970), popularly known as "Dr. Sex," became yet another prominent thinker to advocate Eurasian interracialism. This he did in a controversial proposal for a utopian world organized on "the principles of beauty."[56]

China's first popular sexologist, Zhang had studied philosophy in France from 1912 to 1919. Thus, like Kang Youwei, Zhang had opportunity to encounter firsthand examples of Chinese–Western couples abroad, and indeed he did not shy away from referencing his own sexual encounters with French women in his writings.[57] In 1920 Zhang began teaching at Beijing University, where he became acquainted with leading intellectuals of the era. In 1924 and 1925, Zhang consecutively published two manifestoes: *A Way of Life Based on Beauty* (*Mei de renshengguan*) and *Organizational Principles for a Society Based on Beauty* (*Mei de shehui zuzhifa*).[58] Taking love as the ultimate principle of beauty, these tracts spell out the means for establishing a society founded on this philosophy. One of the key goals to be realized by the Society Based on Beauty was "racial improvement," and Zhang elaborated a eugenic ideal based on principles of perfection and beauty. Eugenicists like Pan Guangdan (1899–1967) and Zhou Jianren (1888–1984) vigorously denounced his eugenic proposals as false science, but the publicity generated by this controversy only served to increase Zhang's popularity, and *A Way of Life Based on Beauty* was reprinted seven times between 1925 and 1927.[59]

In *Organizational Principles*, Zhang proposes a system of out-marriage as the best means of reaching the goal of Global Great Unity. Echoing Tang Caichang and Yi Nai, he contends that interracial marriage will help to promote mutual understanding between nations and eliminate racial conflict. He further suggests that racial intermarriage will produce vigorous cross-breeds, citing as evidence the historical intermingling of Han Chinese and various frontier peoples like the Xiongnu, which he asserts had produced "mixed-blood heroes." Inter-marriage thus serves both ethical and eugenic purposes, and is funda-mental to the institution of a Society Based on Beauty.

Zhang chooses specific targets for intermarriage. If the "mixed-blood heroes" of the past were the offspring of Han–Xiongnu unions, Zhang now identifies Westerners as the ideal candidates for eugenic intermix-ing. Like the late Qing authors discussed previously, Zhang accepts the Social Darwinian racial hierarchy that placed the white race at the pin-nacle and suggests that Chinese "climb up" to intermarry with whites. Citing a newspaper report that more than one million Russian women on the Sino–Russian border had married Chinese men after the Russian Revolution, he delineates the imagined benefits of such unions. Zhang argues that the racial characteristics of the Russians and the Chinese are complementary: the staunch and tough nature of the Russians compen-sating for the Chinese flaw of gentleness. If the Chinese could absorb the Russians' daring and outgoing natures while simultaneously endow-ing the Russians with their gentle and lenient dispositions, he asserts, it would produce the ideal combination, a race of Sino–Russian hybrids fit to be the masters of an "Asia for Asians."

Zhang also advocates intermarriage with Western Europeans and Americans, though he fears his [male] readers might consider white women out of reach.[60] Refuting the misconception that white women are inacces-sible "swan meat" who disdain the Chinese, Zhang asserts that French women had warmly welcomed Chinese migrant laborers during World War I. Zhang furthermore argues that those upper-class European and American women who *do* look down on the Chinese are far too extrava-gant and ill-tempered to make suitable spouses in any event. Far better, he argues, for Chinese men abroad to look for wives among the common folk. A particular class dynamic is thus inscribed into Zhang's prescription for East–West intermarriage, with the lower-class status of the white wife counterbalancing the lower racial status of the Chinese husband.

Idealizing Western women as efficient homemakers, good mothers, and intellectual companions, he declares that overseas students who bring home Western wives will benefit enormously. They would also render a service to the nation, he argues, because Western wives would indirectly promote reform by exerting cosmopolitan and progressive influences over their husbands. The Western wife, he imagined, could also perform service as an authoritative consultant on Western ways. Presuming modernization along Western lines, Zhang depicts these women as an asset to the modernizing nation, and he claims that their presence in China would speed political reform exponentially. Once again, interracial sexuality is redeemed as it is harnessed for the benefit of the nation.

While Zhang focuses primarily on the marriages of Chinese men with Western women, he also advocates intermarriage for Chinese women. In terms of the national interest, Zhang proposes that Chinese women could be valuable tools in East–West international relations: first, by contracting marital alliances with Westerners; and second, as pawns in the time-honored "beauty's stratagem" (*meiren ji*), a tactic of winning over the enemy through seduction. On a personal level, Zhang argues, Chinese women can liberate themselves by marrying Western men. Idealizing Western men as more romantic, gentle, doting, and interesting than Chinese men, Zhang declares it inevitable that Chinese women, especially New Women, will prefer to marry foreigners. Introducing competition into the system, intermarriage will thereby serve as a stimulus for gender reform in China. As one example of a Chinese woman who had happily married a foreigner, Zhang cites Der Ling (1885–1944), the Eurasian court lady who married American businessman Thaddeus White, becoming a popular writer who marketed herself as "Princess Der Ling" to American audiences. In the end, Zhang argues, all will balance out, since Chinese women of sense and sensibility like Der Ling will desire to marry foreign men, while their male counterparts will desire to marry foreign women. For both Chinese men and women, then, intermarriage with Westerners provides the best opportunity for realizing the individual ideal of love as well as the broader social ideals of improving the Chinese race and ultimately promoting world peace.

In turning to the question of nonwhite races, Zhang accepts intermarriage between Chinese men and women of color but definitively rejects the idea of Chinese women "lowering themselves" by marrying men of darker races. This gendered double standard derives from the patriarchal notion that a woman's status follows that of her husband, and thus Zhang argued that Chinese men who married women from the "inferior races" would render a service to humankind by elevating their racial status. Since Japanese and white colonists are too arrogant to marry native women, he provocatively argued, it is up to Chinese men to perform the service of civilizing the "weak" and "savage" races through racial amalgamation.[61]

Like his late Qing antecedents, Zhang exhibits a marked bias against the darker races, associating dark skin color with cultural inferiority. Zhang thereby endorses what had come to be a prevalent Chinese interpretation of Social Darwinism, which placed the white race at the pinnacle, the yellow race a close second, and the darker races at the bottom. In their intermediate position, the Chinese must aim to "climb up" to the level of the white race or "stoop down" and "pull up" the darker races. Based on this hierarchy, Zhang advances two different hypotheses concerning racial amalgamation: whereas he conceptualizes hybridization between Chinese and Russians as a merging of complementary racial characteristics, he posits amalgamation between Chinese and the darker races as a tool for assimilating and absorbing the latter. This second type of hybridization is not to be an equal exchange or merger but a one-way transformation up the racial hierarchy.

With his admiration for the white and his disdain for the dark, Zhang constructs the Eurasian as the eugenic ideal, combining the best racial characteristics of superior yellow and white parent stock while tempering the racial flaws of each. His conviction that this mixed Eurasian race will one day be the masters of an "Asia for Asians" is an interesting combination of Eurocentric Social Darwinism and pan-Asianist, anti-imperialist rhetoric: for in his formulation, it is only by amalgamation with a white race that an Asian race will achieve regional self-determination.

THE EURASIAN AS THE IDEAL COMBINATION OF EAST AND WEST

Despite their production in radically different historical moments, the late Qing and early Republican proposals examined here share two fundamental ideas: that racial amalgamation can serve as a eugenic tool; and that the Eurasian represents the ideal racial breed of the future. Hence, in sharp contrast to Western eugenicists, who frequently portrayed racial improvement as an effort to preserve the racial *purity* of particular groups, the authors of these proposals conversely theorized racial improvement in terms of the regenerative potential of racial *amalgamation.*[62] Embracing the notion of hybrid vigor, they asserted that the Eurasian stood to inherit the strong points of the parent races while filtering out the weaknesses. Combining not the "vices of both parents," but the "best of both worlds," the resulting new hybrid race would be exceptionally intelligent, strong, fit, and beautiful. These thinkers conceptualized hybridity as a unification or bridging of two elements—similar to the interlocking of yin and yang—thus invoking the notions of compromise and peaceful coexistence rather than those of mixing as pollution, transgression, or degeneration.

Yet it is only the particular amalgamation of yellow and white, or Chinese and European, that is idealized; other forms of hybridity (Chinese-black, black–white, and so on) are either rejected outright or considered subpar. The selective glorification of the Eurasian thus confirms for these writers the special status of white and yellow as superior among the various races of the world. Instead of debunking Social Darwinian notions of racial hierarchy and competition, leading Chinese racial thinkers simply adapted its structure to admit of *two* superior races whose eventual amalgamation would produce the perfected race of the future. The idealization of the Eurasian thus served as one means for Chinese intellectuals to reconcile an emerging sense of racial inferiority generated by Social Darwinism (hence the need to "improve the race") with deeply held convictions of Chinese superiority, whether conceived of in cultural or racial terms (hence the idea of ameliorating whiteness, or preserving the best qualities of Chineseness); and particularly in the twentieth century, with Chinese nationalism.

The various articulations of Eurasian hybridity examined here bring two concepts into play. The first is the concept of yellow and white as proximate races, similar in civilizational attributes, appearance, and native intelligence. The second is the concept of yellow and white as complementary opposites, each one possessing strengths where the other is weak. Although their specific formulations varied, the writers discussed here tended to associate the white race with physical qualities—strength, tall stature, vigor, fair skin, and beauty: a racialization that reflected to a large degree the military and economic strength of the aggressive Western imperialist powers during the Treaty Port era. In contrast, they tended to associate the Chinese race with intellectual or cultural qualities—intelligence, moral sensibility, elegance, and cultivation. Based on these racializations, they conceptualized the Eurasian as the eugenic combination of Western physical strength and beauty with Chinese intelligence, moral capacity, and/or cultural refinement.

We might read this dichotomy as an implicit gendering of the races. However, even if we were to accept the association between physical strength and masculinity, on one hand, and between cultural refinement and femininity, on the other, other terms of the dichotomy (beauty and intelligence, for example) are not necessarily strongly gender coded. Indeed, Yi Nai is the only one of the writers examined here who explicitly represented white and yellow as masculine and feminine. Furthermore, as we saw from earlier chapters, most late Qing and early Republican commentators on the issue tended to represent East–West intermarriage predominantly in terms of Chinese men and Western women. Thus, as I have argued elsewhere, the gendering of the races is a multilayered and sometimes contradictory phenomenon, beyond a simple equivalence of West/masculine and China/feminine.[63]

I argue that these two concepts—of racial proximity on one hand and of binary polarity between Chinese and Westerners on the other—have been key to Chinese historical representations of the Eurasian as a biracial subject, and to a lesser extent to the modern construction of Chinese racial identity itself. In other words, "Chineseness" is constructed not simply in opposition to "Westernness," but also on the premise that Chinese and whites are racially similar relative to the "darker races." As noted in the introduction, the notion of an East/West binary has been integral to the master narrative of modern Chinese nationalism. The notion of yellow–white proximity is obviously at odds with this master narrative. Yet, when we examine discussions of intermarriage and racial hybridity that privilege Eurasians while denigrating Afro-Asians and other "mixes," this important subtext emerges with greater clarity. My reading of these texts thus suggests that modern Chinese racial identity is constituted between the contradictory notions of "not-white" and "like-white," however much the latter idea might be resisted by Han Chinese racial nationalists. We see this quite clearly in the racial writings of Liang Qichao, for example, where the notion of a dichotomy between yellows and whites coexists with the notion of racial proximity: "Only the yellows are not very dissimilar to the whites."[64]

The significance of this "like-white" concept becomes apparent when we view Chineseness beyond the Chinese/Western dyad, in a global framework of multiple races. Rebecca Karl has argued that "it was a growing Chinese sense of identification with the non–Euro-American world at the turn of the [twentieth] century that initially made the modern world visible as a structured totality."[65] While acknowledging the historical importance of this identification (which would eventually find expression in Maoist practices of Third World solidarity) as a basis for anti-imperialism, I argue here that late Qing and early Republican perceptions of the black, brown, and red races as abject, colonized, and/or enslaved, simultaneously served as a basis for Chinese *disidentification* with the "darker races." Many influential Chinese intellectuals reacted to global unevenness with a fervent hope that China could preserve its (precarious) status as "not-black" (understood as not-abject, not-colonized, not-enslaved). Entwined with anti-black racism, this anxiety informed their negative attitudes toward amalgamation with the purportedly "unfit" darker races. Hence, disidentification with the darker races served as a necessary basis for the construction of yellow and white as proximate races.

For the writers examined here, the simultaneously not-white/like-white figure of the Eurasian represented a resolution to the vexing question of how China could modernize and still maintain a distinctively Chinese character, a question that had preoccupied many Chinese intellectuals since the 1860s. By constructing the Eurasian as a perfected combination of East and West, Chinese reformers were able to critique what they saw as the flaws of the Chinese race and embrace the positive elements of the West without accepting white supremacy wholesale. The idealization of the Eurasian hybrid can thus be read as one response to the problem of negotiating Chinese identity in an age of Western dominance, an alternative to the type of visceral Han Chinese racial nationalism espoused by leading Chinese revolutionaries like Zou Rong. For some, the eugenic improvement of the Chinese race involved not racial cleansing and purification, but amalgamation and hybridity. In addition, since Eurasian hybridity as a merging and union of yellow and white suggested a peaceful, nonconflictual resolution to the opposition between the two races, a solution to the global race war, the notion had particular appeal to pacifist thinkers in their attempts to envision a perfected future—whether that was the utopia of One World, the era of Great Peace, or the Society Based on Beauty.

Perhaps the hybrid's very ambiguity is one reason the figure of the Eurasian has remained compelling for certain Chinese intellectuals. The Eurasian can be read as a "Westernized" Chinese or as a "Sinicized" Euro-American. In other words, the "mixed blood" is one who embodies exotic foreignness, but in an acceptable form: simultaneously "like" and "not like." I argue that it is this indeterminacy that has attracted various commentators during a century in which China has seen radical and fundamental sociopolitical change but throughout which time China's relationship to the West remained an inescapable and abiding concern.

In the next chapter, we will see how the idea of hybrid exceptionalism, as a sociological counterpart of hybrid vigor, played out in a very different context: the transnational endeavors of sociologists to map miscegenation in North America and China.

Prologue to Chapter 5

A FIRST DANCE ACROSS SHANGHAI'S COLOR LINE

On the first day of her arrival in Shanghai, Rosalind Phang (1893–1933) met a young American reporter by the name of George Sokolsky (1893–1962). It was 1919, and Rosalind's friends had organized a welcome for her at a restaurant: it would be the first time in Shanghai history that Chinese and foreigners danced together in public, and the party was screened off in a separate area. This was Rosalind's big "homecoming," her first time in the ancestral land that she knew only through her grandmother's tales, for her Hakka family had migrated from Canton to the British West Indies more than a century ago, establishing themselves as merchants and British subjects.

Born in Jamaica, Rosalind was the daughter of Balaclava's leading Chinese merchant, Charles Phang, and also was distinguished as the first ethnic Chinese piano licentiate of the Royal Academy of Music. Having spent much of her girlhood studying in England, in 1919 she traveled with her sister Hilda to China, seeking new opportunities in the cosmopolitan metropolis.[1] Beautiful, talented, wealthy, and decidedly modern, the Phang sisters were soon moving in Shanghai's elite circle, with close ties to the powerful Kwok and Soong families. Eager to contribute to the New China, Rosalind took work at the China Bureau of Public Information and the *Journal of Commerce*.[2] At the journal, Rosalind found herself working with Sokolsky, and soon they began debating the subject of mixed marriages, consulting the opinions of friends—both Chinese and foreign. Finally, in October 1922, Rosalind

Edith Agatha Phang and George Ephraim Sokolsky were married. As Shanghai's *Weekly Review* reported, the unusual nuptials "took place at the synagogue 'Ohel Rachel' 38 Seymour Road, Shanghai, on Thursday afternoon, October 19, at three o'clock, in the presence of a large number of friends," the bride having become a "Chinese Jewess."[3]

As it would turn out, she also became stateless. As George recalled a decade later in a famous piece he wrote for the *Atlantic Monthly*, "My Mixed Marriage: A Jewish-Chinese Union," "Then we married—she, Chinese, Christian, British; I, Polish, Jewish, American. She became a woman without a country, for my country would not have her and hers had to let her go; I became part of a mixed world in the East, where the color line is drawn in the foreign settlements."[4] Like Mae Franking, Rosalind suffered marital expatriation for marrying a foreign national, but unlike Mae she was unable to assume her husband's nationality. The reason was simple: despite being a British subject, born in Jamaica and educated in England, Rosalind was racially Chinese in the eyes of the U.S. government and therefore barred from naturalization under the Chinese Exclusion Act.

George, for his part, found himself increasingly marginalized in Shanghai expatriate society.[5] More and more, he placed himself on the Chinese side of the color line. Yet "going native" was not entirely a loss for George, for Rosalind was well connected among the Kuomintang (KMT) elite, providing the ambitious journalist with valuable network capital.[6]

The Sokolskys returned to New York in 1930, bringing with them their son, Eric Solomon, who had been born in Shanghai in 1927, and a Chinese nursemaid from Ningbo. Although Rosalind had been debarred from taking U.S. citizenship, she was able to enter the country as the wife of a U.S. citizen. Eric had been conferred U.S. citizenship through his father, and although immigration records show that Rosalind and the nursemaid were required to pay a head tax, Eric was exempt. Paternal privilege meant more than an exemption from the head tax, for whereas Rosalind and the nursemaid were demarcated Chinese under the "race or people" column, Eric was classified as American like his father, with the parenthetical explanation that he was "1/2 Hebrew, 1/2 Chinese."[7]

Transplanted into a new social environment, the Sokolskys found themselves facing many of the same old prejudices. Thus George was compelled to take up his pen and compose an eloquent defense of inter-marriage for the *Atlantic Monthly*, producing yet another antidote to the scandalous miscegenation dramas that had first become popular in American newspapers during the 1880s and multiplied after the turn of the century.[8] In this frequently republished piece, Sokolsky laid out the dilemmas of intermarriage and the prejudice faced in both countries but asserted that "marriage involves, not races and nationalities, but individuals."[9]

Yet, race, nationality, and religious identity could not be so easily dismissed, Sokolsky worried, when it came to the children of such marriages, who would inevitably encounter prejudice from those around them. And thus he concluded that the "most pressing problem" in a mixed marriage "is the child."[10]

Reversing the Sociological Lens

*Putting Sino-American "Mixed Bloods" on
the Miscegenation Map*

Writing for the *American Journal of Sociology* in 1936, Herbert Day
Lamson made this bald pronouncement concerning "The Eurasian in
Shanghai":

> Not that they are biologic freaks, but the fact of being "half-caste" gives
> them a position in the social structure which interferes with their mobility
> and social contacts even in a so-called cosmopolitan society. For this reason
> this intermixture has important sociological consequences.[11]

In casting the "human hybrid" as an object, not of fear and loathing,
but of social scientific interest or importance, early twentieth-century
sociologists like Lamson and his mentor Robert E. Park sought to distance themselves from the biological discourse that dominated nineteenth-century accounts of race mixing (see chapter 3).[12] As such, they
were not concerned with the issues that had so consumed racial theorists of an earlier era—degeneration, reversion, abnormalities, and the
all-important question of hybrid fertility—but rather with the *sociological consequences* of intermixture, and they brought a different set of
inquiries to bear on the "problem" of miscegenation. Turning their
focus away from bodies, and eschewing methods such as anthropometric measurement and photography, they granted a new importance to
life histories—transforming, in their quest for knowledge, the narratives
of people like Mae Franking, George Sokolsky, and many others into
sociological data.[13]

With the emergence of new sociological understandings, the 1920s and 1930s may be regarded as an important turning point in the development of Anglo-American discourses on mixed race.[14] Robert Park and the Chicago School, along with anthropologist Franz Boas, are often credited with reorienting the discourse on racial mixing away from its earlier biological emphasis to a focus on the social.[15] But how far were they really able to shift the discourse?[16] As we will see later in the chapter, biological conceptions of race and identity could never be entirely erased from their work. Moreover, if the great nineteenth-century debate between polygenists and monogenists had pivoted on the question of human hybridity, the issue was once again at the center of the new discourse on race relations: the "human hybrid" still served as a symbol onto which larger meaning was loaded, a portent of the future, for better or worse.[17]

Indeed, Park viewed racial hybrids as the key to understanding race relations, arguing for their significance on two grounds: first, racial hybrids offered "the most obvious and tangible evidence of the extent and character of European cultural contact"; and second, their numbers and position in the social structure were "indices of the character of existing race relations."[18] Park believed that mixed-race populations enabled sociologists to read the degree of assimilation that had taken place over time between the parent races. On this basis he proposed that sociologists chart a "miscegenation map of the world," which, in locating the places where race mixture had occurred or was underway, would facilitate comparative study of the phenomenon.[19] Hence, whereas American nativists of the era viewed miscegenation primarily as a problem for the nation (see chapter 3), Chicago School sociologists like Park theorized race mixture as a *universal* phenomenon of "frontiers," spaces in which different groups of people, possessing different cultures, come into contact, and they thus turned their attention beyond U.S. borders.

Within this burgeoning interest in the sociological implications of racial hybridity, two researchers working under Park's tutelage helped to put Chinese Eurasians on the "miscegenation map." One was Herbert Day Lamson (1899–?), an American student who wrote his dissertation on the American community in Shanghai; and the other Wu Jingchao (1901–68), a Chinese student who wrote his dissertation on American Chinatowns. A juxtaposition of their work provides a window onto the sociological turn in scholarly discourses on mixed race and furthermore demonstrates the definitively transnational character of this enterprise during the 1920s and 1930s. The new project of mapping miscegenation was transnational not only in geographic scope, but also in the involvement of non-Western researchers like Wu and the transnational and translingual circulation of ideas.[20] In order to probe the transnational circuits—from the United States to China, and from China to the United States—along which the sociological discourse on Sino-American miscegenation developed during this time, this chapter compares the writings of Lamson and Wu, two students working in very different settings but each located at the nexus of transnational exchanges between the United States and China.

A comparison of their work prompts us to ask, after Edward Said and James Clifford: What happens to theory when it "travels"? Lamson's study in particular provides us with an interesting opportunity to examine the implications of transposing American sociological theory to China, of reversing a sociological lens that had been trained on immigrants in America, and setting the focus on the American expatriate community in China. As I show, although Lamson applied Park's "marginal man" concept to Shanghai's Eurasians, he did not simply extend North American research agendas wholesale to China but actively sought to negotiate the tension between universal theory and local context. Thus, whereas the previous chapter examined how Chinese intellectuals adapted Western racial theories for their own purposes, producing in the process hybridized theories of eugenic intermixing, the critical focus of this chapter centers on the question of how Lamson's encounter with China shaped his understanding of the sociological significance of racial hybridity. I argue that the idea of "Chinese difference"—seen through an Orientalist lens—played a central role in Lamson's analysis of racial and cultural hybridity in Shanghai, ultimately prompting him to challenge the universal paradigms of American sociological giants like Robert Park and E. B. Reuter and to problematize the use of the racial hybrid as a cipher or index. Hence, even as Lamson's study of interracialism in China added empirical data to the notional global miscegenation map, he critiqued the very premises on which such a project was predicated.

A CHINESE STUDENT IN CHICAGO: WU JINGCHAO PUTS THE CHINESE DIASPORA ON THE MISCEGENATION MAP

In 1923, a young graduate from China's elite Tsinghua University in Beijing arrived in the United States, set to study sociology.[21] A brilliant student, Wu Jingchao (known as Ching Chao or "CC" Wu) was soon taken under the wing of Robert Park at the University of Chicago, drawn into the orbit of an ambitious endeavor to investigate Asian immigrant communities in North America, the Survey of Race Relations (SRR) on the Pacific Coast. Underwritten by missionary social reformers and philanthropists, and directed by Robert Park, this multiyear study (1924–26) was dedicated to understanding the so-called "Oriental problem" on the North American Pacific Coast. Although broad in scope, an investigation of intermarriage was central to this survey. As Henry Yu has demonstrated in his study of American Orientalism and the Chicago School, American sociologists of this era displayed an intense fascination with interracial sex and marriage between "Orientals" and "whites," elevating texts like Emma Fong Kuno's tabloid-style narrative "My Oriental Husbands" to the status of a major document in race relations studies. Although not entirely immune from the prurient curiosity that drove the demand for such stories (see chapter 2), sociologists like Robert Park were, Yu argues, deeply interested in intermarriage as "the distillation and symbol of two different cultures coming into intimate contact."[22] Intermarriage became for the SRR a key indicator of the Oriental's assimilation into American society, with researchers and their supporters keen to determine whether racial intermixing could serve as the ultimate solution to the "Oriental problem." Rather than decrying miscegenation as an unnatural abomination, they took it for granted as a given of intercultural contact—though with varying sociological consequences. Whereas miscegenation appeared threatening to American nativists (see chapter 1), then, in the reformers' eyes intermarriage was a hopeful sign of the diminishing social distance between so-called Orientals and Americans. Concerns about inclusion, and not exclusion, drove their agenda.

Against this backdrop, Wu began work on a master's thesis on "Chinese Immigration in the Pacific Area," which he completed in 1926. Under Park's guidance, Wu highlighted intermarriage as a key index of race relations across different human ecologies. Yet his approach differed from the SRR in some fundamental respects. First, Wu adopted a different framework: the transnational framework of the Chinese diaspora. Extending beyond the North American Pacific Coast, this comparative scope allowed Wu to generate key insights, anticipating in some ways Park's call for a global "miscegenation map." Second, Wu was less interested here in the implications of intermarriage for

American society than in the effects on Chinese immigrants. Broadly surveying Chinese migration across different ecologies, Wu identified intermarriage as a core feature of overseas Chinese communities, found everywhere from Malacca to Hawaii, Mexico, and Peru.[23] Viewing local marriages as a natural outcome of the unequal sex distribution among Chinese migrants, Wu found the relative *infrequency* of intermarriage between Chinese and whites (in the United States, Canada, and Australia) to be an aberration—one he explained by white racial prejudice. The issue of intermarriage thus served as a compelling way for Wu to demonstrate that race relations were fundamentally different for Chinese migrants in the human ecology of the "white countries," which he saw as overwhelmingly shaped by practices and ideologies of discrimination and exclusion.

Under the mentorship of SRR researchers, Wu went on to write his PhD dissertation on American Chinatowns, drawing heavily on the life histories and interviews collected by the survey. The central aim of *Chinatowns: A Study of Symbiosis and Assimilation* (1928) was to analyze Chinese immigrant experiences in terms of the Chicago School's theory of the assimilation cycle. Again, intermarriage was taken as a key index of race relations, but also as a central feature of Chinese migration: "Wherever the Chinese immigrants go, they show no scruples against marrying with other racial groups."[24] Although noting once more that racial prejudice kept the rate of intermarriage in the United States comparatively low, Wu nonetheless concluded that "amalgamation follows racial contact just as naturally as [cultural] assimilation."[25]

In keeping with Chicago School theories of assimilation, Wu portrayed intermarriage as the last step in the full integration of Chinese immigrants. Cultural assimilation alone, he argued, could not do the job, even in the case of native-born Chinese Americans. Race consciousness could only be erased, he concluded, "if it is to be erased at all, not by further assimilation, but by amalgamation."[26] Yet Wu remained pessimistic about intermarriage as a cure for "race problems." Analyzing a variety of cases, including those of Mae Franking and Emma Fong Kuno, Wu identified seven difficulties associated with Chinese–white intermarriage: race prejudice; religious differences; differences in the standard of living between East and West; the problem of acclimatization; the matter of citizenship; attitudes of the parents; and finally what he called "the fate of Eurasians."[27] Indeed, like Park and so many other sociologists of his era, Wu viewed the Eurasian as a tragic figure—a paradigmatic example of the "marginal man."

THE MARGINAL MAN: A NEW MODEL
OF HYBRID PATHOLOGY

The sociological concept of the marginal man was introduced by Robert Park and subsequently developed by many of his students. In "Human Migration and the Marginal Man," Park described this type as a "cultural hybrid" living between two distinctive groups and never completely accepted by either.[28] Park identified the "mixed blood" as the paradigmatic marginal man, reifying the connection between racial and cultural hybridity.[29] For Park, this "typical marginal man" was one "who by the very fact of his racial origin is predestined to occupy a position somewhere between the two cultures." Park further argued that mixed bloods who exhibited physical evidence of their dual origins would inevitably possess "a specific type of mentality—i.e. intellectual and moral qualities which are characteristic of the cultural hybrid or the marginal man."[30] Everett Stonequist, who further developed the theory, similarly identified mixed-race individuals as "the most obvious type of marginal man. . . . His very biological origin places him between the two races."[31] As such, the racial hybrid became a symbol for a particular social process.[32]

Jayne Ifekwunigwe has argued that with this model early twentieth-century sociologists merely replaced the old biological paradigm of hybrid degeneracy with a new paradigm of mixed-race pathology rooted in social maladjustment theory.[33] Indeed, Stonequist and Park characterized the marginal man as pathologically doomed to "spiritual instability, intensified self-consciousness, restlessness, and *malaise*."[34] In extreme cases, this developed into suicidal tendencies, as noted in several of the SRR documents.[35] E. B. Reuter similarly argued that racial hybrids were beset by divided loyalties, internal conflict, and maladjustment, which could only be resolved by identification with "the backward group."[36] Yet Park's original conceptualization of marginality had a positive dimension as well. For Park, the marginal man was a greater intellectual, with critical distance and sensitivity, a cosmopolitan citizen of the world. In Park's words, "The marginal man is always relatively the more civilized human being."[37] Ambivalence thus surrounds the concept of the marginal man.

Wu dedicated a chapter of his dissertation to the marginal man, distinguishing two types: the "cultural hybrid," a product of cultural fusion; and the "biological hybrid," a product of "the fusion of blood." Wu described the marginal man as lost and confused, feeling within himself the conflict of two cultures. But Wu also noted that the marginal man had a key role to play as an interpreter of cultures (of China to the Americans, and of America to the Chinese) and potentially as a reformer (especially in China). He saw Eurasians, however, as beset by a particular set of "problems."

Drawing a distinction between those with Chinese fathers (predominant in the United States) and those with American fathers (predominant in China), Wu asserted that it was generally only the latter group who experienced internal conflict. The American convention of hypo-descent, he argued, was the source of this conflict: for no matter whether the child of an American father and Chinese mother identified as American, American society would treat him or her as Chinese. Citing evidence from SRR case studies, Wu declared that this clash of perspective causes Eurasians to become bitter, and even suicidal. In contrast, Wu asserted that Eurasians with Chinese fathers "do not develop those symptoms as the other types of hybrids."[38] Given that the majority of Chinese Eurasians in the United States were born to Chinese fathers, Wu argued that the "Eurasian problem" was not a serious issue in American society. Wu concluded that the mental "disorganization" observed in some mixed-race individuals was in fact a product of *cultural* conflict, and "not caused, as some persons choose to believe, by the supposed fact that they inherited the bad traits of two races."[39] Wu thus firmly dismissed the notion of hybrid degeneracy promoted by Louis Beck and other nineteenth-century writers (see chapter 3).

Wu's work was enthusiastically promoted by Robert Park and endorsed by Eliot G. Mears, executive secretary of the SRR, who cited Wu as an authority on Chinese migration and miscegenation in his *Resident Orientals on the American Pacific Coast: Their Legal and Economic Status* (1928). Unfortunately, Wu's dissertation was never published, and many of his insights on mixed race were overlooked, even as leading sociologists like Everett Stonequist cited his work. In the end, it was in China, and not the United States, that Wu's influence was strongest.

RETURNING TO CHINA: BRINGING AMERICAN
SOCIOLOGY TO A CHINESE AUDIENCE

Wu returned to China after completing his dissertation, and he quickly became one of China's most prominent sociologists, teaching at Jinling University in Nanjing and at Tsinghua in Beijing. Serving as an adviser to the government, Wu turned his attention to new topics like industrial planning, but he brought back to China his interest in intermarriage, introducing Chinese readers to his work through a series of short articles on "Researches on Sino-American Intermarriage" published between December 1928 and January 1929 in the popular *Life Weekly* magazine.[40] *Life Weekly* subsequently republished the work in its entirety in 1933.[41]

With the international marriages of public figures such as Princess Der Ling and her brother (who took a French wife), and the passage of successive governmental bans on intermarriage for overseas students (see chapter 2), the issue was very much *au courant* among Chinese intellectuals of the early Republican era, especially among the returned student set.[42] Capitalizing on public curiosity, in 1927 *Life Weekly* published a serialized translation of Mae Franking's *My Chinese Marriage* (see chapter 2), followed by a translation of Louise Jordan Miln's fictional *Mr. and Mrs. Sen*. In the following year, Thomas Ming-Heng Chao's *Shadow Shapes: Memoirs of a Chinese Student in America*, an interracial love story originally published in 1926 in the *Chinese Students' Monthly*, was published in Beijing.[43]

Building on reader interest, Wu Jingchao added his voice to the debate. His short articles explained to readers the fundamental distinction between biological and sociological theories of miscegenation, and introduced Chinese audiences to both Anglo-American and Chinese viewpoints (pro and con) on the subject. Wu further used this platform to censure anti-Chinese prejudice, citing American anti-miscegenation statutes as evidence of racial discrimination. Although this article essentially summarized his dissertation findings, Wu approached interracialism from a different angle, setting aside the question of Americanization and emphasizing intercultural understanding. Referencing *My Chinese Marriage*, which had been a favorite among *Life Weekly* subscribers, and further citing the narratives of Emma Fong Kuno and Sui Sin Far, Wu suggested that interracial marriage had the potential to counter anti-Chinese prejudice on an individual level. In discussing intercultural understanding, Wu was less concerned here with bringing Chinese closer to Western culture than with bringing *Westerners* closer to *Chinese* culture. As such, Wu saw hope expressed in transculturated individuals like Mae Franking.

Yet, Wu diverged from intellectuals who presented a utopian vision of interracialism as the solution to global racial conflict (see chapter 4). Adopting instead the "social problems" approach of sociology, Wu dwelt on the difficulties faced by mixed families on both sides of the

Pacific, particularly the children, whom he portrayed as caught between two worlds and bound to suffer discrimination whether in the United States or in China. As an example, he cited the Chinese term *zazhong* ("mongrel" or "bastard"), a common appellation for the hybrid, which was also a highly offensive curse word. Wu suggested instead that a new term be adopted, *tongshengzi*, or "inter-bred children." Although the term never caught on, Wu's attempt to coin this neologism is a noteworthy example of his translingual practice.

AN AMERICAN STUDENT IN SHANGHAI: HERBERT LAMSON PUTS CHINA ON THE MISCEGENATION MAP

By 1926, the Survey of Race Relations was wrapping up, and American sociologists began to carry their interest in East–West contact across the Pacific, by way of Hawaii (viewed as a virtual "experimental laboratory" of race mixing), to Asia. As part of this movement, in 1927 Herbert Day Lamson, a graduate student from Harvard, traveled to Shanghai to begin fieldwork on his dissertation. Lamson was in many respects an interesting counterpart to Wu Jingchao. Similarly influenced by Robert Park, who served as an unofficial adviser on his dissertation, Lamson essentially reversed the trajectory traveled by Wu, setting out from the United States to study the American expatriate community in Shanghai.

While conducting his dissertation fieldwork, Lamson taught sociology at the University of Shanghai, where he would remain in residence until 1933. Lamson soon grew dissatisfied with the use of American sociology textbooks, and he compiled, and later published, his own textbook focused on local case studies.[44] Lamson also took part in several research projects conducted under the aegis of the Chinese government and published in Chinese journals. These experiences informed the writing of his PhD dissertation on *The American Community in Shanghai*, a wide-ranging work from which "The Eurasian in Shanghai" and another article on Sino-American miscegenation were drawn.[45] Based on years of fieldwork and participant observation, Lamson's work still stands as the most detailed sociological investigation of Eurasians in China.[46]

By the time that Lamson arrived in China, the "Eurasian problem" had been a subject of long-standing concern among Shanghai's Anglo-American expatriate community. As early as 1869 the *North China Herald* had warned that a looming social problem was "daily thrusting itself before us into ever greater prominence." This problem was the anomalous position of Eurasians, an issue that had proven troublesome in India and now threatened to do the same in China. Cautioning that it "would be a fatal error" to turn a blind eye to miscegenation and neglect "these half castes," the *North China Herald* called on the international community to deal frankly with the issue of race mixing in its early stages and "direct the lives of the intermediate race that is arising."[47]

As reflected in this editorial, Anglo-American discourses on the "Eurasian problem" in China focused on two main concerns: the anxiety that Eurasians might pose a threat to white racial prestige, which rested upon a sharp division between European and native; and the realization that children of European parentage had a moral claim to support and recognition, for which they might agitate, as they had in British colonial India. The *North China Herald* suggested what it saw as an easy solution to both dimensions of the problem: the establishment of a special Western-style boarding school for Eurasians in Shanghai. A separate school would allow these children, many of whom were poor and orphaned, to be transformed into "civilized men and women," rescued from the detrimental influences of native mothers and "Chinese ignorance and superstition." The newspaper called for Eurasian children to be educated as Europeans, but taught Chinese as well as English, in order to train this "intermediate race as a civilized link between Foreigners and Chinese." In this manner, the foreign community could kill two birds with one stone: fulfilling its moral obligations to the children of European parentage while introducing "a valuable civilizing influence" among the Chinese.[48]

Concerns over this issue were widespread enough that an American missionary woman, Mrs. Samuel Bonney, founded a Eurasian School in September 1870, with backing provided by a charitable committee and significant resources from an Englishman, Mr. Thomas Hanbury. Manifesting the "tension of empire," the school's mission was premised on the belief that Eurasian children should be educated "as nearly up to the European standard as possible," yet segregated from "Europeans of pure blood."[49] In the words of the *First Yearly Report of the Shanghai Eurasian School*, "There are many reasons for dealing with Eurasian children as a class by themselves, at least during the earlier years of their education."[50] With a population that expanded—by official counts—from 8 to 519 between 1876 and 1900, the Eurasian School served a growing segment of Shanghai's International Settlement (fig. 11).[51] Such discourses concerning the Eurasian problem were well ingrained in the Anglo-American expatriate community by the time that Lamson conducted his fieldwork.

FIGURE 11. Thomas Hanbury School, Shanghai, ca. 1889.
Harvard University Widener Library, WID-LC DS796.S243 P36;
p. 37.

In many crucial respects, Lamson's project paralleled the sociological investigations of Chinese American communities. Sharing their interest in interracial contact, assimilation, and cultural hybridization, Lamson took many of the same theoretical questions posed by the SRR but turned his lens on Americans in Shanghai. Thus, Lamson asked seemingly familiar questions such as: To what degree is there cultural continuity in the American community? Does intermarriage promote native–alien social approach? Can the racial hybrid serve as an index of cultural fusion? The linked issues of racial and cultural fusion were again at the heart of his study, but this time, it was the Occidentals and not the Orientals who were under scrutiny.

Yet, Lamson's study was not a simple reversal of the SRR, a mere flip-flop in which Americans became the aliens and Chinese the natives.

Indeed, a comparison of the two projects reveals how American sociologists brought different sociopolitical concerns to bear on their investigations of Asians in America, and Americans in Asia. Whereas the primary concern in the United States was the "problem" of assimilating Asian immigrants into American society, the overriding concern of sociologists in China was to understand cultural change in the opposite direction: in Lamson's words, not "nativeward," but "alienward."[52] Thus, although *alien* and *native* changed places in the sociological equation, the power dynamics between East and West remained the same. Dedicated to the ideal of cosmopolitanism, Lamson immediately recognized the ethnocentrism inherent in this shift of the paradigm. He wrote, "Americans in Shanghai claim for themselves the right to a cultural continuity which they deny to minority groups in the United States. The unassimilated minority national or racial group in the United States tends to be an object of suspicion and dissatisfaction because of its 'unassimilability,' but this same quality we find in our Shanghai alien American community. This fact heightens the importance of our contention that American culture expects other civilizations to change their ways in its direction."[53]

Lamson thereby linked his work to sociological studies of immigrant assimilation in the United States, all the while aware that attempts to draw parallels were fundamentally limited by the power asymmetry between China and the West. As we will see later in the chapter, this insight would serve as the basis for a pointed critique of the Chicago School.

REVERSING THE LENS, REVERSING
THE GENDER EQUATION

The effects of reversing the sociological lens between America and Asia immediately become evident when we consider the intersections of race and gender in the formulation of research agendas. As Yu has demonstrated, sociologists of North American race relations were particularly interested in the pairing of Asian men and (white) American women. In contrast, sociological studies of race mixing in Asia focused on relations between European men and Asian women. This reversal had a demographic basis (in both cases it was predominantly men who traveled), but it cannot be explained by empirical reasons alone, because, as Lamson showed in his dissertation, reliable statistical data on interracialism in China were virtually nonexistent. Rather, it was also determined by the biases researchers brought to the framing of their studies.

In the United States, the framework for reading intermarriage was defined by the "problem" of immigration and race relations, and further seen against the backdrop of popular miscegenation dramas calling for the protection of white women's purity against the imagined threat posed by Chinese male immigrants (see chapter 1).[54] American sociologists studying Asia did so within the framework of Western economic and cultural imperialism, and they viewed miscegenation through this lens. Park's comparative surveys of "racial hybrids," for example, conceptualized "half-castes" around the globe as "products and indices of Europe's social frontier."[55] Within this context, the Eurasian problem was linked to the supposed threat posed by immoral native women to white men's scruples.

If both paradigms placed the white racial group—whether as majority or minority, native or alien—at the center of the story, Wu Jingchao had offered another (Sinocentric) perspective. Using the framework of the Chinese diaspora, Wu placed Chinese migrants at the center of his narrative, measuring his racial frontiers through the distances covered by Chinese migrants. Yet precisely because he placed the issue of Sino-American intermarriage squarely within the framework of Chinese migration, Wu still focused his attention on relations between Chinese men and American women, dismissing rather summarily the couplings of Western men and Chinese women that had taken place in China.[56]

Bridging the research on Chinese immigrants with the literature on colonial societies, Lamson's work on Shanghai's "racial hybrids" went much farther than Wu Jingchao in dealing with *both* the children of European fathers and Chinese mothers *and* the children of Chinese fathers and European mothers. This marked a significant departure from the existing sociological literature: following British colonial convention, sociological analyses of Asia typically defined Eurasians as the offspring of European fathers (lumping the children of Asian fathers with the "natives"). As Kumari Jayawardena has pointed out, this gendered paradox has rendered both white mothers and their mixed-race children invisible in colonial and postcolonial historiography.[57] Sociologists of Lamson's era similarly reinforced the privileging of paternal heritage because they theorized particular forms of hybridity while rendering others invisible.

Lamson's decision to use an inclusive definition allowed him to generate many interesting comparative insights, ultimately enabling him to critique E. B. Reuter's model of the racial hybrid as a universal sociological type. Dividing the "mixed bloods" of Shanghai into two cohorts,

Lamson noted that the first group had been established in Shanghai from the 1840s on as a product of local liaisons (mainly extramarital) between Western men and Chinese women. The second grouping did not emerge as a cohort until after 1900 and was primarily comprised of the children of Chinese returned students who had married Western women abroad, not locally. As Lamson demonstrated, these two cohorts differed substantially. The first had its own distinct social organizations, such as the Eurasian School, a Sunday school, and a basketball team.[58] In contrast, children of Chinese fathers and white mothers followed an altogether different pattern: they took their fathers' nationality, wore Chinese clothes, spoke Chinese, and attended Chinese schools. Considered "Chinese," Lamson argued, they occupied an entirely different position in Shanghai's social structure and did not suffer from the same social ostracism. Lamson further identified a third cohort: the children of European fathers and Chinese mothers who had "become Chinese culturally," thereby "blending back," as he put it, into Chinese society.

While recognizing the diversity among Shanghai's mixed-race population, Lamson primarily focused his discussion on the first cohort and thus painted a general portrait of Shanghai Eurasians as a group that lived in European style, wore European clothes, and for the most part reflected "the alien's anti-Chinese viewpoints."[59] Hence, Lamson represented the Shanghai Eurasian as a marginal man: "He is marginal, belonging really to neither parental group, not wholly acceptable either to the 'white' or the 'yellow' communities, but on the whole tending to ape the alien and to claim nationality under some European or 'white' aegis."[60] Like Wu, Lamson asserted sociological, not biological, causes for this marginality, identifying prejudice as the primary factor.[61] As an example of this prejudice, Lamson cited an American military chaplain who declared, "I am from the South where we don't want intermarriage between whites and blacks to get a 'high yaller,' and out here I don't propose to be instrumental in raising a batch of Eurasians."[62] Lamson's American and British interviewees expressed definitive biases: the Eurasian was thought to embody the worst qualities of the parent races; he was "crooked," "morally deficient," and "did not amount to much."

Lamson identified various sociological explanations for this discrimination. Foremost is the stigma of illegitimacy, a strong bias that carried over even onto legitimate children. A related factor was the stereotype of low-status origins—the sailor father, the prostitute mother. Most important, he argued, was the deep-seated cultural taboo against miscegenation in Anglo-American society. Lamson found that his American and British interviewees frequently justified their objections to mixed-race children by expressing sheer repugnance at the thought of miscegenation. Lamson argued that ostracism of mixed couples and their Eurasian children served as a form of social sanctioning that punished those who violated the taboo against crossing racial boundaries. According to Lamson, Anglo-American "racial exclusiveness" marginalized mixed couples and relegated them to the "native" group. Citing George Sokolsky's "My Mixed Marriage," Lamson related the effects of "white prejudice against Chinese." As Sokolsky wrote of his marriage to Rosalind Phang, "The result is that in such a mixed marriage as ours the social relationships tend to be limited to the wife's people. In the husband, resentment grows against the discrimination and condescension which he sees frequently manifested toward her people. . . . More and more the man finds himself tied to his wife's people."[63]

Foreign prejudice, Lamson emphasized, was only one-half of the picture: the other half was "native" attitudes. Although Lamson conceded that Chinese opinion on the matter was divided, with many disapproving of the "dilution of blood" with foreigners in Shanghai, overall he asserted the Chinese were relatively "less exclusive" and more tolerant of intermarriage than the British and Americans.[64] Lamson fully acknowledged the differences between rural and urban opinion, noting that attitudes among the "natives" in Shanghai and other urban centers were already being shaped by liberal returned students. Thus Lamson asserted that tolerance toward intermarriage was most frequently expressed by modern, educated Chinese, many of whom approved of interracial marriage "theoretically as an instrument in the breakdown of interracial and international prejudice."[65] Noting that such a viewpoint was informed by the (imported) romantic notion of "Love conquers all," and also influenced by Western biologists who argued for hybrid vigor, Lamson nonetheless portrayed Chinese intellectuals as active agents in appropriating such ideas for their own purposes.

An editorial "On Mixed Marriage" that appeared in the *China Critic* in February 1930—possibly authored by the American-educated sociologist and eugenicist Pan Guangdan—provides a perfect example of such creative appropriation.[66] Weighing in on the issue "which [has] been in the minds of many Chinese, and which will undoubtedly influence our own social structure to an appreciable extent," the *China Critic* outlined for readers the pros and cons of the matter, listing various impediments to mixed marriages, including class and cultural differences, and the perennial question of whether foreign women could satisfactorily acclimatize to China. On the other side of the argument, biological theories were invoked in favor of intermarriage, much as in the utopian visions examined in the previous chapter. Referring to such experts as Edward M. East and Griffith Taylor, the editorial set forth arguments for racial intermixing as a means of increasing variability and vitality. As evidence, the author pointed to Shanghai's Eurasians:

> Look around yourselves; there are more beautiful Eurasian girls and handsome Eurasian boys in Shanghai than there are beautiful girls and handsome boys amongst all the foreign communities here combined. Of course, physical appearance is not the whole thing, but this alone goes a long way in improving the human race. And the mental aspect of the question is an argument decidedly for intermarriage between peoples of different nationalities. This holds true even in China. Many offsprings of such unions are decidedly superior in mentality, not only above their own mixed parents, but also over and above the general level any where.[67]

Noting this general tolerance among urban Chinese intellectuals, Lamson nonetheless found opinion tempered by patriotic sentiment and the fear that out-marriage would entail a loss of devotion to China. Echoing the concerns of an earlier generation (see chapter 1), one Chinese student stated, "A man who marries an American woman usually forgets his own country."[68] Faced with this divided opinion, Lamson identified a gendered split in local attitudes: "While some Chinese heartily disapprove of such unions, yet to some it gives a feeling of satisfaction in that it helps to raise their own group in its own estimation, because the native is sensitive to foreign criticism and if a foreign woman in America is willing to marry 'one of our Chinese men' then this very fact is an admission on the part of the foreigner that there are admirable qualities in the Chinese which certain foreign women have not been able to resist."[69]

These attitudes were similarly projected onto interracial children. Lamson argued that Eurasians with Chinese fathers were more acceptable in the "Chinese cultural milieu" than those with European fathers. Here again is an example of how Lamson's comparison of the two cohorts generated insights into the intersectionality of race and gender.[70]

THE SHANGHAI EURASIAN: "HOW HE APES HIS SIRE"

Lamson's treatment of Eurasian marginality is seemingly sympathetic as he attempted to distance himself from attitudes of racial snobbery among Anglo-American expatriates in China, and also from the labeling of hybrids as "biologic freaks." Yet, Lamson also repeatedly refers to Eurasians as "European aping hybrids" throughout his text, revealing his ultimately derisive attitude toward his subject. This suggests Lamson as a complex figure, a person who attempted to rise above the racism of his time but who also saw fit to denigrate certain groups based on their perceived cultural or social inferiority. Lamson in fact blamed Eurasians for drawing scorn upon themselves by mimicking European ways and manners. Indeed, he contended that the Chinese dislike of Eurasians was chiefly a reaction to the latter's tendency to emulate foreigners' haughty treatment of the Chinese. As he wrote, "When Chinese meet Eurasians who try to cover up their Chinese ancestry and appear totally foreign, tending to look down upon the Chinese, it naturally makes natives feel unfriendly toward the mixed blood."[71] Chinese discrimination against Eurasians therefore arises not so much from an aversion toward racial hybridity per se but rather from a nationalistic reaction against an "imitation foreigner" in the body of a "part-Chinese."[72]

What becomes evident in Lamson's text is that he shared the "native disgust" at the pretensions of the "European-aping Eurasian." Lamson blamed Eurasian marginality on the fact that they "hitch their wagons to the wrong star, the alien instead of the native."[73] It was among the natives, Lamson believed, that mixed bloods had the best chance, and he approved heartily of those who "blended back" into Chinese society; they "might be very poor, but at least they would 'belong' to Chinese society, and could get along better and with less prejudice than the Chinese-hating Eurasian."[74] On this point, Lamson's analysis accords with the conclusions of Wu Jingchao's dissertation. Although Wu had less opportunity to fully compare the offspring of Chinese mothers with those of Chinese fathers, he concluded that the "problems" of Eurasians in American society could be solved by "a determination to throw their fate with the Chinese, to be known and to be treated as such."[75]

RACIAL INTERMEDIARY AND INTERPRETER:
HYBRID EXCEPTIONALISM

Lamson, like Wu, followed Park in representing the Eurasian as a marginal man. Yet, Lamson did not entirely walk in step with the dominant sociological theories of his time. Indeed, the central theoretical thrust of "The Shanghai Eurasian" was to challenge E.B. Reuter's paradigm of the racial hybrid as a universal sociological type. In "The Hybrid as a Sociological Type," Reuter had argued that the racial hybrid occupied a distinctive intermediary position, a particular status that derived from his anomalous physical appearance. This status allowed the racial hybrid to play a special role: as a cultural or political intermediary; a harmonizer; or a buffer. For Reuter, the racial hybrid was not only different, but, in certain respects, superior. As he wrote, "In all cases these hybrid groups resulting from the amalgamation of physically divergent races are superior in social position and intellectual achievement to one racial element of their ancestry."[76] While Reuter admitted to diversity in the status of racial hybrids in different countries, these local variations were overridden for him by the notion that "every mixed-blood group conforms, psychologically and culturally, to type."[77]

Based on his analysis of Eurasians in Shanghai, whom he viewed as markedly different from the American "mulattos" that Reuter had studied, Lamson disputed this idea of a single, universally applicable formula.[78] Lamson's contention that there were, rather, multiple types was further supported by his identification of key differences between the two cohorts of Shanghai Eurasians. For example, Lamson challenged Reuter's bold declaration that "the desire of the mixed-blood man is always and everywhere to be a white man; to be classed with and become a part of the superior race."[79] Lamson debunked this claim by demonstrating that in Shanghai this desire was evident only among Eurasians of European paternity.[80]

Moreover, Lamson believed that Reuter underestimated the role of social ostracism in determining the hybrid's status. In Shanghai, he contended, ostracism precluded Eurasians from bridging the gulf between the races. As he argued, "The alien is brought no nearer to native culture because of a class of alien-aping hybrids whom he despises and ostracizes. The native is brought no nearer to an understanding and appreciation of alien culture because of a class of native-despising hybrids who ape the alien."[81] On this basis, Lamson seriously questioned the degree to which Shanghai Eurasians facilitated, as Reuter had contended, "cultural contacts and . . . the spread, acceptance, and fusion of culture heritages."[82] Instead, Lamson argued that it was the "modernized pure-blood Chinese," and *not* the "racial hybrid Chinese-foreigner," who was the most effective agent for the transmission of Western culture to China.[83]

But more than anything else, Lamson objected to the hybrid exceptionalism inherent in Reuter's theory. Reuter had already become infamous for contending that the "mulatto" was superior to "pure-blood" African Americans in intellect and achievement and hence served as the natural leader of this group. This notion of hybrid exceptionalism heavily informed Reuter's theorization of the universal hybrid type as an "intellectual, social, and economic aristocracy."[84] Lamson was particularly irked by Reuter's contention that "in every biracial situation the hybrids ... have erupted a percentage of intellectually capable men far in excess of that furnished by the native element of their racial ancestry. Everywhere they have risen to positions of leadership and relative social success in larger numbers than have the full-blooded individuals."[85] Challenging this hypothesis, Lamson denied the superiority of Shanghai Eurasians over the native Chinese and suggested that they might, in fact, be considered *inferior*: they were less educated, less capable, and perhaps even less intelligent, he claimed, than the "modernized pure-blood Chinese." Ultimately, then, Lamson took issue with the hybrid exceptionalism implicit (to varying degrees) in the work of Chicago sociologists like Park, Reuter, and Stonequist, who claimed that the racial hybrid's notional in-betweenness placed this figure in a special role—whether as cultural intermediary, harmonizer, buffer, connecting link, or natural aristocracy.

Disputing Reuter's universal formula, Lamson urged that new variables be added to the analysis, and one of these was biological inheritance. Whereas Reuter had sought to remove biological explanations from the picture, Lamson argued that biological inheritance could not be ignored entirely, and that "selection among the parent stocks" (in class terms) must be taken into account as *one* determining factor of the hybrid's status. Although he considered social environment to be the most important determinant, he also argued that the inferior social position of Eurasians could partially be explained by biological inheritance. On this point, Lamson once more drew a fundamental distinction between European-fathered and Chinese-fathered hybrids. As he wrote, "We have no way of knowing positively whether the mixtures in Shanghai have been from below-average biological stock, but there seems to be some possibility that this is so. This could hardly be said of the hybrids now in childhood who are the offspring of relatively recent matings of returned Chinese male students and white women. . . . "[86] Again favoring the hybrid offspring of Chinese fathers and white mothers, Lamson suggested that class origin trumps racial origin, even as he figured class as "biological stock."[87]

The most important variable, however, Lamson argued, that Reuter had failed to consider was *the quality of traditional native culture* (emphasis in original) in the biracial situation, for Chinese culture, he claimed, was essentially different from the "backward cultures" Reuter described, limiting the applicability of his model to China. This is where a notional "Chinese difference" becomes key to Lamson's theorization of cultural contact and hybridization. Lamson argued that the Chinese cultural background was "certainly backward from the white man's set of values, but there was a massive literary cultural tradition, and sets of values in the Chinese native culture which were not present in the Filipino, Negro, or Amerind. The Chinese traditional reverence for the scholar and the student was an element in China's favor. . . ."[88] Here we see an implicit hierarchy of civilizations, with Chinese culture lower down the scale than the "white man's" but superior to that of other "colored" races. In Lamson's eyes, "traditional" Chinese values favored rapid modernization led by the native, educated elite, thereby diminishing the opportunity for the hybrid to step into this role. Under such conditions, Lamson asserted, it was Western-educated Chinese, and *not* Eurasians, who were fit to be the natural leaders in modern Chinese society.[89]

Lamson's critique of universal models was further informed by his perception of a second crucial difference in the local ecology. As he put it, "The cosmopolitanism of Shanghai is not the same as the cosmopolitanism of Chicago." This came down to a matter of the power relations that prevailed in semicolonial Shanghai. As Lamson pointed out, the alien minority in Shanghai perceived itself as a "ruling group," whereas the alien minority in Chicago lived under a sense of "being ruled." This differential power dynamic shaped the expectation that cultural change should be nativeward in Chicago but alienward in Shanghai. Hence Lamson argued that the racial hybrid should not be regarded as a uniform sociological type, but as a plurality of types varying according to local conditions.[90]

Having debunked Reuter's universal sociological type, Lamson asserted Shanghai as an important counterexample to dispute Park's use of the racial hybrid as an index of cultural fusion.[91] Insisting on a notional *Chinese difference*, Lamson questioned some of the fundamental presumptions of authoritative sociological discourse and challenged what he saw as the Chicago School's conflation of racial and cultural hybridity.

Unfortunately, in arguing that cultural fusion and racial fusion proceed on separate tracks, Lamson drew a fundamental distinction between two cohorts based on "blood." Although he identified sociological, and not biological, factors as the root cause of Eurasian inferiority to the "modernized pure-blood Chinese," the very fact that he referred to the latter in terms of blood is telling. The phrase "modernized pure-blood Chinese" excluded by default all "mixed bloods," even those who were socially Chinese (whether through paternal inheritance or by active choice to "become Chinese culturally"). Thus Lamson rendered invisible Eurasians like Morrison and Bartlett Yung, Chen Xiru (Toney Afong, 1859–1936) and his son Chen Yongshan (1887-1924), and Robert Ho (He Shili, 1906-98), men who had in fact taken leadership roles, either civil or military, in the young republic.[92] In Lamson's eyes, returned students and Chinese Americans were icons of cultural hybridity without racial hybridity. Elevating these figures enabled Lamson to develop his theoretical point that biological race should be separated from culture, but also reinforced (wittingly or unwittingly) the privileging of "pure blood" over "mixed blood."

CONCLUSION: THE BIRACIAL ICON REVISITED

As this chapter has demonstrated, the sociological interest in Chinese–white interracialism went far beyond the parameters of the nation-state that framed the "Chinese Question" (see chapter 3). A transnational perspective allows us to recognize the contributions of Chinese sociologists like Wu Jingchao to the sociological discourses on mixed race during the 1920s and 1930s, and reminds us that such discourses circulated in China as well as the United States, through Sinophone as well as Anglophone texts. Even a brief comparison of Lamson and Wu demonstrates how the traffic of ideas concerning interracialism at this time was no longer unidirectional—as was largely the case with the works examined in the previous chapter—but circular. As I have argued, even as Lamson and Wu worked to put Sino-American interracialism on the "miscegenation map," they both, each in his own way, resisted the totalizing impulse of this global project, offering vital critical insights that are still relevant today.

Wu Jingchao played a pivotal role in the transnational flow of ideas concerning Chinese–Western interracialism. He made an important contribution to the American scholarship on Chinese–Western interracialism by positioning the issue within the framework of the Chinese diaspora, challenging the North America–centric orientation of the SRR. Treating interracial marriage not as taboo, but as an ordinary outcome of sex imbalance in migrant communities, Wu further offered a stringent critique of white racism by highlighting the relative absence of Chinese creole communities in the particular human ecologies of North America and Australia. If racial frontiers were to be found the world over, then, as Park theorized, Wu demonstrated that from the standpoint of Chinese migrants the experiences and meanings of these frontiers diverged widely. Like Lamson, Wu thereby suggested that universal theory had critical limitations. His work poses for us the possibility of charting an alternative miscegenation map, one that would place Chinese migrants, and not European imperialists, at the center.

On the Chinese side, Wu helped bring the Chicago School approach to race relations to Chinese audiences. With popular articles informing a broad readership of the sociological turn in studies of mixed race, Wu did his part to shift the discourse in China, even as eugenics remained a strong interest among sociologists like Pan Guangdan and other contemporaries. Wu's Chinese-language publications furthermore helped to introduce Chinese readers to some of the central texts that had shaped the American reading public's understanding of Chinese–Western interracialism: to the works of Emma Fong Kuno, Sui Sin Far, and Wong Chin Foo, among others.

Like Wu Jingchao, Herbert Day Lamson was a pivotal figure in the transnational circulation of ideas, a scholar and teacher who not only brought American sociology to China but also brought China back—insisting that China had something valuable to offer American sociology, both as case study *and* as critical lens. Lamson made a crucial critical intervention by questioning the Chicago School's use of the racial hybrid as an index. He furthermore brought back from his experiences in China a self-reflexive critique of American attitudes of cultural and racial superiority. Challenging the privileging of whiteness that was inherent in notions of hybrid exceptionalism, Lamson went further than many Americans of his time in championing Chinese culture. In addition, like George Sokolsky, Lamson played a role in informing American audiences about Chinese attitudes toward interracialism, offering an indirect critique of American racism by demonstrating that mixed families were less apt to face social ostracism from the Chinese (at least in a cosmopolitan city like Shanghai).

Lamson's critical intervention rested on his conviction in China's fundamental difference, a notion no doubt informed by certain Orientalist preconceptions. Yet Lamson emphasized Chinese difference in the service of an anti-racist agenda that was not unlike Wu Jingchao's. Moreover, by placing the American community in Shanghai under the same lens as Chinese immigrant communities in the United States, Lamson exposed the ethnocentrism inherent in American discourses concerning immigrant assimilation. Critiquing presumptions concerning the directionality of cultural change resulting from intergroup contact, Lamson's work speaks to the question of whether assimilation can be a "two-way street," much as did Mae Franking's narrative (see chapter 2).

It is unfortunate that in disputing the notion of hybrid exceptionalism propounded by sociologists like E. B. Reuter, Lamson found it necessary to demean Shanghai Eurasians. Yet, there are, nonetheless, important lessons one can draw from his work. Indeed, a juxtaposition of Lamson's Shanghai study with Wu's Chinatowns study demonstrates the pivotal role of gender in theorizing intermarriage, an insight that is not immediately evident from the SRR alone, because Chinese–white relations in North American were predominantly of a single pattern (Chinese men married to white women). Comparison across gender lines (Chinese fathers versus Chinese mothers) was precisely what enabled Lamson to dispute universal theories of the "mixed blood." For Lamson, these two groups were fundamentally divided in terms of social status, cultural orientation, national identification, and even intelligence. Through such comparisons, Lamson's project served to bridge sociological investigations of Eurasians in North America and colonized Asia—which Park himself curiously failed to do in his wide-ranging "Race Relations and Certain Frontiers." In Lamson's work we can read a productive dialogue between immigration studies and studies of colonialism as racial frontiers, through which gender (especially parental gender) emerges as an important dynamic.

Moreover, a reading of Lamson's work also provides us with an opportunity to reexamine Jayne Ifekwunigwe's contention that the new sociological discourse did little more than replace the pathological discourse of hybrid degeneracy with a new pathological discourse rooted in social maladjustment theory (see introduction).[93] Lamson's critique of Reuter and Park serves as a reminder that the discourse of hybrid exceptionalism, as expressed through the sociological model of the racial intermediary or aristocracy, coexisted with hybrid pathology in leading sociological theories of the early twentieth century. Thus, I argue that twentieth-century sociological discourse on "mixed race" was not just about pathology, but also about exceptionalism, a dualism inherent in the very model of the marginal man. By thus theorizing the ambivalence toward the "half-caste" discussed in chapter 3, the new sociological discourse on mixed race did, in fact, represent a significant break with nineteenth-century scientific racism, even as the turn away from biology was incomplete.

Relying on life histories as key sources, sociologists also went farther than their predecessors in giving their subjects a voice. Yet these voices were always subordinated to theory. In part III, we turn from Eurasians as objects of research to Eurasians as producers of knowledge.

PART THREE

Claiming Identities

Prologue to Chapter 6

HARRY HASTINGS: OF BORDER CROSSINGS
AND RACIAL SCRUTINY

Harry Hastings was an intrepid traveler: born in China circa 1874, he would travel to Hong Kong, Formosa, the Philippines, Hawaii, Fiji, and as far afield as Europe and Africa. Hastings would even cross Siberia six times. He would eventually migrate to Canada. But this fearless globe-trotter would never in his life, ever, visit the United States—to the great puzzlement of his friends.

When the Survey of Race Relations (SRR) found Hastings in British Columbia in 1924, he had already earned a reputation as the "half-breed Chinese intellectual of Victoria." The son of a Chinese woman and a British man, Hastings was raised in China but educated in European ways. Sent away from his mother as a child, he attended a boys' school in Canton with other Eurasians and later matriculated at Oxford. Returning to Asia, he worked in Hong Kong and China for many years before emigrating to Canada in 1912. In Victoria, Hastings worked as a merchant and lawyer, and he was soon reputed to be one of the most knowledgeable men in international law.

Like George Sokolsky, Hastings was another hybrid figure whose story had caught Everett Stonequist's eye when he wrote *The Marginal Man*. In his interview with SRR researchers, Hastings explained why he refused to visit the United States, recounting with lingering bitterness an incident that had occurred at the U.S. Immigration Office in Vancouver: "They asked me questions, I said I was a British subject, a merchant, my father was British, my mother was Chinese. They told me I must go to the Chinese Immigration Department. I said, 'I will not do this.' Instead of going to the United States I will take a boat that will take me straight to Honolulu."[1]

After this confrontation with the immigration officers, Hastings determined never to travel to the United States, though he hid the reason for his stubborn refusal from his American friends. In his words: "I did not explain because then everyone would have known."[2]

In the era of Chinese exclusion, the borders of the American nation became a place where racial identifications were assigned, negotiated, and policed. Under the Exclusion Act, all Chinese were interrogated at points of entry, and Chinese Americans seeking to exit and reenter the country had to provide proof of citizenship by birth. At such border crossings, Eurasians faced potential inquests into their racial status, birthplace, and citizenship, often at the whims of immigration officials.

When the U.S.-born See children traveled to China in 1901 and 1919, their parents ensured that they, like others of Chinese descent, obtained certificates permitting them to reenter the United States.[3] When Yung Wing's son Morrison traveled abroad in 1906, 1909, and 1916, he did not obtain such certificates, though he shows up in immigration records reentering the United States listed among the "alien passengers," despite his possession of U.S. citizenship.[4] The treatment of Eurasians, however, was inconsistent. When Morrison's brother Bartlett entered the port of New York in 1913, returning from China via Southhampton, he cleared immigration on the U.S. citizen list.[5]

The anxiety of border crossing took on an additional meaning for those who were attempting to pass as white. Thus Hastings chose to forgo ever visiting the United States rather than risk being outed. And yet, as Hastings told SRR researchers, sometimes passing elicited an emotional pain of its own. Speaking animatedly and "with a good deal of vehemence," as his interviewer noted, Hastings recounted this story:

> I was in Africa one time. We were sitting out on the porch after dinner, a friend of mine, and a physician and I. This physician didn't know who I was and he talked, as such people will talk, about the Eurasian, who combines within himself the vices of both the parent races. I listened, I let him talk.
>
> Then I said, "Any child of mixed parentage should have the legal right to shoot his father and his mother and himself if he cares to when he is 21."[6]

As if to justify his younger self, Hastings went on to tell his interviewer of the "situation" faced by "half-breeds," as he saw it. Hastings related a story of schoolmate from Canton. Excelling in school and athletics, the boy had been placed by his British father in a docking company in Canton where he was quickly promoted. After the arrival of some "English boys" at the firm, however, he found himself increasingly ostracized. He took up gambling and smoking. The headmaster sent Hastings to talk to his old classmate. "I said," Hastings recalled, "you shouldn't do this, you are hurting the name of the whole Eurasian colony. You should make a fight." Filled with despair, his friend retorted: "Hastings," he said, "that isn't fair, you have your father's house to go to. You are accepted everywhere on his account. I can find no society at all. What have I to fight for?"[7] As Hastings recalled with cynical laughter, it all ended when his friend took raw opium and committed suicide.[8] Hastings further related stories of how he himself took pleasure in exacting petty revenges on the newly arrived "English boys," flaunting his wealth in spiteful ways.

Whereas Hastings had lived among Europeans in China, and passed for white in Africa, in Victoria the locals saw him in another light. As Hastings told the SRR interviewer, "They speak of me as a Chinese, because I have taken the part of the Chinese so openly."[9] Hastings was referring here to his role in the Chinese students' strike of 1923–24, when Chinese students staged a boycott against school segregation. Hastings had taken a leading role in this strike, crafting legal memos in the name of "the Chinese parents." Although Hastings never declared himself as such, his frequent letters to the newspapers on behalf of the Chinese community led Victorians to interpolate him as Chinese.[10]

Despairing about his situation, Hastings wondered if he should return to China and live with the Chinese. He quickly dismissed this option, however, stating, "If I did that, I would have to fight my father's people, and perhaps, who knows, bring nearer the inevitable conflict, between the East and West, and I don't want to do that."[11] Hastings thus saw himself not as the embodiment of the best of both worlds, combining within himself "the metaphysics of the East and the practicality of the West," as one of his European friends saw it, but as an agent of global racial conflict.

Instead of returning to China, then, Hastings dreamed of retiring to an island of his own in the Pacific where he would be able to "forget all about this thing in which I have been involved" and devote himself to writing.[12]

The "Peculiar Cast"

*Navigating the American Color Line in the
Era of Chinese Exclusion*

In 1895, three full years before Louis Beck published his account of the
infamous "half-breed" George Appo, a fledgling reporter wrote a piece
on "Half-Chinese Children: Those of American Mothers and Chinese
Fathers" for the *Montréal Daily Star*, describing the lives of Eurasian
children in the Chinatowns of New York and Boston. The article
informed readers that "the white people with whom these children
come in contact, that is, the lower-class, jibe and jeer at the poor little
things continually, and their pure and unadulterated Chinese cousins
look down upon them as being neither one thing nor the other—neither
Chinese nor white." Still, the reporter noted, in a departure from the
dominant representations of the time, "the sneers and taunting words
which are their birthright . . . do not prevent these children from developing and becoming as fine a lot as a globe trotter could wish to see."[13]

This article can be read as part of the burgeoning North American
interest in miscegenation and the "Chinese problem," as discussed in
chapter 3, but with one important difference: the young journalist was an
aspiring Eurasian author, Edith Maude Eaton (1865–1914), the daughter
of Edward Eaton and Lotus Blossom, who had crossed the color line to
marry in Shanghai in 1863 (see chapter 2). By the time that Beck published *New York's Chinatown*, both Edith and her younger sister Winnifred (1875–1954) had penned several pieces, fiction and nonfiction, on
the subject of interracialism for North American periodicals. For Edith,
these early publications represented a start toward realizing her child-

hood ambition of writing a book about the "half-Chinese," an ambition, she would later explain to *Boston Globe* readers, that arose from her "sensitiveness to the remarks, criticisms and observations on the half Chinese which continually assailed [her] ears."[14] Driven to convey to the world "all that [she] felt, all that [she] was," Eaton sought to be a Eurasian voice justifying her kind in a world dominated by pathological images of the "half-caste."[15] Whereas journalists like Beck and Wilson portrayed the Eurasian as "a problem," then, Eaton turned the tables and focused on the problems and troubles *faced by* Eurasians, who had to live with labels such as "half-breed" thrust upon them.

Better known today by the Chinese pen name that she adopted in 1896—Sui Sin Far—Edith Eaton is undoubtedly the most famous Eurasian author in North America today, with her sister Winnifred in close second place. Her works are a powerful testament to the efforts of one writer, writing against accusations that the Chinese–white miscegen was a "hybrid of the most despicable, a mongrel of the most detestable that has ever afflicted the earth," to act as a public voice for the "half-Chinese."[16] Yet, the Eaton sisters, as celebrated as they are today, were not the only Chinese Eurasians to offer their voices to curious readers, social reformers, and sociologists. In fact, one of these was none other than George Appo himself, whose autobiographical sketch "as told to" the author, was published in reformer Frank Moss's *The American Metropolis: Knickerbocker Days to the Present Time, New York City Life in All Its Various Phases* (1897).

The publication of Appo's brief life narrative by 1897 is noteworthy, for it underscores the fact that Beck never allowed Appo to "speak for himself" in his text (despite using Appo as an informant).[17] How many others have been silenced or fallen into obscurity, their experiences subjected to the historical erasure described in Kumari Jayawardena's *The Erasure of the Euro-Asian* (see chapter 5)? In part III of this book I turn from examining the Eurasian as an *object* of discourse to consider Eurasians as *producers* of their own discourses on the question of mixed race. As we will see, their attempts to articulate their own claims to identity were highly individual, varying not only from place to place, from one historical moment to the next, but even among siblings. There is no better example of this, perhaps, than the Eaton family, for even as Edith adopted the Chinese pen name Sui Sin Far and championed the Chinese in North America, Winnifred would make her literary career by masquerading as a Japanese Eurasian, selling romance novels under the pen name Onoto Watanna.

By recuperating a broader range of Chinese Eurasian voices beyond the canonical works of the Eaton sisters we can gain a more nuanced understanding of the diverse ways in which biracial subjects negotiated their identities within the constraints of American racial hierarchies that were shaped both by a notional color line dividing white and nonwhite and the particular racialization of Chinese during the Exclusion era.

THE PROBLEM OF THE COLOR LINE REVISITED

"The problem of the twentieth century is the problem of the color line."[18] With words that would reverberate across time, W. E. B. Du Bois made this famous declaration in an essay published in the *Atlantic Monthly* in 1901. The color line has been a central problematic in American ethnic studies, and yet the relationship of mixed-race Asians to this notional line is still not fully understood. Scholars have frequently asserted that American society prior to 1967 was rigidly monoracial, assigning people either a white or nonwhite identity without giving recognition to mixedness, with hypodescent operating as the normative convention.[19] A pioneering historian of Asian Americans and mixed marriages, Paul Spickard has argued that prior to the 1960s conventions of hypodescent meant that "as far as whites were concerned, such [Asian-white mixed-race] people were consigned to the Asian group."[20] Yet, as Daniel Sharfstein has shown, for much of U.S. history the one-drop rule did not in fact constitute a bright-line rule, because the "courts were not absolutist about blood purity, regularly turning to other criteria in drawing the color line."[21] Critiquing widespread presumptions concerning the dominance of the one-drop rule, Sharfstein further argues that the legal history of race "is incomplete when divorced from the social context of racial migration," the process by which people of color assimilated into white communities.[22]

Although not focused on racial migration per se, this chapter similarly attempts to bring nuance to our understanding of the one-drop regime through attention to social context as evidenced by Eurasian life narratives. Hypodescent was certainly the logic we see employed in a long history of racial prerequisite cases from 1878 until 1952, when racial requirements for naturalization were removed.[23] It is the same logic employed in a 1930 census directive instructing enumerators to report "mixed races" according to the nonwhite parent.[24] The story of Harry Hastings further illustrates the powerful ways in which conventions of hypodescent determined the relationship of Chinese Eurasians to the North American color line and to exclusionary immigration laws that constrained their mobility. Yet, as his story also suggested, Hastings's relation to the color line—as he traveled the globe and performed various acts of racial migration—was far from clearcut, an ambiguity he sometimes exploited for his own ends. Thus, an examination of Eurasian life narratives in conjunction with other sources, including early census and immigration records, reveals that Eurasian experiences of the American color line in the late nineteenth and early twentieth centuries were in fact far more ambiguous and complex. Life narratives suggest that the color line had very different meanings for "half-Chinese" born to Chinese fathers and those born to Chinese mothers, two cohorts frequently lumped together in the literature (see chapter 5). They further indicate that Eurasian life experiences were not solely determined by the color line but were shaped by what Shirley Geok-lin Lim calls the "hybridity matrix" of race, gender, and class.[25]

Placing the legal history of race in relation to social context and the lived experiences of Chinese Eurasians in North America, this chapter reassesses the problem of the color line. I begin by examining how the U.S. government attempted to define and classify these mixed-race peoples, delineating both their place within American racial hierarchies and the scope of their rights. I then consider how Eurasians themselves attempted to navigate the color line, using self-representation as one means to contest their "half-caste" racial status. I argue that while the notion of the color line structured the racialization of Eurasians during the Exclusion era, in terms of day-to-day lived experience, this line was not fixed but rather fluid and unstable. This slippage between racial ideology and practice opened a space for Chinese Eurasians to navigate their social identities (within limited constraints). This slippage also suggests that the tension between inclusion and exclusion, theorized by Ann Stoler as a "tension of empire" (see introduction), was similarly at work in the settler societies of Exclusion-era North America. Finally, I argue that inconsistencies in census categorizations of Eurasians demonstrate that despite the U.S. government's obsessive interest in orderly racial classification, this project foundered in the face of the messy realities of a nation forged through immigration, border crossings, interracial unions, and racial migration.[26]

STRADDLING THE COLOR LINE: CALCULATING
"MIXED RACE"

As we saw in chapter 3, almost from the very beginnings of Chinese
immigration the American media expressed concerns regarding the
"bewildering" picture of "half-Chinese" children.[27] What would such
children be? Chinese or American? White or nonwhite? A definitive
legal answer to this question did not come until 1909, in the case of *In
re Knight*.[28] In this case, a New York District Court judge was asked to
rule whether an applicant, surnamed Knight, was eligible for naturalization as a U.S. citizen. Knight had been born on a British schooner off
the coast of China, to an English father and a Chinese-Japanese mother,
and had served honorably for more than twenty-five years in the U.S.
Navy. Owing to the racial prerequisites for naturalization, the case
hinged on the question of whether Knight qualified as a "white person."
Lacking precedent, District Judge Chatfield conceded the difficulty he
faced: "No case to which the attention of the court has been drawn
seems to specifically determine what percentage of Mongolian blood
will exclude the applicant from classification as a white person." He
therefore looked to cases involving "colored persons" for precedent,
concluding that "a person, one-half white and one-half of some other
race, belongs to neither of those races, but is literally a half-breed."[29]
The court denied Knight's application on the basis of this determination
that he was not white, and with specific reference to the Chinese Exclusion Act, which barred Chinese from naturalization. As Ian Haney
López shows, *In re Knight* marked a major turning point. During the
following decade, several other naturalization cases involving Eurasian
immigrants were heard by the courts, and in each case the applicants
were deemed "not white."[30]

Despite these racial bars to naturalization, however, the tradition of
jus soli remained strong in American law, meaning that any children
born on U.S. soil were citizens by birthright. Hence, whereas British-
born Edith Eaton was a British subject, her U.S.-born siblings, Grace,
Sara, Ernest George, and Christina Agnes, were U.S. citizens. In the
Franking family, Michigan-born Nelson was a U.S. citizen, whereas his
Chinese-born siblings, Alason and Cecile, were for much of their lives
"aliens ineligible for naturalization." Chinese as a racial group were not
permitted to naturalize until the lifting of Chinese exclusion in 1943.

Beyond the question of citizenship, the color line had other important
implications, for various other legal rights (varying from state to state)

also depended on one's racial classification as white or nonwhite—including the right to testify in court, the right to attend whites-only public schools, and the right to marry a white person. Blood quantum rules in U.S. history are complex, varying from state to state, year to year, and by racial group. With regard to the ethnic Chinese, blood quantum rules were inconsistent.[31] Oregon's anti-miscegenation statute, for example, targeted persons having one-fourth or more "Chinese blood," whereas Nebraska and Mississippi employed a stricter definition of one-eighth or more "Chinese blood." It was not until the act of December 17, 1943, which repealed Chinese exclusion, that federal government regulations explicitly defined "Chinese persons" (in relation to section 2 of the act) as "persons who are of as much as one-half Chinese blood."[32]

The U.S. Census likewise lacked uniformity. Tchen's research shows that late nineteenth-century census takers followed no set formula in classifying the children of Chinese fathers and white mothers, who were sometimes designated "Chinese," sometimes "white," and sometimes "mulatto."[33] My research on the families whose stories are told in this book has shown similar inconsistencies. In the Hartford census of 1900, Bartlett Yung was returned as "Chinese."[34] Edith Eaton, who was living as a lodger in Seattle in that year, was returned as "white," an identity that probably seemed consistent with her English surname and birthplace.[35] The 1910 census of Washington, D.C., showed the children of Chinese diplomat Yung Kwai and his wife Mary (née Burnham) returned as "Chinese"(see frontispiece).[36] In 1920, the Yung children were returned "white," and in 1930, "Chinese" again.[37] The 1930 census directive on "other mixed races" was an attempt to clarify such discrepancies. Conforming to this institutionalization of hypodescent, the 1930 census for Los Angeles recorded Eddie and Florence See as "Chinese."[38] The new directive notwithstanding, however, the Franking children were returned "white" on the 1930 census of Ann Arbor, Michigan, as was Eric Sokolsky on the 1940 census of New York City.[39] Such evidence supports Ian Haney López's contention that "whiteness" as a legal construct remained a moving target in this era.[40]

Although much has been written about the role of blood quantum in American constructions of racial identity, paternal descent was profoundly important for foreign-born (marital) children, as evidenced through various immigration cases. In 1908, for example, when a Norwegian laborer living in China petitioned to immigrate to the United States with his Chinese wife and two daughters, U.S. Secretary of Commerce and Labor Oscar Strauss declared that "the Chinese exclusion laws must be held not to operate against the Chinese wife and minor children of a Norwegian." Strauss's logic, in the case of the children, was that they were "entitled to come in by reason of their relationship to the father."[41] Similarly, when Thaddeus C. White and Der Ling (see chapter 4) brought their Shanghai-born son, Thaddeus Reymond, to the United States in 1922, wife and child freely entered the country as dependents of a U.S. citizen, Thaddeus Reymond furthermore deriving citizenship through his father.[42] And as we saw (chapter 5), when Eric Sokolsky entered the United States in 1930, immigration officials classified him as belonging to the American "race or people" like his father.[43] In these cases, the gender privilege inherent in patriarchal family structures trumped the racial bar (and even class in the case of the Norwegian laborer's family), demonstrating that hypodescent was not the only game in town.

Oscar Strauss's opinion in the case of the Norwegian laborer and his family can be seen as consistent with a pattern that Peggy Pascoe identified in Reconstruction-era legal cases upholding marriages between white men and black women. Pascoe shows that such decisions, in the face of widespread opposition to miscegenation, were not intended to promote racial equality, but rather primarily to protect the rights of white men as husbands—their right to freely choose their marriage partners and to bequeath property to their spouses and/or children upon their deaths. What was at stake in these cases, Pascoe argues, was the upholding of marriage law, "which guarded the rights and responsibilities of White men as husbands."[44] Similarly, Strauss made clear in his opinion that the grounds for thinking about the immigration status of this mixed family revolved solely around the husband's fundamental right to the company of his family.[45]

Although we cannot assume that administrative and legal constructions of race corresponded perfectly to social constructions, as Melissa Nobles has demonstrated in her study of the U.S. Census, these definitions have nonetheless been critical to the racialization of minorities and furthermore circumscribed the options for negotiation of one's social identity.[46] These negotiations were complex, because whereas court decisions of this era tended to racialize Eurasians as nonwhites, discrimination created compelling incentives for claiming whiteness. Thus, it is not surprising that some Eurasians—there is no telling how many—attempted to "pass," making lives for themselves on the empowered side of the color line, where educational, professional, and other opportunities were available.

In the next section of the chapter, I turn to various works of life narrative, focusing in particular on Edith Eaton's outspoken protests against the injustices of the color line. Through these diverse life stories, I seek to complicate Paul Spickard's contention that the monoracialist impulses of both the Euro-American majority and Asian American minority communities prior to the 1960s left those of mixed race "with no place to be."[47]

GEORGE WASHINGTON APPO: A CRIMINAL MADE, NOT BORN

Although life narratives provide a unique source for understanding an individual's perspective on his or her times, it is crucial to take into account the context surrounding their production and the motivations behind the autobiographical act. George Appo produced at least three versions of his autobiographical story, all aimed at explaining his life of crime for different purposes. The first, "The Full History of My Life," was authored in 1895 at the prompting of his attorney Frank Moss, on the theory that a first-person account of Appo's pitiful childhood and turn to crime might persuade a sympathetic judge to leniency. Hoping to promote the agenda of the Society for the Prevention of Crime (SPC), Moss later paid Appo for a longer version of his life story, which he published in *The American Metropolis*.[48] Moss believed that this true story of the making of a criminal genius would support his contention that criminals were not "born," as Beck would claim, but formed by their environment. Years later, between 1911 and 1915, while working for the SPC in New York, Appo wrote (he had learned to write in prison) a full-fledged autobiography, which was unfortunately never published in his lifetime.[49] Speculating on Appo's motivations for writing this record of his life, Gilfoyle writes that "perhaps he wanted to refute the multiple, negative images of being a 'mongrel,' 'hybrid,' and 'half-breed.'"[50]

Unfortunately for our purposes, Appo's life narratives contain little information about his perception of his racial identity, though he was certainly forthright about his origins. "My father," he wrote in *Autobiography of George Appo*, "a Chinaman . . . came to this country in the year of 1847."[51] But this fact was of little consequence to Appo, it appears, in contrast to the subsequent events of his life: his father's imprisonment ("It was about the year 1869 when I first met or knew I had a father living"); the loss of his mother and sister; and his life as an orphan in "gloomy and bad surroundings," raised by "a very poor family named Allen."[52] Yet the silence speaks volumes: in sharp contrast to Louis Beck, who portrayed George Appo as a case study in hybrid degeneracy, Appo himself did not represent race as a factor in his criminal career. Appo's life narratives further contrast sharply with Beck's attempt to racialize Appo by associating him with Chinatown and the Chinese Question. As Timothy Gilfoyle contends in his study of Appo's unpublished autobiography, "Like the polyglot world of Baxter Street where he grew up, Appo never labeled himself by a single ethnic category."[53]

Whereas the notional color line shaped Beck's view of 1890s New York, such a line apparently held little meaning for Appo, born in 1856, for his world was the mixed and shifting world of Manhattan's Five Points, where lived, by Appo's own account, "poor people of all nationalities."[54] As Appo recalled, his formative years had been spent in this neighborhood, where the Chinese all lived next door to Black Mike's Saloon, on the floors above Cohen's secondhand clothing shop. "Such was Donavan's Lane [sic]," Appo mused.[55] The opium dens Appo later frequented were similarly spaces for intermingling across racial, gender, and class lines. As Appo wrote, "The place was crowded day and night by opium habitués from all stations in life, both men and women, some of good social and financial standing."[56] Trying to make his way in a world with no family, Appo made alliances with anyone, from Chinatown "Mayor" Tom Lee to Crosby Street fence Barney Maguire, who could help. At the end of the day, for Appo, Gilfoyle writes, it mattered little that he was Chinese, Irish, and Roman Catholic; what mattered to him was the code of ethics by which he lived.[57] Resisting Beck's obsessive focus on race and miscegenation, Appo narrated his life along a trajectory shaped by poverty and hard luck.

If Appo's autobiography can be viewed primarily as an attempt to write back against the popularly circulating image of him as a "born criminal," Edith Eaton's autobiographical works more directly took on the issue of racism and the color line, for her aim as an author was to convey to readers her "experiences as an Eurasian" and thereby generate sympathy for all those who had been castigated as "half-caste."[58]

EDITH EATON: PLANTING A FEW EURASIAN THOUGHTS IN WESTERN LITERATURE

Edward Eaton and Lotus Blossom, we will recall (see chapter 2), had returned to England shortly after the birth of their first son. There,

Edith was born. But Edward quarreled with his parents—probably over his unusual marriage—and the family soon set off on what would turn out to be a long series of moves between England, the United States, and Canada, ever in search of a place to call home. Edward's dreams of making it rich in the China trade had faded, and the family fell on hard times. Against this backdrop of downward mobility, Edith was sent out to work early. By eighteen, she had found work as a typesetter, and then began a career as a stenographer and journalist, all the while struggling to publish short fiction.

Attempting to establish herself, Edith became a "bird on the wing," moving back and forth between the United States and Canada, and criss-crossing the North American continent multiple times (with a brief stint as a reporter in Jamaica). From 1898 on, she made the United States her home, living in San Francisco, Los Angeles, Seattle, and Boston, with regular visits to her family in Montréal. Thus, in sharp contrast to Harry Hastings, Edith Eaton crossed the U.S.–Canadian border effortlessly and multiple times. Hastings may have enjoyed the privileges of his wealth, but Eaton, for all her financial woes, enjoyed the privilege of cross-border mobility that came with an ability to pass for white.

Yet Eaton also suffered under the heavy weight of what she called the "cross of the Eurasian," and she sought to give expression to her griev-ances through writing. Beginning with her early article "Half-Chinese Children," Eaton made many attempts to plant "a few Eurasian thoughts in Western literature."[59] An opportunity arose when the *Independent*, a progressive weekly magazine of national readership, published her auto-biographical piece "Leaves from the Mental Portfolio of an Eurasian" in 1909. "Leaves" suited perfectly the agenda of the *Independent*'s chief editor, Hamilton Holt, the notable progressive who helped found the NAACP in 1909. As editor of the New York–based magazine from 1897 until 1921, Holt undertook to promote a form of short of autobiogra-phy that he called the "lifelet." Believing that such narratives would be of "deep human interest and perhaps some sociological importance," Holt published a long-running series of lifelets representing the lives of ordinary Americans, including immigrants and people of color, "told in their own words."[60] Committed to representing diverse ethnic and racial "types," Holt would have seen Eaton's lifelet as a natural fit. Indeed, the reception was so favorable that the *Independent* published a second life-let, "The Persecution and Oppression of Me," in 1911.[61]

If the early "Half-Chinese Children" had been a measured defense of the "new hybrid brood," contending that environment, and not heredity,

FIGURE 12. Sui Sin Far (Edith Eaton), pictured in the *Independent*, 1909.

Courtesy of Harvard University Widener Library P 231.16 F; *The Portrait of Sui Sin Far, Independent* Vol. 66 (1), 1909, p. 125.

was primarily responsible for the sorry condition in which so many found themselves in American Chinatowns, Eaton's lifelets went much farther in condemning racism by asking readers to step into the Eurasian's shoes. A fragmentary compilation of memories, "Leaves" takes us from Eaton's early childhood in England through her experiences in the United States, Canada, and Jamaica, together creating a composite picture of "Eurasian experiences." "The Persecution and Oppression of Me" is a similar set of anecdotes, picking up where "Leaves" left off and focusing on the author's experiences as an adult in the United States.

Although Eaton by this point in her career already had a long track record of speaking out against anti-Chinese sentiment, I argue that her lifelets adopt a different rhetorical strategy: that is, attacking racism by demonstrating that the one who has been treated as "different" is, in fact, very much "like" the readers themselves. It was a strategy that would already have been familiar to middle-class American readers through the tradition of abolition literature. As Werner Sollors has demonstrated, the figure of the biracial person (who is at once like and not-like) is pivotal to this rhetorical strategy. The photographic portrait of Eaton (fig. 12) published with her first lifelet is consistent with such a strategy: the portrait shows the author in European dress, conveying an image that would have been reassuringly familiar to her audience, which was primarily white middle class. Highlighting sameness rather than difference, this image stands in sharp contrast to the exotic photographic portraits of a kimono-clad Winnifred that publishers used to market "Onoto Watanna's" Orientalist fiction.

THE DOUBLE-CONSCIOUSNESS OF THE EURASIAN: RACIAL SCRUTINY AND "TELLTALE SIGNS"

Eaton begins the narration of "Leaves" with a scene made famous by critics in Asian American studies. Recalling herself as a small child of four walking in an English lane, the narrator suddenly overhears her nurse tell another that her mother is Chinese: "'Oh, Lord!' exclaims the informed. She turns me around and scans me curiously from head to foot. Then the two women whisper together." Eaton identifies this moment as the day on which she first learned that she "was something different and apart from other children."[62]

In many key respects, this scene resembles an even more famous scene from W. E. B. Du Bois's essay on "double-consciousness," published in the *Atlantic* magazine in August 1897.[63] In this essay, Du Bois recalled a childhood experience in which it "dawned upon [him] with a certain suddenness that [he] was different from the others; or like, mayhap, in heart and life and longing, but shut out from their world by a vast veil." Such experiences, one after another, led him to perceive his double-consciousness as an African American. "It is a peculiar sensation," wrote Du Bois, "this double-consciousness, the sense of always looking at one's self through the eyes of others, measuring one's soul by the tape of a world that looks on in amused contempt and pity."[64] "Leaves" bears remarkable similarities to Du Bois's text in terms of narrative structure, wording, and theme, and it is not inconceivable that Eaton, as a well-read and aspiring author, would have been influenced by Du Bois's work.[65] Like Du Bois, Eaton represented the accumulation of such experiences as formative in her sense of identity as one who is "different," and hence imbued with double-consciousness, always looking at herself through the eyes of others.

Eaton expresses this double-consciousness through another scene in which the "merry romping child" is suddenly made aware of the veil separating her from the others.[66] This incident must have played a powerful role in shaping Eaton's self-understanding, because she reworked the scenario several times in various genres, including her early newspaper article "Half-Chinese Children."[67] In this incident, a small girl plays happily at a party until she is suddenly called to be inspected by a gentleman who is greatly surprised to find the child's Chinese ancestry revealed upon close scrutiny:

> "Ah, indeed!" he exclaims. "Who would have thought it at first glance. Yet now I see the difference between her and other children. What a peculiar coloring! Her mother's eyes and hair and her father's features, I presume. Very interesting little creature!"[68]

The child who was passing for *same* is discovered to be *different* from the other children, given away by her "peculiar coloring," which is uniquely mixed. If Eaton's initial response to this humiliating incident, as she tells readers in "Leaves," was to hide herself away, as an adult she would use her platform as a journalist and fictionist to publicly protest the demeaning experience of being made an object of inspection, crying out against being examined "from head to toe as if [she were] a wild animal."[69]

Racial scrutiny calls attention to the biracial subject's *differentness*, which Eaton represents as the fundamental condition of Eurasianness—being different from other children, being different from both Europeans and Chinese, different from one's own father and mother. "Leaves" is punctuated by scene after scene in which the Eurasian child is "inspected," "surveyed," and "scanned from head to foot," indicating the centrality of the scrutinizing gaze (and hence the social experience of "differentness") in the formation of Eaton's biracial identity.

The figurative veil that separates the "half-Chinese" child from the others takes the form in Eaton's writings as a "peculiar cast" across the child's face. Through this image Eaton brings together two issues that are central to her: racial scrutiny and passing. In "Half-Chinese Children," Eaton the reporter had warned readers that half-Chinese children might be virtually indistinguishable from whites, except for the "peculiar cast." Recalling the racialist logic of the one-drop rule and the threat that "blood will tell," she proclaimed, "This cast is over the face of every child who has a drop of Chinese blood in its veins. It is indescribable—but it is there."[70] The "peculiar cast" functions in Eaton's work as a racial sign, as described by Werner Sollors in his analysis of European and American interracial literature. Sollors demonstrates that a particular obsession evolved from the mid-nineteenth through mid-twentieth centuries with detecting minute traces of "dark" ancestry in seemingly white characters revealed through a "bluish tinge in the halfmoon" of the fingernails. This literary motif emerged from the desire to fix an identifiable sign of essential difference between whites and blacks, even among mixed-race individuals who appeared phenotypically white. Sollors explains that the motif of "telltale" racial signs "was useful to racialists in helping to create the illusion that racial distinctions are permanent, natural, objective, biological, and always subject to discovery."[71] The motif of telltale racial signs—"Chinese hair," "almond eyes," a "yellowish tinge" to the complexion, a "peculiar cast," and so forth—was similarly common in American literary depictions of Chinese Eurasians. The obsession with racial signs as a means of reading racial ambiguity, of revealing the "truth" of blood, is symptomatic of anxieties surrounding passing during this era.

Whereas the obsession with racial signs evolved from a desire to fix the racial identity of the hybrid and thereby ease the anxiety that a nonwhite might pass as white, Eaton characteristically approached the issue of passing from the standpoint of the Eurasian. From the perspective of the biracial subject, it is not *passing* that is a source of anxiety, but conversely the fear of *discovery* that leads the passer to live in "nervous dread," as we will see later in the chapter.

Double-consciousness is further engendered when Eaton and her siblings are publicly labeled "Chinese," which conflicted with the Eaton family's own sense of their Englishness. Among Eaton's earliest childhood memories are moments when she is called out as Chinese. In Hudson City, New York, for example, Edith and her brother Edward Charles are taunted by a group of children chanting "Chinky, Chinky, Chinaman, yellow-face, pig-tail, rat-eater."[72] When the family later arrives in Canada, they are surrounded by curious onlookers who peer at them murmuring "Chinoise, Chinoise."[73]

Initially, young Edith has trouble attaching meaning to the word *Chinese*, because the only Chinese person she has known is her Anglicized mother. When she and Charlie encounter a group of working-class Chinese in Hudson City, Edith recoils "with a sense of shock," asking her brother, "Are we like that?"[74] Chineseness thus first becomes apparent as something external to herself, a word that is whispered, a "mocking cry." Eaton's memories in "Leaves" circle around this repeated racial interpellation as "Chinese" and her own move from disidentification ("Are we like that?") to identification, which emerged gradually in her adult life. As Eaton told the *Boston Globe* in 1912, a turning point came when she accompanied her mother on a visit to a young Chinese woman who had just arrived in Montréal. "From that time," she wrote, "I began to go among my mother's people, and it did me a world of good to discover how akin I was to them."[75] "Leaves" traces this trajectory from disidentification to recognition.

THE TEMPTATION TO PASS

Progressing from memories of racial scrutiny and taunting, Eaton's leaves of memory open onto scenes that elucidate the diverse ways in which Eurasians attempted to navigate the color line through strategies of passing. Eaton recounts numerous incidents, many of which can be tied back to her own siblings. As she wrote, "I meet a half Chinese, half white girl. Her face is plastered with a thick white coat of paint and her eyelids and eyebrows are blackened so that the shape of her eyes . . . is changed. . . . It is not difficult, in a land like California, for a half Chinese, half white girl to pass as one of Spanish or Mexican origin. This the poor child does, tho she lives in nervous dread of being 'discovered.'"[76] She further tells of other Eurasians who chose to pass as Japanese Eurasians (a clear reference to her sister Winnifred) because Japanese were in those years held in higher esteem. Eaton portrays passing not simply as a form of racial treachery and opportunism, but as part and parcel of the "troubles and discomforts" foisted upon Eurasians by a racist society, declaring, "Are not those who compel them to thus cringe more to be blamed than they?"[77]

Yet, Eaton herself was sharply critical of passers, and she distanced herself from the phenomenon, which she called cowardly. A condemnation of passing is central to "The Persecution and Oppression of Me." While dealing with similar themes, Eaton's second lifelet differed in notable respects from her first. For example, whereas the focus of "Leaves" is on the Eurasian's experiences of being racialized as Chinese, as Other, "Persecution" conversely presents a series of scenes in which the narrator is mistaken for white, perceived as "same" rather than "different." It is only when her difference is revealed, Eaton contended, that she was subjected to "persecution and oppression."

Eaton asserts that this phenomenon explains why the temptation to "pass as wholly white" was so widespread among Eurasians. The temptation was certainly seen in Eaton's own family. According to Eaton's biographer, Annette White-Parks, the Eaton family in Montréal "maintained a public image as English Canadian."[78] Certainly, growing up with an Anglicized mother and with few opportunities to meet other Chinese until later in life, Edith and her siblings were raised as British Presbyterians: never learning to speak Chinese, and learning little about Chinese culture. Nonetheless, it would be inaccurate to say that the family was passing, for Grace was highly visible as a Chinese woman who was active in her church, and Edward maintained relationships with Chinese merchants, a network that later allowed Edith to gain introductions to Chinese merchants in the United States. Her Chinese connections furthermore helped the fledgling journalist secure the "local Chinese reporting" for the Montréal newspapers.[79]

Yet, in adulthood most of Edith's siblings opted to live on the white side of the color line, and some even hid their Chinese heritage, no doubt to escape from the racism they experienced as children.[80] As Winnifred's granddaughter, Diana Birchall, has written, "One by one during the 1890s, they married and became absorbed into the white community."[81] Edith alone found herself increasingly drawn to her Chinese heritage. As noted previously, Edith began to do Chinese mission work with her mother, and she continued to work in Chinatown missions during the years she lived in the United States. Gradually, she came to feel herself "at home" among the Chinese. Edith found outlets for her Chinese interests by writing newspaper articles about immigrant life and protesting anti-Chinese sentiment. By championing their cause, Eaton earned the trust and gratitude of many Chinese, including prominent merchants. Moreover, among the literary works she had attempted to publish beginning in the 1880s, it was her "Chinese stories" published under the pen name of Sui Sin Far that "took off" and eventually earned her fame. Thus "Chineseness" was not simply a source of shame but also a kind of capital that Eaton could use to her advantage as a journalist and author.

Whether in reaction to her siblings' choices, or to their criticisms of her own, Eaton vehemently castigates passing in both her lifelets. Acknowledging that passing "makes living easier," she yet vowed that she would never attempt to pass for white, Mexican, or Japanese Eurasian, declaring, "I will not be that sort of half breed, and prefer to reflect honor upon those who are of mixed Asiatic and European nationality."[82] Eaton took particular pride in "self-outing" as a mark of her integrity. In one of the most famous incidents from "Leaves," Eaton recounts how she outed herself in a small midwestern town where she worked as a stenographer. At dinner with her employer, "Mr. K," she found the conversation turn to a racist discussion of the "Chinaman." As Eaton wrote, "A miserable, cowardly feeling keeps me silent. I am in a Middle West town. If I declare what I am, every person in the place would hear about it the next day." Eaton portrayed herself facing a difficult choice, in danger of losing her job and possibly worse. Yet she chose, with "great effort," to courageously tell her employer, "The Chinese people may have no souls, no expression on their faces, be altogether beyond the pale of civilization, but whatever they are, I want you to understand that I am—I am a Chinese."[83] After a lengthy silence, Mr. K stands up and apologizes.

Critics have interpreted this scene as an example of Edith Eaton's great moral integrity and her choice to identify with the Chinese, despite their low status. Yet, I argue that Eaton's decision to declare "I am Chinese" must be understood primarily as a rhetorical gesture of protest against the ignorant prejudice of the midwesterners who allege to hate the Chinese even as they have never met one. Indeed, as "Sui Sin Far" herself made amply clear in "Leaves," her claims to Chineseness were tenuous at best, as I elaborate following.

Such scenes of self-outing are replayed over and again in "Persecution," with sometimes frightening, sometimes humorous consequences. Eaton recounts, for example, an experience in a Boston boarding house when her landlady confides her dislike of "the negro race," and then declares that she hates the Chinese even more. The author retorts, "You do, do you? . . . Well, I am Chinese!"[84] In this instance, Eaton receives no apology, but rather a desperate plea that she not reveal her nationality to the other boarders lest it ruin the landlady's business.

In this manner, Eaton exposed the duality of Euro-American attitudes toward passing: passing is feared and despised, but also *expected* of the biracial subject, who should, after all, aspire to the higher racial status of whiteness. Eaton records several instances when Euro-Americans are shocked to discover she is not "pure" white, and then even more shocked (and offended) to find out that she does not *want* to pass. As she recalled from her Boston days, "One day my landlady inquired if I did not think that the reason why I was brighter than the ordinary Chinese was because I had white blood in my veins. I answered that I hadn't the slightest doubt that the reason why I was superior to a great many *whites* was because I had *Chinese* blood in my veins."[85]

"SO I STAND"

Yet, despite this purported pride in her Chineseness, Eaton's relationship to Chinese American communities was ambivalent at best. Moving across the country, Eaton always lived in boarding houses in white neighborhoods, and while she may have declared herself Chinese to Mr. K, the narrator of "Leaves" elsewhere represented herself as an outsider among Chinese. She described, for example, the reaction when she canvassed San Francisco's Chinatown for newspaper subscriptions: "I find that the Chinese merchants and people generally are inclined to regard me with suspicion. They have been imposed upon so many times by unscrupulous white people. Another drawback—save for a few phrases, I am unacquainted with my mother tongue. How, then, can I expect these people to accept me as their own countrywoman? The American-ized Chinamen actually laugh in my face when I tell them that I am of their race."[86] The apparently simple claim that "I am a Chinese"— which accords perfectly with the American logic of hypodescent—is here undercut by the mocking laughter of the "Americanized China-men." Instead of claiming Chineseness, then, the author here associates herself with white people, who are regarded with suspicion in this ethnic enclave. Eaton further relates how the Chinese, too, subject her to racial scrutiny, though less to uncover her racial otherness than to discern if she is one of their own. "Some little women discover that I have Chinese hair, color of eyes and complexion," she writes, "and also that I love rice and tea. This settles the matter for them."[87] Although Eaton is ultimately embraced by these women, this experience once again reminds her of her outsider status. Several factors would have made Chinatown residents inclined to regard Eaton as an outsider: she did not speak Chinese; she had not been raised in the Chinese commu-nity; and most important, her father was European.

In "Persecution," Eaton further notes that her decision to live outside Chinatown raised questions among some of her Chinese friends. As they accused her, "You have the Chinese hands, the Chinese voice, the Chinese hair. Back of your head you look just like the Chinese, and you have the Chinese little figure. You are more Chinese than white. You know more about the Chinese than the Chinese know themselves. But you live with the white people and you must like them best."[88] Rather defensively, Eaton explained her choice of associations both in terms of her upbringing and in terms of class: "It is hard for me to explain to them that there are class distinctions as well as race, and that it would be quite beneath my dignity, and certainly be of little benefit to them, for me to tramp around with them to 10-cent shows and Chinese ban-quets."[89] Eaton's emphasis here on the importance of class in addition to race in determining her associations makes evident the "hybridity matrix" of race, class, and gender that Shirley Geok-lin Lim analyzes in her reading of "Leaves."[90]

Indeed, despite her professed antipathy toward passing, in actual-ity Eaton appears to have practiced this survival strategy at various points in her life. While adopting a Chinese authorial persona as Sui

Sin Far, Eaton simultaneously took advantage of her British nationality, her European surname, and her ability to pass for white in order
to effect numerous border crossings between Canada and the United
States during the era of Chinese exclusion. In addition, Eaton allowed
herself to be taken for white in order to live in neighborhoods that
were considerably more genteel than Chinatowns. In Boston, she similarly hid her nationality from the other lodgers even after confronta-
tionally declaring to her landlady, "I am Chinese!" Her ability to
convincingly perform whiteness, or a European cultural identity,
most likely also facilitated her employment as a courtroom stenographer and journalist. Eaton's attitude toward passing may thus best
be described as ambivalent and strategic, despite her literary self-
presentation. Indeed, as she conceded in "Persecution," although she
was proud to be "Chinese as well as white," she did not "believe in
being aggressively Chinese."[91]

Whereas critics have tended to read Eaton's literary work, including
"Leaves," as a denunciation of anti-Chinese sentiment, and have viewed
her adoption of the pen name Sui Sin Far as an expression of her identification as Chinese American, the works I have examined here in fact
express a particular Eurasian subjectivity that was simultaneously critical of both white and Chinese prejudice.[92] Eaton's double-consciousness
as a Eurasian is thus forged between the dominant society, on one hand,
and the Chinese immigrant community, on the other.

Hence, rather than reading Sui Sin Far's life narratives as a testament
of what it meant to be Chinese during the Exclusion era, as many have
done, I would argue that these texts are also simultaneously narratives
of Eaton's relationship to whiteness, a relationship that was conditioned
by provisional acceptance as well as exclusion and was thus characterized by the "tension of empire." In light of Eaton's self-positioning as
one who stands between two communities, I contend that her practices
of self-outing as represented in her lifelets were less an attempt to claim
Chinese identity than an anti-racist gesture aimed at critiquing white
prejudice—a gesture that fit perfectly with the *Independent*'s liberal
agenda and its white, middle-class readers.

"KNOWN TO THE WORLD AS CHINESE"

Eaton's place within the Chinese American community may have been
tenuous, seeming to confirm Paul Spickard's contention that before the
1960s, "there was no place" for multiracial people in Chinese America.[93]

Yet Eaton's work, as valuable as it is, does not provide a definitive portrait of the social experiences of the half-Chinese in North America, for there was a significant gap between the experiences of her family and the lives led by Eurasians of Chinese paternity. An indication of this gap is evident in Eaton's assertion that "few, if any, of the half Chinese women and men, living in America, save those who live with the Chinese side of the family and are dependent upon it, are known to the world as Chinese."[94] This offhand remark reveals an important lacuna in Eaton's autobiographical accounts, for even as the Eurasian characters in Sui Sin Far's *fiction* are uniformly the Chinatown children of Chinese men and white mothers, her life writing was fundamentally based on the experiences of Eurasians with European fathers. Eaton did proclaim her sense of kinship with the "half-Chinese children" born to Chinese fathers and American mothers, but on a day-to-day level, such Chinese-surnamed children had vastly different social experiences that are not reflected in Eaton's works, revealing the limitations of her insider perspective even as she presented herself as an expert on the "half-Chinese." Such limitations are suggested in a letter received by Wu Jingchao in response to a story he sent (quite possibly "The Persecution and Oppression of Me") to an American woman of Chinese father and Irish mother who flat-out rejected the image of the troubled Eurasian. As she wrote, "Frankly, that example sent in your letter certainly stirred up the above-mentioned Irish in me! I'm very proud of my Chinese blood and my ability to make others anxious to know me and my family."[95]

So what of those who lived with the Chinese side of the family? How did their experiences differ? Lisa See's family history, *On Gold Mountain*, which recounts the saga of the Eurasian children of Fong See and his wife Ticie growing up in Los Angeles during the 1910s and 1920s, vividly demonstrates that there *was* in fact a place for those of mixed race in the Chinese American community: generations of See children lived and worked in Chinatown, playing and eating alongside their "pure Chinese" cousins and neighbors.[96] This place was not automatic, but was earned through ties of friendship and familiarity, and most important, kinship. As Lisa See explains in the case of her father Richard, who was one-fourth Chinese by blood quantum, "Although [his cousins] saw him as definitely Caucasian, they accepted him because he was a relative."[97] See's account suggests that the Chinese American community was less concerned with blood quantum and racial purity than with distinguishing family from outsiders. This

188 | Chapter 6

picture is consistent with Mary Ting Yi Lui's contention that mixed families were an integral part of New York's Chinatown up through the 1910s, when families began to move to the suburbs.[98]

For comparative purposes, let us take a closer look at one mixed family who lived "on the Chinese side": the Huie family of New York. As recounted in his *Reminiscences* (1932), Huie Kin was an immigrant from Canton who arrived in California in 1868, converted to Christianity, and in 1885 became New York's first Chinese ordained to the ministry. In New York, Huie Kin met a young Dutch American missionary, Louise Van Arnam, and over the objections of her parents, they were married in 1889. The Huie family home became the hub of the Chinese community in New York, a home away from home for everyone from the humblest laundrymen to Ivy League students and visiting VIPs. Huie Kin was actively engaged with pastoral life, Chinese overseas student activities, and the Chinese Boy Scouts and YMCA. In the role of pastor's wife, Louise was equally active in the Chinese community and kept busy with a large brood of children: Irving, the oldest child, was born in 1890, followed by Tom (1891), Harriet Louise (1893), Alice (1895), Caroline (1897), Helen (1899), Ruth (1901), Dorothy (1902), and twins Albert and Arthur (1905).[99]

The Huie children were raised in a home that was bicultural, but also very definitively a part of the Chinese community. Hence, in sharp contrast to the "half-Chinese" described by Eaton in "Persecution," the Huie family was undoubtedly "known to the world as Chinese." Unlike the Eatons, the Huie children were immersed in the Chinese immigrant community: they were active in their father's Chinese mission work and overseas student activities; and the children all had Chinese names. In college, the children were active in the Chinese Students' Club: one daughter was elected vice president in 1915–16, while another served as treasurer.[100]

Yet, it would be too simple to say that Huie family lived on the non-white side of the color line. Although the Reverend Huie's flock was defined as New York's Chinese community, the mission and family home were never located in Chinatown, but always in neighborhoods that the census shows as predominantly white.[101] What motivated the Huies' decision to live in white neighborhoods even while serving the Chinese community? Their reasons probably had much to do with class, as Edith Eaton suggested in her own case. Or perhaps the choice of location was driven by the fact that Huie's flock included both Chinatown's working-class immigrants as well as the Chinese students at Columbia University and other schools.

Was it the location of the Huie home that prompted the inconsistencies continually exhibited by census enumerators in their classification of the Huie family? On the 1900 census, the children were returned "white," but on the 1910 census, they were designated "Chinese."[102] On the 1920 census, there was evident confusion, as demonstrated by the multiple entries, crossed out and reentered, under the "color or race" column, but it appears that the children were ultimately returned "white."[103] By 1930, Irving, living in Saugerties, New York, with his Euro-American wife, was designated "white," as were the twins, Albert (in White Plains, New York) and Arthur (in North Branford, Connecticut).[104] Similarly, Irving's draft registration card for World War I showed him designated as "Caucasian."[105]

With the family home serving as a "spiritual and social center" for the New York Chinese community, the Huie children were raised in a very different world from the Eatons. Yet, as adults, they too made very different life decisions: all six daughters married Chinese overseas students and returned with them to China; the three sons, in sharp contrast, married Euro-American women and settled in the United States.[106]

Whereas legal cases like *In re Knight* demonstrate how the state attempted to fix the color line, life narratives provide equally important insights into how individuals attempted to navigate this line and claim identities for themselves. A juxtaposition of the Huie family with the Eatons demonstrates that Eurasian experiences of the American color line did not follow a single pattern. While we might expect the one-drop rule to determine the place of Eurasians, we see instead that experiences of the color line varied across time and space, being dependent not only on blood quantum but also on factors of class, upbringing, cultural capital (British cultural capital in the Eatons' case and Chinese cultural capital in the Huies' case), and phenotype as well as paternal descent. Hence, whereas the courts may have been content to declare a man like Knight "nonwhite," pure and simple, the lived experiences of Chinese Eurasians in North America during the Exclusion era give lie to such a cut-and-dried interpretation. Thus this chapter has offered an alternative perspective to the literature in mixed-race studies that portrays the one-drop rule as the sole "American regime of race" prior to 1967. Like Sharfstein, I show instead that the "history of the color line is one in which people have lived quite comfortably with contradiction."[107]

It is also important to note that Eurasian responses to the color line were highly individual: some, like Edward Charles Eaton, chose to pass as white; others, like Harriet Louise Huie and Milton See, identified as Chinese. Yet others, like George Appo and Harry Hastings, saw such a binary choice as meaningless. As Harry Hastings declared to SRR researchers, "I'm not Chinese, I'm not British, I'm an international-ist."[108] Individual experiences further suggest the need to critically inter-rogate paradigms such as "passing." Let us take the case of Yung Kwai's son, Addison Kwai Young (1902–89, Yale class of 1924) as an exam-ple. Given the double surname Yung Kwai at birth, Addison legally changed his name to Addison Kwai Young in 1927, with Kwai used as a middle name. According to his son, Dana Bruce Young (b. 1938, Yale class of 1960), this change was motivated by "a desire to 'fit' more eas-ily within American society." And yet, as Young recalls, his "father was always open in acknowledging his half-Chinese descent to his two sons, and, as far as I know, to his friends and acquaintances as well (if they ever bothered to ask)."[109] Passing is clearly inadequate to encapsulate such choices.

Like Hastings, Edith Eaton had similarly asserted in "Leaves," "After all I have no nationality and am not anxious to claim any. Individuality is more than nationality."[110] Thus Eaton reclaimed the Eurasian's nei-ther/nor condition and transformed it into a claim for individuality: prefiguring, by many decades, a Zeitgeist brought into being by the multiracial movement of the 1990s.[111]

. . .

If Harry Hastings had dreamed of one day escaping from it all on a small island of his own, Edith Eaton dreamed of one day getting to China. As she told her readers, "As my life began in my father's country it may end in my mother's."[112] An early death in 1914 prevented Eaton from realizing this hope, even as it cut short her ambition of writing a book about the half-Chinese. If she had gone to China, Eaton would likely have been very surprised by the different lives led by Eurasians on the other side of the Pacific—the subject of the next chapter.

Prologue to Chapter 7

ADVENTURES OF A DEVOTED SON IN HIS FATHER'S LAND

In the spring of 1912, the same year that Harry Hastings arrived in Canada, a dashing young man set off from Hartford, Connecticut, bound for adventure in the newly established Chinese republic. Excited that his father's long-held dream of a New China had at last come true, Bartlett Golden Yung placed his company, the Rotary File and Machine Company of Brooklyn, New York, in the hands of a Yale classmate and signed on as the East Asia representative for Colt's Patent Firearms. For Yung Wing's younger son, this was not only an opportunity to see his father's native land for the first time but also a chance to test his mettle.[1]

As soon as Bartlett safely landed his cargo in China, he made immediately for Canton to meet with Sun Yat-sen, who awaited his arrival. Bartlett had written to the great man immediately after he was instated as president of the Chinese Republic, offering his congratulations and placing himself at the service of the new nation.[2] As Bartlett informed Sun, he had the following credentials: he was Yung Wing's son; a Yale graduate of 1902 (fig. 13); and a mechanical engineer; with experience in the New York State National Guard, he was willing to serve in the Chinese Army.

Bartlett was buoyed after a successful interview with Sun Yat-sen, but he was soon greeted with the news that his father had passed away on April 21.[3] While Joseph Twichell presided over the burial at Cedar Hill Cemetery in Connecticut, Bartlett spoke these words at a memorial service for revolutionary martyrs in Canton:

FIGURE 13. *(left)* Bartlett Golden Yung, Yale College class of 1902.

Yale College Class Book 1902. Manuscripts and Archives, Yale University.

FIGURE 14. *(right)* Morrison Brown Yung, Yale College class of 1898.

1898 Class Book of the Sheffield Scientific School, Yale University. Manuscripts and Archives, Yale University.

> This is, of course, to me a very sad occasion and yet I am glad of the opportunity to be present here to represent, in some senses, my father's memory. I can only say in conclusion that as my father's thoughts and aim in life were the welfare of his countrymen and the upbuilding of China, his sons—my brother and myself—should and do intend to take at least a humble part in the glorious work of preserving China for the Chinese.[4]

Indeed, Yung Wing's sons, Rong Jintong (Morrison Brown) and Rong Jinhuai (Bartlett Golden), did much to promote this "glorious work." With degrees in mining engineering from Yale (1898) and Columbia (1901), Morrison (fig. 14) worked to help develop mining in southern China, gaining renowned expertise that would lead him to be appointed head of Sun Yat-sen's Mining Department. Bartlett inherited his father's entrepreneurial flair, helping to modernize China's arms manufacturing before establishing his own import-export and engineering consulting business in Shanghai.[5] Although they spent much time traveling between East and West, the Yung brothers eventually decided to settle East: Morrison in Hong Kong and Bartlett in Shanghai. Morrison died in Beijing in 1934 and Bartlett in Shanghai in 1942.

One can only imagine that if Morrison and Bartlett had stood out at Yale, in China they must have appeared equally "foreign"—especially

Prologue to Chapter 7 | 193

Bartlett with the thick mustache he sported in 1912. Their foreignness must have been reinforced by the fact that neither spoke any Chinese before they arrived in China. Contemporary Chinese accounts frequently emphasize the Yung brothers' patriotic "return" to China and their decision to marry ethnic Chinese women, but such a narrative surely simplifies the shifts in identity that their migrations entailed.[6]

Bartlett addressed this question in his travelogue, "'Drumming' Revolutionary China," a magazine article based on his lectures to the Yale Club of New York in January 1914. "I have been asked," Bartlett wrote, "whether my feelings are Chinese or American." As he explained:

> Though my father was Chinese, all my life was spent in the United States until two years ago, when I visited China for the first time, as the agent of an American corporation. . . . My mother's people came to America in the *Mayflower* and fought for the flag in the Revolutionary and Civil wars. Perhaps it is this, perhaps because I was born and brought up in the States, but anyway, whenever I saw the stars and stripes out in faraway China, the big lump would always come in my throat. This will answer the question as well as I can.[7]

Bartlett must have felt like an outsider indeed when he first arrived in China: his Western clothing and demeanor, his distaste for Chinese food, and his halting and fragmentary Chinese—all marked him as a "foreign devil."[8] Yet, Bartlett also told of a shift in his sense of identity that he underwent during eight months he spent in Canton, his father's home province. Having been made a major-general in the Chinese Army, Bartlett was placed at the head of a large Cantonese arsenal, and his perception of the country and people gradually changed. As he explained, "The Chinese disregard almost entirely the maternal side of the family, so that I now was permitted to enjoy the pleasant side of social life because I was looked upon by the Cantonese as one of their own people."[9]

Bartlett's ethnic ambiguity nearly cost him his life. As readers of the *Hartford Courant* would learn, on the night of September 14, 1913, Bartlett Yung was summarily arrested in Beijing and thrown in a military jail, where he was threatened with death without trial for purportedly conspiring with revolutionists in Canton. Bartlett informed his jailers that he was an American citizen and demanded to be taken to the American Legation, but the gendarme only spat on his American passport and threw it to the ground in contempt. Fate was clearly on Bartlett's side, however, for his life was saved by a Hartford "Old Boy," Tsai Ting Kan, who had been made an admiral and aide to President

Yuan Shikai. Reporting on the American citizen's close brush with death, the *Hartford Courant* explained the outrage by stating that Bartlett, with his mixed parentage, "was undoubtedly mistaken for a Chinese."[10] But Bartlett himself had a different interpretation of events, believing that his "foreign appearance" and papers had led his jailers to treat him cautiously.[11] Did Bartlett's ambiguous looks endanger or save his life on that terrifying Beijing night? God alone knows.

On Not Looking Chinese

Chineseness as Consent or Descent?

In 1934, a pious lady of great gentility brought distinction to her family by publishing the *Travelogues of Famous Mountains* (*Mingshan youji*), a collection of essays recording a lifetime of travels to more than twenty sacred mountains and Buddhist temples—no simple accomplishment given her tiny bound feet. Written in terse but elegant classical Chinese, the text closely followed the conventions of an established genre among Chinese scholars, and one might be forgiven for thinking that there was nothing much exceptional about this slim volume. But the author was, in fact, as exceptional for her time as were Edith and Winnifred Eaton (see chapter 6): like the Eaton sisters, Lady Clara Ho Tung was Eurasian.

Travelogues of Famous Mountains and the appended autobiographical sketch may be read as works of self-representation, as the author's attempt to represent herself as a devout lay Buddhist and a traditional "wise wife and good mother." With prefaces contributed by Chinese government officials and eminent Buddhist monks, and photographs of the Buddhist free school she established, this text further serves to represent Lady Clara and her husband as established members of the Chinese gentry being commemorated for their local philanthropy (see fig. 9 in chapter 4).[12] Yet, given that Clara was a second-generation Eurasian whose most famous ancestor was Thomas Ash Lane of Scotland, such a reading deserves to be complicated.[13]

Whereas the Eaton sisters, struggling to establish themselves as writers in North America, negotiated their public and private identities against the backdrop of Chinese exclusion, on the other side of the Pacific Eurasians like Lady Clara and her family faced very different contexts. What constraints did they encounter in negotiating their identities in Hong Kong, or in China—both societies in which Han Chinese formed the majority? And why did prominent Eurasians like the Ho Tungs in Hong Kong and the Princess Der Ling in China choose to project public images as Chinese and downplay their European roots? If Edith Eaton had claimed in the 1910s that Eurasians in North America were generally tempted to "pass as wholly white," Hong Kong Eurasian Eric Peter Ho (b. 1928, Commander of the Order of the British Empire) recalled a popular saying passed down among his elders: "It is better to walk at the head of the humans, than to follow behind the [foreign] devils' tail."[14] In choosing this affiliation, some Eurasians even tried to deny their "foreign blood," thereby reversing the phenomenon discussed in the previous chapter.

Focusing on Chinese-identified Eurasians, this chapter takes up some of the questions concerning Chineseness posed in the introduction, namely the tension between descent and consent in conceptions of Chinese identity. A consideration of the ways in which "mixed bloods" articulated their claims to Chineseness allows us to revisit debates in the field over whether Chinese identity is best described by models of Confucian culturalism or by descent-based models of "we-group" definition. I approach this question through a reading of Eurasian life narratives, analyzing the diverse *grounds* on which individual Chinese-identified Eurasians in China and Hong Kong claimed Chineseness. In order to compare how such claims differ between those with Chinese descent in the maternal line and those with Chinese descent in the paternal line, I focus on two authors: Hong Kong's Irene Cheng (1904–2007), the daughter of Sir Robert Ho Tung and Lady Clara; and China-born Han Suyin (1917–2012), the daughter of Chinese engineer Zhou Yingtong and his Belgian wife, Marguerite Denis. I demonstrate that the pathways for claiming Chinese identity differ significantly between the two but contend that each has a foundation in long-established Chinese practices of reckoning we-group membership. For comparison's sake, I also briefly discuss the case of Irene's father, Ho Tung, perhaps the single most famous Eurasian of the Treaty Port era. Probing the limitations of racially bounded notions of Chineseness—such as suggested by Lisa See's confrontation with the accusation "You don't look Chinese" (see introduction)—my analysis demonstrates that the category of "Chinese" has itself been unstable, creating a space for negotiations of identity.

NATIONALITY, RACIAL CLASSIFICATION, AND SOCIAL IDENTITY

As we saw in chapter 5, Eurasians during this era faced prejudice from both the Chinese and expatriate communities, though this prejudice was also mitigated by a certain degree of privilege, as I discuss in the next chapter. Thus, Eurasians occupied what Henry Lethbridge called an "ambiguous and uncertain" status, an ambiguity perhaps most aptly summed up in the words of Shanghai-born Eurasian, Joyce Anderson Symons (1918–2004): "I was not totally accepted at best by either culture, nor totally despised at worst."[15]

Eurasians on the China Coast frequently led lives of great mobility, which took them between mainland China, Hong Kong, Macao, and Singapore as well as farther-flung destinations. Lady Clara, for example, was born in Hong Kong but grew up in Shanghai and Jiujiang, following her father's career trajectory.[16] On the other end of the class spectrum, Ng Akew, the abandoned partner of James Endicott, moved with her children between Canton, Macao, and Hong Kong in search of opportunity. In each place, Eurasians faced different legal and social environments.

As we saw in chapter 2, the Qing promulgated its first nationality law in 1909, with nationality primarily defined according to the bloodline principle (*jus sanguinis*). Privileging paternal descent, Qing nationality law automatically extended Chinese citizenship to children born of Chinese fathers regardless of birthplace. Secondarily, children born on Chinese *soil* to Chinese mothers and foreign fathers could claim Chinese nationality if their fathers did not legally recognize them or were stateless.[17] After the fall of the Qing, nationality laws of the Republic of China (ROC) continued to privilege paternal descent in according nationality through *jus sanguinis*.[18]

Eurasians born in Hong Kong faced a different legal regime. In contrast to the Chinese privileging of *jus sanguinis*, British law privileged *jus soli*. As a result, Eurasians born in the colony were technically considered British subjects. However, not being of "pure European descent," Eurasians had ambiguous legal status, and they did not enjoy the full rights and privileges of British citizens.[19] In 1898, the British instituted the category of "British Protected Person," a status that applied to non-marital children born outside the colony to British subject fathers and Chinese subject mothers.[20] The imprecise status of Eurasians was indicative of the "tension of empire," manifested as a conflict between an inclusive model of British imperial subjecthood and exclusionary practices based on race and birthplace.[21] Given the circumstances, some Eurasians opted to claim Chinese nationality.

Despite these fundamental differences neither the Chinese nor the British colonial system used blood quantum as a criterion for defining the legal status of Eurasians (see chapter 6). As C. G. Alabaster reported to the *Eugenics Review* in 1920, Eurasians in Hong Kong were classified based on a host of factors, "the least of which would be the quantum of blood admixture." According to Alabaster, Eurasians could easily be divided into three distinct groups—the Portuguese, the Chinese, and the British—according to criteria that were largely cultural and social. Alabaster wrote, "One would have no difficulty in giving a Chinese classification to a half-caste, even though his father were English, who wore Chinese clothes and the queue, who passed under the name of Wong or Chan, who had married according to Chinese custom a 'Kit Fat' (wife) and three concubines." Similarly, he noted that a Eurasian who used an English surname, wore European clothing, and lived as a European "would not be regarded legally as a Chinese, although his parentage might affect him socially."[22] Finally, Alabaster declared that phenotype was not a basis for ethnic classification, explaining that any man using a Portuguese surname, practicing Roman Catholicism, and affiliated with Portuguese schools and clubs would not be considered Chinese "even though he was Oriental in feature and had only a fraction of European blood in his veins."[23] Ethnic affiliations thus trumped blood quantum.

Aside from the distinct Portuguese Eurasian minority, the majority of Hong Kong Eurasians appear to have lived as Chinese.[24] As Cedric Dover explained, many Eurasians in Hong Kong, even those with British paternity, chose to adopt Chinese social identities "to avoid prejudice and gain economic opportunity."[25] In other words, despite British colonial privilege in Hong Kong, Eurasians found it better to identify with the Chinese than to endure the degraded position of "half-caste" that was their lot if they allied themselves with the Europeans. One might add that since many Hong Kong Eurasians were raised within their mothers' natal families, their Chinese identification may not have been a matter of "choice" but a product of early childhood socialization.

In contrast, when Herbert Lamson did his field study of Eurasians in Shanghai during the late 1920s and early 1930s, he found a significant cohort of Eurasians who identified with their European fathers, even as he noted the untold numbers of mixed-race children who had "blended back" into the Chinese community (see chapter 5).[26] Socio-logical studies and memoirs suggest that there were more options for negotiating a Eurasian identity in Shanghai and other cosmopolitan cit-ies in China than in Hong Kong, where the color line was more rigidly upheld (see chapter 8).[27]

Although Eurasians in China and Hong Kong were able to claim Chinese nationality, legal inclusion did not automatically translate into social acceptance. Chinese Eurasians were sometimes reviled as *gwei-jai* ("foreigner's offspring"), *gwei-lo* ("foreign devil"), and *zazhong* ("mon-grel," "bastard") among other choice epithets.[28] The degree of prejudice faced by individual Eurasians depended on various factors of timing, location, class, gender, and whether one's father was Chinese or foreign (see chapter 5). In short, to be the marital child of a Chinese diplomat and an educated French woman was altogether different than being the nonmarital child of a Norwegian sailor and a Chinese prostitute. Thus, Li Mo argues that Chinese–Western intermarriage had a somewhat elite aura in China during the late nineteenth and early twentieth centuries, when it was viewed as a phenomenon chiefly initiated by (male) over-seas students and diplomats.[29] In Hong Kong, in contrast, the majority of Eurasians were descended from the liaisons between foreign men and Chinese "protected women," who were held in low regard by the Chinese.[30] Hence, the prejudice against Eurasians during this time stemmed not only from the "impurity" of foreign blood, but also from the stigma of (imputed) illegitimacy and the bias against relationships between Chinese women and foreign men.

Chinese Racial Nationalism in the Revolutionary Era

The Revolution of 1911 has been identified as a major watershed event for Eurasians, affecting even those in Hong Kong.[31] This new era of ris-ing Chinese nationalism led to backlash against Eurasians and a ques-tioning of whether they should continue to be counted as Chinese, as I elaborate in the next chapter.[32] The racialized character of modern Chi-nese nationalism had a distinctly negative impact on Eurasians, calling into question their Chineseness and making issue of their descent from the foreigners who had subjected China to humiliation.

As discussed in chapter 4, the invention of the *Hanzu* (Han race or lineage) as a racialized concept was crucial to the formation of modern Chinese racial nationalism. Drawing on a traditional discourse of lineage affiliation, racial nationalists promoted the notion of the Hanzu as a lineage sharing common descent from the mythical Yellow Emperor. The new racialized discourse marked the revolutionaries' rejection of the Confucian model of culturalism and resulted in what Rebecca Karl has called a "narrowed recentering of 'Chinese-ness' around ethnicity."[33]

In their appeals to primordialism, revolutionaries privileged notions of shared descent, blood, and kinship.[34] As Sun Yat-sen, for example, wrote, "The greatest force is common blood. The Chinese belong to the yellow race because they come from the blood stock of the yellow race. The blood of ancestors is transmitted by heredity down through the race, making blood kinship a powerful force."[35] Blood and kinship were thus mobilized as compelling metaphors of group unity. Yet, as Peter Zarrow notes, revolutionaries like Zhang Binglin did not base the notion of Hanzu solely on descent but rather drew a conceptual linkage among blood, land, and culture.[36]

In tandem with the rise of racial nationalism, as we saw in chapter 2, this era witnessed a surge of heated rhetoric against Chinese–Western intermarriage. Xenophobia also led many to question the loyalty of Eurasians, with their "foreign blood" and their familial and business connections to the foreign devils, and those who extolled racial purity furthermore denigrated Eurasians as "mongrels."

CLAIMING CHINESENESS

Within this evolving context, what were the mechanisms by which Chinese-identified Eurasians claimed their Chineseness? Did they appeal to culturalist or ethnic conceptions of Chineseness: to Chineseness as consent or descent? Interesting insights can be gained through an examination of three specific case studies: Ho Tung, a Eurasian with maternal Chinese descent; Irene Ho Cheng, a second-generation Eurasian; and Han Suyin (pen name of Zhou Guanghu), a Eurasian with paternal Chinese descent. Cheng and Han have both authored life narratives, and I therefore focus on their works, analyzing how each claims Chineseness on her own terms. Although Ho Tung unfortunately never wrote a memoir, leaving us no firsthand evidence "in his own words" regarding his ethnic identification, a brief discussion of his case is nonetheless warranted by his historical importance. Moreover, a comparison between Ho Tung and his daughter Irene allows us to consider generational change within a Eurasian family. As in the previous chapter, each of these three case studies is to be understood as an individual story and not as representative of Eurasians in general. Indeed, both the Ho family and the Zhou family are excellent examples of the range of individual identifications displayed by Eurasians, even within the same family. In the Ho family, Irene's sister Jean (see fig. 9 in chapter 4) was strongly British identified, whereas her brother Robert joined the ROC military.[37] Similarly, Han Suyin became an ardent spokesperson for China, but her elder brother and younger sister chose to adopt European identities. This makes our authors' choice to "claim Chineseness" even more striking.

Sir Robert Ho Tung: Chinese Mother, European Father

According to Sir Robert's daughters, despite their father's strikingly Western appearance, for all his adult life he chose to present himself as Chinese (see fig. 8, chapter 4). His daughters have further noted that his origins were a source of some pain for Sir Robert, and a subject the stern patriarch rarely discussed.[38] As we saw (see chapter 4), Ho Tung's life was a quintessential rags-to-riches story. With a sharply honed instinct for negotiating the bilingual and bicultural environment of colonial Hong Kong, Ho Tung rose to become the richest man in Hong Kong, and a powerbroker with significant political influence in China as well.[39]

Although he was known to be Eurasian, the image Ho Tung crafted for himself was essentially that of a Chinese gentleman. As his daughter Florence explained, "Eurasians were not accepted well in society in those days, and to be successful one had to make a choice to be Chinese or European. Father chose to be Chinese so he took on a Chinese name—Ho Tung."[40] Florence not only notes the monoracial logic of British colonial racial ideology, which forces the Eurasian to "choose sides," but also highlights the pivotal role of the name in this process. Ho Tung's choice contrasted sharply with his younger brother, who took the name of Walter Bosman after he left Hong Kong to study in England (see chapter 4).[41] Bosman would later marry an Englishwoman, move to South Africa, and "pass."

Numerous sources attest to the crucial role of the surname in establishing a Chinese identity. Patricia Ebrey argues that ties of patrilineal kinship, as signified through surnames, have operated as a key metaphor of Han Chinese ethnic identity, of membership in the we-group. Examining the long history of ethnic assimilation in China, whereby non-Han became Han, Ebrey demonstrates that the adoption of a Han Chinese surname, in addition to acculturation, was essential to this transformation. Eurasians born to European fathers had two options:

they could use their mother's surname or assume a new surname. Eric Peter Ho records that most took the latter course, which more closely conformed to Chinese patrilineal custom.[42] In order to support their claim to Chineseness, many Eurasians thus fabricated Chinese lineages for themselves, giving Chinese names to their European ancestors and placing these names on ancestral tablets and gravestones. According to Ho Tung's daughter Irene, their family would make ritual offerings according to Chinese custom at the gravesite of the "Ho family ancestors" at the Chiu Yuen Cemetery.[43] The imposing joint tomb is actually the burial site for Madam Sze, and although the inscription implies that Bosman is also interred there, the tomb contains only a few articles of his clothing as proxy for his body (as per Chinese custom). The construction of this joint tomb demonstrates that surnames are important because they are essential to lineage and to ancestor worship, two crucial aspects of Chinese identity. By these means of accommodation to the Chinese privileging of the patrilineal descent group, and through the practice of ancestor worship, a mixed family could "become Chinese" within a generation or two.

A second strategy Ho Tung pursued was the claiming of Chinese nationality. As his daughter Jean wrote, "He decided to claim Chinese nationality—possibly because he knew that the Chinese would not be so discourteous as to disown him openly but I think it was chiefly due to the fact that he knew, with his English education, he would have a distinct advantage over his contemporaries in his dealings with the British."[44] Jean thus indicates that there was a strategic element to claiming Chineseness.

Dress also provided a means through which Ho Tung signified his Chinese identification. Although he had worn European clothes in his youth, as an adult Ho was known for always wearing traditional Chinese clothes, and usually Chinese shoes and a skullcap. He also wore the queue before the Revolution of 1911, as did his eldest sons.

Consistent with his Chinese social identity, Ho Tung ran his family as a strict Confucian patriarch and according to traditional mores. He took two equal co-wives (see fig. 9), married according to Chinese custom, and a concubine. Both his wives were Eurasians who had similarly been raised in Chinese households and used Chinese surnames—Mak and Cheung. As noted previously, the family practiced ancestor worship, and there was also a Buddhist shrine in the home. Since Lady Clara was a devout Buddhist, the family ate vegetarian food on the first and fifteenth of every lunar month. Important dates were recorded by the family according to the lunar calendar and the reign years of the Qing emperors.

Another factor central to Ho Tung's "claiming Chineseness" was his public role as a philanthropist and supporter of political causes. Ho Tung's business success, wealth, and charitable donations allowed him to become a leader of the Hong Kong Chinese community as well as an important representative to the British of "Chinese sentiment." In 1898, Ho Tung became chairman of the board of the Tung Wah Hospital, the leading Chinese charitable organization, and in 1899, he helped found the Chinese Club and became its first president. A year later, he and his brother Ho Fook (see fig. 9) established the Chinese Chamber of Commerce.[45] He furthermore supported Lady Clara's Buddhist philanthropic activities, including the founding of a Buddhist temple, medical clinic, and free schools for girls.

Sir Robert's interests were not confined to Hong Kong but also extended to China, where he traveled regularly for business dealings, holidays, and family visits. The most symbolic of these visits was taken in 1909 or 1910, when the extended Ho family went in search of their mother's ancestral home on Chongming Island, near Shanghai.[46] Ho Tung was deeply concerned with the political future of China after the 1911 revolution and engaged in various political causes, extending his network beyond the famous reformer Kang Youwei (see chapter 4) to include Sun Yat-sen, Chiang Kai-shek, and other leading political figures. In recognition of his service to China, the Chinese government awarded him numerous prestigious honors.[47] In 1921, he was appointed honorary adviser to China's president, and he remained a senior adviser to the ROC government throughout the 1930s and 1940s.[48] His son Robert (He Shili) became an important ROC lieutenant general.

Despite these various efforts to claim Chineseness, however, Ho Tung was not necessarily accepted by others, and his daughters have recorded various incidents of discrimination he faced.[49] Irene recounts one encounter that occurred when Ho Tung applied for a post with the Chinese Maritime Customs in Canton, a competitive position that required command of both Chinese and English: "When the applicants all lined up outside, there were obviously many who were older and perhaps wiser than Father—erudite scholars and other learned people. There were even some who did not like Father because he was Eurasian. His hair was not pure black so it was easy to see that he was not pure Chinese. One of them said: 'You don't stand a chance. Why do you even bother?'"[50]

These incidents only steeled Ho Tung's determination to "make good" and establish himself as a leader of the Chinese community, an exemplar of Confucian conservatism, and a benevolent patron, through Lady Clara, of Buddhist charitable works. When he died in 1956 at the ripe old age of ninety-three, Ho Tung left behind a vital legacy, carried on by his descendants to this day.[51]

Irene Cheng: Second-Generation Eurasian

The sixth child of Sir Robert and Lady Clara, Irene (He Ailing) authored two books on her family, *Clara Ho Tung: A Hong Kong Lady, Her Family and Her Times* (1976) and *Intercultural Reminiscences* (1997).[52] Following in her parents' footsteps, Irene (see fig. 9) accomplished numerous achievements of her own. Pursuing the field of education, she earned degrees from the University of Hong Kong, Teachers' College of Columbia University, and London University (PhD 1936). While studying in London she did volunteer work with young British Eurasians but found it so emotionally stressful, because she had "not yet come to terms with [her] own Eurasian background," that she was obliged to stop.[53] Like her father, she was recognized for her service to Hong Kong, and she was appointed as an Officer of the Order of the British Empire in 1961. Cheng further followed her father in publicly emphasizing her Chinese identity.

Cheng begins her memoir, *Intercultural Reminiscences,* with an assertion of her family's Chineseness, even as she discusses the topic of interculturalism. The memoir opens with the explanation that "although we were Eurasians, ostensibly we were brought up in the Chinese tradition. We spoke Cantonese at home, honoured Chinese festivals, and lived according to the lunar calendar."[54] As Cheng explained in her biography of Lady Clara, owing to European prejudice, the "majority [of Eurasians] therefore identified themselves with the Chinese and tried in every way to be as 'Chinese' as possible."[55] In concrete terms, this meant using Chinese names, attending Chinese schools, wearing Chinese clothes (see figs. 8 and 15), eating Chinese food, and perhaps most important, practicing ancestor worship.[56]

For Cheng, a cornerstone of Chineseness lies in education, particularly the mastery of the Chinese written language and the Chinese classics—which we might call the acquisition of Chinese cultural capital. As she writes, "The families which identified themselves with the Chinese usually sent their sons first to Chinese schools where the curriculum was

FIGURE 15. Catherine Anderson, ca. 1905.

Courtesy of Dr. Bruce Chan, a relative of Catherine Anderson.

based on a study of the Confucian classics."[57] Cheng's own family emphasized classical Chinese education—a fact that she notes with pride.

Cheng's self-representation as Chinese furthermore foregrounds her thorough understanding of the intricacies of Chinese kinship networks and relations. Cheng represents herself as deeply embedded in these relations, which structure her sense of who she is in the world. In addition, she invokes the Confucian principle of filial piety in order to justify her father's taking two wives.[58] Filial piety is also key to Cheng's self-fashioning, and her narrative continually highlights her own role as a filial daughter.

Religion also features prominently in Cheng's portrait of her family's Chineseness. Cheng proudly claims that the family resolutely refused to convert to Christianity, with Lady Clara staunchly rebutting missionary assertions of Christian superiority.[59] Cheng identifies herself as a Confucianist, her eldest sister Victoria as a dedicated Buddhist, and her Fifth Uncle as an expert geomancer.[60] Interestingly, she makes no mention of the fact that her sisters Jean and Florence became devout Christians. Perhaps Cheng fears that such an admission would disrupt the representation of her family's essential Chineseness, which she is compelled to overemphasize due to their acknowledged "mixedness." Yet, despite emphasizing her parents' firm insistence on upholding Chinese traditions, Cheng acknowledged that the family was gradually becoming Westernized. After the move to the exclusive Peak district in 1906, the children began wearing European clothes. Given a bilingual education, their generation commonly used English names, and they were avid players of European sports like tennis. Connected as it was to modernity and class status, Westernization was a tide that could not be stemmed, especially in Hong Kong. Thus the Ho household exhibited many bicultural influences, from furnishings to food and holidays. Funerals were conducted in the Chinese style, while weddings for the second generation were conducted in a fashionable Western style (see fig. 9). Nonetheless, Cheng represents these changes as consistent with her own Chineseness, and not as symptomatic of her in-betweenness. As she wrote, "Hong Kong at the time was becoming cosmopolitan, and many Chinese families were accepting Western influences."[61]

Cheng further acknowledged cracks in the family's Chinese public image. Twice her narrative recalls a painful episode concerning identity from her youth. Apparently, while teaching at Lingnan University in Canton during the 1930s, Cheng attempted to pass as fully Chinese. This had a hurtful effect on her youngest sister, Florence, who was attending Lingnan at the time. As Florence recalled in her memoir, *My Memories* (1989), "There was a great problem welling up within me. At school in Hong Kong, I was known to be Eurasian and not pure Chinese. But my family, especially Irene, told me to say that I was pure Chinese. This puzzled and confused me. . . . I had light brown hair and brown eyes, my skin was fairer, whereas Chinese people have black hair and black eyes. Chinese people can be very snobbish about race and I was made to feel an outcast."[62] Unaware of her sister's sentiments at the time, Cheng sought to pass, possibly motivated by her burgeoning Chinese nationalism, which was awakened by political events in China during the 1930s and perhaps also by her location in "China proper," away from the British colony.

Indeed, the geographic space of China plays a distinct role in Cheng's self-representation of her Chineseness. Earlier on, Cheng's identification with China, as a geographic territory and a font of culture, had been spurred on by a "grand tour of China" that she completed in the summer of 1926. It was on this trip that young Irene met her future husband, Hsiang Hsien Cheng, a northern Chinese. Irene's eventual marriage to Cheng helped to consolidate her Chinese identity.

Cheng's identification with China as a source of roots is revealed in chapter 18 of *Intercultural Reminiscences*, "Return to the New China." The notion of return is a critical concept in discourses of Chinese identity, as Elizabeth Sinn, Andrea Louie, and others have noted. To be Chinese is to *return*—to ancestral hometown, to roots, to motherland— to a place viewed as the ultimate source of familial and ethnic identity. In "Return to the New China," Cheng links the concepts of home and roots to mainland China, not to Hong Kong, and she explicitly proclaims China as her "mother country," even as her paternal lineage in fact traced back to Europe.[63] In the first paragraph of the chapter, Cheng explains that her Chineseness derives not just from "blood," but from her cultural learning and patriotism. Despite having become a U.S. citizen, she muses that she ultimately regarded herself "as a Chinese who through exposure had become something of a citizen of the world. The Chinese side of my personality was not simply a matter of genetics. It had been developed through the influence and example of my parents during my formative years and through the early training I received from old Master Chiu. One way it manifested itself was a genuine concern I felt for the welfare of China and its people."[64] In "Return," Cheng's loyalty to her mother country is displayed in a defense of Communist China; she presents numerous favorable firsthand observations of the "New China" in order to counter what she called Western "misunderstandings." Chinese identity is thus ultimately a matter of childhood training, education, and patriotic sentiment, with "genetics" deliberately deemphasized.

Han Suyin: Chinese Father, Belgian Mother

Born September 1917 in Henan, China, Zhou Guanghu (Elizabeth Kuanghu Chow) was raised and educated in China, attending Yenching University before leaving to pursue medical studies in the West (fig. 16). Returning to China to practice medicine, she simultaneously became an author, adopting the pen name Han Suyin and writing in English to inform Western readers about the situation of wartime China. After the Chinese Communist Revolution of 1949, Han lived and worked in Hong Kong, but she eventually settled in Europe. Even as Han continued to practice medicine, she became a prolific and world-renowned author. Among her numerous writings, Han authored a five-volume autobiography (published between 1965 and 1980), linking her own story to the history of modern China.[65]

Like Irene Cheng, Han grew up in a large family with siblings who chose different cultural orientations—some identifying primarily as European and others as Chinese. Han's own identification underwent various changes during the course of her lifetime as she grappled with the ambiguity of Eurasianness and discrimination from both sides, but she ultimately chose to proclaim her Chineseness and took on the role of a spokesperson for China to the West. Yet, Han Suyin also expressed repugnance at having to masquerade as either "pure" Chinese or "pure" European and hide her Eurasian identity, which she came to embrace with defiance.

Throughout the five volumes of her life narrative, Han defines herself as essentially Chinese: "It is from Papa, from being born in China, from all my childhood and growing up there that I have this inescapable passion and obsession with China. In this I have been . . . a Chinese intellectual of my generation."[66] Of these various factors, Han granted primacy to her inheritance of Chinese identity through her father. Similarly, Han's first husband, an ultranationalist Kuomintang officer, Tang Paohuang, whom she married in 1938, declared that he considered his wife fully Chinese due to paternal inheritance: "Your blood is Chinese, blood comes from the father, the mother is only a receptacle."[67] Here, the notion of blood is interwoven with the privileging of paternal

FIGURE 16. Han Suyin (née Elizabeth Kuanghu Chow), by Ida
Kar, 1958.

© National Portrait Gallery, London.

inheritance, which is regarded not as a matter of cultural transmission
or legal status but of biological transmission. In both cases, the mother
is rendered irrelevant, placed under erasure. This recalls Bartlett Yung's
earlier contention that "the Chinese disregard almost entirely the maternal side of the family."[68]

Yet, if blood defines her Chineseness, it also becomes a source of
anxiety for Han and her nationalist husband. As Han recounts, some

among his military associates called her "mixed blood" in a derisive manner, while others jeered at her for having "foreign blood." Tang worried that this would jeopardize his career chances among his xeno-phobic and fascist-leaning peers and urged his wife either to masquer-ade as a pure Chinese or to hide herself away. On one occasion Tang's friends confronted him: "'There is foreign blood in her, one can see that. . . .' 'Not at all, she is pure Chinese,' retorted Pao."[69] The idea of blood can thus be used alternatively to signify Han's Chineseness, or conversely her "impurity" and foreignness.

In order to compensate for this impurity, Tang exhorts Han to act more "Chinese." As Han writes, "I was too European, I must learn to become more Chinese. . . . I must also learn these Ancient Virtues, and one of them was obedience. . . ."[70] This exhortation to "act Chinese" functions as an appeal to culturalist arguments of Chinese identity. In similarly culturalist terms, Han had been conversely complimented by a Chinese nationalist during her student years in Belgium (1935–38) for having kept up her Chinese. In the eyes of this man, her *linguistic* abilities translated into patriotism, qualifying her for membership in the local branch of the Chinese Resurrection Society in Belgium: "We have decided . . . that you are a patriotic and upright spirit, and that you can be of great use to your Motherland."[71] Tang, however, evaluated Han's Chineseness in specifically gendered terms, viewing her as "too European" because she was educated and independent-minded, refusing to play the role of an obedient wife. In Tang's eyes, to "become more Chinese" meant to adhere to the "Ancient Virtues" of conservative Con-fucianism as defined by the extremist New Life movement of the 1930s, with its four pillars of propriety, righteousness, integrity, and chastity.

Hence, when Chinese culturalism is invoked as a model of Chinese identity, it is important to interrogate the contents of the black box known as "Chinese culture." As we saw previously, Irene Cheng defined Chinese tradition in concrete terms such as speaking Cantonese, cele-brating Chinese festivals, living according to the lunar calendar, study-ing the Chinese classics, obeying precepts of filial piety, and perhaps most important, practicing ancestor worship. She did not define it in narrow, politicized terms, as did Tang Paohuang. In short, "acting Chinese" means different things to different people.

Rejecting the New Life movement's ultraconservative interpretation of culture, Han takes patriotism as the ultimate measure of Chinese-ness. In other words, "loving China" trumps "acting Chinese." Han's patriotism drives her desire to "do" something for China, to serve the people—both as a doctor and as a writer. As she wrote in *Birdless Summer*, Han longed to "accomplish something, prove my usefulness, and especially prove myself a Chinese, ready to die for China . . . even though, at times, a wince, a twinge, from deep down within me reminded me that to many Chinese I was a Eurasian, and not always acceptable."[72] Mixedness, therefore, necessitates "proving" her Chineseness.

Han ties this sense of patriotism and duty back to the notion of blood or biology. Recalling the Japanese invasion of China during the 1930s, she wrote, "This old biological stir took over: I could *not* stay in peace in Europe, studying, when there was war in China. . . . I returned to China."[73] Further explaining her decision to return to China and dedicate herself to the Chinese people, Han declared, "It is almost biological. . . . I had to live by what was imprinted in my cells."[74] If being "half-blood" problematizes Han's Chineseness, then, it is also this very blood that underlies her claim to inherited, essential, even genetic, ties to China.

Thus Han links the notion of racial blood to the concept of Chineseness as a territorialized identity. At various stages of her life, Han would describe the "call" of China to her, especially in times of national crisis. For her, this call is not only a matter of duty, but also of love, of affective ties to place. Without China, she declares herself lost, deprived, "an inelastic living mummy," and hence she must return to China, again and again, despite the risks of war and revolution.[75] Once more we see the notion of return playing a central role in her imagining of Chineseness, reinforcing the territorial aspects of Chinese identity. Like Irene Cheng, Han imagines herself linked or tied to the "millions" of Chinese people. It is to this imagined community of Chinese people, and second, to "the land" more than to the state, that she renders her ultimate allegiance. The notion of Chineseness as a territorialized identity is also consistent with Han's emphasis on her birth in China as one reason for her continuing obsession with the nation. Han thus bases her claim to Chineseness on both the principles of *jus sanguinis* and *jus soli*, a matter of both ancestral and territorial origin.

From Self-Representation to Reception: Claiming Han Suyin as a "Chinese Writer"

In the final section of this chapter I turn from self-representation to reception. Due to the relative lack of critical work on Irene Cheng, my analysis is limited to Han Suyin, a writer of tremendous global celebrity, especially in the 1950s and 1960s. With renewed interest in "overseas Chinese" writers in China during the post–1980s reform era, there has been a flurry to translate Han Suyin's works into Chinese, drawing significant attention from critics and journalists.[76]

Han Suyin's "Chineseness" is a recurrent theme in both media and scholarly articles produced between the 1980s and the 2000s. A favorite formula among writers is to introduce Han as an author who at first superficially strikes one as Western—her physical appearance is European, she writes in English, she has English nationality, and/or she lives in the West—but who upon closer inspection turns out to be authentically Chinese in heart, soul, or mind. The outer is thus contrasted with the inner, formal notions of citizenship with affective ties. In addition, various critics invoke the discourse of roots to reclaim this "global" Anglophone writer as a "Chinese author." In the eyes of Chinese critics, what is it that makes Han Suyin Chinese? I have identified several general themes, many of which echo those in Han's own writing: blood, paternal inheritance, affective territorial ties, culture, childhood experience and education, and patriotism. Again, these themes are often intertwined in a discourse of Chinese identity that links race, culture, nation, and territory.

In terms of blood, various critics emphasize that the "Chinese blood" flowing through Han Suyin's veins makes her Chinese and draws her to China. Several quoted Han herself as saying, "In my body flows Chinese blood, I belong to China. . . ."[77] As another wrote, "Almost every year she wants to return to the embrace of her ancestral land. This is not only because half of the blood that runs through her veins is Chinese blood, but also because her entire life has been bound together with the joys and sorrows of China."[78] Similarly, other writers invoked the notion of Han's "Chinese bones," again locating Chineseness in the physical body.

Paternal inheritance is also a key theme: numerous critics assert that Han is Chinese by virtue of her father's nationality. Some even claim Han as a Sichuan native based on paternal inheritance, despite the fact that she was born in Henan and raised mostly in Beijing. In the words of one writer, "She is a native of Pi county, Sichuan, because her father was born there. . . ."[79] In Sichuan today there are also efforts to claim this famous writer as a native daughter. Again, such discourses render the mother irrelevant, a mere "receptacle." Critics also quote Han herself as saying, "In my heart there is only one country—China. One could say, my Dad belonged to China all of his life, it is the same for me. . . ."[80]

Critics have further mobilized a roots discourse that emphasizes affective ties to native place, a concept that once again links the lineage to a territorialized identity. We see over and over references to the facts that Han's birthplace is China; her "hometown" is in China; her "ancestral land" is China; her extended family is in China; she "returns" to China regularly; and finally, the straightforward claim that her "roots" are in China. Several praise Han as someone who understands the value of not "forgetting one's roots." For these critics, Chineseness is a matter of primordial ties, something into which one is born, and which goes back in history and lineage. It is also territorial, as suggested by the metaphor of roots sinking down into the soil, and the emphasis on birthplace, the hometown, and the act of return. There are two aspects of this territorialized identity: the first is belonging to a native place (local); the second is belonging to China (nation). Within this territorialized concept of identity, return is a ritual act that confirms one's Chineseness. Return links territory, as native place, with family and lineage. As one critic claims, "Every time [Han] comes back to China now, she always wants to find an opportunity to go back [to Sichuan] and visit her extended family. This shows that she has a deep native soil consciousness, and also that she is someone who grew up under Chinese traditions."[81]

In contrast to critics who emphasize Han's Chinese blood, or paternal inheritance, others emphasize the fact that Han was raised and educated in China, which suggests Chineseness as a product of social experience rather than a given of birthright. Similarly, various writers stress Han's understanding of Chinese culture and tradition (Confucian values, fluency in Mandarin, love of green tea [!]), as a measure of her Chineseness. Her respect for elders, for example, is taken as an index of her inheritance of "the superior traditions of the Chinese people (*Zhongguo renmin*)."[82] To be Chinese, then, is rooted in a particular value system and set of behaviors, even behaviors as specific as choosing green tea over coffee.

Most important of all, however, is Han's patriotism, an idea that is hammered home by critics time and again. This patriotism is described not so much in terms of loyalty, sacrifice, and duty, but predominantly in terms of sentiment and affective ties—love, feeling, longing, attachment, and concern (about China's future, about the people, about her hometown). Writers further praise Han's "Chinese heart" or "Chinese soul." As one proclaimed, "She has attached her own Chinese heart to the fate of the Chinese race."[83] Critics declare that patriotism drove Han to return to China during the war with Japan, and later after the Communist Revolution, in order to "do" something for China. Hence, it is not enough to have Chineseness "in the heart": true dedication to

China must be confirmed through the ritual act of return. Ultimately, it is this patriotism and devotion to China, I argue, that makes Han Suyin a *Zhongguoren* in the eyes of her admirers.

As mentioned previously, much of this discourse is aimed toward reclaiming Han as a Chinese writer, despite outward attributes that would seem to tie her to the West. One critic for example, noted Han's place, as an Anglophone author, in the Western literary canon, while asserting, "But, deep in her soul she is Chinese (*Zhongguoren*), one who possesses the attainments of traditional Chinese culture, and China is also the foundation of her emotional sustenance. In this way, her works of literature can also be considered a part of Chinese literature."[84] Similarly, another declared, "Americans call her a 'Global Woman,' but she herself actually declares: 'my roots are in China!'"[85] Cultural authenticity and racial primordialism are thus invoked to expand the canon of modern Chinese literature. Such rhetoric echoed the official discourse that was adopted by the People's Republic of China (PRC) government during the reform era of the 1980s in order to encourage the "overseas Chinese" to develop ties (and to remit funds) to their native place.[86]

Indeed, as scholars from Ling-chi Wang to Shu-mei Shih and Ien Ang have argued, hegemonic discourses of Chineseness are not only narrowly exclusionary but may be coercively inclusive as well—claiming as "Chinese" various people (Tibetans, Chinese Americans or Indonesian Chinese, and so on) who may not necessarily identify with this label.[87] This tendency in canon formation appears to be particularly pronounced in the current era of China's globalization, moving outward to claim for the motherland as much as it can from the diaspora, including Anglophone writers like Han Suyin and Shirley Geok-lin Lim.

CONCLUSION: PUTTING THE "BLOOD" BACK IN "MIXED BLOOD"

In sum, although Irene Cheng and Han Suyin both make claims to Chineseness, they do so on rather different terms. Cheng emphasizes her cultural credentials, especially in terms of what we might call "everyday" practices of Chinese culture and in terms of ritual. She does not emphasize paternal descent or the notion of Chinese blood, in fact deliberately downplaying her genetic inheritance in favor of her cultural attainments. Moreover, relative to Han Suyin, territorial ties to China play a minor role in her life narrative. National loyalty is also minimalized, with loyalty to Hong Kong balancing loyalty to China. In short, we might summarize Cheng's claim as "I am Chinese because I act Chinese." Han Suyin, in contrast, bases her claims to Chineseness primarily on paternal descent, blood, birth on Chinese soil, native place, and the ritual act of return. Moreover, she emphasizes her experiences growing up and attending school in China, formative years that her elder brother, who attended school in Belgium, missed. The Chinese language plays a minor role in Han's claims to Chineseness, possibly because much of her secondary and higher education was in English and French. Finally, patriotism and loyalty to the nation play a much larger role in Han's life narrative, as does the notion of Chinese nationality. Han's complex claims to Chineseness might best be summarized as "I am Chinese both by birth (place and paternal descent) and by loyalty." Juxtaposing these two cases makes apparent that each articulated their claims to Chinese identity based on the types *most possible* in their individual circumstances, given their particular biographical trajectories. Patricia Ebrey has demonstrated that patrilineal descent has historically been the preferred route for claiming Chineseness, even in cases in which claims to such descent are invented. Han Suyin mobilizes precisely this claim. Irene Cheng, in contrast, emphasizes other grounds for asserting her Chineseness, understanding, no doubt, the tenuousness of her claim to Chinese identity through patrilineal descent. Instead, Cheng foregrounds her possession of Chinese cultural and linguistic capital, which Han, raised as a Roman Catholic by parents who did not practice ancestor worship, is less able to claim.

As we might conclude from the examples in this chapter, it is not necessary to "look Chinese" to be Chinese. Rather, claims of cultural affiliation, language, hometown, and political allegiance can outweigh the importance of phenotype—depending on context. These cases indicate that in sharp contrast to the common American ideology of hypodescent, as examined in the previous chapter, in the Chinese context being "mixed" did not automatically exclude one from we-group membership. Thus, as noted in the introduction, purity and blood quantum never assumed the importance they did in American racial schemas. In the words of Patricia Ebrey, "Chinese were never preoccupied with notions of creoles or half-breeds."[88] That is, one can be "mixed" and still be "Chinese," whereas in the U.S. context, one cannot be "mixed" and still be "white." Indeed, as is evident in their life narratives, Irene Cheng and Han Suyin represent their mixedness as coexisting with their Chineseness. Nonetheless, these narratives also indicate that Eurasians might be considered by others a lesser or diminished form of Chinese, who must work extra hard to prove their Chineseness and loyalty.

We might say, therefore, that to be a Chinese of "heart," "mind," or "soul" is more important than biology and blood—vindicating the culturalism model. Yet, at the same time, the examples considered here suggest that the notion of blood *is* in fact important, and that Chineseness is not just a cultural category. As we have seen, the Eurasian's so-called Chinese blood plays a vital role in defining Chineseness, even if this blood is "mixed" or "half."

In addition, it is evident that paternal inheritance (which carries with it the Chinese surname and lineage affiliation) is a crucial factor in delineations of group membership. The privileging of paternal over maternal heritage was particularly strong before the reform of Chinese nationality laws in the mid-twentieth century. Despite the removal of legal sanction, however, this privileging has not entirely disappeared today. The qualification rules of the "Miss Chinatown USA" pageant, for example, stipulate that contestants' fathers must be of Chinese descent.[89] Descent, ancestry, lineage, and blood are therefore crucial criteria in the Eurasian's Chineseness, which becomes a matter not just of culture but also race.

Nonetheless, I argue that *physical appearance*, or race as phenotype, is less important for those who would claim Chineseness when compared with historical American constructions of whiteness. As we saw in the previous chapter, American conceptions of whiteness, as articulated through racial prerequisite cases, blood quantum laws, and even in literature, placed great weight on "purity" of blood and appearance, fetishizing the "trace" or "taint" of nonwhite blood. In contrast, the notion of race as lineage was more compelling for Chinese than that of race as phenotype, particularly before the advent of more extreme forms of racial nationalism such as exemplified in the New Life movement. Phenotype is certainly not irrelevant: as we saw from the examples of Ho Tung, Irene Cheng, Florence Yeo, and Han Suyin, not "looking Chinese" (or conversely showing the evidence of "foreign blood") created dilemmas at various points of their lives—marking them as anomalous despite their cultural fluency. Such dilemmas notwithstanding, I contend that in comparison to the Anglo-American conceptions of race examined in the previous chapter, the body assumes relatively less importance as a criterion for group membership or classification.

In the next chapter we will see how Hong Kong Eurasians, long accustomed to following a Chinese lifestyle, began to claim a new Eurasian identity for themselves in the 1920s and 1930s.

Prologue to Chapter 8

CECILE FRANKING: OF CENSUS TAKERS AND POETS

When census enumerator Nellie Thornton knocked on the door at 911 Monroe Street, Ann Arbor, Michigan, on January 12, 1920, she must have faced quite a surprise. 911 Monroe was home to Mr. and Mrs. Henry O. Watkins, ages sixty-two and fifty-nine, respectively; a young widow who looked white but was Chinese by nationality; and three young children, one born in the United States and two in China. Ms. Thornton settled on returning the entire family as "white." The issue of mother tongue posed a conundrum. Ms. Thornton marked "English" for Alason and Cecile, then crossed it out and wrote "Chinese" before crossing the entry once again and leaving an illegible mess.[1] Did Ms. Thornton return the children "white" as a gesture to uniformity in a household headed by a white man, set in an all-white neighborhood? Or did she perceive their whiteness, like their "mother tongue," to be a maternal inheritance? Or was she merely documenting what she saw before her, three phenotypically and culturally white children—in her eyes?

The Franking children had traveled a long distance to the house on Monroe Street. Nelson had left Ann Arbor when he was but a baby, and Alason and Cecile had been born in the Middle Kingdom. Cecile entered the world in 1917, just at the time the family was moving back to Kulangsu, her father's ancestral home. Doted on by their grandmother and a house full of servants, at Kulangsu the children led a "sheltered and happy existence," playing within the high stone walls that encircled the Huang family's grand estate.[2] In these carefree childhood days, Cecile and Alason spoke only Chinese, leaving Nelson as their mother's sole English-speaking companion aside from callers from the foreign settlement. If foreigners sometimes looked askance at the Franking children, dressed in Chinese clothes and chattering in Amoy dialect, they were unquestioningly accepted in the Huang family because their father was Chinese and they belonged to the lineage. As Mae wrote her mother back in Ann Arbor, "[Cecile's] grandma in showing her off to the neighbors always tells them that she looks just as Tiam used to when he was little."[3]

Cecile's idyllic life would change abruptly when her father was posted to the Chinese consular service in San Francisco in 1918. With the impending separation, Grandfather requested that one of the children be left with them, according to custom. Would it be Cecile, "thousand pieces of gold"?[4] Or Nelson, who already attended a Chinese school? In the end, all three set sail for America with their parents—with Grandfather's exhortation that the children must not forget their Chinese and "in four more years, all come back together."[5]

But it was not to be. Tragically, Tiam died of influenza a few months after their arrival in San Francisco. A grief-stricken Mae took the children (fig. 17) to live with her parents in Ann Arbor, where they were matter-of-factly welcomed into the Watkins family home, a small, neat house with a large front porch. In their new "well-ordered world," as Cecile remembered it, just as in Kulangsu, there were loving grandparents and largess at the holidays. But now there were peppermint candy canes and walnuts instead of rice cakes and sesame brittle—and much else that was different.[6]

If we are tempted to infer from census records that the Franking children were "passing" (the census taker in 1930 again returned them as "white"), Cecile's poetic reminiscences serve as an important corrective.[7] From Cecile's poetry we learn that the Franking children were very publicly Chinese in Ann Arbor: "Teachers always said [Papa was] a Diplomat / And looked [him] up in all the books on China."[8] Reading the poetic record against the bureaucratic, we also see days like the one when a boy called Cecile a "Chink," sending her running to find solace with gentle Granddad.[9]

Being called a "Chink" was all the more mysterious to Cecile because China was a fading memory.[10] Her links to China were cut off even further after her mother died of tuberculosis in 1926. The Huang grandparents sent word through the missionary network, asking that the children be sent home to Kulangsu.[11] But Nelson decided they should stay put with Gram and Dad Watkins, their "rock of stability."[12]

FIGURE 17. Mae Franking with Nelson, Alason, and Cecile, Michigan, ca. 1920.
Courtesy of Christopher N. Wu and William F. Wu.

Perhaps it was curiosity about her "childhood's unknown half" that inspired Cecile to attend the Chinese Students' Club in 1935, her freshman year as an Oriental Studies major at the University of Michigan.[13] Club member William Q. Wu (b. 1910) recalled of that evening, "Many people, including myself, were curious about her presence there. Actually, she created a sensation. She was very attractive; her face possessed

FIGURE 18. Wedding of Cecile M. Franking and William Q. Wu, Trinity Episcopal Church, Washington, D.C., August 19, 1945.

Courtesy of Christopher N. Wu and William F. Wu.

some Caucasian features with a touch of Asian influence, and she was slender and well-proportioned with pretty legs."[14] The following year, William plucked up his courage and invited Cecile to the October 10 celebration of the Republic of China's national day.

When William Q. Wu graduated medical school in 1939, he wrote his parents in China that he planned to marry Cecile and bring her to Beijing. Knowing what Tiam had suffered when he told his parents of his engagement to Mae, William was surprised when his father, an old imperial scholar, wrote back that "a girl with parentage from two hemispheres might add much to our family tree."[15] But war interrupted their plans. In 1942, William joined the U.S. Army and shipped overseas to China while Cecile worked in Washington, D.C., as a coordinator of the China Unit of the Army Map Service and then as a Chinese analyst for the State Department.[16] Gram moved down to Washington to take care of Cecile. It would be several long years until August 19, 1945, when Cecile and William finally wed (fig. 18).

If the war had derailed their plans, it also unexpectedly led to an opportunity denied Cecile and William all their lives: in March 1943,

First Lieutenant William Q. Wu, native of Canton, gained his U.S. citizenship along with other Chinese servicemen in the mass naturalizations of the war.[17] Desperately needed at the Army Map Service, Cecile was granted U.S. citizenship by an act of Congress, making her at long last a citizen of the country that one of her ancestors had fought to establish in 1776.[18]

Cecile had made her life between exclusion and inclusion, between the laws of a country that had prohibited her naturalization and the steadfast love of her Watkins grandparents. Had Nellie Thornton made a "mistake" when she returned Cecile as "white" that January day in 1920? The only other choice, to return Cecile as "Chinese," would not have been more accurate. Yet such were the only options available in the monoracial enumeration system that helped to uphold the fiction of the color line, rendering Eurasians invisible as a statistical class and obscuring the history of racial mixing.

CHAPTER 8

"No Gulf between a Chan and a Smith amongst Us"

Charles Graham Anderson's Manifesto for
Eurasian Unity in Interwar Hong Kong

On December 23, 1929, a meeting of prominent Eurasians was convened in Hong Kong. Prompted by a spontaneous donation of $10,000 by an anonymous Eurasian donor—possibly Sir Robert Ho Tung—they were joined together by a common purpose: to discuss the establishment of an association to take charge of the welfare needs of Eurasian families in the colony. Yet, something greater than relief of the destitute was at stake. Invited by the chair to take the stage, C. G. Anderson, a man whose oratorical prowess was well known to his friends, delivered a rousing address in which he declared:

> We Eurasians, being born into this world, belong to it. We claim no privileges but we demand our rights for which we must contest to the last ditch. With the blood of Old China mixed with that of Europe in us, we show the world that in this fusion, to put it no higher, is not detrimental to good citizenship. . . . In this part of China, we are a force to be reckoned with, a force to be respected and a force to be better appreciated when it is shown that we can look after, not only ourselves, but also the destitute of our kith and kin.[19]

As Anderson's speech makes clear, the founding of the Welfare League (*Tongren hui*), which had its genesis in the meeting that night, was motivated not simply by philanthropic intentions but also by the aspiration for Eurasian rights and human dignity. As such, it can be regarded as part of a movement that was taking place among Eurasian groups across Asia during the interwar years. Like other Eurasian organizations that were founded during this time, the Welfare League represented a significant effort to demonstrate that Eurasians were not a "problem" awaiting colonial or missionary intervention but could be part of their own constructive solution.

The founding of the Welfare League was a watershed event in the institutionalization of Eurasian identity in pre–World War II Hong Kong. Eurasians had long been active in leading Chinese philanthropic and social organizations in the colony, everything from the Tung Wah Hospital to the Chinese Recreation Club. But this was the first time in Hong Kong history that Eurasians had formally organized an association *of* their own, *for* their own—despite the fact that there had been calls to do so since at least 1895. The formation of such an organization depended on a critical mass of Eurasians within the local population, but just as important it also required acceptance of the *idea* of a "Eurasian community" as a distinct communal group. Hence, the heart of Anderson's historic speech was a call for Eurasian unity.

What was to be the basis for this unity? On what terms did Anderson attempt to claim a particular Eurasian identity? The task of Eurasian unity in an era when "half-caste" status was still stigmatized was in fact no easy one. Campaigners like Cedric Dover and Kenneth Wallace faced insurmountable challenges in India, with its larger and more established mixed community.[20] In Hong Kong, where Eurasians were not officially recognized as a communal group, the Welfare League had to contend not only with this virtual administrative invisibility, but also with the fact that many of the "leading" Eurasians publicly claimed Chinese identity, as we saw from the previous chapter. Given these challenges, the formation of the Welfare League and its continuing existence until this day cannot be taken for granted, and suggests instead the successful institution of a sense of collective identity among its members—one that has survived the postwar diaspora of its core constituency.

As a founding member of the Welfare League and the orator tasked with inspiring his community to action, C. G. Anderson played a key role in generating this sense of collective identity. In order to understand the terms within which Anderson attempted to mobilize a unified Eurasian identity, this chapter examines the inaugural address he delivered on the evening of December 23, 1929, which I read as an act of self-representation and a gesture toward self-determination. Reading Anderson's address in conjunction with the memoirs of other Welfare League members, including Anderson's own daughter, Joyce Anderson Symons, I place his historic speech within the context of important social and political changes taking place in Hong Kong during the interwar era. I argue that the formation of the Welfare League can be viewed as part of an ethnic shift that emerged during these years among Hong Kong Eurasians. An examination of this shift confirms Melissa Brown's contention that sociopolitical experience, and not ancestry or shared culture, is the most important factor in constituting ethnic groups, and that ethnic identity can have a different basis locally than it does at the level of the larger society.[21]

Before examining C. G. Anderson's manifesto, I first present a biographical sketch of his family to illustrate the complex sociopolitical experiences that shaped elite Eurasian identity in Hong Kong during this era. I show that this group faced both particular conditions of social mobility and a set of racialized constraints. The founding of the Welfare League represented one strategy for negotiating the paradoxical position of privilege and denigration, inclusion and exclusion, that the Eurasian bourgeoisie occupied in prewar Hong Kong.

THE ANDERSON FAMILY: EURASIAN UPWARD MOBILITY AND THE GLASS CEILING

Charles Graham ("Carl") Anderson (1889–1949) was born in Hong Kong, the fifth son of thirteen children born to Eurasians Hung Kam Ning (also known as Henry Graham Anderson, ca. 1862–1919) and Chan Lai Kau/Mary Mackenzie (1861–1941). Hung Kam Ning was the son of a Scotsman, most likely John Graham Anderson.[22] Hung Kam Ning and his brother Hung Kam Shing (ca. 1858–1907) were both interpreters for the Hong Kong colonial government, a key avenue of professional mobility for Chinese on the China Coast. Their success, along with others of their generation, set the foundation for the emergence of a Eurasian elite in Hong Kong, and hence it is worth understanding the path they trod to upward mobility.

The Hung brothers were prize-winning students at Government Central School, Hung Kam Shing enrolling in the same year (1873) as Ho Tung.[23] Here they received the bilingual instruction that proved the first crucial step in their upward mobility. As Carl Smith has demonstrated, English-language schools were the first "rung on the ladder to elite status" for Hong Kong Chinese in the nineteenth century.[24] According to Smith's research, by the late 1800s, Government Central School (founded 1862; name changed to Queen's College in 1894) and the Diocesan Boys' School[25] (DBS, founded 1869) had become the leading institutions for training Hong Kong's Anglophone Chinese elite.[26] Many famous Eurasians, such as the Ho brothers, Sin Tak-fan, Wong Kam-fuk (1870–1931), and others linked to them by intermarriage, attended Central/Queen's. Among the latter was the uncle of Carl Anderson, Chan Hong Key (1855–1942).[27] In this fashion emerged a group of Eurasians linked by kinship and/or school ties.

The bilingual training offered by these schools opened up several main avenues of employment: Hong Kong government service (usually as a clerk or interpreter); employment in a European trading firm, leading to the position of compradore; and the Chinese Imperial Customs Service. As Smith has noted, these positions all held open the possibility of wealth and power.[28] Whereas Ho Tung's path after Central, as we have seen, took him through the Chinese Customs Service to the compradoreship at Jardine's, the Hung brothers followed instead the route of Hong Kong government service.[29] In 1887, Hung Kam Shing and Hung Kam Ning were appointed first and second Chinese interpreter at the Supreme Court, respectively. When Hung Kam Shing resigned in 1892, he was replaced by Hung Kam Ning.[30]

Interpreters played a vital role in colonial Hong Kong, where all legal matters were transacted in English.[31] The early involvement of Eurasians like the Hung brothers as court interpreters set the foundation for later Eurasian connections with the legal profession in Hong Kong. Sin Tak-fan was another famous Eurasian who made his start as an interpreter, entering government service as a Chinese clerk and interpreter at the Registrar General's Department in 1878, before rising to prominent positions in prestigious British private legal firms.[32] Hung Kam Ning's grandson, Donald Anderson, would become the first Eurasian barrister at the Hong Kong Supreme Court, and subsequently, the first local magistrate.[33]

As interpreters, the Hungs entered into the role of intermediary between the British colonial administration and the Chinese populace, a role for which the British believed "half-castes" were uniquely suited. As elsewhere in the empire, the British maintained a contradictory attitude toward "half-castes," denigrating their racial "impurity" on one hand, while simultaneously considering them more trustworthy, loyal, and capable than the "natives" on the other.[34] By the late nineteenth century, the British administration had come to rely on educated and bilingual Eurasians, with their connections to the Chinese community, as valuable intermediaries. In searching for Western-educated Chinese to serve in various positions as representatives of the Chinese community, the British frequently set their sights upon Eurasians as the most "qualified" and "responsible."[35] Hence, the particular success of Eurasians in Hong Kong was enabled by many of the distinct features of colonial society, even as it manifested the "tension of empire" (see introduction).

In intermediate positions, some Eurasians came to enjoy a degree of colonial privilege—being paid more than Chinese in European firms, for example. But this privilege was more than balanced by the discrimination meted out against those not "of pure European descent," as many Eurasians have recalled with bitterness in their memoirs. Thus, despite the particular channels for mobility open to educated Eurasians, this mobility was also limited by the color bar. Until World War II, positions for the senior civil service, for example, were reserved for expatriate British of "pure European descent."[36]

Queen's College had been critical to the success of the Hung brothers, and they sent their sons to the school in turn. While at Queen's, Carl Anderson went by the name of Hung Iu-chi, and his brothers by Hung Iu-fan and Hung Iu-kwong. His cousins, the sons of Hung Kam Shing, were Hung Kwok-leung (1880–1940, Joseph Overbeck Anderson), Hung Kwok-chi (1890–1935, Charles Graham Overbeck Anderson), and Hung Kwok-wah (William Graham Anderson). The second generation enjoyed notable academic success, with Hung Kwok-leung/Joseph Anderson being among the first graduates to be sent (in 1903) to the United Kingdom for further studies. Studying law at the prestigious Lincoln's Inn, he went on to Shanghai, where he became a member of the Mixed Court, then later a legal and political adviser to the mayor of Shanghai.[37] He eventually moved to Beijing and became a judge at the Chinese Supreme Court.[38] Hung Kwok-chi/Charles Graham Overbeck Anderson was a school tennis champion who attended Cambridge University and became a lawyer in Shanghai. He later worked for the British Consulate there. Hung Iu-chi won several prestigious scholarships and an appointment to the Hong Kong Land Court in 1906. Hung Iu-kwong entered the Tangshan Mining and Engineering College in north China that same year.[39] Thus the second generation enjoyed expanded educational and professional opportunities that had not been available to their fathers.

While at Queen's, the Hung boys were considered Chinese. The possession of a Chinese social identity had important educational consequences; beginning in 1893 the Upper School established separate classes for its non-Chinese pupils, who were exempted from the Chinese curriculum. Anxious to avoid "the problems that might otherwise have arisen in the case of the numerous Eurasian students," the school divided students solely on the basis of dress—with those in Chinese dress classed as Chinese, and those in European classed as non-Chinese.[40] The division provided incentive for Eurasians to adopt a Chinese social identity in order to receive the bilingual training that was advantageous in career terms. The Hung boys apparently wore Chinese gowns, and possibly the queue before 1911.[41] They nonetheless excelled at British sports, with Hung Kwok-leung named the first Chinese captain of the Cricket Eleven in 1902. Carl was known as an avid cricketer and tennis player, and he remained a keen sportsman throughout his life.[42]

At some point, however, the Hung family joined the untold numbers of Hong Kong Eurasians who practiced "name changing." In some cases, this change was from a European to a Chinese name; in other cases, the change was the reverse. After his retirement from government service in 1896, Hung Kam Ning began to use the name Henry Graham Anderson, and other family members later followed suit.[43] Why the name change? Was it because Anderson, in his private life, was no longer compelled to play the public role of a "Chinese representative" for the British government? Did he begin to think that his children, some of whom were redheaded, could enjoy better status as Europeans? Was it motivated by his move to Shanghai, where he died in 1919—his English (but not Chinese) name recorded on the register of British National Overseas deaths?[44] I return to the phenomenon of name changing later; suffice it to say for now that the change marked a shift in the Hung/Anderson family's identity, but one that was far from straightforward.

In 1910, Carl married Lucy Eleanor Perry (1892–1979), the daughter of Annie Overbeck and Edward Lionel Perry, who was descended on his father's side from an American named Perry.[45] Born and raised in Macao by a strict family, Lucy was tutored at home in Chinese but was forbidden to learn English. The couple had an elaborate Chinese-style wedding in Macao, and then moved to Shanghai where other members of the extended Anderson family were living.[46] With this union, and the marriage of Carl's sister Catherine/Hung Wan Chi (1885–1964, see fig. 15) to Ho Tung's adopted son Ho Sai-Wing (1883–1946), the Anderson/Hung family was drawn even more closely into the complex Eurasian "web" linking them to others like the Chan/Mackenzie, Gittins, Greaves, Hall/Sinn, Ho, Overbeck, and Paterson/Tai Yuk Ching families.[47]

In Shanghai, the Andersons enjoyed a time of family prosperity. Carl soon found work as a stockbroker and moved his family to a grand home with a spacious garden and tennis courts in a western suburb just beyond the French Concession. With his cousins employed in influential positions, Carl enjoyed an active sporting and social life. While emulating the Shanghai expatriate lifestyle, he was also infected by the enthusiasm of young intellectuals who were dedicated to building a New China and became passionately involved in political discussions of Sun Yat-sen's socialist ideals. By all accounts, the Shanghai years were good ones.[48]

Not long after the birth of their third child, Catherine Joyce, in August 1918, the family fell on hard times and decided to move back to Hong Kong. As Joyce recalled in her memoir, the family immediately noticed the difference between Shanghai and Hong Kong "so far as the status of Eurasians was concerned."[49] According to Joyce, in cosmopolitan Shanghai, Eurasians were considered one among many groups of "non-Chinese." In contrast, Joyce asserted, "in Hong Kong throughout the colonial period, people were either expatriates or Chinese—no one mentioned Eurasians."[50] This silence, a product of the British attempt to maintain the fiction that the color line in Hong Kong was firmly upheld, effectively subjected them to erasure. Returning to Hong Kong, Carl found this difference a painful shock, which gradually led to an identity crisis.

In her memoir, Joyce recalled how her father became increasingly unhappy during this time. As Joyce wrote, "Father missed the vitality of his Shanghai life-style, which had regularly included political discussions with radical young friends, inspired by Sun Yat-sen. Father often remembered those ardent socialists who were often found at our house, arguing and enthusing many long hours about socialism and the new world order."[51] Carl also grew bitter about the exclusiveness of Hong Kong expatriate society, a resentment sharpened by the downward mobility he experienced. Joyce remembered how her father grew to intensely "dislike and disapprove of the expatriate foreigners and started to accentuate his Chinese heritage."[52] This led to a growing estrangement from his wife as he began to spend more and more time at the Chinese Club. As Joyce wrote, "As he grew older he looked increasingly Chinese in his appearance, while Mother, on the other hand, was drawn to the West."[53] Whereas Carl found comradeship at the Chinese Club, Lucy sought solace at St. Peter's Church, an Anglican church with a large congregation of Eurasians.

Family life stabilized somewhat after Carl's business prospects improved, and he became manager of the French Insurance Company and the International Saving Society while also working as a newspaper reporter.[54] His heart, however, was not in business but in politics. Joyce recalled that a high point in her father's life was his involvement with the Anti-Mui Tsai Society, where he gained recognition for his leadership role.[55] The society was founded in 1921, initially by a group of Chinese Christians, to campaign for an end to the practice of buying young girls as servants, or "Mui Tsai."[56] The campaign attracted much public attention and signaled a new confrontational turn in social activism.[57] With a reputation for leadership and oratorical prowess thus established, it is no wonder that Carl was invited to address the group of Eurasians that gathered on the evening of December 23, 1929.

C. G. ANDERSON'S INAUGURAL ADDRESS: A MANIFESTO FOR EURASIAN UNITY

Although the primary purpose of Anderson's speech was to convince the group to establish a charitable organization for "the provision of succour and relief to Eurasians," Anderson turned his address to a stirring appeal for Eurasian unity. For Anderson, Eurasian unity was imperative not only for the sake of providing organized welfare relief, but more important, for Eurasians to prove their detractors wrong. Hence, Anderson's plea for Eurasian unity was also a plea for Eurasian rights, which he urged his audience to "contest to the last ditch."[58]

In calling for unity, Anderson invoked a notional "Eurasian community," drawing on the British colonial conception of communal groups. Yet, the existence of such a community cannot be taken for granted, because Eurasians were not an officially recognized communal group, being generally subsumed under the category of Chinese.

A central argument of this chapter is that there was a wide gap between external and internal perceptions of the Eurasian community in Hong Kong, a gap that Anderson sought to close by contesting colonial representations of Eurasians as a "dangerous element" "left on the dunghill of neglect" or as degenerate hybrid offspring.[59] Instead, Anderson described Eurasians as a "numerically small community," but one with great achievements, having produced "business magnates like Sir Robert [Ho Tung], large-hearted philanthropists like Mr. Wong Kam-fuk, brilliant men of affairs like Dr. [Robert] Kotewall and ornaments of the learned professions like Mr. [Man Kam] Lo."[60] Anderson further described the community as "a community with a moral conscience," one dedicated to philanthropic activity in the colony. Highlighting Eurasian achievements and their vital contributions to the development of Hong Kong, Anderson emphasized not Eurasian marginality but rather their centrality to the colony; not the potential danger they posed, but their contributions to colonial stability. Thus, Anderson argued, Hong Kong Eurasians had proved to the world "that in this fusion [of European and Chinese], to put it no higher, is not detrimental to good citizenship."[61] This underlying sense of pride in Eurasian achievements and contributions served as a foundation for the unified Eurasian identity that Anderson sought to build.

As Stevan Harrell and Melissa Brown have demonstrated, governments or ethnic leaders frequently attempt to portray ethnic identities as fixed and natural in order to bolster their agendas, typically asserting claims to ethnic identity based on purported common culture and/or common descent.[62] In sharp contrast, in mobilizing a unified Eurasian community, Anderson notably invoked neither a shared culture, nor shared origins, in the conventional sense, as a basis for this identity. Indeed, Anderson and the other leaders of the Welfare League understood well enough that Eurasian unity would have to be constructed in the face of cultural and religious diversity as well as a diversity of origins.

In the absence of such primordial claims, we might expect Anderson to have relied on shared interest as the basis for Eurasian unity. Instead, he invoked metaphors of kinship—"brethren" and "kith and kin"—and a notional common "extraction." When Anderson refers to Eurasians as "those of our extraction," he suggests a biological basis for Eurasianness, asking his audience to imagine a community bound together not by common origins or ancestry in a literal sense, but rather by the shared experience of mixed origins.[63] Instead of *shared blood*, or the myth of shared descent from the Yellow Emperor, which we saw from the previous chapter, was invoked as a basis for Han Chinese imagined community, Anderson portrays Eurasians as a group united by the common condition of *mixed blood*: a community "with the blood of Old China mixed with that of Europe in us."[64] Anderson thus invokes the social concept of blood, rather than shared culture, as the force that binds the community together.

Hence, even as Anderson attempted to reclaim racial hybridity from its strong associations with degeneration and the conflict of "warring blood," he did not do so by denying the biological basis of "mixed race" (see chapter 5), but by portraying this fusion as a harmonious unification of opposites. Steering clear of eugenic arguments and the notion of hybrid vigor, Anderson invokes blood primarily as a metaphor for cultural inheritance, casting the Eurasian as the embodiment of the positive fusion of Old China and Europe, bridging East and West, tradition and modernity.

Through this embodiment of the "best of both worlds," Eurasians could lay claim to a unique historical role, Anderson proclaimed, as harbingers of international peace. "If 'Peace on Earth and Goodwill towards Men' is not to be mere gibberish," Anderson continued, "then the Eurasians within the seven seas are some of the people sent into this world to assist in the accomplishment of this ideal."[65] Transcending the particularities of race and nation, Eurasians should, Anderson exhorted, claim a belonging to the world at large: "We Eurasians," Anderson told his gathered comrades, "being born into this world, belong to it."[66] This claim upon the world, he emphasized, was not a claim for privileges, but a demand for equal rights.

Hence Anderson's manifesto reminds Eurasians that they bear a special burden of proving themselves against their detractors. "Gentlemen," Anderson declared to his audience, "it has been said of us that we can have no unity, and . . . [this] is a challenge to be faced and an insult to be wiped out."[67] Without unity, Eurasians could gain no recognition as a distinct communal group, and therefore no basis on which to contest their marginality between the dominant groups. As we saw in the previous chapter, within the context of colonial Hong Kong, elite Eurasians like Ho Tung attempted to improve their status by claiming membership in the Chinese community. As one of Ho Tung's daughters recalled, despite Chinese residents' second-class status in the colony, this was nonetheless better than being "half-caste."[68] The claim of a Eurasian community as a distinct group of its own, with its own coherent "unity," while paradoxically acknowledging the "mixed" origins for which Eurasians were stigmatized, would at least serve as a basis for their demands for communal recognition and rights.

Anderson's repeated calls for Eurasian unity and brotherhood were intended both to transcend the division between rich and poor within the notional Eurasian community and to bridge the divide between those with Chinese surnames and those with European. As he proclaimed, "Our detractors little know . . . that, after all, there is no gulf between a Chan and a Smith amongst us and that underlying the superficial differences in names and outlook, the spirit of kinship and brotherhood burns brightly."[69] What did it mean, in a context in which the gulf between Europeans and Chinese was vast indeed, and where names served as important ethnic markers, for Anderson to contest the significance of such a divide?

THE PUZZLE OF EURASIAN NAMES

Anderson's assertion that "there is no gulf between a Chan and a Smith amongst us" flies in the face of the notion that there was an easy distinction between Chinese Eurasians and British Eurasians. As we saw in the previous chapter, C. G. Alabaster in his report to the *Eugenics Review* asserted that Hong Kong Eurasians could be easily categorized into three distinct groups—the Portuguese, the Chinese, and the British—with surnames, and not blood quantum, providing the key to this classification system. Contemporary historians have often echoed the view that Eurasians were divided based on surnames. Carl Smith, for example, distinguished two groups of Eurasians based on surname usage, correlating this distinction with class: Eurasians bearing English surnames, he argued, were usually the offspring of "foreigners with a low social status" who often remained in the colony, while those bearing Chinese surnames were usually the children of higher-status Euro-Americans, who did not remain permanently.[70]

Yet Alabaster lamented that this easy distinction had begun to break down after 1911, leading to the emergence of a "Eurasian problem." Alabaster complained that the increasingly ambiguous identity of Hong Kong Eurasians had blurred the boundaries between groups and suggested that the Hong Kong legislature ought perhaps to pass anti-miscegenation or blood quantum laws to clarify the lines.[71] Alabaster's evident irritation on this point indicates that the tendency to create rules for demarcating different "types" of Eurasians stems from a desire to instill order, to make sense of the ambiguity created by border-crossing Eurasians and definitively decree them "one race or another." Yet these rules cannot account for the complexity of Eurasian sociopolitical experiences.

In place of rules, I argue, we can gain insights from examining the actual usage of names among some of the prominent Eurasian families in Hong Kong. As discussed in the previous chapter, during the early years of the colony, when there was little choice but to be European or Chinese, most Eurasians elected to assume a Chinese social identity because they suffered less ostracism that way. One cannot be Han Chinese without a Han surname. Thus *Bosman* became *Ho*; *Rothwell* and *Roberts* became *Lo*; *Hall* became *Sin*; and *Tyson*, upon the advice of a fortuneteller, became *Chan*.[72] While the adoption of a Chinese name was the dominant pattern, some families did use European names publicly. As Eric Peter Ho recalls, "Every family followed its own instinct for survival. However, even here they would also be known by a Chinese name among their Chinese friends."[73] This resulted in many families using two names: the Zimmerns, for example, were known to their friends as Shi.[74]

Although many Eurasian families have maintained their Chinese names until this day, some families gradually began to use Western names. If there were strong incentives to use a Chinese name in the early years of British rule, there were multiple reasons for adopting a European or Anglicized name. Travel or study abroad was one. Even Ho Tung, the self-styled Chinese patriarch, used the name H. T. Bosman when he traveled to New York.[75] Others sought to take advantage of career or business opportunities that were opening up as the environment changed.[76] Those who worked for European firms also found they could receive higher pay than the Chinese. For the older generation, success was found through the professions of compradore or interpreter, where Chinese affiliations and networks were valued, but many in the British-educated younger generation chose other professional routes—physician, architect, engineer, stockbroker, accountant, lawyer—in which Western training and certification were valued.[77] A European name may have enhanced one's professional mobility. Some individuals changed their names in order to pass for white. Finally, the rise of Chinese racial nationalism, which became especially pronounced after 1911, led some to question the authenticity of Eurasians as Chinese and their right to serve as representatives of the Chinese, no doubt prompting more than a few to change their names.[78]

Thus, the notion of clear and easily legible lines of demarcation between Chinese Eurasians and British Eurasians based on surnames gives way to the complexity of Eurasian historical experiences in Hong Kong. These lines were, rather, fluid and situational. The choice of names, like dress, could be part of a familial or individual strategy of survival and social mobility. The notion that name changes could be strategic, and not necessarily ideological or indicative of an ethnic shift, is confirmed by the fact that some Eurasians changed to Chinese names during World War II in order to avoid volunteer service with the British, while many more changed during the Japanese occupation in order to avoid being interned as British.[79] The practice of name changing made Eurasians vulnerable to accusations of opportunism—though they were hardly alone in the practice of adopting new names.[80]

When Anderson dismissed the differences between Chan and Smith as superficial, he suggested a distinction between insider and outsider understandings of Eurasian identity, between the "community" and its "detractors" who "little knew" the reality. Given his own family history, Anderson knew all too well that the Eurasian with a Chinese surname and the Eurasian with a Western surname could be part of a single family unit, or even, as with Hung Kam Ning/Henry Graham Anderson, one and the same person. In short, while Eurasians utilized surnames as ethnic markers, surnames in and of themselves did not divide the Eurasian community into distinct ethnic groups. Instead, "the web" of Eurasian kinship networks connected Chinese-surnamed and Western-surnamed Eurasians, Buddhists, and Christians, whatever ideological differences may have existed among them.[81]

C. G. Anderson's historic speech called upon Eurasians to recognize their underlying kinship, whether actual or "spiritual." For Anderson, the differences in names and "outlook" were outweighed by the commonality of Eurasianness. Indeed, if we examine the roster of names of the founders of the Welfare League, the diversity is evident. The names include: Lo Cheung-shiu, Hung Tsze-leung, Henry Gittins, Ho Leung, S. M. Churn, W. H. Peters, J. L. Litton, J. D. Bush, J. Kotwall, A. E. Perry, M. K. Lo, Fung Tsok-lam, J. McKenzie, J. F. Grose, Wong Tak-kwong, Ed Law, P. Abesser, J. F. Shea, H. K. Hung, and C. G. Anderson, among others.[82] Thus, despite possessing names that served as outward markers of European, Chinese, or even Parsi identity, the participants in the Welfare League perceived a common interest that drew them together to form an organized society on behalf of their "community."[83]

In place of the divide between Chan and Smith, Anderson asserted instead a unitary Eurasianness, called up through the words *We Eurasians*. This simple utterance was in fact profoundly significant, because Anderson was calling on his "brethren" to embrace the label *Eurasian*, often regarded as a "dirty word." In calling for unity under the banner of "We Eurasians," Anderson urged his audience to acknowledge their mixed origins openly, and perhaps even with pride—no short order in a time when many Eurasians treated their origins as a "family secret," as Eric Peter Ho recalled.[84]

Anderson also provided Eurasians with a purpose for uniting: on the face of it, this purpose was charity. But charity, for Anderson, was ultimately linked to rights. As he forcefully proclaimed, "In this part of China, we are a force to be reckoned with, a force to be respected and a force to be better appreciated when it is shown that we can look after, not only ourselves, but also the destitute of our kith and kin."[85] Thus, Anderson asserted a direct link between responsibility and rights, representing charitable work as a vehicle through which Eurasians could gain respect and social standing as a communal group within the colony, and South China as a whole.

RIGHTS AND RESPONSIBILITIES: EURASIANS AND
HONG KONG SOCIAL ORGANIZATIONS

Indeed, as Anderson noted in his speech, Eurasians had participated widely in the colony's philanthropic activities—though they did so *qua* Chinese. From the start, Eurasians had been active in the three leading charitable and voluntary organizations that served vital functions in Hong Kong colonial society and furthermore came to represent the "voice" of the Chinese community: the Tung Wah Hospital, the District Watch Force, and the Society for the Protection of Women and Children.[86] Essentially modeled on traditional Chinese gentry organizations, these institutions, as John Carroll has written, "helped establish Chinese merchants as the Chinese gentry of a British colony."[87] As such, membership in these organizations became important markers of class status in colonial Hong Kong.

Eurasians also took a leading role in founding important organizations such as the Chinese Chamber of Commerce (1896), the Chinese Club (1899), and the Chinese Recreation Club (1912), which had been formed in response to racial segregation at exclusive clubs like the Hong Kong Club.[88] As Carroll demonstrates, these associations were fundamentally different from the Tung Wah Hospital and the District Watch Force in that they no longer sought confirmation from the Chinese government for fulfilling traditional gentry functions. Instead, they were a new type of organization based on Western colonial models and "offer[ed] affluent Chinese a new way to flaunt their status and wealth."[89] Carroll argues that the formation of these institutions demonstrated that the Chinese bourgeoisie in Hong Kong was neither willing to passively accept racial discrimination nor willing to overtly challenge it: hence, they created their own separate and parallel world. Eurasians were not only active in the establishment of these various organizations, but also well represented in the leadership, helping to consolidate their status as members of the Chinese community.[90]

In contrast to both types of institution, I argue that the move to found the Welfare League represented something altogether different— the first time that Eurasians in Hong Kong had come together to form a formal association *qua* Eurasians on behalf of Eurasians as a distinct communal group. The need for such an association had been felt as early as 1895, when an anonymous Eurasian reader sent a letter to the *Hong Kong Telegraph* protesting the immorality of European men who abandoned their protected women and children in the colony.[91] The letter writer called for the establishment of a welfare organization for these women and children. He also issued a plea for wealthy Eurasian patrons to build a nonsectarian temple that Eurasians could use for worship and as an ancestral hall.[92]

Although nothing seems to have come from this letter, the founding of the Chiu Yuen Cemetery for Eurasians in 1897 did at least meet the need for a place to carry out ancestor worship. The cemetery's founding can be regarded as an important precursor to the Welfare League because it reflected an incipient sense of communal identity among Hong Kong Eurasians, and also the realization that they could not rely on the government to provide for their needs.[93] The desire for such a cemetery arose from the fact that the colonial government had provided burial grounds for Europeans (separate for Protestant and Roman Catholic) as well as for the colony's other minority groups—the Parsis, Muslims, and Jews—but had done nothing for the Eurasians. In 1896, after burying their mother at the Chinese cemetery at Mount Davis, Ho Tung and Ho Fook as justices of the peace applied to the governor for a grant of land around the vicinity of her grave (where other Eurasians had already been buried) as a Eurasian cemetery. With Ho Tong and Ho Fook named trustees, a Eurasian cemetery was officially authorized at Mount Davis in 1897.[94] As families over the years buried their dead at Chiu Yuen, gathering regularly to perform ancestor worship, a sense of communal identity—distinct from the British and distinct from the Chinese—was produced and reinforced.

THE FORMATION OF COMMUNAL IDENTITY

The founding of the Eurasian cemetery points to the emergence of an incipient sense of communal identity already in the 1890s, even as much of the community publicly identified as Chinese. The context within which this took place is crucial. Although Eurasian identity can be viewed as a product of racism, a response to the discovery, in Eric Peter Ho's words, that one is "somehow different," as we have seen in previous chapters, this consciousness did not always lead to the formation of a communal identity.[95] Instead, we must take into account factors of time and place and the size of the population. In Hong Kong, the long-standing practice of endogamous marriage among China Coast Eurasians, which complexly interlinked families, helped to produce a sense of belonging to a distinct community. [96] This endogamous "web" was further strengthened by the shared business networks among Eurasians who worked for European trading firms and in the Chinese Customs Service (see fig. 10, chapter 4). Eurasians were also connected by the strong alumni networks of Central/Queen's College and the Diocesan Boys' and Girls' Schools (DBS and DGS). Indeed, many of the founders of the Welfare League were Central/Queen's "Old Boys"— Robert Ho Tung, Robert Kotewall, M.K. Lo, C.G. Anderson, and J.F. Grose, to name only a few.

But why the long gap between the founding of the Eurasian cemetery in 1897 and the historic meeting on the evening of December 23, 1929? According to Anderson, the economic downturn of the 1920s prompted the formation of the league.[97] But other factors may have contributed. The interwar years were a time of burgeoning social activism and anticolonial movements throughout the colonial world. In Hong Kong, anti-British sentiment had been growing among the Chinese population since the Chinese Revolution of 1911, which had given rise to a strong current of Chinese nationalism. A series of anti-British protests, most famously the 1922 seamen's strike and the general strike and boycott of 1925–26, rocked Hong Kong during the 1920s. Although Hong Kong never developed a serious anticolonial movement, racial discrimination was coming under fire. Anderson's exhortation that Eurasians should "demand [their] rights" and contest them "to the last ditch" accorded with anticolonial rhetoric and demands for inclusion that were spreading throughout the empire.

THE ETHNIC SHIFT

The timing of the league's founding can also be correlated with an ethnic shift that was emerging within Hong Kong's Eurasian community. If I have argued that the practice of adopting European names alone is not indicative of an ethnic shift among Hong Kong Eurasians, other sources, for example, the Hong Kong census, provide additional evidence. Eurasians were perennially undercounted in the Hong Kong censuses. The census nonetheless provides vital information concerning changes in the way that the administration classified mixed-race peoples, as well as trends in the ways in which Eurasians identified themselves to the enumerators.[98]

From the start, the census did not adopt a uniform approach to enumerating the racial composition of the colony, and there was frequent confusion between the terms *race* and *nationality*. Like the annual enumeration of births and deaths, the census was always primarily concerned with documenting the relative sizes of the Chinese and European populations, and the approach to populations classed as "other" changed over time. "Eurasian" appeared for the first time as a distinct category in an interim census of 1897, though the registrar general lamented, "The return of the number of Eurasians is distinctly unsatisfactory. I am afraid that the arrangements made were not such as to ensure getting the correct number. It is quite evident that the 272 who have entered themselves as such in the census schedules form a very small portion of the Eurasian community. No doubt the large majority are included among the Chinese. In the Settlement of Singapore the Eurasians in 1891 numbered 3589."[99] In his report, the registrar general classed Eurasians among "races other than European, American and Chinese." When the census was conducted in 1901, the registrar general again expressed concern over the undercount of Eurasians: "The number was ascertained to be 267. This is five less than in 1897. The large majority of Eurasians . . . live in Chinese fashion, and would certainly return themselves as Chinese. Those who have called themselves Eurasians in this Census probably only represent the small majority who have been brought up as Eurasians. . . . The Chinese consider the term one of reproach. If enumerators were instructed to find out the numbers of Eurasians themselves, it is obvious that this would inevitably lead to abuses, and present great opportunities for the exercise of private spite."[100]

By 1911, when a paltry forty-two residents returned themselves as "Eurasian," the registrar general despaired that "the number of persons who return themselves as Eurasians gets fewer every census." The census report discussed Eurasians (along with Portuguese, Japanese, and Filipinos) as a subcategory of "Non-Chinese Races" but distinct from "British, European and American." However, in the race tables, both Portuguese and Eurasians were listed on the table for "European and American," with "Eurasian" singled out at the very bottom of the table.

Unfortunately for our purposes, in 1921 census officials decided *not* to ask questions concerning birthplace and race for the non-Chinese population, as had been done on the previous census, but only for birthplace and nationality.[101] Hence, "Eurasians" disappeared once more from the census entirely. They were back with a vengeance, however, in

1931, when the colonial administration restored the race question, arguing that "race is of much more importance in some respects than nationality."[102] To cover all bases, the 1931 census asked for birthplace, race, and nationality.[103] This time, the number of people returned "Eurasian" jumped to 835 persons, though census officials still expressed concern that Eurasians were largely undercounted. The largest age cohort was the "early adult life" (ages 21–44) cohort, which showed 250 persons. In sharp contrast the age 65 and over cohort showed only three persons.[104]

The perennial undercounting of the Eurasian population suggests the stigma associated with this label and a lack of incentives for individuals to claim this identity. The census further demonstrates how British colonial racial hierarchies and practices of racial classification tended to render the mixed population invisible. At the same time, the census also makes evident that although Hong Kong's color line was drawn between the two dominant groups of "Chinese" and "Europeans and Americans," there were also officially recognized groups of "others," including "local Portuguese," Indians, and Japanese, who fell outside these categories. Individuals returned "Eurasian" were counted as members of the "non-Chinese" community but were consciously marked off from the "European and American" category and classed among the colony's ethnic Others.[105] From the perspective of the colonial administration, to claim Eurasianness was to claim a non-Chinese identity. But, as evidenced by Eurasian memoirs such as examined in the previous chapter, this is not necessarily how Eurasians perceived themselves.

Although inconsistencies in the census make longitudinal comparisons difficult, the figures indicate that by 1931, roughly correlating with the founding of the Welfare League, there had emerged a significant number of people in Anderson's age cohort identified as Eurasian for such official and public purposes as the census. This was the age cohort that served as the driving force and energy behind the league, even as senior members of the community like Ho Tung and Robert Kotewall were named to the top positions.

This ethnic shift that I have suggested was prompted by a complex convergence of social changes during these years. First was the rise of Chinese nationalism, which proved a double-edged sword for Hong Kong Eurasians. Like other Chinese in the colony, Chinese-identified Eurasians were inspired by a sense of nationalism and mounting antagonism against the racial hierarchy underpinning the colonial status quo. At the same time, however, the rise of Chinese nationalism, and the rhetoric of racial purity that accompanied it, led to mounting hostility against Eurasians (especially those with European fathers) as the spawn of "foreign devils," "tainted" by the pollution of foreign blood. Alabaster reported that the growth of Chinese racial nationalism during this time gradually led many Hong Kong Chinese to form "the idea that the Eurasian Chinese should no longer be classed as Chinese, or at any rate as the leaders of the Chinese community and the exponents to the British of Chinese thought and sentiment."[106]

In addition, the revolution led to the removal of several important ethnic markers—the queue, in particular—that had previously enabled Eurasians to claim Chineseness, in some cases despite a markedly "foreign" phenotype. As Qing Dynasty garb was discarded, and more and more Chinese adopted Western-style clothing, the "simple solution" that Queen's College had once employed to distinguish Chinese from non-Chinese pupils was no longer tenable. Although these changes affected the Chinese community as a whole, in the case of Eurasians the removal of important ethnic markers of Chineseness may have prompted an ethnic shift. As Melissa Brown has argued in the case of Taiwan, evidence demonstrates that Plains Aborigines became Han Chinese after Japanese colonial authorities banned footbinding, effectively removing the last remaining major boundary marker between the two groups.[107] Similarly, for China Coast Eurasians, the abolition of the queue may have marked a turning point in their identification. For some Eurasians, as we saw from the previous chapter, this resulted in increased pressure to perform their Chineseness. For others, perhaps especially the redheaded members of the Anderson family, a growing sense that they could not be fully accepted as Chinese may have prompted them to claim their Eurasianness instead.

C.G. Anderson's daughter Joyce described the cultural aspects of this ethnic shift in her memoir. As Joyce wrote, "The typical Eurasian life-style, food, and, certainly female dress, were mainly Chinese, but some expatriate ideas and habits were admired, and gradually assimilated when a family could afford to move up the social (and financial) scale. This pattern of grafting a Western culture onto the indigenous ethnic culture was evident for many decades in Hong Kong and the ports of Shanghai, Tientsin, Amoy, and Swatow, and penetrated even as far as Hankow, on the mighty Yangtsekiang River in the heart of central China."[108] As noted in the previous chapter, some Eurasians viewed these cultural changes as consistent with elite Chinese identity in Hong Kong. Others, like Joyce, viewed these changes as a step toward becoming British.[109]

FIGURE 19. Sir (Reginald) Edward Stubbs; Sir Robert Ho Tung; Margaret, Lady Ho Tung; Marjory, Lady Stubbs; J.E. Warner; Mrs. Julius Ralph Young, photographer unknown, Kowloon, 1920.

© National Portrait Gallery, London.

The colonial crises of the 1920s also changed the Eurasian relationship to the British administration. As David Pomfret writes, "While these crises reinforced official perceptions of the precariousness of colonial rule they also prompted the administrative elite to address with greater urgency the challenge of cultivating good relations with the colony's Eurasian elite."[110] Eurasians, in fact, played a major role in the crises of the 1920s. With his close connection to Hong Kong Governor Sir Edward Stubbs (fig. 19), Ho Tung was said to have settled the seamen's strike of 1922 through his personal intercession.[111] Although the British administration continued to rely upon Eurasian elites during these years of crisis, they also began to worry that the power of the "half-castes" might be growing out of hand. During the 1922 strike, Governor Stubbs lamented, "We can rely on nobody except the half-castes and even they will throw in their lot with the Chinese if they think they will be on the winning side."[112] While seeking to maintain good relations with this intermediary group, then, the colonial administration also became wary of their influence.[113]

Other developments during the 1920s simultaneously challenged the special claims of Eurasians to bilingualism and biculturalism. In particular, expanded educational opportunities meant that growing numbers of Chinese had access to English-language education. In addition, foreign-born or foreign-educated Chinese were beginning to return to the "New China" to take advantage of new opportunities, and many found their way to Hong Kong. With such competition, and mounting discrimination prompted by the rise of Chinese racial nationalism, Eurasians may have sensed the need to band together to protect their group interests and assert their right for recognition.

Facing these changes, a distinctive sense of Eurasian identity, one that was neither fully Chinese nor wholly European, even as it was both, came to the fore. Reinforcing this shift may have been the fact that increasing numbers of Eurasian children began to attend the DBS and DGS instead of Central/Queen's, as they had in Hung Kam Ning's generation. Unlike the secular Queen's (which actually taught a healthy dose of Confucianism), the diocesan schools were Christian, and furthermore had a smaller population of Chinese students, with the majority being, in Joyce's memory, "a crowd of Eurasians, Portuguese, Indians and expatriates."[114] While Hung Iu-chi, attending Queen's in his long Chinese gown and skullcap, was part of a group that was lumped together as "Chinese and Eurasians," his daughter Joyce Anderson found herself lumped at DGS not with the Chinese but with a multiethnic "crowd" of Hong Kong's ethnic Others.[115]

THE FOUNDING AND FUNCTION OF THE WELFARE LEAGUE

The founding of the Welfare League can be viewed as part and parcel of this ethnic shift. Whether moved by the stirring speech delivered by Anderson, or by practical necessity, the group of Eurasians gathered on that December evening voted to establish a formal society instead of a simple charitable fund. A subcommittee of twelve, including C. G. Anderson and other eminent men such as M. K. Lo, was charged with drawing up a constitution. On July 29, 1930, a general meeting was convened, and the name "The Welfare League" was formally approved, with a Chinese name of *Tongren hui*. Sir Robert Ho Tung was elected president and the Honorable R. H. Kotewall, vice president. C. G. Anderson would serve as secretary from the league's inception until World War II.[116] In forming the Welfare League, these men asserted the existence of a Eurasian community on whose behalf they should act. The league was thus at once a response to discrimination and an attempt to claim a new Eurasian identity. As I discuss later, this attempt met with difficulties.

Despite the fact that Anderson had employed the rhetoric of "rights" in his inaugural address, the aims that the league ultimately adopted were squarely focused on charity and not on political agitation after the fashion of the Anti-Mui Tsai Society. Moreover, the specific charitable works outlined in the league's mandate corresponded to those traditionally undertaken by Chinese voluntary associations, namely providing relief to the needy, scholarship funds, and free burials for the destitute.[117] The league was thus founded as a modern organization, complete with constitution and elected board, but with a squarely Confucian vision and a traditional scope of activities. Like the older voluntary associations, often formed on the basis of common surname or native place, the league limited its charitable efforts to a specific in-group—in this case, the Eurasian community.

DRAWING THE LINES OF COMMUNITY

In the absence of any administrative or statutory definitions of "Eurasian," how was this community to be defined? The organization's historian, Eric Peter Ho, wrote that "in applying the test of eligibility for assistance from the League's funds, 'Eurasian' is deemed to mean the offspring of a union where the mother is Chinese and the father is Occidental. Where either parent is Eurasian, as defined, the child is eligible regardless of its other parent."[118]

"Eurasian" was thus not defined in biological terms, simply as a notional combination of European and Asiatic blood, as suggested in Anderson's inaugural address. Moreover, the issue of blood quantum is studiously avoided. Rather, the league followed British colonial convention in defining Eurasians as the children of European fathers and Asian mothers. However, they explicitly excluded "local Portuguese or Macanese" under the rationale that they had their own established relief organizations.[119]

Although the league's definition of "Eurasian" may appear to be rigid, in comparison to other mixed communities in Asia at the time, it was actually flexible.[120] Eurasian identity, for example, could be inherited through either a Eurasian mother or father. In addition, the league's history noted that they *did* occasionally grant assistance to persons with Chinese fathers and Occidental mothers.[121] This flexibility reflected the diversity of the community, which included people like Robert Kotewall (of partial Parsi descent), the Choas (descended from Malaccan Chinese in the paternal line), and the Kews (descended from an Australian Chinese man).[122] Thus, I argue that *community* and kinship relations, and not biological race or bloodlines, assumed central importance in the formation of this Eurasian we-group.

If the founding of the Welfare League can be taken as evidence of an emerging new communal identity for Eurasians in interwar Hong Kong, this identity was not without its limits. Carl Anderson once confided to Joyce that four prominent men in Hong Kong society, all publicly known as Chinese, were secret members of the league.[123] Indeed, as Eric Peter Ho has recorded in the league's official history, from the beginning membership was always a problem. In 1930, the league had a membership of twenty-nine, which rose to a peak of seventy-six by 1933. However, the numbers were down to fifty-three in 1936, prompting various suggestions for increasing the membership.[124] In 1946, the league considered shutting down due to the fact that "it had become increasingly difficult to enlist 'fresh blood' and 'new brains.'"[125] Such difficulties suggest that there were many who did not subscribe to the idea of a Eurasian community, or at least were not willing to jeopardize their Chinese status by affiliating themselves with such. Yet despite the ongoing issue of membership, the league survived the disruption of World War II and the ensuing diaspora of the Eurasian community, and with sound financials, has continued in operation until this day, a testament to the strength of the "web," to use the words of Peter Hall.[126]

This chapter has argued that the founding of Hong Kong's Welfare League represented the institutionalization of a distinct Eurasian identity that was neither Chinese nor European but acknowledged its mixedness. The formation of this Eurasian community, one that would "take care of its own," supports Steven Masami Ropp's contention that "the way in which [mixed-race subjects] challenge the social construction of race is limited."[127] While mixed race *destabilizes* the boundaries between races, calling into question the meaning of fixed racial categories, the formation of the Welfare League indicates that the effect does not always ultimately serve to *deconstruct* race, as is frequently suggested by mixed-race studies scholars and activists.[128] Instead, as we saw from the ideal of Eurasian unity articulated in C.G. Anderson's inaugural address, embracing mixedness can also lead to the production of new communal or caste identities, with boundaries of inclusion and exclusion drawn on new lines.

Coda

Elsie Jane Comes Home to Rest

In 2009, the remains of Elsie Jane Yung made a final journey to their resting ground alongside her venerable ancestors.[1] It would have been a familiar ritual to the old-time sojourners on Gold Mountain, who arranged when they could to have their bones shipped back home to China for reburial. From the days of the "Railroad Chinese," organizations like the Kong Chu Company of San Francisco had specialized in the ritual collection and transport of "Chinese bones," sending agents across America to gather the remains of their deceased countrymen.[2] The practice continued until it was interrupted by the Japanese invasion of China and World War II.

But Elsie Jane Yung did not die "overseas." She died in Zhuhai, China, the birthplace of her grandfather—Yung Wing. Her "Chinese bones" did not travel back to a village burial ground, but were flown instead across the oceans to Hartford, Connecticut, and interred in the Cedar Hill Cemetery. The daughter of Yung Wing's second son, Bartlett Golden Yung, Elsie Jane had been born and raised in Shanghai, where her father had been a successful businessman and engineering consultant. As reported in the *Hartford Courant*, which had carried the announcement of Yung Wing's marriage to Mary Kellogg so many years ago, Elsie Jane had spent the twilight of her life in a nursing home in Zhuhai, where her grandfather's fame made her a minor local celebrity. Yet, in the end she chose bucolic Cedar Hill as her final home, where she rests in the shadow of her revered ancestors, Yung Wing and

FIGURE 20. Headstone of Elsie Jane Yung and monument for
Yung Wing and Mary Kellogg Yung, Cedar Hill Cemetery,
Hartford, Connecticut.

Photograph by author, July 2012.

Mary Kellogg (fig. 20). With her final earthly journey, Elsie Jane thereby
paid tribute to both her Chinese and American roots, roots that have
woven together not only family, but national histories as well.[3]

· · ·

What became of the Eurasian families of a bygone era? Families that,
like the Yungs, had emerged from the nexus of cultural, economic,

educational, and labor flows between the United States and China? What happened to the once-flourishing Eurasian communities on the China Coast—communities that had produced such luminaries as Sir Robert Ho Tung, Sir Robert Kotewall, and Han Suyin? Whence vanished the "new tribe" of hybrids that Louis Beck once predicted would people America's Chinatowns?

The Pacific War above all else precipitated the eventual breakup of the China Coast Eurasian communities, with their vital centers in Shanghai and Hong Kong. When the Japanese invaded Shanghai, many Eurasian families fled to Hong Kong, taking refuge with relatives and business colleagues. Others left for the United States, the Philippines, and elsewhere—wherever their passports and finances could take them. When war reached Hong Kong, this community too was "torn asunder," as Peter Hall recalls.[4] Many Eurasians joined the Hong Kong Volunteer Defense Corps, serving with "superb gallantry" in the Battle for Hong Kong, where so many were lost.[5] Others joined the war effort in China: Lieutenant General Robert Ho went to fight on the Chinese front, while his sister, Dr. Eva Ho, commanded a unit of the Chinese Red Cross.[6] While many lost their lives during the war, others were interned by the Japanese in either prisoner of war or civilian internment camps in Hong Kong and China.[7] The Japanese came after Bartlett Yung one day, not knowing that tuberculosis had already claimed his life in October 1942.[8] To avoid internment, some Hong Kong Eurasians assumed Chinese identity; others escaped into Free China or found alternative routes for survival. As Joyce Symons recalled, C. G. Anderson went to the "Third Nationals" Bureau established by the Japanese in Hong Kong and obtained visas for his family—as neither British nor Chinese—to Macao.[9] Thus began the dispersal of the once close-knit Eurasian communities on the China Coast.[10]

After the war, many internment survivors were taken to the United Kingdom or Australia, beginning a process of diaspora that only accelerated with the Chinese Communist Revolution and its aftermath.[11] Diaspora took China Coast Eurasians also to North America, as immigration laws gradually liberalized. Hence, as Vicky Lee has recalled, even the traces of the Eurasian community that could still be seen in Hong Kong during the 1950s and 1960s had largely disappeared by the 1970s, though the Ho family still remains a vital presence there today.[12]

War and diaspora were not the only factors contributing to what Peter Hall has called "the split up of the once closely related Eurasian families who were originally in the web."[13] Changing attitudes toward intermarriage and mixed race around the world in the postwar era also led to a gradual abandonment of the old tradition of Eurasian endogamy. As Peter Hall has written, "None of my ten married first cousins, from my mother's side, or the three of us in our family, has married an Eurasian!"[14] Similarly, Irene Cheng has written, "Oddly enough, none of the eighteen [Ho Tung] grandchildren married Eurasians."[15]

World War II also marked a major turning point for the "half-Chinese" in the United States. With China an important American ally, the government was forced to change its discriminatory stance toward the Chinese. Chinese exclusion, which had shaped the lives of so many mixed families, was finally repealed in 1943. Chinese were granted the right to naturalize and were given a small immigration quota. Another important development for the Chinese American community was the passage of the War Brides Act in 1945, which enabled Chinese wives of U.S. citizens to freely immigrate to the United States. This new immigration helped balance the once-skewed sex ratio of the Chinese American population. Whereas mixed families had a significant presence in American Chinatowns at the beginning of the twentieth century, when families were a rarity, in the postwar years they became a distinct minority. With the passage of time, many forgot that, in the words of Bruce Edward Hall, "the first generation of Chinese children in New York [was] actually Eurasian."[16]

But as the Chinese Eurasians of a bygone era have faded from the scene there has arisen something, phoenix-like, to take their place: memory. Memory to take the place of silence. For so many years, Eurasian families on both sides of the Pacific had been taught to live with shame, to hide their origins. As Eric Peter Ho recalled of his childhood in 1930s Hong Kong, "In bits at a time, we were told that our great-grandfather was a Dutchman called Bosman. . . . As this was sinking in we also heard that our maternal great-grandfather was an Englishman called Thomas Rothwell, and there was a photograph of his grave in the English Cemetery at Hankow. We were told solemnly not to disclose these family secrets to anyone. That we should be stunned into silence is understandable. . . ."[17]

Silence is no longer the order of the day. Beginning with official postwar disavowals of racial ideologies and the concept of race, changing attitudes have gradually led to the dismantling of the color line and the old creed of "East is East, and West is West." The UNESCO "Statement on 'Race,'" drafted in 1949, avidly refuted the notion of hybrid degeneracy and proclaimed that "evidence points unequivocally to the fact that race-mixture does not produce biologically bad effects." It further declared there is "no possible biological justification for prohibiting inter-marriage between persons of different racial groups."[18] In 1967, the U.S. Supreme Court struck down the last of the anti-miscegenation laws, leading to a new tolerance of intermarriage, with acceptance increasing year by year.[19] These changes paved the way for the emergence of a mixed-race social movement that began to form in the 1980s, primarily in the United States and Great Britain, but in other countries as well. Across Asia, for example, mixed-race advocates are now speaking out against racial discrimination and calling for reform of nationality laws.[20] The increasing visibility of rhetoric celebrating the "best of both worlds" has enabled many mixed families to come to terms with their origins. Many are now proud to let old skeletons out of the closet and proclaim their dual heritages.

Many of the descendants of the early mixed families examined in this book are among those who now publicly affirm diverse pedigrees. In the United States, Lisa See, the redheaded great-granddaughter of Chinese immigrant Fong See and Ticie Pruett, is proud to declare her Chineseness—and equally proud to state that she learned it from her Euro-American grandmother.[21] Ever pleased to claim himself "one-quarter Chinese," Dana Bruce Young has dedicated himself to making known the history of his eminent grandfather Yung Kwai and other students of the Chinese Educational Mission.[22] William Franking Wu (b. 1951), the grandson of Mae Franking, has become a nationally recognized science fiction author, inventing new forms of hybridity while embracing his bicultural background.[23] In Hong Kong, Ambassador Eric Hotung (b. 1926), Commander of the Order of the British Empire, proclaims with pride his "Anglo-Chinese lineage" and his "noble heritage" as the eldest grandson of Sir Robert Ho Tung. Currently the ambassador at large for Timor-Leste, he has maintained the Hotung name, in all its unabashed hybridity, even as most of his family has opted for the traditional Chinese single-character "Ho."[24] In China's new open climate, Chen Jitong's descendants now freely acknowledge their "French blood," and in Montréal, Edith Eaton's grandnephew, L. Charles Laferrière, whose namesake, Edward Charles Eaton, tried so hard to pass for white, proudly signs himself "1/8 Chinois."[25]

These examples belie Edith Eaton's prediction in her "Half-Chinese Children" regarding the future generations of mixed families: "In some families, one daughter is married to a Chinaman, another to an American. It gives food for thought—the fact, that a couple of centuries from now, the great grand children of the woman who married an American will be Americans and nothing else, whilst the descendants of her sister, who married a Chinaman and probably followed her husband to his own country will be Chinamen, pure and simple."[26] It is indeed true that many descended from the early mixed families established on both sides of the Pacific have effectively assimilated into their communities, as noted previously. Yet, at the same time, the social identities adopted by individuals like Lisa See, Eric Hotung, Dana Young, William Franking Wu, or Elsie Jane Yung cannot in the end be reduced to either "American and nothing else" or "Chinese, pure and simple." Some reject altogether the distinction between mixed and pure—in Lily's words: "Defining people as 'pure' or 'mixed' is an attempt to confine people to stereotypes. I just have no use for it."[27]

Changing attitudes toward mixed race have also provided impetus for a global movement to reclaim the histories of mixed families and communities: to reclaim genealogies, creole languages, and even cherished recipes. Indeed, if Paul Spickard identified a "biracial biography boom" in the United States during the 1990s, we seem to be currently in the midst of a "Eurasian publishing boom" that spans the globe from Asia to Australia, Europe, and the United States.[28] This publishing trend includes not only a growing number of academic books, but also memoirs, family biographies, genealogies, websites, dictionaries, musical CDs, and cookbooks.

Much of this effort to document the past represents a desire to reclaim histories and identities in the face of the historical erasure described earlier.[29] Peter Hall, for example, declared his motivation "to produce a personal history so that the very significant contribution from my 'family' Eurasians would not be lost for future generations of interested parties."[30] Facing fading memories and a disappearing past, Eurasian memoirists and community historians have thus labored to ensure that the record of "who they were, what they had done" would not vanish beyond recall.[31]

. . .

Having dutifully accompanied Elsie Jane's remains on this her last earthly journey, a journey that retraced Yung Wing's voyage from China to America with the Reverend Samuel R. Brown more than a century and a half ago, loyal cousin Frank Yung saw her laid to rest in the family plot in Cedar Hill Cemetery, with the headstones of her parents Bartlett and Elsie Yung beside her, before flying back to Asia.[32]

Epilogue

"Can Mongrelized Mixed-Bloods *Really* Improve the Chinese Race?" Such was the inflammatory title of online pundit Shangguan Tianyi's column, posted on *Duowei zhoukan* in August 2001—the very word *mongrelized* (*zajiao*) signaling to readers his obvious distaste for the notion. Directed at a transnational Chinese audience, the editorial opened consideration of this issue by contrasting the racial thinking of the past with contemporary attitudes. In the past, Shangguan wrote, German Nazis had "promoted the idea of Aryan superiority on the basis of the notion of racial purity," but nowadays, "ironically, people take an avid interest in racial intermixing as a means of improving the Chinese race, and of producing a more intelligent new generation. . . . Decades after [the Nazi era], the mongrelized mixed-blood has unexpectedly become a figure of admiration."[1] Elaborating on the vogue for racial intermixing, Shangguan asked, "Are we talking about interbreeding with blacks, American Indians, Australian Aborigines or Pacific Islanders? No. Essentially, the scope of intermixing is limited to whites, preferably Americans."[2]

Having opened with this deliberately provocative rhetoric, Shangguan proceeded to critique what he perceived to be a new interest in intermarriage as a tool for genetically reengineering the Chinese race and the concomitant fetishization of Eurasians. As noted at the outset of this book, this fetishization is readily apparent in the transnational Chinese media, particularly in the entertainment industry, where

Eurasian models, actors, and athletes are hot commodities.[3] Decrying the absurdity of "blind faith" in Eurasian physical and intellectual superiority, Shangguan proclaimed that only a geneticist in a lab could create the ideal child.

Shangguan's strident critique appears sharply out of step with the celebratory discourses on hybridity current in both popular media and academic circles. Yet, despite his contempt for the vogue of hybridity, Shangguan shares one fundamental tendency with these discourses; that is, the tendency to represent the positive valuation of hybridity as a break with the past, a rupture with an old order that privileged purity (whether cultural, racial, or discursive).

The theoretical concept of hybridity as a metaphor for the new transcultural forms produced out of the colonizer–colonized relation has become fashionable in academic circles since the late 1980s, thanks to the influential work of Homi Bhabha, among others. Bhabha's theorization of hybridity as a disruptive force with the power to subvert or undermine colonial authority has lent the concept cachet as a critical tool. Indeed, hybridity has become one of the most widely employed (and hotly disputed) concepts in postcolonial studies and has frequently been cited as a defining characteristic of "the postcolonial condition."[4] Hybridity, certain theorists promise, allows us to evade "the replication of the binary categories of the past."[5]

Whereas postcolonial theorists have largely conceptualized hybridity in cultural or discursive terms, mixed-race studies as it emerged during the 1990s focused on racial hybridity, analyzing the "mixed-race experience" and "mixed-race identity." Due to its association with activism and identity politics, mixed-race studies has largely tended to construct racial intermixing as a socially progressive and liberal phenomenon. As in postcolonial theory, hybridity is treated as a disruptive or destabilizing force, with "mixed-race" identity promising to break down racial boundaries and bring an end to racism, which is equated with the ideology of racial purity.[6] As one of the leading pioneers of the field, Maria Root, has asserted, "the presence of racially mixed persons defies the social order predicated upon race, blurs racial and ethnic group boundaries, and challenges generally accepted proscriptions and prescriptions regarding intergroup relations. Furthermore, and perhaps most threatening, the existence of racially mixed persons challenges long-held notions about the biological, moral, and social meaning of race."[7] Hybridity, then, seemingly holds the promise of moving us beyond the old identity politics of white and black, colonizer and colonized, toward a boundary-less future where indeterminacy, in-betweenness, and ambivalence reign supreme.

Yet, as the chapters of this book have demonstrated, contrary to Shangguan's assertion, the interest in racial hybrids is not a recent, post–Nazi era phenomenon, but rather one with a long and complex history, both in Greater China and in the United States. Eurasians were not only constructed as a "problem," but were also considered by some as a potential solution: the embodiment of two civilizations, harbingers of international peace, the race of the future. Alongside the privileging of racial and cultural purity, then, there were also those who espoused counter-discourses privileging hybridity and fusion, either as a eugenic or a sociological ideal. Within this context, Eurasians on both sides of the Pacific often suffered racial discrimination and ostracism but they might at times also be accorded a special role as racial intermediaries.

Thus, a central contention of this book is that far from being an ironic reversal (or even a progressive disavowal) of older racialist ideas, as Shangguan would have it, the new trendy discourse on Eurasian "mixed bloods" actually unconsciously replicates the racial thinking of the past in certain key ways. Shangguan's strongly presentist critique thereby prompts us to reexamine some of the contemporary claims concerning the disruptive and/or antiracist potential of hybridity.

EUGENICS REVISITED: RACIAL PURITY AND HYBRID VIGOR

Indeed, there are uncanny similarities between late nineteenth- and early twentieth-century Chinese treatises on eugenic amalgamation and the contemporary fetishization of Eurasian intermixing. Whether promoting models and actresses like Maggie Q or Li Jiaxin, or athletes like Xie Hui and Hua Tian, the contemporary transnational Chinese media frequently employ the notion of hybrid vigor or the "best of both worlds" theme, often in terms that evoke the writings examined in chapter 4. Such is the case when authors idealize, for example, the specific combination of notional "Caucasian" physical qualities (height and whiteness) with purportedly "Chinese" mental prowess or cultural refinement. In this manner, recipes for eugenic hybridity (for example, Chinese brains + Caucasian physiques, or African athleticism + Chinese grace) serve only to reinscribe stereotypical notions about the fixed "racial characteristics" of the "pure races" rather than helping us to deconstruct the notion of race altogether.[8]

The media furthermore frequently represent Eurasians as embodiments par excellence of the East–West cultural hybridity characteristic of contemporary society in Greater China. Portraits of Eurasian pop idols often highlight their bicultural and bilingual fluency, qualifications that seemingly promise success in a global world, where capitalizing on "Westernness" alone is no longer enough. With the hypothetical ability to move seamlessly between East and West, to speak both English and Chinese, the Eurasian stands as a paragon of upward mobility in the transnational capitalist system.[9] At a time when China and the West are becoming increasingly integrated, both economically and culturally, the idea of Eurasian hybridity thus holds particular appeal as a media trope. If late Qing and early Republican thinkers projected their visions of Eurasian hybridity into the future, then, for contemporary media pundits that future seems to have arrived.

Such celebratory discourses appear, on the face of it, to represent a major reversal of the racial thinking of the past. Nonetheless, I argue that it is worth paying attention to the historical stemma of these contemporary images. The notion of Chinese–Euro-American hybridity as a means for the eugenic improvement of the Chinese race—the idea attacked so vehemently in Shangguan Tianyi's editorial—is an extreme expression of the contemporary media fetishization. In debunking this eugenic proposal, Shangguan is right to point out the absurdity of valorizing only the particular form of Eurasian hybridity. (Not immune to gross racial stereotyping himself, he facetiously suggests that intermarriage with the "athletic" black race would do more for the physical improvement of the Chinese race.) He is also right to question the clichéd "best of both worlds" formulation, which is nothing more than an inversion of the colonial-era "vices of both races" formula. But Shangguan misses something important in his monodimensional understanding of the past: that is, as I have shown in this book, the notion of improving the Chinese race through eugenic amalgamation was advocated by leading thinkers in China as early as the late Qing, even as the preservation of white racial purity was becoming a dominant concern in Western eugenic thinking.

This is not simply a matter of Shangguan getting his history right. There is a danger inherent in equating the "old" eugenic thinking solely with the idea of preserving racial purity without recognizing the role that ideas about selective interbreeding have played in the history of eugenics discourse. Setting eugenics as hybridity in opposition to eugenics as purity, as Shangguan does, obscures their mutual imbrication. For those of us who reject Shangguan's brand of Han Chinese racial chauvinism, it becomes easy to uncritically embrace the "good" eugenics of hybridity, which seems to be in tune with the antiracist spirit of the multicultural present, even as we distance ourselves from the "bad" eugenics of a racist past. Once we understand the role of Social Darwinist thought in the genealogy of Chinese idealizations of the Eurasian, however, it becomes clear that the eugenics of hybridity can be every bit as problematic as the eugenics of purity. Regardless of whether we ultimately critique or celebrate the notion of "mixedness," then, it is crucial that we acknowledge the roots of this concept in historical racialist discourse and the fact that hybridity and purity are really two sides of the same coin.

The late Qing and early Republican theorizations of racial amalgamation examined in this book reveal that privileging hybridity can serve illiberal cultural politics as easily as liberal tolerance. The idealization of Eurasian hybridity, for example, may serve, consciously or unconsciously, to promote the notion of yellow-white exceptionalism vis-à-vis other races. In addition, as we saw perhaps most blatantly in the case of Kang Youwei's proposal for "equalizing the races," racial amalgamation does not necessarily imply the *equal* mixing of races in the production of a third type. Rather, hybridity can also be formulated as a means of elevating (or even genetically phasing out) "inferior races" through the process of racial assimilation or "breeding up." In such cases, hybridization does not challenge the existing racial order but rather reinforces notions of racial hierarchy while playing into the politics of "lightening." Thus, if these idealizations of the Eurasian disrupt the boundary between yellow and white, they simultaneously create a new boundary between the yellow–white and the "darker races": hybridity's effect is less a disruption of binary categories than a displacement.

Yet, although there are certain recurrent themes between past and present representations of Eurasian hybridity, there are also some important differences. What is new this time around is that the fetishization of Eurasians is far more pervasive. No longer the product of avant-garde thinkers, it has entered the realm of popular culture and media cliché. In addition, thanks to new technologies of communication and accelerated global migration, the new fashion for hybridity has a decidedly transnational character, with "ethnically ambiguous" models and pop icons like Maggie Q garnering attention on both sides of the Pacific. Further promoting such convergence, the Internet and social media have provided a means for the global constitution of Eurasian identities through online communities such as EurasianNation, Eurasians World-wide, and mixedasians.com, and sites such as Everything Eurasian.[10] Claiming a membership of more than three thousand, EurasianNation sought to galvanize Eurasians worldwide by convening the "Largest Eurasian Nation Meet Up Group" in Kuala Lumpur, Malaysia, in 2011. One hundred and seventy-two Facebook members from countries around the world pledged to attend.[11] Through such social media Eurasians have formed global networks and given themselves the voice that Edith Eaton/Sui Sin Far once struggled to make heard.

Such changes are revolutionary indeed, as we saw in the coda. Yet, as far as we have come, we must also be mindful of claims that increasing rates of intermarriage will lead to the demise of racism. As we saw from the stories in this book, the mere existence of racial "mixing" in and of itself is not enough to overcome racism and prejudice. Indeed, despite the tremendous increase in rates of intermarriage in the United States (see introduction), Americans remain divided on the benefits for the nation. A Pew Research Center study issued in 2012 found that while 43 percent of Americans consider the increase to be good for society, another 44 percent say it has "made no difference" (with 11 percent considering it a change for the worse).[12] Although biracial icons have proved to be powerful public symbols for our desire to heal racial divides, it is overly idealistic, I argue, to expect hybridity alone to do the hard work of antiracism. Perhaps rather than projecting intermixing into the future we should do more to reclaim the intermixing that has shaped our past, and in doing so recognize the interconnectedness of our present. To fully recognize such interconnectedness would be to acknowledge that no one is "pure," and no one "hybrid."

CULTURAL HYBRIDITY REVISITED: ASSIMILATION AS A TWO-WAY STREET

Can cultural hybridity do more than racial hybridity to move us beyond the binary categories of the past? Here the examples of Mae Franking and Ticie See (see chapter 2) provide food for thought. Embodying the seemingly incongruous position of being simultaneously "white" and "Chinese," these women represent a form of hybridity that has received scant attention in the critical literature. Although their experiences reflect a bygone era, I argue that they can nonetheless help us to think through the contemporary cultural politics of assimilation and ethnic nationalism, particularly where Chinese and Chinese Americans are concerned.

Even as my Chinese American students vociferously assert the rights of Chinese immigrants to "become American," and protest the equation of "American" with "white" ("It's how you act, and not how you look"), they adamantly insist that a Euro-American could never "become Chinese." Decrying the assimilation of the "banana" (yellow on the outside, white on the inside), they assert that true Chineseness is a matter of culture and not of race (again, "It's how you act, and not how you look"). Yet, many are uncomfortable with the notion that a white person might be considered Chinese, no matter how fluent in the language and culture. There may be individuals who are "eggs" (white on the outside, yellow on the inside), but they are not "real Chinese." To be authentically Chinese, they finally contend, "You have to have the looks *and* the culture." Multiculturalism, it appears, is not a two-way street.

I raise these issues in order to note that the tendency to conflate biology with culture has not entirely disappeared, even in an age that has supposedly disavowed scientific racialism.[13] To put it another way, despite the fact that contemporary discourse purports to be culturalist, the shadow of race still lurks beneath the surface, especially when it comes to non-Western or minority identities. I also raise these issues to point out that the contemporary discourse on diaspora, assimilation, and multiculturalism is largely a one-way street: that is, although Asian immigrants to the West make claims for the right to be full members (legally and culturally) of multicultural Western societies, these same immigrants often resist the notion that the process could work in reverse, that non-Asians could assume Asian identities. As a result, whereas there is much debate concerning the question of Westernization and assimilation (Is it good? Bad? How much?), the reverse issue of, for example, Sinicization (what might have been called "going native") is rarely raised today, because the general presumption is simply that Westerners can never become Chinese. This presumption is widespread among Westerners and ethnic Chinese alike, both at home and abroad. Even as we contest the equation of American with white, then, we are generally comfortable equating Chinese with yellow. This is one of the paradoxes produced by the unresolved tension between ethnic nationalism and multicultural ideologies in contemporary cultural politics.

This paradox is particularly acute among diaspora Chinese, who, as Hsu Cho-yun writes, tend "to insist upon their Chinese identity even more strongly than Chinese in China," and among whom there is a certain defensive tendency to safeguard a putative Chinese cultural and racial purity in the face of rising rates of "out-marriage" and assimilation among the second generation.[14] This ethnic nationalism is founded on a mythical image of China as a racially homogeneous nation, conveniently erasing the fact that the People's Republic of China is a self-declared "multinationality" state of tremendous diversity. Thus, "Chinese" becomes equated with "Han Chinese" (see chapter 7), a form of identity rooted not only in culture, but also, as we saw, in "blood" and myths of shared descent.

This asymmetry between American and Chinese as forms of identity has delimited the ways in which we conceptualize cultural hybridity. In other words, if the term *Huayi Meiren* (Chinese American, literally "American of Chinese descent") has already become a common part of the modern Chinese vocabulary, the reverse term *Meiyi Zhongguoren* (Chinese of American descent) is essentially nonexistent. Likewise, most Americans would not find the term *American-Chinese* immediately intelligible, and would most likely take it to mean the same thing as *Chinese-American*. Even as the expansion of global migration and the rise of multicultural ideologies in various nations have led to the proliferation of hybrid identities, still, I argue, only certain kinds of hybrid identities are readily available.[15]

Part of this asymmetry derives from the fact that whiteness and Westernness are generally associated with privilege and power, but the other half of the problem lies in the racial boundedness of Chinese identity, which is often left unproblematized even by advocates of multiculturalism.[16] The United States is thus constructed as a privileged site of multiculturalism, while China is imagined as an older model of nationhood wherein the boundaries of race, culture, and nation are coterminous.[17]

Is "Chineseness" any more than "Americanness" a racially bound concept? The notion of "Cultural China," as articulated by Tu Weiming, provides an interesting perspective from which to consider this question. Tu defines Cultural China as an "emergent cultural space" that extends beyond the boundaries of the Chinese nation-state and includes three "symbolic universes": the first includes mainland China, Taiwan, Hong Kong, and Singapore, societies populated by ethnic Chinese majorities; the second includes "overseas" Chinese, now more commonly known as the "Chinese diaspora"; the third is comprised of non-ethnic Chinese individuals who try to understand China.[18] Tu argues that the meaning of Chineseness is produced in the continuous interaction among these three symbolic universes.

Tu's model of "Chineseness" has given rise to much controversy, with many disputing his contention that Confucianism is the core essence of "Chineseness." Critics have also pointed out that the idea of Cultural China as a global network reinforces presumptions that Chinese in the diaspora(s) are essentially and eternally Chinese. Relatively little attention has been paid, however, to what is perhaps the most radical and provocative suggestion of Tu's model: the third symbolic universe.

The notion of the third symbolic universe acknowledges the vital role that non-ethnic Chinese have played in shaping contemporary ideas of Chinese identity. As Tu admits, "There is undoubtedly a whiff of Orientalism . . . in the third symbolic universe."[19] However, Tu also contests the strict dichotomy between foreign and indigenous representations of China, pointing to examples of Chinese who are "supposedly" Westernized and Westerners who are "apparently" Sinified. "Being Chinese," Tu writes, "is as much an attainment as a given."[20] Tu's third symbolic universe thereby opens up the racial boundaries of Cultural China to the membership of non-ethnic Chinese.

Although I do not subscribe to Tu's brand of neo-Confucianism, I find his argument that Chineseness is not just inherited but also "attained" to be thought provoking, because it opens up assimilation as a two-way street, with Sinicization running parallel to Westernization. Tu would thus agree with my students that "it's how you act, not how you look," but he is willing to extend this argument to its logical conclusion: that anyone who "acts" Chinese can be considered Chinese regardless of how they look. Yet, this provocative dimension of Tu's paradigm is rarely discussed by critics.

But if we shift our focus away from "biological" notions of Chineseness defined by racial *descent* and consider the possibilities of Chineseness (like Americanness) as a matter of *consent,* then we must take seriously Mae Franking's claims to identity as a "real Chinese wife." We must similarly give weight to Lisa See's claims that she is Chinese "in the heart," her red hair and freckles notwithstanding. Tu Wei-ming's "third symbolic universe" of Chineseness thus becomes useful as an interpretive concept, because it allows us to begin thinking of Chineseness beyond the limitations of racial descent and to invent labels of bicultural identity like "American-Chinese." Whereas Tu's analytical focus was on the discursive role played by non-Chinese in shaping ideas about Chineseness, what I emphasize here is the possibility for treating the "egg" as something other than an object of derision. The cultural politics surrounding the "egg" will only increase in importance as growing numbers of inter-married couples are choosing to settle in China rather than the West.[21]

By examining hybridity in the figure of a Sinicized Westerner—an "American-Chinese woman"—I hope to have demonstrated the need to reconsider what asymmetries govern our reluctance to critique the racial boundedness of Chinese identity, even as we advocate pluralism in American society. Do we not privilege U.S. national identity as the modern notion of "consent" while relegating Chinese identity to the "old world" notion of "descent"? Do we not ironically reinforce the superordinate–subordinate relations between the West and China by treating assimilation as a cultural process that flows in only one direction?

Perhaps we can take heart from the example of Edith Eaton/Sui Sin Far, who wrote in 1909, "I give my right hand to the Occidentals and my left hand to the Orientals, hoping that between them they will not utterly destroy the insignificant 'connecting link.' And that's all."[22]

Notes

PRELUDE

1. In 1967, the U.S. Supreme Court declared all remaining anti-miscegenation laws unconstitutional.

2. Nancy Kwan was an early example. On the history of Eurasians in the Miss Hong Kong pageant, see "Wuyuan yingtan de liushi niandai gangjie" [Not fated for the cinema world: the sixties' Miss Hong Kong], *sina.com.cn*, August 7, 2001, ent.sina.com.nc/m/2001–08–07/52918.html. On the popularity of Eurasian models, see "Xianggang: hunxue mote 'da hunzhan'" [Hong Kong: Mixed-race models "mix it up"], *zhoumo.com.cn*, October 11, 2001, www. longhoo.net/e/ca76981.htm; and "Maggie Q—Xianggang hunxue xinggan mote" [Maggie Q—Hong Kong's sexy mixed-blood model], *people.com.cn*, July 2, 2001, www.people.com.cn/GB/shenghuo/77/117/20010702/501865.html.

3. See Shangguan Tianyi, "Zajiao hunxue zhen neng gailiang Zhongguo ren-zhong?" [Can mixed-blood hybrids *really* improve the Chinese race?], *Duowei zhoukan [chinesenewsweek.com]*, August 24, 2001, www.chinesenewsweek. com/65/ Commentary/4870.html, 1.

4. See Homi K. Bhabha, *The Location of Culture* (New York: Routledge, 1994); Ien Ang, *On Not Speaking Chinese: Living Between Asia and the West* (New York: Routledge, 2001); Ruth La Ferla, "Generation E.A.: Ethnically Ambiguous," *New York Times*, December 28, 2003, sec. 9, p. 1; Stanley Crouch, "Race Is Over," *New York Times*, September 29, 1996, sec. 6, p. 170.

5. For example, "Zhongguo titan de bada hunxue'er" [The eight great mixed-bloods of the Chinese sports world], http://sports.163.com/special/00052G98 /zghx.html. "Eurasian Invasion," *Time*, April 23, 2001.

6. For Chinese reporting on this topic, see "Meiguo jiazhou yu 1/10 de yayi shi hunxueren" [More than one in ten Asian Americans in California are

mixed], *Da jiyuan shibao [epochtimes.com]*, July 21, 2002, www.epochtimes.
com/b5/2/7/21/n203769.htm.

7. See Michael Omi, "Foreword," in *The Sum of Our Parts*, ed. Teresa Williams-León and Cynthia L. Nakashima (Philadelphia: Temple University Press, 2001).

8. Ang, *On Not Speaking Chinese*, 3, and see Bill Ashcroft et al., ed., *The Post-Colonial Studies Reader* (New York: Routledge, 1995).

9. See Barrett Seaman, ed., *Time: Special Issue: The New Face of America*, Fall 1993. For a critical discussion of this piece, see David Palumbo-Liu, *Asian/American: Historical Crossings of a Racial Frontier* (Stanford, CA: Stanford University Press, 1999).

INTRODUCTION

1. "Lily," oral communication, May 18, 2010. Let me state from the outset that I do not believe in the notion of "pure" races. The term *mixed*, once derogatory, has now come to be embraced by the mixed-race movement and many of mixed heritage. It is in this critical spirit that I use "mixed" throughout this work.

2. Diana Birchall, *Onoto Watanna: The Story of Winnifred Eaton* (Chicago: University of Illinois Press, 2001), 19.

3. Eric Peter Ho, *Tracing My Children's Lineage* (Hong Kong: University of Hong Kong, 2010), 8.

4. Melissa Brown, "Changing Authentic Identities: Evidence from Taiwan and China," *Journal of the Royal Anthropological Institute* 16 (2010): 466.

5. See Philip A. Kuhn, *Chinese among Others: Emigration in Modern Times* (Lanham, MD: Rowman & Littlefield), 2008.

6. My use of the term *intersecting diasporas* draws on the use of "overlapping diasporas" in Vivek Bald, "Overlapping Diasporas, Multiracial Lives: South Asian Muslims in U.S. Communities of Color, 1880–1950," *Souls: A Critical Journal of Black Politics, Culture, and Society* 8.4 (2006): 3–18.

7. Rebecca Karl, *Staging the World: Chinese Nationalism at the Turn of the Twentieth Century* (Durham, NC: Duke University Press, 2002).

8. The Act of December 17, 1943, 57 Stat. 600 (1943) repealed Chinese exclusion.

9. The term *Amerasians* refers to people of Asian and (racially diverse) American descent. In contrast to the era discussed in this book, the majority of Amerasians born after World War II were born to Asian mothers and American fathers.

10. Although this book focuses on Euro–Chinese intermarriages, it should be made clear that Chinese immigrants married women of diverse ethnicities, including African American, Native American, Mexican, and others.

11. In Singapore, for example, a Eurasian Association was founded in 1919 to advance community interests. In this book, I define *Eurasian* as a person of Asian and European ancestry, while not excluding people who were multiply "mixed," with diverse heritages.

12. See Carl Smith, "Ng Akew, One of Hong Kong's 'Protected' Women," *Chung Chi Bulletin* 46 (June 1969): 13–27, and Carl Smith, "Abandoned into

Prosperity: Women on the Fringe of Expatriate Society," in *Merchants' Daughters: Women, Commerce, and Regional Culture in South China*, ed. Helen F. Siu (Hong Kong: Hong Kong University Press, 2010), 129–42.

13. The Portuguese government encouraged colonists to marry with local women in order to create a loyal population baptized as Roman Catholics. Portuguese established families in Macao, giving rise to a population known as the Macanese (*Aomen tusheng*).

14. Based on my sources, I use the terms *European, white, Occidental,* and *Western* to refer to people of European ancestry who were racialized as white during the era this book discusses. On the relationship between whiteness and Asian exclusion, see Kornel Chang, "Enforcing Transnational White Solidarity: Asian Migration and the Formation of the US-Canadian Boundary," *American Quarterly* 60.3 (September 2008): 671–96.

15. Smith, "Ng Akew," 16.

16. Xing Long, "Qingmo minchu hunyin shenghuozhong de xinchao" [New trends in marriage during the late Qing and early Republican era], *Jindaishi yanjiu [Contemporary historical studies]* 3.63 (May 1991): 168–83.

17. Robert Park estimated that there were more than 60,000 Sino-Russian children in the Manchurian Railway Zone in the 1930s. Park, "Race Relations and Certain Frontiers," in *Race and Culture Contacts*, ed. E.B. Reuter (New York: McGraw-Hill, 1934), 57–85.

18. See Kristin Collins, "*Guyer v. Smith*, Personal Status Laws, and the Practice of Citizenship," unpublished paper.

19. See John Kuo Wei Tchen, *New York before Chinatown: Orientalism and the Shaping of American Culture, 1776–1882* (Baltimore: Johns Hopkins University Press, 1999).

20. See Mary Ting Yi Lui, *The Chinatown Trunk Mystery: Murder, Miscegenation, and Other Dangerous Encounters In Turn-of-the-Century New York City* (Princeton, NJ: Princeton University Press, 2005). See chapter 3.

21. The specific history of intermarriage in Hawaii is beyond the scope of this work.

22. Timothy Gilfoyle, *A Pickpocket's Tale: The Underworld of Nineteenth-Century New York* (New York: Norton, 2006), 90–91.

23. See, for example, Lisa See, *On Gold Mountain: The One-Hundred-Year Odyssey of My Chinese-American Family* (New York: Vintage, 1995).

24. Sucheng Chan, *Asian Americans: An Interpretive History* (New York: Twayne, 1991), 103.

25. Peter Moss, *Bye-Bye Blackbird: An Anglo-Indian Memoir* (New York: iUniverse, 2004), 1–2.

26. See Sui Sin Far, "Sui Sin Far, the Half Chinese Writer, Tells of Her Career," *Boston Globe*, May 5 1912, 6.

27. Emmanuelle Saada, *Empire's Children: Race, Filiation, and Citizenship in the French Colonies* (Chicago: University of Chicago Press, 2012), 43.

28. Ann Laura Stoler, "Sexual Affronts and Racial Frontiers: European Identities and the Cultural Politics of Exclusion in Colonial Southeast Asia," in *Tensions of Empire: Colonial Cultures in a Bourgeois World*, ed. Frederick Cooper and Ann Laura Stoler (Berkeley: University of California Press, 1997), 199.

29. On Eurasians who worked as interpreters for Customs, see Mae M. Ngai, *The Lucky Ones: One Family and the Extraordinary Invention of Chinese America* (Boston: Houghton Mifflin Harcourt, 2010), and Survey of Race Relations on the Pacific Coast, Minor Document 35, Wu Jingchao, *Chinatowns: A Study of Symbiosis and Assimilation*. PhD dissertation, University of Chicago, 1928.

30. See Cooper and Stoler, *Tensions of Empire*.

31. Stoler, "Sexual Affronts," 198.

32. See Robert Young, George Stocking, Nancy Stepan, and others.

33. See Robert Young, *Colonial Desire: Hybridity in Theory, Culture, and Race* (New York: Routledge, 1995).

34. See Frank Furedi, *The Silent War: Imperialism and the Changing Perception of Race* (New Brunswick, NJ: Rutgers University Press, 1998).

35. Jayne O. Ifekwunigwe, ed., *"Mixed-Race" Studies: A Reader* (New York: Routledge, 2004), 8.

36. Harriet Ritvo cautions against monodimensional understandings of the past, which assume consensus among experts "on issues where there was actually intense disagreement." Harriet Ritvo, "Animal Consciousness: Some Historical Perspective," *American Zoologist* 40.6 (December 2000): 847–52, esp. 847.

37. See Prasenjit Duara, *Rescuing History from the Nation: Questioning Narratives of Modern China* (Chicago: University of Chicago Press, 1995), and Rebecca Karl, *Staging the World*.

38. This problematic is still evident in contemporary understandings of "Chineseness," as demonstrated by the 2009 "Chocolate Angel" controversy in Shanghai.

39. See Tchen, *New York before Chinatown*; Lui, *The Chinatown Trunk Mystery*; Henry Yu, *Thinking Orientals: Migration, Contact, and Exoticism in Modern America* (New York: Oxford University Press, 2001); and Nayan Shah, *Stranger Intimacy: Contesting Race, Sexuality, and the Law in the North American West* (Berkeley: University of California Press, 2011).

40. Peggy Pascoe, *What Comes Naturally: Miscegenation Law and the Making of Race in America* (New York: Oxford University Press, 2009).

41. See Saada, *Empire's Children*, and Durba Ghosh, *Sex and the Family in Colonial India: The Making of Empire* (New York: Cambridge University Press, 2006).

42. Ian Haney López, *White by Law: The Legal Construction of Race* (New York: New York University Press, 1996), 27.

43. Daniel J. Sharfstein, "Crossing the Color Line: Racial Migration and the One-Drop Rule, 1600–1860," *Minnesota Law Review* 91 (2007): 592–656, 596.

44. Chinese nationality was granted to children born to Chinese mothers, if they were not recognized by their foreign fathers. The Miss Chinatown USA pageant still bases its qualifications on paternal descent, with no reference to blood quantum. www.chineseparade.com/pdf/2012_miss_chinatown_application_form.pdf

45. See Patricia Ebrey, "Surnames and Han Chinese Identity," in *Negotiating Ethnicities in China and Taiwan*, ed. Melissa Brown (Berkeley: University of California Press, 1996), 11–36.

46. See Haney López, *White by Law*.

47. See C. G. Alabaster, "Some Observations on Race Mixture in Hong-Kong," *Eugenics Review* 11 (1920): 247–48.

48. On the English common law tradition, see Sharfstein, "Crossing the Color Line." On Eurasian reactions to this contradiction, see Emma J. Teng, "Zaizao jiaxiang: Ouyayiren jiyilu zhong de yidong yixiang" [Reinventing home: images of mobility and returns in Eurasian memoirs], *Hanxue yanjiu* [Center for Chinese Studies research series] 12 (Taipei: Center for Chinese Studies, October 2009): 355–87.

49. Frank Dikötter, *The Discourse of Race in Modern China* (Stanford, CA: Stanford University Press, 1992).

50. James L. Watson's study of an emigrant community in the New Territories demonstrates how Eurasian and Chinese-Jamaican sons were ritually accepted into their fathers' lineage in their home village. James L. Watson, *Emigration and the Chinese Lineage: The Mans in Hong Kong and London* (Berkeley: University of California Press, 1975), 149-50. Such evidence supports the argument that lineage trumps racial purity or phenotype. I argue that the popular definition of Han Chinese as a people with "black hair, black eyes, and yellow skin" was a twentieth-century phenomenon, related to the rise of Chinese racial nationalism.

51. Adam McKeown, *Chinese Migrant Networks and Cultural Change: Peru, Chicago, Hawaii, 1900–1936* (Chicago: University of Chicago Press, 2001).

52. Kinship ties between Hong Kong Eurasians and Eurasians from mainland China are extensive, as Peter Hall and Eric Peter Ho reveal. See Peter Hall, *In the Web* (Birkenhead: Appin Press, 2012), and Ho, *Tracing My Children's Lineage*, 166.

53. The same could be said about "whiteness." However, I see my main contribution as an effort to further mixed-race studies within Chinese and Chinese American studies, and not as a contribution to whiteness studies, a field of equal importance in its own right.

54. See Lisa See, "The Funeral Banquet," in *Half-and-Half: Writers on Growing up Biracial and Bicultural*, ed. Claudine Chiawei O'Hearn (New York: Pantheon, 1998), 125–38.

55. I am grateful to Lisa See for e-mail correspondence and feedback on these topics.

56. See Tu Wei-ming, ed., *The Living Tree: The Changing Meaning of Being Chinese Today* (Stanford, CA: Stanford University Press, 1994).

57. See www.huaren.org/home.

58. See www.huaren.org/Text/11246910846136097/Chinese-Communities.

59. See, *On Gold Mountain*, xx.

60. Ibid.

61. See, "The Funeral Banquet," 135.

62. My use of the phrase "one-eighth Chinese" in the following paragraphs deliberately references the contentious question of blood quantum.

63. For a biography of Princess Der Ling, see Grant Hayter-Menzies, *Imperial Masquerade: The Legend of Princess Der Ling* (Hong Kong: Hong Kong University Press, 2008).

64. See Werner Sollors, *Beyond Ethnicity: Consent and Descent in American Culture* (New York: Oxford University Press, 1986).

65. Wendy Wang, "The Rise of Intermarriage: Rates, Characteristics Vary by Race and Gender," Pew Research Center for Social and Demographic Trends (Washington, DC: Pew Research Center, February 16, 2012), 1.

66. Ibid.

67. See www.apiidv.org/files/2010Census-WHIAAPI-2011.pdf.

68. Recent research shows that more and more mixed families are choosing to stay in China. James Farrer, "From 'Passports' to 'Joint Ventures': Intermarriage between Chinese Nationals and Western Expatriates Residing in Shanghai," *Asian Studies Review* 32 (March 2008): 7–29.

69. Paul Spickard, "Who Is an Asian? Who Is a Pacific Islander? Monoracialism, Multiracial People, and Asian American Communities," in *The Sum of Our Parts*, ed. Teresa Williams-León and Cynthia L. Nakashima (Philadelphia: Temple University Press, 2001), 18.

70. See Steven Masami Ropp, "Do Multiracial Subjects Really Challenge Race?: Mixed-Race Asians in the United States and the Caribbean," *Amerasia* 23:1 (1997): 1–16.

CHAPTER 1

1. See Carl T. Smith, *Chinese Christians: Élites, Middlemen, and the Church in Hong Kong* (Hong Kong: Oxford University Press, 1985).

2. Samuel R. Brown, *Chinese Repository*, vol. X (1841), 583; quoted in Ibid., 14.

3. See William Elliot Griffis, *A Maker of the New Orient: Samuel Robbins Brown, Pioneer Educator in China, America, and Japan: The Story of His Life and Work* (New York: F.H. Revell, 1902).

4. See Yung Wing, *My Life in China and America* (New York: H. Holt and Co., 1909). Yung's memoir has been translated into Chinese numerous times since 1915.

5. Ibid., 23.

6. Mary was the granddaughter of the eminent Reverend Bela Kellogg and Reverend John Bartlett.

7. *New York Times*, March 2, 1875. The wedding took place on February 24, 1875.

8. Joseph Hopkins Twichell, Journal, vol. 1, February 24, 1875, 60, Yale University, Beinecke Rare Book and Manuscript Library.

9. For more on Yung Wing and the CEM, see Edward J.M. Rhoads, *Stepping Forth into the World: The Chinese Educational Mission to the United States, 1872–81* (Hong Kong: Hong Kong University Press, 2011); Thomas E. LaFargue, *China's First Hundred: Educational Mission Students in the United States, 1872–1881* (Pullman: State College of Washington, 1942); and the CEM Connections website, http://www.cemconnections.org. On Yung Wing's view of America; see K. Scott Wong, "The Transformation of Culture: Three Chinese Views of America," *American Quarterly* 48.2 (1996): 201–32.

10. On the recent efforts to commemorate Yung Wing, see "Zhuhai Carries Spirit of Yung Wing," *Zhuhai Daily News*, November 22, 2010, http://deltabridges.com/news/zhuhai-news/zhuhai-carries-spirit-yung-wing.

11. See Peggy Pascoe, *What Comes Naturally: Miscegenation Law and the Making of Race in America* (New York: Oxford University Press, 2009).

12. Yung's appointment came on December 11, 1876.

13. John Kuo Wei Tchen, *New York before Chinatown: Orientalism and the Shaping of American Culture, 1776–1882* (Baltimore: Johns Hopkins University Press, 1999).

14. Pascoe, *What Comes Naturally*, 85–94.

15. Twichell, Journal, vol. 1, February 24, 1875, 59.

16. Pascoe, *What Comes Naturally*, 1.

17. J. Hector St. John de Crèvecoeur, *Letters from an American Farmer* (New York: Duffield, 1782, 1908 reprint), 51.

18. Such an inclusive vision was for the most part implicitly limited to immigrants from western and northern Europe.

19. Revised naturalization statutes of 1870 were worded to "apply to aliens, being free white persons, and to aliens of African nativity and to persons of African descent."

20. Chinese were first ruled ineligible for naturalized citizenship in 1878.

21. See *Yankee Notions*, March 1858.

22. David G. Croly, *Miscegenation: The Theory of the Blending of the Races, Applied to the American White Man and Negro* (New York: H. Dexter, Hamilton & Co., 1864), 19. US 10703.17, Harvard University, Houghton Library. This pamphlet was originally written as a hoax during the election of 1864. See Sidney Kaplan, "The Miscegenation Issue in the Election of 1864," *Journal of Negro History*, 34.3 (July 1949): 274-343. Thank you to John Kuo Wei Tchen for discussion of this issue.

23. *North China Herald*, January 18, 1870, p. 49.

24. Lorelle, "The Battle of the Wabash: A Letter from the Invisible Police," *Californian* 2 (October 1880): 364–76.

25. William Franking Wu, *The Yellow Peril: Chinese-Americans in American Fiction, 1850–1940* (Hamden, CT: Archon, 1982).

26. By 1910, anti-miscegenation statutes affecting Chinese had been passed in Arizona, California, Mississippi, Montana, Nevada, Oregon, and Utah. Between 1910 and 1950, Wyoming, South Dakota, Georgia, Idaho, Maryland, Missouri, Nebraska, and Virginia added such statutes. See Hrishi Karthikeyan and Gabriel Chin, "Preserving Racial Identity: Population Patterns and the Application of Anti-Miscegenation Statutes to Asian Americans, 1910–1950," *Asian Law Journal* 9.1 (May 2002): 1-40, and Pascoe, *What Comes Naturally*.

27. Asiatic Exclusion League, "Proceedings of the Asiatic Exclusion League, San Francisco" (San Francisco: Asiatic Exclusion League, October 1910), 64. Harvard University, Widener Library, Collection Development Department.

28. Asiatic Exclusion League, "Proceedings of the Asiatic Exclusion League, San Francisco" (San Francisco: Asiatic Exclusion League, April 1908), 19. Harvard University, Widener Library, Collection Development Department.

29. Ibid., 23.

30. See Tchen, *New York before Chinatown*.

31. See *New York Sun*, February 16, 1874, and Tchen, *New York before Chinatown*, 299.

32. "The Chinese," *New York Daily Tribune*, January 1869.

33. *New York Times*, December 26, 1873.

34. This is probably a reference to Norman Asing. Hab Wa and Tong A-chick, "Letter of the Chinamen to His Excellency Gov. Bigler," reprinted in the *New York Times*, June 5, 1852.

35. Wong Chin Foo, "The Chinese in New York," *Cosmopolitan* 5 (March–October, 1888): 297–311.

36. Twichell, Journal, vol. 1, February 24, 1875, 60.

37. See "Yung Wing a Yale Man," *New York Times*, August 5, 1898.

38. On Lee, see Amy Ling, "Yan Phou Lee on the Asian American Frontier," in *Re/Collecting Early Asian America*, ed. Josephine Lee, Imogene L. Lim, and Yuko Matsukawa (Philadelphia: Temple University Press, 2002), 273–87.

39. *Hartford Daily Courant*, July 7, 1887, p. 2.

40. *New York Times*, July 7, 1887, p. 1.

41. See Tchen, *New York before Chinatown*.

42. William Lyons Phelps, "Chinese Students in America," *Chinese Students' Monthly* 6.8 (June 10, 1911): 705–9.

43. See J. H. Trumbull, *The Memorial History of Hartford County, Connecticut, 1633–1884* (Boston: E. L. Osgood, 1886).

44. See Timothy Hopkins, *The Kelloggs in the Old World and the New* (San Francisco: Sunset Press and Photo Engraving Co, 1903).

45. Hawaiian society remained relatively tolerant of intermarriage, and by the 1920s American sociologists were portraying the island as a paradise of racial fusion.

46. On Chen Fang, see Bob Dye, *Merchant Prince of the Sandalwood Mountains: Afong and the Chinese in Hawaii* (Honolulu: University of Hawaii Press, 1997).

47. John Chock Rosa, "'The Coming of the Neo-Hawaiian American Race': Nationalism and Metaphors of the Melting Pot in Popular Accounts of Mixed-Race Individuals," in *The Sum of Our Parts*, ed. Teresa Williams-León and Cynthia L. Nakashima, 49–56.

48. See James McKinney Alexander, *The Islands of the Pacific: From the Old to the New* (New York: American Tract Society, 1895).

49. Caspar Whitney, "The Passing of the Native Hawaiian," *Harper's Weekly*, condensed for *Public Opinion*, April 27, 1899, p. 535.

50. Wang Yanwei, ed., *Qingji waijiao shiliao* [Historical sources relating to the foreign relations of the Qing Dynasty], vol. 1 (Taipei: Wenhai chubanshe, 1963), 300–302.

51. See Yung, *My Life*.

52. Huang Zunxian, "Ba Meiguo liuxuesheng ganfu" [An elegy on the overseas students recalled from America], 1881, collected in Huang Zunxian, *Renjinglu shicao jianzhu* [Poems from the hut in the human realm, annotated] (Shanghai: Shanghai guji chubanshe, 1981), 310.

53. Zhuhai.gov.cn/xxfw/zzjg/szsydw/sbwg/ronghong/gyrh/rhsp.

54. See Emma Jinhua Teng, "Wangguo? Ruguoji? Guoji Hunyin, Guojia Rentong Yu Wenhua Huiliu: Qingmuo Minchu De Zhongxi Lianyin Wenti" [Forgetting the nation? adopting the nation?: Chinese-Western intermarriage, dependent citizenship, and the question of national identity in the late Qing], in *Qingdai zhengzhi yu guojia rentong* [Qing dynasty politics and national identity], ed. Liu Fengyun, Dong Jianzhong, and Liu Wenpeng (Beijing: Shehui Kexue Wenxian, 2012), 665–75.

55. See Xu Ke, *Qingbai leichao* [A classified compendium of Qing anecdotes] (Shanghai: Shangwu, 1928).

56. This motif of loyal sacrifice appeared in the famous late Qing political novel, *Flowers in a Sea of Sin (Niehaihua*, 1905), the story of Sai Jinhua, who purportedly saved China by sleeping with the commander-in-chief of the foreign armies during the Boxer Uprising.

57. See Li Mo, *Bainian jiating bianqian* [One-hundred years of change in the family] (Nanjing: Jiangsu meishu chubanshe, 2000).

58. See Weili Ye, *Seeking Modernity in China's Name: Chinese Students in the United States, 1900–1927* (Stanford, CA: Stanford University Press, 2001).

59. Caleb Carr, *The Devil Soldier: The Story of Frederick Townsend Ward* (New York: Random House, 1992), 212.

60. Ibid., 203.

61. A second famous example was Sir Halliday Macartney (1833–1906), a Scottish medical doctor who entered the Chinese service and also joined the Ever-Victorious Army. Macartney married a Chinese lady in Suzhou in 1864. It was said that this union raised Macartney's status among the Chinese, who granted him many distinctions during his lifetime. Demetrius Charles de Kavanagh Boulger, *The Life of Sir Halliday Macartney, KCMG: Commander of Li Hung Chang's Trained Force in the Taeping Rebellion, Founder of the First Chinese Arsenals, for 30 Years Councillor and Secretary to the Chinese Legation in London* (London: J. Lane Co., 1908), 140.

62. Richard J. Smith, John K. Fairbank, Katherine F. Bruner, eds., *Entering China's Service: Robert Hart's Journals, 1854–1863* (Cambridge, MA: Harvard University, Council on East Asian Studies, 1986), 128.

63. See Smith et al., *Entering China's Service*, 128, 218; and Richard J. Smith, John K. Fairbank, Katherine F. Bruner, eds. *Robert Hart and China's Early Modernization: His Journals, 1863–1866* (Cambridge, MA: Harvard University, Council on East Asian Studies, 1991).

64. Hart and Ayaou had three children between 1858 and 1865. They were later sent back to England for education as Hart's "wards." Smith et al., *Entering China's Service*, 193.

65. See Lin Zixun, *Zhongguo liuxue jiaoyu shi: yibasiqi zhi yijiuqiwu* [History of Chinese overseas education: 1847-1975] (Taipei: Huagang chuban, 1976); Wang Huanchen, *Liuxue jiaoyu: Zhongguo liuxue jiaoyu shiliao* [Overseas education: historical sources relating to Chinese overseas education] (Taipei: Guoli bianyiguan, 1980); and Shu Xincheng, *Jindai Zhongguo liuxue shi* [History of modern Chinese overseas education] (Shanghai: Shanghai shudian, 1989).

66. Xing, "Qingmo minchu hunyin," 168–83.
67. Xu, *Qingbai leichao*, 165.
68. *Shen Bao*, September, 22, 1881.
69. Liang Qichao, "Xindalu youji jielu" [Selected memoir of travels in the new world], in *Yinbingshi wenji* [Collected writings from an ice-drinker's studio] (Shanghai: Zhonghua shuju, 1926), j. 38, 34b. Liang estimated that about one in twenty Chinese men in the mainland United States had married an American wife, and even more in Hawaii. Liang Qichao, "Xindalu youji," j. 39, 5a.
70. See Wu Jingchao, *Chinese Immigration in the Pacific Area*, MA thesis, University of Chicago, 1926.
71. Kuhn, *Chinese among Others: Emigration in Modern Times* (Lanham, MD: Rowman & Littlefield), 2008, 70–71.
72. Many overseas students came to view marriage with a Western woman as a definitive break with outmoded traditions, including arranged marriage, polygamy, and extended family. See Zou Taofen, *Yiyu xiantan* [Idle talk following translation] (Shanghai: Xuelin chubanshe, 2000).
73. Jerome Chen, *China and the West: Society and Culture, 1815–1937* (Bloomington: Indiana University Press, 1979), 140.
74. Chen Tianhua, "Alarm Bells," Ian Chapman, trans., *Renditions: A Chinese-English Translation Magazine* 53 & 54 (2000): 240. The tract was originally published in 1905.
75. An early writer on the theme of Sino–Western romance was a close acquaintance of Yung Wing, pioneering journalist Wang Tao (1828–97).
76. See Yi Nai, "Zhongguo yi yiruo weiqiang shuo" [China should take its weakness for strength], in *Xiangbao leicuan* [Classified compilation of articles from the *Xiangbao*], vol. 1 (Taipei: Taiwan datong shuju, 1968), 18–24.
77. Ibid., 6a.
78. Ibid., 23a.
79. "The Funeral of Mrs. Yung Wing," *Hartford Daily Courant*, June 1, 1886, p. 2.
80. Yung, *My Life*, 222–23. For a glimpse into Mary's last days, see her letter to her mother dated March 20, 1886. Yale University Library, Manuscripts and Archives, Yung Wing Papers (MS 602).

CHAPTER 2

1. *Huakai chengyi* [The blossoming of satisfaction and happiness], *Dianshizhai huabao* [Dianshizhai pictorial] 27 (Shanghai, 1892), 2, 9ab. Based on original translation by Min-Min Liang.
2. Chen Jitong was most famously satirized in Zeng Pu's *Niehaihua* [Flowers in a sea of sin], 1905.
3. See Sui Sin Far, "Leaves from the Mental Portfolio of an Eurasian," *Independent* 66 (1909): 125–32, and Annette White-Parks, *Sui Sin Far/Edith Maude Eaton: A Literary Biography* (Chicago: University of Illinois Press, 1995).
4. Lisa See, *On Gold Mountain: The One-Hundred-Year Odyssey of My Chinese-American Family* (New York: Vintage, 1995).

5. Ibid., 85.

6. Figure 6 represents the same photograph that was published in the *Chung Sai Yat Po* (Chinese daily newspaper), December 13, 1913.

7. Tiam's surname name in Amoy dialect was "Ng." The name "Franking" derives from "Frank Ng," Frank being Tiam's English name. William F. Wu, e-mail correspondence, October 19, 2012.

8. Mae Franking letter to Tiam Hock Franking, April 28, 1914, in Holly Franking, *Mae Franking's My Chinese Marriage: An Annotated Edition* (Austin: University of Texas Press, 1991), 82. Three versions of the text were used in preparing this chapter: the original text as serialized in *Asia* magazine in 1921; the Duffield edition of 1927; and this edition edited by Mae's granddaughter.

9. Franking, *Mae Franking's My Chinese Marriage*, 82.

10. Herbert Day Lamson, "Sino-American Miscegenation in Shanghai," *Social Forces* 14.4 (May 1936): 576.

11. Franking, "Introduction," *Mae Franking's My Chinese Marriage*, xix–xxxi, 1–2.

12. Ibid., 70–76.

13. See David H. Fowler, *Northern Attitudes towards Interracial Marriage: Legislation and Public Opinion in the Middle Atlantic and the States of the Old Northwest, 1780–1930* (New York: Garland, 1987).

14. Tiam H. Franking, "Letter to the Editor," *Ann Arbor Times*, September 15, 1912, in Franking, *Mae Franking's My Chinese Marriage*, 76.

15. "A Concrete Reason for the Race Prejudice at Ann Arbor," *Ann Arbor Times*, September 1912, in Franking, *Mae Franking's My Chinese Marriage*, 71.

16. Tiam's letter to Mae, October 12, 1912, in Franking, *Mae Franking's My Chinese Marriage*, 77.

17. Ibid.

18. See Franking, *Mae Franking's My Chinese Marriage*, xxiii.

19. See Leti Volpp, "Divesting Citizenship: On Asian American History and the Loss of Citizenship through Marriage," *UCLA Law Review* 52 (2005), 405–83, and Nancy F. Cott, "Marriage and Women's Citizenship in the United States, 1830–1934," *American Historical Review* 103.5 (December 1998): 1440–74.

20. Personal status and citizenship laws differed for nonmarital children. See Kristin Collins, "*Guyer v. Smith*, Personal Status Laws, and the Practice of Citizenship," unpublished paper.

21. See Volpp, "Divesting Citizenship."

22. See Ibid., and Cott, "Marriage and Women's Citizenship."

23. Under Chinese exclusion, all ethnic Chinese who wished to reenter the United States after traveling abroad were required to provide proof of their legal entitlement to enter the United States, either as members of the exempt classes and their dependents, or as U.S. citizens by birthright.

24. See, *On Gold Mountain*, 110.

25. 1910 Federal Census, Manhattan, New York, Enumeration District 1248.

26. 1930 Federal Census, Los Angeles, Enumeration District 19–175.

27. 1920 Federal Census, Ann Arbor, Michigan, Enumeration District 139.

28. See Dong Lin, *Zhongguo guojifa* [Chinese nationality law] (Chongqing: Guomin tushu chubanshe, 1943).

29. See Lin Man-houng, "Overseas Chinese Merchants and Multiple Nationality: A Means for Reducing Commercial Risk (1895–1935)," *Modern Asian Studies* 35.4 (2001): 985–1009.

30. See Volpp, "Divesting Citizenship."

31. See Dong, *Zhongguo guoji fa*; Zhang Zhiben and Lin Jidong, eds., *Zuixin liufa quanshu* [The newest complete book of six legal codes] (Taipei: Da Zhongguo tushu gongsi, 1987); and Wang Jiayi et al., eds., *Zuixin xiangming liufa quanshu* [The newest clear and precise complete book of six legal codes] (Tainan: Dawei shuju, 1989).

32. Patricia Ebrey, "Surnames and Han Chinese Identity," in *Negotiating Ethnicities in China and Taiwan*, ed. Melissa Brown (Berkeley: University of California Press, 1996), 33.

33. See Franking, *Mae Franking's My Chinese Marriage*, 114–15.

34. Mary Ting Yi Lui, *The Chinatown Trunk Mystery: Murder, Miscegenation, and Other Dangerous Encounters in Turn-of-the-Century New York City* (Princeton, NJ: Princeton University Press, 2005), 150–52.

35. Report from Amos P. Wilder, American consul general in Hong Kong to assistant secretary of state, Washington, DC, January 25, 1908, in Numerical and Minor Files of the Department of State, 1906–1910, RG59, M862, Roll 803, Case Number 12205, National Archives.

36. Lamson, "Sino-American Miscegenation," 576.

37. Han Suyin, *The Crippled Tree: China, Autobiography, History* (New York: G. P. Putnam's Sons, 1965), 278–79.

38. Wilder concluded that these women were on the whole well treated by their husbands and rarely were subjected to physical abuse. Wilder to assistant secretary of state, January 25, 1908, 4.

39. Ibid., 1.

40. Ibid., 2–3.

41. Ibid., 6.

42. Lui, *The Chinatown Trunk Mystery*, 151–52.

43. Wilder to assistant secretary of state, January 25, 1908, 4.

44. Mary Gaunt, *A Broken Journey, Wanderings from the Hoang-Ho to the Island of Saghalien and the Upper Reaches of the Amur River* (Philadelphia: J. B. Lippincott, 1919), 17.

45. Shu, *Jindai Zhongguo liuxue shi* [History of modern Chinese overseas education] (Shanghai: Shanghai shudian, 1989), 176.

46. See Lin Zixun, *Zhongguo liuxue jiaoyu shi: yibasiqi zhi yijiuqiwu* [History of Chinese overseas education: 1847–1975] (Taipei: Huagang chuban, 1976); Wang Huanchen, *Liuxue jiaoyu: Zhongguo liuxue jiaoyu shiliao* [Overseas education: historical sources relating to Chinese overseas education] (Taipei: Guoli bianyiguan, 1980); and Shu, *Jindai Zhongguo liuxue shi*.

47. Yung Kwai married Mary Burnham of Springfield, Massachusetts, on May 23, 1894. See *Hartford Courant*, May 24, 1894, p. 1. Yung Kwai was a distant cousin of Yung Wing.

48. *Donghua xinbao*, August 26, 1899, in Kate Bagnall, *Golden Shadows on a White Land: An Exploration of the Lives of White Women Who Partnered Chinese Men and Their Children in Southern Australia, 1855–1915*, PhD dissertation, University of Sydney, 2006, 251.

49. Wang, *Liuxue jiaoyu*, 742, and Shu, *Jindai*, 178.

50. Punishments were withdrawal of the government stipend and withholding of the diploma. See Lin, *Zhongguo liuxue jiaoyu shi*.

51. See Lin, *Zhongguo liuxue jiaoyu shi*; Wang, *Liuxue jiaoyu*; and Shu, *Jindai Zhongguo liuxue shi*.

52. Franking, *Mae Franking's My Chinese Marriage*, 8.

53. This stereotype was supported both by Western missionary discourses and Chinese Occidentalism. See Emma Jinhua Teng, "The West as a Kingdom of Women: Woman and Occidentalism in Wang Tao's Tales of Travel," in *Traditions of East Asian Travel*, ed. Joshua A. Fogel (London: Berghahn Books, 2006).

54. Xu Ke, *Qingbai leichao* [A classified compendium of Qing anecdotes] (Shanghai: Shangwu, 1928), 165.

55. Tiam's letter to Mae, March 12, 1918, in Franking, *Mae Franking's My Chinese Marriage*, 108.

56. A number of Chinese returned students who married foreign women during this time period would go on to become prominent members of the Nanjing government (1928–37). See Jerome Chen, *China and the West: Society and Culture, 1815–1937* (Bloomington: Indiana University Press, 1979).

57. Franking, *Mae Franking's My Chinese Marriage*, 92.

58. Ibid., 104.

59. Wu Tingfang, "Zhongguo," in Wu Tingfang, *Wu Tingfang ji* [Collected works of Wu Tingfang] (Beijing: Zhonghua shuju, 1993), 410.

60. See Wu Tingfang, *America, Through the Spectacles of an Oriental Diplomat* (New York: Stokes, 1914).

61. Wu Tingfang met the Huie Kin family in China in 1919. See Stacy Bieler, "The Xu Family," in *Salt and Light: Lives of Faith That Shaped Modern China*, vol. 2, ed. Carol Lee Hamrin and Stacy Bieler (Eugene, OR: Wipf and Stock, 2010). It is also likely that they met earlier when Wu was in the United States.

62. Franking, *Mae Franking's My Chinese Marriage*, 20.

63. Ibid.

64. *Chicago Daily Tribune*, May 1921.

65. Porter not only worked with Mae's original manuscript, but also visited her in Ann Arbor, interviewing her and taking dictation.

66. "Contributors and Contributions," *Asia* 21.8 (August 1921): 657–58.

67. Constitution of the American Asiatic Association as quoted in Ibid., 658.

68. Franking, *Mae Franking's My Chinese Marriage*, 8.

69. "Contributors and Contributions," *Asia*: 657–58.

70. Porter's name was not attached to the work until 1953. Franking, "Introduction," *Mae Franking's My Chinese Marriage*, xix.

71. *Hartford Courant*, May 2, 1922, p. 3.

72. See Emma Fong Kuno, "My Oriental Husbands," *San Francisco Bulletin*, May 25–June 19, 1922.

73. See Henry Yu, *Thinking Orientals: Migration, Contact, and Exoticism in Modern America* (New York: Oxford University Press, 2001).

74. *Boston Globe*, February 20, 1926.

75. Zou Taofen, *Yige Meiguoren jiayu yige Zhongguoren de zishu* [The memoir of an American woman who married a Chinese man] (Taipei: Longwen chubanshe, 1994), 38.

76. J. S. Tow, "Book Review," *Chinese Students' Monthly* 17.5 (March 1922): 421–22, and Chao Ying Shill, "Book Review," *Chinese Students' Monthly* 19.5 (March 1924): 72.

77. See Zou Taofen and Han Song, *Shenghuo zhoukan duzhe xinxiang waiji* [Letters to the editor of *Life Weekly*, vols. 1 and 2] (Shanghai: Shenghuo shudian, 1933), 1.

78. Zou, "Yiming xiaozhuan" [Short biography of anonymous], in *Yige Meiguoren*, 1.

79. See Zou and Han, *Shenghuo zhoukan duzhexinxiang*.

80. As she tells us, "I had taken my vow to obey, having specified that the word was not to be omitted from the marriage ceremony." Franking, *Mae Franking's My Chinese Marriage*, 10–11.

81. Ibid., 17.

82. Ibid.

83. See Frantz Fanon, *Black Skin, White Masks* (New York: Grove Press, 1967).

84. Wilder to assistant secretary of state, January 25, 1908, 4. Wilder also noted that some of the American wives worked in the fields alongside Chinese peasant women.

85. Franking, *Mae Franking's My Chinese Marriage*, 20.

86. Christine M. E. Guth, "Charles Longfellow and Okakura Kakuzō: Cultural Cross-Dressing in the Colonial Context," *positions: east asia cultures critique* 8.3 (Winter 2000): 606.

87. See Herbert Day Lamson, *The American Community in Shanghai* (PhD dissertation, Harvard University, 1935).

88. Wilder to assistant secretary of state, January 25, 1908, 2.

89. Franking, *Mae Franking's My Chinese Marriage*, 34.

90. Ibid., 55.

91. Ibid., 57–58.

92. Ibid., 59.

93. Tow, "Book Review," 421.

94. Wilder to assistant secretary of state, January 25, 1908, 6.

95. Franking, *Mae Franking's My Chinese Marriage*, 91.

96. See Wu Jingchao, *Chinatowns: A Study of Symbiosis and Assimilation*. PhD dissertation, University of Chicago, 1928, 326, and see Lamson, *The American Community in Shanghai*.

97. See Han Suyin, *The Crippled Tree*.

98. See Esther H. Jian, *British Girl, Chinese Wife* (Beijing: New World Press, 1985), (Chinese translation: Esther H. Jian, Bodun Jian, and Junyu Zhang, *Yi*

ge Yingguo funü zai Zhongguo [Beijing: Huaxia chubanshe, 1997]); and Eleanor Cooper and William Liu, *Grace in China: An American Woman beyond the Great Wall, 1934–1974* (Montgomery, AL: Black Belt Press, 1999).

99. See Melissa J. Brown, *Is Taiwan Chinese? The Impact of Culture, Power, and Migration on Changing Identities* (Berkeley: University of California Press, 2004).

100. See correspondence in Franking, *Mae Franking's My Chinese Marriage*, 61–115.

101. See Zou and Han, *Shenghuo zhoukan duzhexinxiang.*

102. Zou, *Yige Meiguoren*, 38.

CHAPTER 3

1. *New York Times*, December 26, 1856.

2. George Appo, *Autobiography of George Appo*, ca. 1915, Society for the Prevention of Crime Papers, box 32, Columbia University in the City of New York, Rare Book & Manuscript Library, 1.

3. Walter Lowrie, *Memoirs of the Rev. Walter M. Lowrie: Missionary to China* (New York: R. Carter & Brothers, 1850): 274–75.

4. Ibid., 275.

5. *New York Times*, June 20, 1859. See also Louis J. Beck, *New York's Chinatown: An Historical Presentation of Its People and Places* (New York: Bohemia Publishing, 1898); John Kuo Wei Tchen, *New York before Chinatown: Orientalism and the Shaping of American Culture, 1776–1882* (Baltimore: Johns Hopkins University Press, 1999); Tyler Anbinder, *Five Points: The Nineteenth-Century New York City Neighborhood That Invented Tap Dance, Stole Elections and Became the World's Most Notorious Slum* (New York: Free Press, 2001); and Timothy Gilfoyle, *A Pickpocket's Tale: The Underworld of Nineteenth-Century New York* (New York: Norton, 2006).

6. As John Kuo Wei Tchen, Tyler Anbinder, and others have demonstrated.

7. See Tchen, *New York before Chinatown*, 91.

8. *New York Times,* December 26, 1856.

9. Beck, *New York's Chinatown*, 9.

10. *New York Times*, June 15, 1899; *Hartford Courant*, October 4, 1895.

11. Timothy Gilfoyle, "Staging the Criminal: *In the Tenderloin*, Freak Drama and the Criminal Celebrity," *Prospects: An Annual of American Cultural Studies* 30 (2005): 285–307.

12. For more on George Appo, see Gilfoyle's biography, *A Pickpocket's Tale.*

13. Beck, *New York's Chinatown*, 1.

14. Ibid., 250. Appo was actually born in New Haven in 1856.

15. Ibid., 259.

16. Wong Chin Foo, "The Chinese in New York," *Cosmopolitan* 5 (March–October 1888): 297–311.

17. See, for example, Werner Sollors, ed., *Interracialism: Black-White Intermarriage in American History, Literature, and Law* (New York: Oxford University Press, 2000), and Robert Young, *Colonial Desire: Hybridity in Theory, Culture, and Race* (New York: Routledge, 1995).

18. *Yankee Notions* VII, no.3 (March 1858).

19. Tchen, *New York before Chinatown.*

20. The Chinatown census of 1900 recorded 82 Chinese men married to non-Chinese women, including 43 native-born white American women; 12 women of Irish descent; nine of English descent; 9 of German descent; and 2 each from Scottish, Canadian, French, Spanish, and African American backgrounds. Fifty-one Chinese men were married to Chinese women. Mary Ting Yi Lui, *The Chinatown Trunk Mystery: Murder, Miscegenation, and Other Dangerous Encounters In Turn-of-the-Century New York City* (Princeton, NJ: Princeton University Press, 2005), 155–56.

21. Based on figures from the U.S. Census, Julius Drachsler's study of New York intermarriage found ten cases of registered intermarriages involving Chinese between 1908 and 1912, with the wives virtually evenly distributed among German, British Canadian, French, Irish, Norwegian, Russian, Scottish, and Spanish ancestry. Julius Drachsler, *Intermarriage in New York City: A Statistical Study of the Amalgamation of European Peoples* (New York, 1921), 106. According to Shepard Schwartz, between 1908 and 1924 approximately 55 percent of Chinese in New York were in interracial marriages. Shepard Schwartz, "Mate-Selection among New York City's Chinese Males, 1931–38," *American Journal of Sociology* 56.6 (May 1951): 562–68. See also Lui, *The Chinatown Trunk Mystery*, 155–57.

22. Willard B. Farwell, *The Chinese at Home and Abroad Together with the Report of the Special Committee of the Board of Supervisors of San Francisco, on the Condition of the Chinese Quarter of That City* (San Francisco: A.L. Bancroft & Co., 1885), 14–16; and see Jacob Riis, *How the Other Half Lives: Studies among the Tenements of New York* (New York: Scribner, 1890, 1902 reprint).

23. *Harper's Weekly*, November 22, 1890, p. 910.

24. *New York Times*, November 22, 1896.

25. Beck, *New York's Chinatown*, 260.

26. *Chicago Daily Tribune*, December 27, 1897.

27. Wong, "The Chinese in New York," 308.

28. *New York Times*, November 22, 1896.

29. *New York Daily Tribune*, January 4, 1869.

30. *New York World*, January 30, 1877.

31. See Tchen, *New York before Chinatown.*

32. I borrow the term "racial migration" from Daniel J. Sharfstein, who defines it as the "social process by which people of African descent became white," including, but not limited to, passing. Daniel J. Sharfstein, "Crossing the Color Line: Racial Migration and the One-Drop Rule, 1600-1860," *Minnesota Law Review*, Vol. 91 (2007): 592-656, esp. 595 n. 12.

33. See Frank Moss, *The American Metropolis: Knickerbocker Days to the Present Time, New York City Life in All Its Various Phases*, vol. 3 (New York: P.F. Collier, 1897).

34. Nancy Stepan, *The Idea of Race in Science: Great Britain, 1800–1960* (New York: Macmillan, 1982), 1–5.

35. See Beck, *New York's Chinatown.*

36. See Tchen, *New York before Chinatown*, and Anbinder, *Five Points*.

37. Tchen, *New York before Chinatown*, 285.

38. See Beck, *New York's Chinatown*.

39. "Chinamen in New York," *New York Times*, December 26, 1856.

40. See Anbinder, *Five Points*.

41. See Gilfoyle, *A Pickpocket's Tale*.

42. The term "China Town" began to be used in the New York press in 1880. See Tchen, *New York before Chinatown*, and Anbinder, *Five Points*. On the demographics of Five Points see Anbinder, 42–50.

43. George Appo, *Autobiography*, 2.

44. See Sander Gilman and Edward Chamberlin, *Degeneration: The Dark Side of Progress* (New York: Columbia University Press, 1985).

45. See Ibid.

46. See Cesare Lombroso, *Criminal Man*, trans. Mary Gibson and Nicole Hahn Rafter (Durham, NC: Duke University Press, 2006); and Gilman and Chamberlin, *Degeneration*.

47. Gilfoyle, *A Pickpocket's Tale*.

48. Lombroso, *Criminal Man*.

49. Stepan, *The Idea of Race in Science*.

50. Charles White, *An Account of the Regular Gradation in Man, and in Different Animals and Vegetables* (London: C. Dilly, 1799), 123. Harvard University, Houghton Library, HOU-LC/GN60.W5. Charles Darwin similarly noted that racial crossing had produced piebald children, Charles Darwin, *The Descent of Man, and Selection in Relation to Sex* (New York: Appleton, 1898), 176.

51. Young, *Colonial Desire*, 18.

52. Josiah Nott, "The Mulatto a Hybrid—Probable Extermination of the Two Races If the Whites and Blacks Are Allowed to Intermarry," *American Journal of the Medical Sciences* (1843): 255.

53. Robert Knox, *The Races of Men: A Philosophical Enquiry into the Influence of Race over the Destinies of Nations* (London: Henry Renshaw, 1862), 497.

54. John H. van Evrie, *Subgenation: The Theory of the Normal Relation of the Races: An Answer to "Miscegenation,"* 2nd ed. (New York: Bradburn, 1864), 25.

55. Charles Darwin, *The Variation of Animals and Plants under Domestication*, vol. 2 (London: J. Murray, 1868), 21.

56. McClellan noted the presumption that Eurasians were "human nondescript[s]." Roland Guy McClellan, *The Golden State: A History of the Region West of the Rocky Mountains* (Philadelphia: William Flint and Co., 1876), 474–75.

57. *Debates and Proceedings of the Constitutional Convention of the State of California, Convened at the City of Sacramento, Saturday, September 28, 1878*, E. B. Wills and P. K. Stockton, official stenographers (Sacramento, CA: State Printing, 1880–81), 632.

58. Chinese Exclusion Convention, *For the Re-enactment of the Chinese Exclusion Law. California's Memorial to the President and the Congress of the United States* (San Francisco: Star Press, J. H. Barry, 1901), 4.

59. Letter of Herbert Spencer to Baron Kaneko Kentaro, August 26, 1892, published by the *London Times*, January 22, 1904, quoted in Wu, *Chinatowns*, 292.

60. See John H. van Evrie, *White Supremacy and Negro Subordination* (New York: Garland, 1868).

61. Beck, *New York's Chinatown*, 254.

62. For more on this play see Robert G. Lee, *Orientals: Asian Americans in Popular Culture* (Philadelphia: Temple University Press, 1999).

63. Thomas S. Denison, *Patsy O'Wang: An Irish Farce with a Chinese Mix-up* (Chicago: Denison, 1895), 78.

64. Ibid., 104.

65. The Jekyll and Hyde trope of Eurasian hybridity also had a darker side, which would find expression in stock villains from pulp fiction and Hollywood cinema.

66. See Young, *Colonial Desire*, and Stepan, *The Idea of Race*.

67. See J. C. Pritchard, *Researches into the Physical History of Mankind*, 4th ed., vol. 1 (London: Sherwood, Gilbert, and Piper, 1851).

68. See Carl Vogt, *Lectures on Man: His Place in Creation, and in the History of the Earth* (London: Longman, Green, Longman, and Roberts, 1864).

69. See Frank Norris, "Among Cliff-Dwellers: A Peculiar Mixture of Races from the Four Corners of the Earth," *Wave* (May 15, 1897).

70. See Ibid.

71. *Yankee Notions* (March 1858).

72. See Tchen, *New York before Chinatown*.

73. Beck, *New York's Chinatown*, 154.

74. Ibid., 252.

75. Ibid., 260.

76. Ibid., 269.

77. Ibid., 286–89.

78. Ibid., 289.

79. Beck reports that Appo attended the Oliver Street school and spent his childhood in the area of Oliver, St. James, Catherine, and Cherry streets. Beck, *New York's Chinatown*, 252–53.

80. Ibid., 11.

81. See Gilfoyle, *A Pickpocket's Tale*.

82. Beck, *New York's Chinatown*, 250.

83. Ibid., 252.

84. Young, *Colonial Desire*, 16.

85. Armand de Quatrefages, *The Human Species* (New York: D. Appleton and Company, 1879), 280.

86. See, for example, Sidney L. Gulik, *Mixing the Races in Hawaii: A Study of the Coming of the Neo-Hawaiian American Race* (Honolulu: Hawaiian Board Book Rooms, 1937).

87. John Chock Rosa, "'The Coming of the Neo-Hawaiian American Race': Nationalism and Metaphors of the Melting Pot in Popular Accounts of Mixed-Race Individuals," in *The Sum of Our Parts: Mixed-Heritage Asian Americans*,

ed. Teresa Williams-León and Cynthia L. Nakashima (Philadelphia: Temple University Press, 2001), 49–56.

88. *Boston Globe*, December 14, 1893.

89. *New York Times*, March 9, 1885.

90. *New York Times*, August 2, 1898.

91. Bob Dye, *Merchant Prince of the Sandalwood Mountains: Afong and the Chinese in Hawaii* (Honolulu: University of Hawaii Press, 1997), 225.

92. *New York Times*, September 28, 1906.

93. Indicative of the gendered dimensions of the discourse on interracialism, the notion of exceptional hybrid beauty was most commonly associated with women. Yet, George Appo's example demonstrates that the notion could be extended to men.

94. "Chinamen in New York."

95. *New York Daily Tribune*, January 4, 1869.

96. *The World*, January 30, 1877.

97. See Jayne O. Ifekwunigwe, ed., *"Mixed Race" Studies: A Reader* (New York: Routledge, 2004).

98. Harriet Ritvo, "Animal Consciousness: Some Historical Perspective," *American Zoologist* 40.6 (December 2000): 847.

CHAPTER 4

1. Eric Peter Ho, *Tracing My Children's Lineage* (Hong Kong: University of Hong Kong, 2010), 42.

2. See Ibid.

3. See Frances Tse Liu, Terese Tse Bartholomew, and Frances McDonald, *Ho Kom-Tong: A Man for All Seasons* (Hong Kong: Compradore House, 2003).

4. Employment in the Chinese Customs Service required bilingual skills and the ability to serve as an intermediary between Chinese and Europeans and, like the position of compradore, drew many Eurasians.

5. Yen-p'ing Hao, "The Compradors," in *The Thistle and the Jade: A Celebration of 150 Years of Jardine, Matheson and Company*, ed. Maggie Keswick (London: Octopus Books, 1982), 85–102.

6. See Irene Cheng, *Clara Ho Tung, A Hong Kong Lady: Her Family and Her Times* (Shatin: Chinese University of Hong Kong, 1976).

7. Ibid., 26.

8. See Jean Gittins, *Eastern Windows—Western Skies* (Hong Kong: South China Morning Post, 1969); Irene Cheng, *Intercultural Reminiscences* (Hong Kong: Hong Kong Baptist University, David C. Lam Institute for East-West Studies, 1997); and Zheng Hongtai and Wong Siu-lun, *Hejia nüzi: sandai funü chuanqi* [The women of the Ho family: the remarkable story of three generations of women] (Hong Kong: Joint Publishing, 2010), 254. See also Zheng Hongtai and Wong Siu-lun, *Xianggang dalao: He Dong* [The grand old man of Hong Kong: Ho Tung] (Hong Kong: Joint Publishing, 2007); and Zheng Hongtai and Wong Siu-lun, *Xianggang jiangjun: He Shili* [A Hong Kong general: He Shili] (Hong Kong: Joint Publishing, 2008).

9. Eva and Irene were among the first female students to attend the University of Hong Kong.

10. "He Luo Shi Xian Cai, nü buyou jiawai." Ho, *Tracing My Children's Lineage*, 11.

11. Peter Hall, *In the Web* (Birkenhead: Appin Press, 2012).

12. See Ho, *Tracing My Children's Lineage*.

13. See Ibid.

14. See Cheng, *Intercultural Reminiscences*. Among the best-known members of the Ho lineage today are Ho Fook's grandson, Stanley Ho/He Hongsun (1921–), Officer of the Order of the British Empire, a prominent businessman and casino magnate in Hong Kong and Macao; his granddaughter, Elaine Ho, who joined Jardine's in 1945 as a third-generation member of the Ho family to serve the firm; and Ho Tung's grandson Eric Hotung/He Hongzhang (1926–), Commander of the Order of the British Empire, ambassador at large of the Democratic Republic of Timor-Leste.

15. Yung Wing, *My Life in China and America* (New York: H. Holt and Co., 1909), 241.

16. Ibid., 241–43; and Mao Haijian, *Cong jiawu dao wuxu: Kang Youwei "woshi" jianzhu* [From 1894 to 1898: an annotated edition of Kang Youwei's "my history"] (Beijing: Sanlian shudian 2009); J. Y. Wong, "Three Visionaries in Exile: Yung Wing, K'ang Yu-wei and Sun Yat-sen, 1894–1911," *Journal of Asian History* 20.1 (1986): 1–32.

17. See Mao, *Cong jiawu dao wuxu*, and Cheng, *Clara Ho Tung*.

18. On Kang's travels, see Mao, *Cong jiawu dao wuxu*; Kang Wenpei, *Kang Nanhai (Youwei) xiansheng nianpu xubian* [A supplement to a chronological biography of Mr. Kang Nanhai (Youwei)] (Taipei: Wenhai chubanshe, 1972); and Kang Youwei, *Kang Nanhai ziding nianpu* [Kang Nanhai's chronological autobiography] (Taipei: wenhai chubanshe, 1966).

19. Kang's letter to Ho Tung is reproduced in Kang Youwei, *Wanmu caotang yigao waibian* [A collection of miscellaneous essays from the grass-roof house among ten-thousand trees] (Taipei: Chengwen chubanshe, 1978), 583.

20. See Rebecca E. Karl, *Staging the World: Chinese Nationalism at the Turn of the Twentieth Century* (Durham, NC: Duke University Press, 2002).

21. William Rowe, *China's Last Empire: The Great Qing* (Cambridge, MA: Belknap Press of Harvard University Press, 2009), 203–4.

22. Jing Tsu, *Failure, Nationalism, and Literature: The Making of Modern Chinese Identity, 1895–1937* (Stanford, CA: Stanford University Press, 2005), 41–42.

23. See Yuehtsen Juliette Chung, *Struggle for National Survival: Eugenics in Sino-Japanese Contexts, 1896–1945* (New York: Routledge, 2002); Karl, *Staging the World,* 110; and Tsu, *Failure,* 36.

24. See Frank Dikötter, *The Discourse of Race in Modern China* (Stanford, CA: Stanford University Press, 1992).

25. See Kai-wing Chow, "Narrating Nation, Race, and National Culture: Imagining the Hanzu Identity in Modern China," in *Constructing Nationhood in Modern East Asia*, ed. Kai-wing Chow, Kevin M. Doak, and Poshek Fu (Ann Arbor: University of Michigan Press, 2001), 47–84.

26. See Chow, "Narrating Nation"; Dikötter, *Discourse of Race*; and articles collected in *Critical Han Studies: The History, Representation, and Identity of China's Majority*, ed. Thomas Mullaney et al. (Berkeley: University of California Press, 2012).

27. Tsu, *Failure*, 41.

28. Peter C. Perdue, "Erasing the Empire, Re-racing the Nation: Racialism and Culturalism in Imperial China," in *Imperial Formations*, ed. Ann Laura Stoler, Carole McGranahan, and Peter C. Perdue (Santa Fe, NM: School for Advanced Research Press, 2007), 160.

29. Young, *Colonial Desire*, 18.

30. Ibid., 16.

31. See Nancy Stepan, *The Hour of Eugenics: Race, Gender, and Nation in Latin America* (Ithaca, NY: Cornell University Press, 1991).

32. Ibid., 138. In Stepan's view, "The failure to apply the notion of hybrid vigor to human populations is a measure of the racism that pervaded science until well after World War II."

33. See, for example, Thomas Griffith Taylor, *Environment and Race: A Study of the Evolution, Migration, Settlement and Status of the Races of Man* (London: Oxford University Press, H. Milford, 1927).

34. See Mullaney et al., eds., *Critical Han Studies*.

35. See Kang Youwei, *Datong shu* [One World treatise] (Beijing: Guji chubanshe, 1956). On the dating of this work, see Tsu, *Failure*, 36.

36. Kang, *Datong*, 119.

37. Ibid., 120.

38. Laurence G. Thompson, *Ta T'ung Shu: The One World Philosophy of K'ang Yu-Wei* (London: George Allen and Unwin, 1958), 148.

39. Kang, *Datong*, 124–25.

40. Ibid., 122.

41. Ibid., 118.

42. Ibid.

43. On yellow and white, see Dikötter, *Discourse of Race*, 55–57.

44. Tang Caichang, *Juedianmingzhai neiyan* [Essays on political and historical matters] (Taipei: Wenhai chubanshe, 1968), 1–38.

45. Ibid., 35b.

46. Ibid.

47. Yi Nai, "Zhongguo yi yiruo weiqiang shuo" [China should take its weakness for strength], *Xiangbao leicuan* [Classified compilation of articles from the *Xiangbao*], vol. 1 (Taipei: Taiwan datong shuju, 1968), 18–24.

48. Ibid., 4a.

49. Ibid.

50. Ibid., 6a.

51. Wu Tingfang, "China," in *Papers on Inter-Racial Problems: Communicated to the First Universal Races Congress, Held at the University of London, July 26–29, 1911*, ed. Gustav Spiller (London: P. S. King & Son, 1911), 129.

52. Ibid.

53. Sir Harry Johnston, "The World-Position of the Negro and Negroid," in Spiller, *Papers on Inter-Racial Problems*, 328–35, esp. 328.

54. Wu, *America*, 185.

55. Ibid.

56. For more on Zhang Jingsheng's work, see Tsu, *Failure*, and Chung, *Struggle*.

57. Tsu, *Failure*, 133.

58. See Zhang Jingsheng, *Zhang Jingsheng wenji* [Collected works of Zhang Jingsheng] (Guangzhou: Guangzhou chubanshe, 1998).

59. Chung, *Struggle*, 114–17.

60. Zhang, *Wenji*, 157.

61. Ibid., 159.

62. Stepan, *The Idea of Race*, 1.

63. See Emma J. Teng, "Miscegenation and the Critique of Patriarchy in Turn-of-the-Century Fiction," *Race, Gender and Class* 4.3 (1997): 69–87.

64. Liang Qichao, "Lun Zhongguo zhi jiangqiang" [On the future power of China], quoted in Dikötter, *Discourse of Race*, 82.

65. Karl, *Staging the World*, 3–4.

CHAPTER 5

1. *Washington Post*, August 27, 1919.

2. *Washington Post*, August 27, 1919; Frank Scully, *Cross My Heart* (New York: Greenberg, 1955), 58–59; *Weekly Review*, vol. 22 (October 21, 1922) (Shanghai: Millard Publishing), 270. For more on the family, see Bryna Goodman, "Semi-Colonialism, Transnational Networks and News Flows in Early Republican Shanghai," *China Review* 4.1 (2004): 55–88; and Warren Cohen, *The Chinese Connection: Roger S. Greene, Thomas W. Lamont, George E. Sokolsky and American-East Asian Relations* (New York: Columbia University Press, 1978).

3. *Weekly Review*, 270.

4. George Sokolsky, "My Mixed Marriage: A Jewish-Chinese Union," *Atlantic Monthly* (August 1933), 137–46, esp. 138.

5. Sokolsky, "My Mixed Marriage," 142. Similar experiences were reported by a writer from Qingdao. An Occidental (pseudonym), "My Chinese Marriage," *China Critic* (December 1934).

6. See Goodman, "Semi-Colonialism, Transnational Networks."

7. List or Manifest of Alien Passengers for the United States, Chichibu Maru, June 19, 1930, Passenger Lists of Vessels Arriving at San Francisco, 1893–1953, Records of the Immigration and Naturalization Service, RG 85, M1410:285, National Archives. 1940 census records for New York City show that Eric Sokolsky was returned as "white." 1940 Federal Census, New York, Enumeration District 31–483.

8. Peggy Pascoe, *What Comes Naturally: Miscegenation Law and the Making of Race in America* (New York: Oxford University Press, 2009).

9. Sokolsky, "My Mixed Marriage," 139. Sokolsky's work was reprinted in numerous places, including *Readers' Digest* 23.137 (September 1933).

10. Sokolsky, "My Mixed Marriage," 143.

11. Herbert Day Lamson, "The Eurasian in Shanghai," *American Journal of Sociology* 41.5 (March 1936): 642.

12. Robert E. Park, "Race Relations and Certain Frontiers," in *Race and Culture Contacts*, ed. E. B. Reuter (New York: McGraw-Hill, 1934), 78.

13. Everett V. Stonequist, *The Marginal Man: A Study in Personality and Culture Conflict* (New York: Russell & Russell, 1961), 222.

14. See Frank Furedi, "How Sociology Imagined 'Mixed Race,'" in *Rethinking Mixed Race*, ed. David Parker and Miri Song (London and Sterling, VA: Pluto Press, 2001).

15. As Frank Furedi has demonstrated, race relations sociology became enormously influential due to the institutional support it enjoyed and its close relationship to policy formation in the United States and Britain. Frank Furedi, *The Silent War: Imperialism and the Changing Perception of Race* (New Brunswick, NJ: Rutgers University Press, 1998), 144. See also Henry Yu, *Thinking Orientals: Migration, Contact, and Exoticism in Modern America* (New York: Oxford University Press, 2001); and Jayne O. Ifekwunigwe, ed., *"Mixed Race" Studies: A Reader* (New York: Routledge, 2004).

16. Sociologists could never distance themselves entirely from the biological discourse. The very terminology they employed, *hybridity* and *mixed blood*, perpetuated the link between culture and bodies. Lamson referred to Eurasians as "mixed bloods" while Wu labeled them "biological hybrids."

17. See Robert J. C. Young, *Colonial Desire: Hybridity in Theory, Culture, and Race* (New York: Routledge, 1995); and George W. Stocking, *Race, Culture, and Evolution: Essays in the History of Anthropology* (Chicago: University of Chicago Press, 1982).

18. Park, "Race Relations and Certain Frontiers," 78.

19. Ibid.

20. The Institute of Social and Religious Research helped fund the development of sociology in China. See Roy Porter, Theodore M. Porter, and Dorothy Ross, *The Cambridge History of Science: The Modern Social Sciences*, vol. 2 (Cambridge, UK: Cambridge University Press, 2003). Park himself also taught at Yenching University in Beijing for a semester in 1932.

21. See Yung-chen Chiang, *Social Engineering and the Social Sciences in China, 1919–1949* (Cambridge, UK: Cambridge University Press, 2001).

22. Yu, *Thinking Orientals*, 61.

23. Wu Jingchao, *Chinese Immigration in The Pacific Area*. MA thesis, University of Chicago, 1926, 16.

24. Ibid., 5.

25. Ibid.

26. Ibid., 290.

27. Ibid., 5.

28. Robert E. Park, "Human Migration and the Marginal Man," *American Journal of Sociology* 33.6 (May 1928): 881–93.

29. See Park, "Race Relations and Certain Frontiers," for example.

30. Robert E. Park, *Race and Culture* (New York: Free Press of Glencoe, 1950), 370–76.

31. Stonequist, *The Marginal Man*, 10.

32. Stonequist wrote his Chicago dissertation (1930) on the marginal man (published 1937).

33. Ifekwunigwe, ed., *"Mixed Race" Studies*, 33.

34. Park, "Human Migration and the Marginal Man," 893.

35. See "Tea with Harry Hastings, the Half-breed Chinese Intellectual of Victoria," May 26 and 30, 1924, Survey of Race Relations Records, Major Document, 24–31, Box 24; and "Interview with Harry Hastings regarding the School Strike and Other Matters," May 26 and 30, 1924, Survey of Race Relations Records, Major Document, 24–32, Box 24, Hoover Institution Archives.

36. E. B. Reuter, *Race Mixture: Studies in Intermarriage and Miscegenation* (New York: McGraw-Hill, 1931), 216.

37. Park, *Race and Culture*, 375–76.

38. Wu Jingchao, *Chinatowns: A Study of Symbiosis and Assimilation*, PhD dissertation, University of Chicago, 1928, 340.

39. Ibid., 343.

40. *Shenghuo zhoukan [Life weekly]* 4.7, 8, and 9.

41. The work was republished as Wu Jingchao, "Zhong Mei tonghun de yanjiu" [Researches on Sino-American intermarriage], *Shenghuo wenxuan* [Collected writings from *Life*], vol. 1 (Shanghai: Shenghuo Shudian, 1933).

42. On the brother's marriage, see *Zhongwai ribao [Universal gazette]*, November 29, 1902, 4.

43. Thomas Ming-Heng Chao, *Shadow Shapes: Memoirs of a Chinese Student in America* (Peking: T. M. C., 1928).

44. See Herbert Day Lamson, *Social Pathology in China: A Sourcebook for the Study of Problems of Livelihood, Health, and the Family* (Shanghai: Commercial Press, 1934).

45. See Herbert Day Lamson, *The American Community in Shanghai*, PhD dissertation, Harvard University, 1935.

46. See Herbert Day Lamson, "Sino-American Miscegenation in Shanghai," *Social Forces* 14.4 (May 1936): 573-81.

47. *North China Herald*, February 6 1869, pp. 69–70.

48. See *North China Herald*, February 6, 1869.

49. See Ibid.

50. See "First Yearly Report of the Shanghai Eurasian School, 1871," *North China Herald*, October 11, 1871.

51. These figures are taken from census surveys of Shanghai's foreign population (excluding the French Concession) conducted by the Shanghai Municipal Council. *North China Herald and Supreme Court and Consular Gazette*, October 19, 1876, p. 401; *North China Herald and Supreme Court and Consular Gazette*, July 18, 1890, p. 80; *North China Herald and Supreme Court and Consular Gazette*, July 12, 1895, pp. 45–50; *North China Herald and Supreme Court and Consular Gazette*, June 27, 1900, p. 1164. It should be noted that the Eurasian population in Shanghai was always undercounted and in some years Eurasians were not enumerated separately. Moreover, Eurasians who lived as Chinese were not counted in these figures. Foreigners were not enumerated on the Chinese census until 1928. Lamson, *The American Community*, 41E, 43. See also Tong Lam, *A Passion for Facts: Social Surveys and the Construction of the Chinese Nation-State, 1900–1949* (Berkeley: University of California Press, 2011).

52. Lamson, "The Eurasian in Shanghai," 646.
53. Lamson, *The American Community*, 390.
54. Pascoe, *What Comes Naturally*, 86.
55. Park, "Race Relations and Certain Frontiers," 61.
56. Wu, "Zhong Mei tonghun," 20.
57. See Kumari Jayawardena, *Erasure of the Euro-Asian: Recovering Early Radicalism and Feminism in South Asia* (Colombo, Sri Lanka: Social Scientists' Association, 2007). H. A. Giles's *Glossary of Reference on Subjects Connected with the Far East* (Shanghai: Kelly & Walsh, 1900) defines *Eurasian* as "the offspring of a European father and an Asiatic mother."
58. The Eurasian School later became the "Thomas Hanbury School and Children's Home."
59. Lamson, *The American Community*, 545.
60. Ibid.
61. Ibid., 544.
62. Ibid., 534.
63. Sokolsky, "My Mixed Marriage," 142.
64. Lamson, "Sino–American Miscegenation," 576.
65. Lamson, *The American Community*, 628.
66. "On Mixed Marriage," *China Critic* 3.9 (February 1930): 196–97. Thank you to Ke Ren for suggesting that the anonymous author might be eugenicist Pan Guangdan.
67. Ibid., 197.
68. Quoted in Lamson, "Sino-American Miscegenation," 579.
69. Lamson, *The American Community*, 572–73.
70. Gender mainly figures in Lamson's dissertation as a matter of parental inheritance—maternal versus paternal. He also accounted, to a lesser degree, for gender differences among Eurasians themselves, particularly when it came to the issue of marriage and sexuality. Lamson, *The American Community*, 591.
71. Lamson, *The American Community*, 627.
72. Lamson, "The Eurasian in Shanghai," 643.
73. Ibid.
74. Lamson, *The American Community*, 590–91.
75. Wu, *Chinatowns*, 342.
76. E. B. Reuter, "The Hybrid as a Sociological Type," *Publications of the American Sociological Society* 19 (1925): 59.
77. Reuter, *Race Mixture*, 211.
78. See E. B. Reuter, *The Mulatto in the United States: Including a Study of the Role of Mixed-Blood Races throughout the World* (New York: Negro Universities Press, 1969).
79. Reuter, *The Mulatto in the United States*, 315.
80. Lamson, *The American Community*, 549.
81. Ibid., 632.
82. Ibid.
83. Ibid., 633.
84. Reuter, "The Hybrid as a Sociological Type," 63.
85. Ibid., 62.

86. Lamson, "The Eurasian in Shanghai," 645.

87. As he put it, so often, their "biological inheritance is low grade" (Ibid., 642).

88. Ibid., 642–43.

89. Lamson, *The American Community*, 639.

90. Lamson, "The Eurasian in Shanghai," 646.

91. Lamson, *The American Community*, 576.

92. On the Yung brothers, see chapter 7. Toney Afong/Chen Xiru, whose full name was Antone Abram Kekapala Keawemauhili Afong, returned to China in 1890. He supported Sun Yat-sen in the revolution and in 1921 was made governor of Canton province. Chen Yongshan (also known as [Afong] Chun Wing-sen) became a general in Canton. Bob Dye, *Merchant Prince of the Sandalwood Mountains: Afong and the Chinese in Hawaii* (Honolulu: University of Hawaii Press, 1997), 230. Robert Ho/He Shili became a lieutenant general in the Chinese Army and later a UN representative. Zheng Hongtai and Wong Siu-lun, *Xianggang jiangjun: He Shili* [A Hong Kong general: He Shili] (Hong Kong: Joint Publishing, 2008).

93. Ifekwunigwe, ed., *"Mixed Race" Studies*, 8, 33.

CHAPTER 6

1. "Tea with Harry Hastings, the Half-breed Chinese Intellectual of Victoria," May 26 and 30, 1924, Survey of Race Relations Records, Major Document, 24–31, Box 24, Hoover Institution Archives, 6.

2. Ibid.

3. Lisa See, *On Gold Mountain: The One-Hundred-Year Odyssey of My Chinese-American Family* (New York: Vintage, 1995), 112.

4. List or Manifest of Alien Passengers, Monterey, August 5, 1906, Passenger Lists of Vessels Arriving at New York, New York, 1820–1957, Records of the U.S. Customs Service, RG 36, M237, National Archives; List or Manifest of Alien Passengers, Havana, February 23, 1909, Passenger Lists of Vessels Arriving at New York, New York, 1820–1957, Records of the U.S. Customs Service, RG 36, M237, National Archives; List or Manifest of Alien Passengers, Princess Victoria, August 19, 1916, Passenger Lists of Vessels Arriving at Seattle, Washington, 1890–1957, Records of the U.S. Customs Service, RG 085, M1383–26, National Archives.

5. List of U.S. Citizens, George Washington, December 22, 1913, Passenger and Crew Lists of Vessels Arriving at New York, New York, 1897–1957, Records of the Immigration and Naturalization Service, T715, Roll 2242, National Archives.

6. "Tea with Harry Hastings," 2.

7. Ibid., 3.

8. Sociologists picked up on this anecdote from the Hastings transcript as confirmation of the "half-caste's" "maladjustment" and suicidal tendencies. See Everett V. Stonequist. *The Marginal Man: A Study in Personality and Culture Conflict* (New York: Russell & Russell, 1961), and Wu Jingchao, *Chinatowns: A Study of Symbiosis and Assimilation*, PhD dissertation, University of Chicago, 1928.

9. "Tea with Harry Hastings," 5–6.

10. "Interview with Harry Hastings Regarding the School Strike and Other Matters," May 26 and 30, 1924, Survey of Race Relations Records, Major Document, 24–32, Box 24, Hoover Institution Archives.

11. "Tea with Harry Hastings," 4–5.

12. Ibid., 5.

13. "Half-Chinese Children: Those of American Mothers and Chinese Fathers," *Montréal Daily Star*, April 20, 1895, in *Mrs. Spring Fragrance and Other Writings*, ed. Amy Ling and Annette White-Parks (Urbana: University of Illinois Press, 1995), 187–91.

14. See "Sui Sin Far, the Half Chinese Writer, Tells of Her Career," *Boston Globe*, May 5, 1912.

15. Ibid.

16. *Debates and Proceedings of the Constitutional Convention of the State of California*, 632.

17. On Beck's use of Appo as an informant, see Timothy Gilfoyle, *A Pickpocket's Tale: The Underworld of Nineteenth-Century New York* (New York: Norton, 2006).

18. W. E. B. Du Bois, "The Freedmen's Bureau," *Atlantic Monthly* (March 1901).

19. Carlos A. Fernandez, "Government Classification of Multiracial/Multiethnic People," in *The Multiracial Experience: Racial Borders as the New Frontier*, ed. Maria P. P. Root (Thousand Oaks, CA: Sage, 1996), 16.

20. Paul Spickard, "Who Is an Asian? Who Is a Pacific Islander? Monoracialism, Multiracial People, and Asian American Communities," in *The Sum of Our Parts*, ed. Teresa Williams-León and Cynthia L. Nakashima (Philadelphia: Temple University Press, 2001), 18.

21. Daniel J. Sharfstein, "Crossing the Color Line: Racial Migration and the One-Drop Rule, 1600–1860," *Minnesota Law Review* 91 (2007): 598.

22. Ibid.

23. See Ian Haney López, *White by Law: The Legal Construction of Race* (New York: New York University Press, 1996).

24. See Melissa Nobles, *Shades of Citizenship: Race and the Census in Modern Politics* (Stanford, CA: Stanford University Press, 2000), 189.

25. See Shirley Geok-lin Lim, "Sibling Hybridities: The Case of Edith Eaton/Sui Sin Far and Winnifred Eaton/Onoto Watanna," *Life Writing* 4.1 (2007).

26. On racial migration see Sharfstein, "Crossing the Color Line," 595.

27. *New York Times*, November 22, 1896.

28. Haney López, *White by Law*, 59–61.

29. In re Knight 171 F. 299 (Eastern District Court of New York, 1909), 1909 U.S. Dist. LEXIS 229 (July 13, 1909).

30. Haney López, *White by Law*, 205–7.

31. Paul Spickard, "What Must I Be? Asian Americans and the Question of Multiethnic Identity," *Amerasia* 23.1 (1997): 47–48.

32. 8 C.F.R. § 110.35 (1944 Cum.Supp.), reprinted in Immigration and Naturalization Service, Immigration and Nationality Laws and Regulations as of March 1, 1944, p. 744.

33. John Kuo Wei Tchen, *New York before Chinatown: Orientalism and the Shaping of American Culture, 1776–1882* (Baltimore: Johns Hopkins University Press, 1999), 228.

34. 1900 Federal Census, Hartford, Connecticut, Enumeration District 158.

35. 1900 Federal Census, Seattle, Washington, Enumeration District 84.

36. 1910 Federal Census, Washington, D.C., Enumeration District 217.

37. 1920 Federal Census, Washington, D.C., Enumeration District 167. 1930 Federal Census, Washington, D.C., Enumeration District 385. On Yung Kwai's eminent career and promotions see "CEM Connections," www.cemconnections.org.

38. 1930 Federal Census, Los Angeles, California Enumeration District 19–175.

39. 1930 Federal Census, Ann Arbor, Michigan, Enumeration District 81–7, and 1940 Federal Census, Manhattan, New York, Enumeration District 31–483.

40. Haney López, *White by Law*.

41. Letter from Oscar S. Strauss, secretary of commerce and labor, to Elihu Root, secretary of state, Washington, D.C., September 14, 1908, in Numerical and Minor Files of the Department of State, 1906–1910, RG59, M862, Roll 923, Case Number 15302, National Archives.

42. List of U.S. Citizens, Empress of Canada, August 14, 1922, Passenger and Crew Lists of Vessels Arriving at Seattle, Washington, 1890–1957, RG 085, M1383.71, National Archives, Washington, D.C.

43. List or Manifest of Alien Passengers for the United States, Chichibu Maru, June 19, 1930.

44. Peggy Pascoe, *What Comes Naturally: Miscegenation Law and the Making of Race in America* (New York: Oxford University Press, 2009), 40.

45. Letter from Oscar S. Strauss to Elihu Root, September 14, 1908.

46. See Nobles, *Shades of Citizenship*.

47. Spickard, "Who Is an Asian?," 18.

48. Frank Moss, *The American Metropolis: Knickerbocker Days to the Present Time, New York City Life in All Its Various Phases*, vol. 3 (New York: P. F. Collier, 1897). Moss was Appo's counsel for the Lexow Committee.

49. Gilfoyle, *A Pickpocket's Tale*, 309–12.

50. Ibid., 309.

51. George Appo, *Autobiography of George Appo*, ca. 1915, Society for the Prevention of Crime Papers, box 32, Columbia University in the City of New York, Rare Book & Manuscript Library, 1.

52. Appo, *Autobiography*, 2; Moss, *The American Metropolis*, 123.

53. Gilfoyle, *A Pickpocket's Tale*, 94.

54. Appo, *Autobiography*, 2.

55. Ibid.

56. Ibid., 9.

57. See Gilfoyle, *A Pickpocket's Tale*.

58. See Sui Sin Far, "Leaves from the Mental Portfolio of an Eurasian," *Independent* 66 (January 21, 1909), 125–32.

59. *Boston Globe*, May 1912. For more on her life see Annette White-Parks, *Sui Sin Far/Edith Maude Eaton: A Literary Biography* (Chicago: University of Illinois Press, 1995).

60. Between 1902 and 1906, seventy-five of these lifelets were published. Hamilton Holt, *The Life Stories of Undistinguished Americans, as Told by Themselves* (New York: J. Pott & Company, 1906), vii.

61. See Dominika Ferens, *Edith and Winnifred Eaton: Chinatown Missions and Japanese Romances* (Chicago: University of Illinois Press, 2002), 195 n. 21 for attribution of "The Persecution and Oppression of Me."

62. Sui Sin Far, "Leaves," 125.

63. W. E. B. Du Bois, "Strivings of the Negro People," *Atlantic* 80 (August 1897): 194–98.

64. Ibid.

65. Eaton's first book, *Mrs. Spring Fragrance* (1912) was published by the publisher of Du Bois's *The Souls of Black Folk* (1903), A. C. McClurg of Chicago.

66. Sui Sin Far, "Leaves," 126.

67. The scene appeared in "Half-Chinese Children," and a short story, "Sweet Sin," published by the California magazine *Land of Sunshine* in 1898.

68. Sui Sin Far, "Leaves," 126.

69. "Half-Chinese Children," 189.

70. Ibid., 187.

71. Werner Sollors, "The Bluish Tinge in the Halfmoon; or, Fingernails as a Racial Sign," in *Neither Black Nor White Yet Both: Thematic Explorations of Interracial Literature*, ed. Werner Sollors (New York: Oxford University Press, 1997), 160.

72. Sui Sin Far, "Leaves," 126.

73. Ibid., 127.

74. Ibid., 126.

75. *Boston Globe*, May 5, 1912.

76. Sui Sin Far, "Leaves," 131.

77. Ibid.

78. White-Parks, *Sui Sin Far/Edith Maude Eaton*, 70.

79. Sui Sin Far, "Leaves," 128.

80. Edward Charles cut off communication with his family after his marriage in 1888 to Isabella Maria Carter. He became a successful businessman and joined several whites-only clubs. Grace married Walter Blackburn Harte in 1891 and moved to New York City, then Chicago. In 1912, she was admitted to the Illinois bar. May moved to San Francisco, where she passed for Mexican before eventually marrying a Euro-American man. She hid her Chinese origins even from her own grandchildren. Agnes married a French Canadian, while Rose married a Frenchman. Sara moved to Boston and married artist Karl Bosse. Winnifred married Bertrand Babcock and then Frank Reeves. Diana Birchall, *Onoto Watanna: The Story of Winnifred Eaton* (Chicago: University of Illinois Press, 2001), 19–21.

81. Birchall, *Onoto Watanna*, 30.

82. Sui Sin Far, "The Persecution and Oppression of Me," *Independent* 71 (August 24, 1911), 421–26, esp. 421.

83. Sui Sin Far, "Leaves," 129.

84. Sui Sin Far, "The Persecution and Oppression of Me," 423.

85. Ibid., 424.

86. Sui Sin Far, "Leaves," 130–31.

87. Ibid., 131.

88. Sui Sin Far, "The Persecution and Oppression of Me," 426.

89. Ibid.

90. Lim, "Sibling Hybridities."

91. Sui Sin Far, "The Persecution and Oppression of Me," 421.

92. Ibid., 426.

93. Spickard, "Who Is an Asian?," 14.

94. Sui Sin Far, "The Persecution and Oppression of Me," 421.

95. Anonymous interview subject, ca. 1928, quoted in Wu, *Chinatowns*, 342. Wu cites "The Persecution and Oppression of Me" as a source in the passage preceding this.

96. Even when they moved elsewhere, Los Angeles Chinatown remained a symbolic home for the descendants of Fong See. See, *On Gold Mountain*. Pardee Lowe's autobiographical account of his own mixed family in Oakland, California, during the 1930s provides further evidence of the place of mixed-race children within the Chinese community. See Lowe, "Mixed Marriage," *Asia* (January 1937), and "The Good Life in Chinatown," *Asia* (February 1937).

97. See, *On Gold Mountain*, 282.

98. Mary Ting Yi Lui, *The Chinatown Trunk Mystery: Murder, Miscegenation, and Other Dangerous Encounters In Turn-of-the-Century New York City* (Princeton, NJ: Princeton University Press, 2005).

99. See Huie Kin, *Reminiscences* (Peiping: San Yu Press, 1932), and Stacey Bieler, "The Xu Family: A Legacy of Service," in *Salt and Light: More Lives of Faith That Shaped Modern China*, vol. 2, ed. Carol Lee Hamrin and Stacey Bieler (Eugene, OR: Wipf and Stock, 2010), 78–106.

100. Bieler, "The Xu Family," 82.

101. Huie Kin, *Reminiscences*, 48, 78.

102. 1900 Federal Census, Manhattan, New York, Enumeration District 103; 1910 Federal Census, Manhattan, New York, Enumeration District 1248.

103. 1920 Federal Census, Manhattan, New York, Enumeration District 889.

104. 1930 Federal Census, Saugerties, New York, Enumeration District 50; 1930 Federal Census, White Plains, New York, Enumeration District 360; 1930 Federal Census, North Branford, Connecticut, Enumeration District 187.

105. World War I Draft Registration Card, Irving Van Arnam Huie, New York, New York, Draft Board 123. Selective Service System, National Archives, M 1509.

106. As Huie Kin recorded proudly in his memoir, all nine children were highly educated and chose professions like engineering, medicine, education, or mission work.

107. Sharfstein, "Crossing the Color Line," 594.

108. "Interview with Harry Hastings Regarding the School Strike," 5.

109. Dana Bruce Young, e-mail communication, November 6, 2012.

110. Sui Sin Far, "Leaves," 132.

111. See Kimberly McClain DaCosta, *Making Multiracials: State, Family, and Market in the Redrawing of the Color Line* (Stanford, CA: Stanford University Press, 2007).

112. Sui Sin Far, "Leaves," 132.

CHAPTER 7

1. See *Achievements of the Class of 1902, Yale College* (New Haven: Yale University Press, 1913), 619–23; "Bartlett Yung Thrills Yale Boys," *Hartford Courant*, January 19, 1914; "Bartlett Yung Visits Hartford," *Hartford Courant*, January 21, 1914.

2. *Rong Jinhuai zhi Sun Zhongshan han* [Letter from Bartlett Yung to Sun Yat-sen], January 2, 1912, *Sun Zhongshan guju jinianguan* [The Museum of Dr. Sun Yat-sen], www.sunyat-sen.org/sunyat/showdis.php?id = 1029.

3. *Achievements of the Class of 1902, Yale*, 621.

4. Ibid., 623.

5. Bartlett Yung, "The Water Supply of Greater Shanghai," *Journal of the Association of Chinese and American Engineers* 11 (1930): 31–37.

6. See "Zuizao he guowai nüzi jiehun de da Qing guanyuan" [The earliest Qing official to marry a foreign woman], December 20, 2009, Blog.sina.com. cn; and "Rong Hong, Zhongguo liuxuesheng zhifu" [Yung Wing, the father of Chinese overseas students], May 1, 2010, bbs.creaders.net/education.

7. Bartlett G. Yung, "'Drumming' Revolutionary China," *The World's Work*, March and April 1914. Quote from March 1914, 533–34.

8. Ibid., March 1914.

9. Ibid., April 1914, 692.

10. *Hartford Courant*, September 16, 1913. See also *Peking Daily News*, September 16, 1913, quoted in Yung, "'Drumming' Revolutionary China," 533; *North China Daily News*, September 17, 1913, quoted in "'Drumming' Revolutionary China," 533; *Hartford Courant*, October 23, November 4, 1913.

11. Yung, "'Drumming' Revolutionary China," April 1914, 698.

12. See He Zhang Lianjue, *Mingshan youji* [Travelogues of famous mountains] (Hong Kong: Donglianjue yuan, 1934).

13. See Josephine Lai-kuen Wong, "The Eurasian Way of Being a Chinese Woman: Lady Clara Ho Tung and Buddhism in Prewar Hong Kong," in *Merchants' Daughters: Women, Commerce, and Regional Culture in South China*, ed. Helen F. Siu (Hong Kong: Hong Kong University Press, 2010), 143–64.

14. Eric Peter Ho, *The Welfare League (Tong Ren Hui): The Sixty Years: 1930–1990* (Hong Kong: Welfare League, 1990), 10; see also Cedric Dover, *Half-Caste* (London: Martin Secker and Warburg, 1937), 166.

15. See Henry Lethbridge, "Caste, Class, and Race in Hong Kong before the Japanese Occupation," in *Hong Kong: Stability and Change: A Collection of Essays* (New York: Oxford University Press, 1978), 163–88; and Catherine Joyce Symons, *Looking at the Stars: Memoirs of Catherine Joyce Symons* (Hong Kong: Pegasus, 1996), vi.

16. See Wong, "The Eurasian Way," and Irene Cheng, *Clara Ho Tung: A Hong Kong Lady, Her Family and Her Times* (Hong Kong: Chinese University of Hong Kong, 1976).

17. Dong Lin, ed., *Zhongguo guojifa* [Chinese nationality law] (Chongqing: Guomin tushu chubanshe, 1943), 62.

18. See Ibid., 72. Current laws of the People's Republic of China and the Republic of China allow children to claim Chinese nationality through either parent.

19. See Symons, *Looking at the Stars.*

20. Robin White, "Hong Kong, Nationality and the British Empire: Historical Doubts and Confusions on the Status of the Inhabitants," *Hong Kong Law Journal* 19 (1989): 25.

21. This ambiguity is a central theme in many Eurasian memoirs. See Emma J. Teng, "Zaizao jiaxiang: Ouyayiren jiyilu zhong de yidong yixiang" [Reinventing home: images of mobility and returns in Eurasian memoirs], *Hanxue yanjiu* [Center for Chinese Studies research series] 12 (Taipei: Center for Chinese Studies, October 2009): 355–87.

22. C. G. Alabaster, "Some Observations on Race Mixture in Hong-Kong," *Eugenics Review* 11 (1920): 247–48.

23. Ibid., 247.

24. "Report on the Census of the Colony for 1901," Registrar General's Office, Hong Kong, August 15, 1901. See similar comment in "Report on the Census of the Colony of Hong Kong for 1931," Census Office, Hong Kong, April 17, 1931, 91.

25. Dover, *Half-Caste*, 166.

26. See Herbert Day Lamson, *The American Community in Shanghai*, PhD dissertation, Harvard University, 1935.

27. See Lamson, *The American Community*; Robert E. Park, "Race Relations and Certain Frontiers," in *Race and Culture Contacts*, ed. E. B. Reuter (New York: McGraw-Hill, 1934), 57–85; Dover, *Half-Caste*; Symons, *Looking at the Stars*; Han Suyin, *A Mortal Flower: China, Autobiography, History* (New York: G. P. Putnam's Sons, 1965); Han Suyin, *Birdless Summer: China, Autobiography, History* (New York: G. P. Putnam's Sons, 1968); Han Suyin, *My House Has Two Doors: China, Autobiography, History* (New York: G. P. Putnam's Sons, 1980); Emily Hahn, *China to Me* (Garden City, NY: Doubleday, Doran & Company, 1944); Peter Hall, *In the Web* (Birkenhead: Appin Press, 2012); Eric Peter Ho, *Tracing My Children's Lineage* (Hong Kong: University of Hong Kong, 2010);; Wu Jingchao, *Chinatowns: A Study of Symbiosis and Assimilation*, PhD dissertation, University of Chicago, 1928.

28. Ho, *Tracing My Children's Lineage*, 8.

29. See Symons, *Looking at the Stars*; Li Mo, *Bainian jiating bianqian* [One-hundred years of change in the family] (Nanjing: Jiangsu meishu chubanshe, 2000), 37–42.

30. See Carl Smith, "Protected Women in 19th-Century Hong Kong," in *Women and Chinese Patriarchy: Submission, Servitude and Escape*, ed. Maria Jaschok and Suzanne Miers (Hong Kong: Hong Kong University Press, 1994), 221–37.

31. See Alabaster, "Some Observations," and Dover, *Half-Caste.*

32. Alabaster, "Some Observations," 248.

33. Rebecca E. Karl, *Staging the World: Chinese Nationalism at the Turn of the Twentieth Century* (Durham, NC: Duke University Press, 2002), 118.

34. See Ibid.

35. Quoted in Frank Dikötter, "Introduction," in *The Construction of Racial Identities in China and Japan* (Honolulu: University of Hawaii Press, 1997), 4.

36. See Peter Gue Zarrow and Joshua A. Fogel, *Imagining the People: Chinese Intellectuals and the Concept of Citizenship, 1890–1920* (Armonk, NY: M.E. Sharpe, 1997).

37. For a discussion of Jean's British identification, see Vicky Lee, *Being Eurasian: Memories across Racial Divides* (Hong Kong: Hong Kong University Press, 2004); and Teng, "Reinventing Home."

38. Irene Cheng, *Intercultural Reminiscences* (Hong Kong: Hong Kong Baptist University, 1997); Jean Gittins, *Eastern Windows—Western Skies* (Hong Kong: South China Morning Post, 1969); and Florence Yeo, *My Memories* (Speldhurst, Kent, UK: Words & Images, 1994).

39. Zheng Hongtai and Wong Siu-lun, *Xianggang dalao: He Dong* [The grand old man of Hong Kong: Ho Tung] (Hong Kong: Joint Publishing, 2007).

40. Yeo, *My Memories*, 12.

41. Even among family in Hong Kong, he was known as "Sixth Uncle Walter."

42. Patricia Ebrey, "Surnames and Han Chinese Identity," in *Negotiating Ethnicities in China and Taiwan,* ed. Melissa Brown (Berkeley: University of California Press, 1996), 11–36, and Ho, *Tracing My Children's Lineage.*

43. Cheng, *Clara Ho Tung*, 94.

44. Gittins, *Eastern Windows—Western Skies*, 10–11.

45. See Yen-p'ing Hao, "The Compradors," in *The Thistle and the Jade: A Celebration of 150 Years of Jardine, Matheson and Company*, ed. Maggie Keswick (London: Octopus Books, 1982, 85–102); John M. Carroll, *Edge of Empires: Chinese Elites and British Colonials in Hong Kong* (Cambridge, MA: Harvard University Press, 2005); Howard L. Boorman and Richard C. Howard, *Biographical Dictionary of Republican China* (New York: Columbia University Press, 1968).

46. Ho, *Tracing My Children's Lineage*, 43.

47. Hall, *In the Web*, 119; Ho, *Tracing My Children's Lineage*, 118.

48. Lee, *Being Eurasian*, 29; Hao, "The Compradors," 96.

49. Cheng, *Intercultural Reminiscences*, 44, 209.

50. Ibid., 44.

51. The name was sometimes rendered Robert Hotung, and thus Hotung became a surname. Usages are inconsistent.

52. Irene's original Chinese name was He Qizi.

53. Cheng, *Intercultural Reminiscences*, 212.

54. Ibid., 1.

55. Cheng, *Clara Ho Tung*, xv–xvi.

56. Ibid., xvi.
57. Ibid.
58. Cheng, *Intercultural Reminiscences*, 1–2.
59. Ibid., 51.
60. Ibid., 22.
61. Ibid., 1.
62. Yeo quoted in Cheng, *Intercultural Reminiscences*, 175.
63. Cheng, *Intercultural Reminiscences*, 384.
64. Ibid.
65. Her books have been translated into Chinese multiple times since the 1980s.
66. Han Suyin, *Phoenix Harvest: China: Autobiography, History* (Reading, UK Triad Panther, 1985), 314.
67. Han, *Birdless Summer*, 22.
68. Yung, "'Drumming' Revolutionary China," April 1914, 692.
69. Han, *Birdless Summer*, 70.
70. Ibid., 49.
71. Han, *A Mortal Flower*, 401.
72. Han, *Birdless Summer*, 22.
73. Han, *Phoenix Harvest*, 315.
74. Ibid.
75. Han, *My House Has Two Doors*, 11.
76. The survey of contemporary Chinese articles on Han Suyin was performed by Betty Zhang in January–March 2008 and updated by myself in July 2008.
77. Wang Xingyuan, "Han Suyin de Zhongguo qingjie" [Han Suyin's obsession with China] *Zhongzhou tongzhan* [The United Front of Henan] 12 (1997): 40.
78. Qiu Jian, "Tade gen yongyuan zai Zhongguo—fang yingji nüzuojia Han Suyin nüshi" [Her roots remain always in China—interviewing British female author Ms. Han Suyin], *Juece yu xinxi* [*Policy and news*] 2 (2000): 25–26.
79. See Ye Junjian, "Zhongguo shi ta ganqing jituo de suozai—ji zhuming yingji zuojia Han Suyin" [China is the foundation of her emotional sustenance—on the famous British author Han Suyin], *Yanhuang chunqiu* [*Yanhuang spring and autumn*] 7 (1994): 56–59.
80. Zhu Jiongqiang, "Zai Ruishi fang Han Suyin" [Interviewing Han Suyin in Switzerland], *Wenhua jiaoliu* [*Cultural exchange*] 6 (2003): 12–13.
81. See Ye, "Zhongguo shi ta ganqing jituo de suozai."
82. Lin Xi, "Wo suo zhidao de Han Suyin" [The Han Suyin I know], *Dangdai wentan* [*Contemporary literature*] 9 (1982): 26–27.
83. Wang Huiqin, "Huajia yanzhong de Han Suyin" [Han Suyin in the artist's eyes], *Yishu jie* [*Art world*] Z3 (1994): 20–21.
84. See Ye, "Zhongguo shi ta ganqing jituo de suozai."
85. See Qiu, "Tade gen yongyuan zai Zhongguo."
86. Andrea Louie, *Chineseness across Borders: Renegotiating Chinese Identities in China and the United States* (Durham, NC: Duke University Press, 2004), 53; Elizabeth Sinn, "Xin Xi Guxiang: A Study of Regional Associations

as a Bonding Mechanism in the Chinese Diaspora. The Hong Kong Experience," *Modern Asian Studies* 31 (1997): 375–97.

87. See Tu Wei-ming, ed., *The Living Tree: The Changing Meaning of Being Chinese Today* (Stanford, CA: Stanford University Press, 1994); Shu-mei Shih, *Visuality and Identity: Sinophone Articulations across the Pacific* (Berkeley: University of California Press, 2007); Ling-chi Wang, "The Structure of Dual Domination: Toward a Paradigm for the Study of the Chinese Diaspora in the US," *Amerasia* 21.1–2 (1995): 149–69; and Ien Ang, *On Not Speaking Chinese: Living between Asia and the West* (New York: Routledge, 2001).

88. Ebrey, "Surnames and Han Chinese Identity," 33.

89. http://www.chineseparade.com/pdf/2013_miss_chinatown_application_form.pdf]

CHAPTER 8

1. 1920 Federal Census, Ann Arbor, Michigan, Enumeration District 139.

2. Holly Franking, *Mae Franking's My Chinese Marriage: An Annotated Edition* (Austin: University of Texas Press, 1991), 49.

3. Ibid., 105.

4. "Thousand pieces of gold" is a Chinese set phrase that refers to daughters.

5. Franking, *Mae Franking's My Chinese Marriage*, 57.

6. Cecile M. Franking, "An Act of Solace," *New Yorker* 29 (1954), 24–25.

7. 1930 Federal Census, Ann Arbor, Michigan, Enumeration District 81-7.

8. Cecile M. Franking, *From Ink and Sandalwood* (Warrensburg, MO: Mid-America Press, 1998), 10.

9. Ibid., 14, 15.

10. Ibid., 10, 12.

11. See "Introduction" in Franking, *Mae Franking's My Chinese Marriage*; see also reader comments in Zou Taofen and Han Song, *Shenghuo zhoukan duzhe xinxiang waiji* [Letters to the editor of *Life Weekly*, vols. 1 and 2] (Shanghai: Shenghuo shudian, 1933.

12. Franking, "Act of Solace," 24.

13. Franking, *From Ink and Sandalwood*, 35, and author's biography (n.p.); see also William Q. Wu, *Monsoon Season: An Autobiography* (Las Vegas: Uni-Star, 1996).

14. Wu, *Monsoon Season*, 83.

15. Ibid., 121.

16. Franking, *From Ink and Sandalwood*; see also Wu, *Monsoon Season*.

17. See Wu, *Monsoon Season*.

18. William F. Wu, e-mail correspondence, October 25, 2012; Franking, *Ink and Sandalwood*.

19. C. G. Anderson, "Address to the Welfare League," in Eric Peter Ho, *The Welfare League (Tong Ren Hui): The Sixty Years: 1930–1990* (Hong Kong: Welfare League, 1990), 9. Thank you to Elizabeth Sinn for helping me obtain a copy of this document.

20. See Kenneth E. Wallace and Cedric Dover, *The Eurasian Problem, Constructively Approached* (Calcutta: Thacker, Spink and Co., 1930).

21. See Melissa J. Brown, *Is Taiwan Chinese? The Impact of Culture, Power, and Migration on Changing Identities* (Berkeley: University of California Press, 2004).

22. Geoffrey Chan, e-mail correspondence, November 6, 2012. See also, Catherine Joyce Symons, *Looking at the Stars: Memoirs of Catherine Joyce Symons* (Hong Kong: Pegasus, 1996). For more on these complex familial relationships, see the pedigree charts in Peter Hall, *In the Web* (Birkenhead: Appin Press, 2012; 1st ed., 1992). I have relied on both the 1992 and 2012 editions of this work.

23. Zheng Hongtai and Wong Siu-lun, *Xianggang jiangjun: He Shili* [A Hong Kong general: He Shili] (Hong Kong: Joint Publishing, 2008), 27.

24. Carl T. Smith, *Chinese Christians: Elites, Middlemen, and the Church in Hong Kong* (Hong Kong: Hong Kong University Press, 2005), 139.

25. See Gwenneth Stokes and John P. Stokes, *Queen's College: Its History 1862–1987* (Hong Kong: Queen's College Old Boys' Association, 1987).

26. See Smith, *Chinese Christians*.

27. See Stokes and Stokes, *Queen's College*; Hall, *In the Web*; John M. Carroll, *Edge of Empires: Chinese Elites and British Colonials in Hong Kong* (Cambridge, MA: Harvard University Press, 2005), 78. Chan Hong Key, known at school as Chan Fook Hing, attended the Central School at about the same time as the Hung brothers. Geoffrey Chan, e-mail correspondence, November 8, 2012, and Dr. Bruce Chan, e-mail correspondence, November 10, 2012.

28. See Smith, *Chinese Christians*.

29. See Stokes and Stokes, *Queen's College*.

30. Geoffrey Chan, e-mail correspondence, November 6, 2012; Smith, *Chinese Christians*, 153–54.

31. See Smith, *Chinese Christians*.

32. Eric Peter Ho, *Tracing My Children's Lineage* (Hong Kong: Hong Kong University Press, 2010), 306–7; Hall, *In the Web*.

33. Symons, *Looking at the Stars*, 1. Thank you to Elizabeth Sinn for sharing the original manuscripts of this work with me.

34. See David Pomfret, "Raising Eurasia: Race, Class, and Age in French and British Colonies," *Comparative Studies in Society and History* 51.2 (2009): 314–43; and Cedric Dover, *Cimmerii: Or Eurasians and Their Future* (Calcutta: Modern Art Press, 1929).

35. See Pomfret, "Raising Eurasia."

36. Frank Welsh, *A History of Hong Kong* (London: HarperCollins, 1993), 381.

37. Stokes and Stokes, *Queen's College*, 334; Symons, *Looking at the Stars*, 2.

38. Stokes and Stokes, *Queen's College*, 294.

39. Stokes and Stokes, *Queen's College*, 256, and Smith, *Chinese Christians*, 263.

40. Stokes and Stokes, *Queen's College*, 39.

41. See Ibid.

42. See Ibid., and Symons, *Looking at the Stars*.

43. See Smith, *Chinese Christians*, 153-54.

44. Information provided by Geoffrey Chan, e-mail correspondence, November 6, 2012, and January 25, 2013.

45. See Hall, *In the Web*.

46. Symons, *Looking at the Stars*, 2.

47. On Catherine's marriage to Ho Sai-Wing, see Smith, *Chinese Christians*, 154. Ho Tung adopted this son from his brother, Ho Fook. On the "web" of Eurasian families, see Hall, *In the Web*. Information on family ties among Anderson/Hungs, Chan Hong Key/Mackenzies, and Tai Yuk Ching (1876–1955)/Patersons from Dr. Bruce Chan, e-mail correspondence, November 8, 2012.

48. See Symons, *Looking at the Stars*.

49. Ibid., 3.

50. Ibid., 2.

51. Ibid., 4.

52. Ibid.

53. Ibid.

54. Ibid., 13.

55. Ibid., 43.

56. John M. Carroll, *A Concise History of Hong Kong* (Lanham, MD: Rowman & Littlefield, 2007), 111–12.

57. Ibid., 110.

58. See Anderson, "Address."

59. Quoted in Pomfret, "Raising Eurasia," 318.

60. Anderson, "Address," 9.

61. Ibid.

62. Melissa J. Brown, "Ethnic Classification and Culture: The Case of the Tujia in Hubei, China," *Asian Ethnicity* 2.1 (2001): 55–72, 53; and Stevan Harrell, "Introduction," in *Negotiating Ethnicities in China and Taiwan*, ed. Melissa J. Brown (Berkeley: Institute of East Asian Studies and University of California Berkeley, Center for Chinese Studies, 1996), 1–18.

63. Anderson, "Address," 8.

64. Ibid., 9.

65. Ibid.

66. See Ibid.

67. Ibid., 9.

68. See Florence Yeo, *My Memories* (Speldhurst, Kent, UK: Words & Images, 1994).

69. Anderson, "Address," 9.

70. Smith, *Chinese Christians*, 169–70.

71. C.G. Alabaster, "Some Observations on Race Mixture in Hong-Kong," *Eugenics Review* 11 (1920): 247.

72. Ho, *Tracing My Children's Lineage*, 12-16, and Hall, *In the Web*.

73. Ho, *Tracing My Children's Lineage*.

74. See Ibid.

75. *New York Times*, April 15, 1901, p. 6.

76. See Alabaster, "Some Observations."

77. See Hall, *In the Web*.

78. See Hall, *In the Web*, and Symons, *Looking at the Stars.*

79. See Symons, *Looking at the Stars*, and Jean Gittins, *Eastern Windows— Western Skies* (Hong Kong: South China Morning Post, 1969).

80. See Alabaster, "Some Observations."

81. See Hall, *In the Web.*

82. See Ho, "The Welfare League."

83. Kotwaj, Kotwall, and Kotewall are Parsi names. Other Eurasians have Armenian names. See Hall, *In the Web.*

84. See Ho, *Tracing My Children's Lineage.*

85. Anderson, "Address," 9.

86. See Elizabeth Sinn, *Power and Charity: The Early History of the Tung Wah Hospital, Hong Kong* (New York: Oxford University Press, 1989), and Carroll, *A Concise History of Hong Kong*, 61.

87. Carroll, *Edge of Empires*, 100, 107.

88. See Hall, *In the Web*, and Carroll, *Edge of Empires.*

89. Carroll, *Edge of Empires*, 107.

90. See Hall, *In the Web*, and Ho, *Tracing My Children's Lineage.*

91. *Hong Kong Telegraph*, September 24, 1895, pp. 289–90, quoted in Carl T. Smith, "Protected Women in 19th-Century Hong Kong," in *Women and Chinese Patriarchy: Submission, Servitude and Escape*, ed. Maria Jaschok and Suzanne Miers (Hong Kong: Hong Kong University Press, 1994), 221–37; and Carl T. Smith, "Abandoned into Prosperity: Women on the Fringe of Expatriate Society," in *Merchants' Daughters: Women, Commerce, and Regional Culture in South China*, ed. Helen F. Siu (Hong Kong: Hong Kong University Press, 2010), 129–42.

92. Smith, "Protected Women," 224 and 234–35.

93. Ho, *Tracing My Children's Lineage*, 334.

94. See Frances Tse Liu, Terese Tse Bartholomew, and Frances McDonald, *Ho Kom-Tong: A Man for All Seasons* (Hong Kong: Compradore House, 2003), and Ho, *Tracing My Children's Lineage.*

95. Ho, *Tracing My Children's Lineage*, 7.

96. Hall, *In the Web*, xvi.

97. Anderson, "Address," 9.

98. Until 1931, the Householder Method was used to collect census data. In 1931, the Canvasser Method was adopted. Yet, enumerators were still permitted to leave forms to be filled out by the householders themselves. In either case, the census report indicates that racial designations were to be based on "descent claimed." See "Report on the Census of the Colony of Hong Kong for 1931," Census Office (Hong Kong, April 17, 1931).

99. "Report on the Census of the Colony for 1897," Registrar General's Office (Hong Kong, June 20, 1897), 468.

100. "Report on the Census of the Colony for 1901," Registrar General's Office (Hong Kong, August 15, 1901).

101. "Report on the Census of the Colony for 1921," Census Office (Hong Kong, November 10, 1921).

102. "Report on the Census of the Colony of Hong Kong for 1931," 91.

103. Ibid., 160.

104. Ibid., 112.

105. "Report on the Census of the Colony for 1911," Census Office (Hong Kong, October 27, 1911).

106. Alabaster, "Some Observations," 248.

107. See Brown, *Is Taiwan Chinese?*

108. Symons, *Looking at the Stars*, 3.

109. See Emma J. Teng, "Zaizao jiaxiang: Ouyayiren jiyilu zhong de yidong yixiang" [Reinventing home: images of mobility and returns in Eurasian memoirs], *Hanxue yanjiu* [Center for Chinese Studies research series], 12 (Taipei: Center for Chinese Studies, October 2009): 355–87.

110. Pomfret, "Raising Eurasia," 328.

111. Ho, *Tracing My Children's Lineage*, 109–10.

112. Quoted in Pomfret, "Raising Eurasia," 329.

113. Ibid., 332.

114. Symons, *Looking at the Stars*, 9; and see Teng, "Reinventing Home."

115. Joyce Anderson Symons later became the longtime head of DGS.

116. See Ho, "The Welfare League."

117. Carroll, *A Concise History of Hong Kong*, 108.

118. Ho, "The Welfare League," 4.

119. See Ibid.

120. See Wallace and Dover, *The Eurasian Problem*.

121. Ho, "The Welfare League," 5.

122. See Hall, *In the Web*; Ho, "The Welfare League"; Ho, *Tracing My Children's Lineage*.

123. Symons, *Looking at the Stars*, 9.

124. Ho, "The Welfare League," 2.

125. Ibid., 3.

126. See Hall, *In the Web*.

127. Steven Masami Ropp, "Do Multiracial Subjects Really Challenge Race?: Mixed-Race Asians in the United States and the Caribbean," *Amerasia* 23:1 (1997): 1.

128. See Maria P. P. Root, ed., *Racially Mixed People in America* (Newbury Park, CA: Sage, 1992), and Root, ed., *The Multiracial Experience: Racial Borders as the New Frontier* (Thousand Oaks, CA: Sage, 1996).

CODA

1. Anne M. Hamilton, "From China to Hartford, A Historic Connection," *Hartford Courant*, June 14, 2009, F7. My account of Elsie Jane Yung's burial is based on the reporting in this *Hartford Courant* story.

2. *Los Angeles Times,* November 7, 1908.

3. "Marriage Announcement," *Hartford Daily Courant*, February 25, 1875, 2; Hamilton, "From China to Hartford," F7.

4. Peter Hall, *In the Web* (Birkenhead: Appin Press, 2012; 1st ed., 1992).

5. Eric Peter Ho, *Tracing My Children's Lineage* (Hong Kong: University of Hong Kong, 2010), 314.

6. See Ibid.

7. The British had treated Eurasians with characteristic inconsistency from the outbreak of the war. In 1941, Eurasians had been denied evacuation from Hong Kong with the other "British" women and children, despite their possession of valid British passports, and yet they were called up for the Volunteers. This was recalled bitterly by many Eurasians years later. See Catherine Joyce Symons, *Looking at the Stars: Memoirs of Catherine Joyce Symons* (Hong Kong: Pegasus Books, 1996).

8. Hamilton, "From China to Hartford," F7.

9. See Symons, *Looking at the Stars.*

10. See Hall, *In the Web,* 1992.

11. The impending return of Hong Kong to China in 1997 drove a large diaspora from Hong Kong in general.

12. See Vicky Lee, *Being Eurasian: Memories across Racial Divides* (Hong Kong: Hong Kong University Press, 2004).

13. Hall, *In the Web,* 123.

14. Ibid.

15. Irene Cheng, *Clara Ho Tung: A Hong Kong Lady, Her Family and Her Times* (Hong Kong: Chinese University of Hong Kong, 1976), 25.

16. Bruce E. Hall, *Tea That Burns: A Family Memoir of Chinatown* (New York: Free Press, 1998), 38.

17. Ho, *Tracing My Children's Lineage,* 8

18. "Statement on 'Race,'" United Nations Educational, Scientific and Cultural Organization, Meeting of Experts on Race Problems, UNESCO House, December 12–14, 1949, 4.

19. See Wendy Wang, "The Rise of Intermarriage: Rates, Characteristics Vary by Race and Gender," Pew Research Center for Social and Demographic Trends (Washington, D.C.: Pew Research Center, February 16, 2012).

20. See Stephen Murphy-Shigematsu, *When Half Is Whole: Multiethnic Asian American Identities* (Stanford, CA: Stanford University Press, 2012).

21. See Lisa See's website, www.lisasee.com.

22. Dana Bruce Young, e-mail correspondence, November 6, 2012. Young is one of the administrators of the "CEM Connections" website, cemconnections.org.

23. www.williamfwu.com.

24. See Eric Hotung website, www.erichotung.com.

25. Diana Birchall, *Onoto Watanna: The Story of Winnifred Eaton* (Chicago: University of Illinois Press, 2001), 11.

26. Sui Sin Far, "Half-Chinese Children: Those of American Mothers and Chinese Fathers," *Montréal Daily Star,* April 20, 1895; reprinted in *Mrs. Spring Fragrance and Other Writings,* ed. Amy Ling and Annette White-Parks (Urbana: University of Illinois Press, 1995), 189.

27. Lily, e-mail communication, November 2, 2012.

28. See Paul Spickard, "The Subject Is Mixed Race: The Boom in Biracial Biography," in *Rethinking "Mixed Race,"* ed. David Parker and Miri Song (London: Pluto Press, 2001), 76–98; Emma Teng, "Naming the Subject: Recovering 'Euro-Asian' History—Reading Kumari Jayawardena's *Erasure of the Euro-Asian: Recovering Early Radicalism and Feminism in South Asia* (2007)," *Journal of Women's History* 22.4 (2010): 257–62.

29. For a discussion of some of these works, see Teng, "Naming the Subject."

30. Hall, *In the Web*, 163.

31. Here I am paraphrasing Peter Moss, *Bye-Bye Blackbird: An Anglo-Indian Memoir* (New York: iUniverse, 2004), 1–2.

32. Hamilton, "From China to Hartford," F7. As noted on the gravestone at Cedar Hill Cemetery, Bartlett Yung's ashes were interred in Shanghai, where he had died in 1942. Several members of the Yung and Kellogg families are buried in this plot at Cedar Hill Cemetery.

EPILOGUE

1. Shangguan Tianyi, "Zajiao hunxue zhen neng gailiang Zhongguo renzhong?" [Can mixed-blood hybrids *really* improve the Chinese race?], *Duowei zhoukan* [*chinesenewsweek.com*], August 24, 2001, www.chinesenewsweek.com/65/ Commentary/4870.html, 1.

2. Ibid.

3. In 2009 *ShanghaiDaily.com* carried a story explaining the perennial popularity of "fusion" models: "There's a perception among Chinese that hun xue are especially attractive and more intelligent than most people." See "Half-and-Half, Chinese and Western, Get Best of Both Worlds," *ShanghaiDaily.com,* 2009, www.shanghaidaily.com/article/print.asp?id = 414154; Jiang Zhaolun, "Shida keren nüxing" [Top ten hottest female stars], *ETtoday.com,* March 13, 2001, www.ettoday.com/2001/03/13/350-398165.htm; "Xianggang: hunxue mote 'da hunzhan'"; "You Say Potato (malingshu), I Say Potato (tudou)!," *Beijing Scene [xin Beijing],* November 12–18, 2001, www.beijingscene.com/v06i005/comrade/comrade.html.

4. See Homi K. Bhabha, "Signs Taken for Wonders: Questions of Ambivalence and Authority under a Tree Outside Delhi, May 1817," *Critical Inquiry* 12.1 (1985): 144–65; Bhabha, "The Third Space," in *Identity: Community, Culture, Difference,* ed. Jonathan Rutherford (London: Lawrence & Wishart, 1990), 207–21; Ella Shohat, "Notes on the 'Post-Colonial,'" *Social Text* 31/32 (1992): 99–113; and Robert J.C. Young, *Colonial Desire: Hybridity in Theory, Culture, and Race* (New York: Routledge, 1995).

5. Bill Ashcroft et al., eds., *The Post-Colonial Studies Reader* (New York: Routledge, 1995), 183.

6. See Maria P.P. Root, *Racially Mixed People in America* (Newbury Park, CA: Sage, 1992); Maria P.P. Root, ed., *The Multiracial Experience: Racial Borders as the New Frontier* (Thousand Oaks, CA: Sage, 1996); and Naomi Zack, ed., *American Mixed Race: The Culture of Micro-Diversity* (Lanham, MD: Rowman & Littlefield, 1995).

7. Root, *Racially Mixed People,* 3.

8. See "Maggie Q—Xianggang hunxue xinggan mote."

9. The 2009 *ShanghaiDaily.com* article cited in n. 3 lauded the bilingual and bicultural assets purportedly possessed by the "half-and-half," which ostensibly opens professional and social opportunities for them in China.

10. See *EurasianNation—Home,* http://eurasiannation.proboards.com/; *Mixed Asians,* www.mixedasians.com/; *Eurasians Worldwide—Uniting Every*

Eurasian, Hapa, and Amerasian in the World, http://eaworld.proboards.com/; *Everything Eurasian*, www.everythingeurasian.com/.

11. See *The Largest Eurasian Nation Meet Up Group* by Charles Stewart Lee, Ryan William, and Raymond Fadli, *Eurasian Nation*, www.facebook.com /events/191890000861608/.

12. Wendy Wang, "The Rise of Intermarriage: Rates, Characteristics Vary by Race and Gender," Pew Research Center for Social and Demographic Trends (Washington, D.C.: Pew Research Center, February 16, 2012), 2.

13. See Andrea Louie, "Pandas, Lions, and Dragons, Oh My!: How White Adoptive Parents Construct Chineseness," *Journal of Asian American Studies* 12.3 (October 2009): 285–320.

14. Hsu Cho-yun, "A Reflection on Marginality," in *The Living Tree: The Changing Meaning of Being Chinese Today*, ed. Tu Wei-ming (Stanford, CA: Stanford University Press, 1994), 239.

15. See Jonathan N. Lipman, "Hyphenated Chinese: Sino-Muslim Identity in Modern China," in *Remapping China: Fissures in Historical Terrain*, ed. Gail Hershatter et al. (Stanford, CA: Stanford University Press, 1996), 113–29.

16. See George Lipsitz, *The Possessive Investment in Whiteness: How White People Profit from Identity Politics* (Philadelphia: Temple University Press, 1998).

17. On the United States as a privileged sight of multiculturalism, see David Palumbo-Liu, *Asian/American: Historical Crossings of a Racial Frontier* (Stanford, CA: Stanford University Press, 1999), 206f.

18. Tu, *The Living Tree*, 13-14.

19. Ibid., 14.

20. Ibid., viii.

21. See James Farrer, "From 'Passports' to 'Joint Ventures': Intermarriage between Chinese Nationals and Western Expatriates Residing in Shanghai," *Asian Studies Review* 32 (March 2008): 7–29.

22. Sui Sin Far, "Leaves from the Mental Portfolio of an Eurasian," *Independent* 66 (January 21, 1909), 132.

Glossary of Chinese Personal Names and Terms

Aomen tusheng 澳門土生
Ba Meiguo liuxuesheng ganfu 罷美國留學生感賦
bai 白
bushou fudao 不守婦道
Chan Fook Hing/Chen Fuxing 陳福興
Chan Hong Key/Chen Kangqu 陳康衢
Chan Kai-ming/Chen Qiming 陳啟明
Chan Lai Kau/Chen Liqiu 陳麗球
Chen Fang (Afong) 陳芳
Chen Jitong 陳季同
Chen Lanbin 陳蘭彬
Chen Tianhua 陳天華
Chen Xiru 陳席儒
Cheung Ching-Yung/Zhang Jingrong 張靜蓉
Cheung Tak Fai/Zhang Dehui 張德輝
Chiang Kai-shek/Jiang Jieshi 蔣介石
Chiu Yuen/Zhaoyuan 昭遠
Chun Wing-sen/Chen Yongshan 陳永善
Chung Sai Yat Po/Zhongxi ribao 中西日報
Datong 大同
Datong shu 大同書
Der Ling/Deling 德齡
Dianshizhai huabao 點石齋畫報
Duowei Zhoukan 多維週刊
Eric Hotung/He Hongzhang 何鴻章
Fong See/Fang Si 方四
Fude Li 輔德里

guoji hunyin 國際婚姻
guojia 國家
guojia rentong 國家認同
gwei-jai/guizai 鬼仔
gwei-lo/guilao 鬼佬
Han Suyin 韓素音
Hanzhong 漢種
Hanzu 漢族
He Ailing 何艾齡
He Luo Shi Xian Cai, nü buyou jiawai 何羅施洗蔡, 女不憂嫁外
He Qizi 何奇姿
he renlei 合人類
He Zhang Lianjue 何張蓮覺
hehua 合化
Ho Fook/He Fu 何福
Ho Kam-chee/He Jinzi 何錦姿
Ho Kom-Tong/He Gantang 何甘棠
Ho Shai-lai/He Shili 何世禮
Ho Tung/He Dong 何東
Ho-lan-yan/Helanren 荷蘭人
Hsiang Hsien Cheng/Zheng Xiangxian 鄭湘先
Hua Tian 華天
Huang Tianfu/Ng Tiam Hock 黃添福
Huang Zunxian 黃遵憲
huangbai hezhong 黃白合種
Huaren 華人
Huayi 華裔
Huayi meiren 華裔美人
Huie Kin/Xu Qin 許芹
Hung Iu-chi/Hong Yaozhi 洪耀芝
Hung Iu-fan/Hong Yaoxun 洪耀勳
Hung Iu-kwong/Hong Yaoguang 洪耀光
Hung Kam Ning/Hong Jinning 洪錦寧
Hung Kam Shing/Hong Jincheng 洪錦城
Hung Kwok-chi/Hong Guozhi 洪國智
Hung Kwok-leung/Hong Guoliang 洪國樑
Hung Kwok-wah/Hong Guohua 洪國華
Hung Wan Chi/Hong Yinzhi 洪蘊芝
hunxue er 混血兒
jia 嫁
jiaji suiji, jiagou suigou 嫁雞隨雞 嫁狗隨狗
Jingshizhong 警世鐘
Kang Youwei 康有為
Kit Fat/faqi 髮妻
Kulangsu/Gulangyu 鼓浪嶼
Li Fang 李方
Li Fang yu Paierli lihun 李方與拍爾利離婚

Li Hongzhang 李鴻章
Li Jiaxin 李嘉欣
Liang Qichao 梁啟超
Mak Sau-Yin/Mai Xiuying 麥秀英
Man Kam Lo/Luo Wenjin 羅文錦
Mei de renshengguan 美的人生觀
Mei de shehui zuzhifa 美的社會組織法
meiren ji 美人計
Meiyi zhongguoren 美裔中國人
Ming-Heng Chao/Zhao Mingheng 趙敏恒
Mingshan youji 名山遊記
Mui Tsai/meizai 妹仔
Ng Akew/Wu Ajiao 吳阿嬌
Niehaihua 孽海花
Ouya hunxue 歐亞混血
pah-kwei/baigui 白鬼
Pan Guangdan 潘光旦
Qingbai leichao 清稗類鈔
Qingmo minchu hunyin shenghuozhong de xinchao 清末民初婚姻生活中的新潮
qu 娶
Rong Jinhuai 容覲槐
Rong Jintong 容覲彤
Sai Jinhua 賽金花
Shangguan Tianyi 上官天乙
Shenbao 申報
Shenghuo Zhoukan duzhexinxiang waiji 生活週刊讀者信箱外集
Shimu 師母
Sin Tak-fan/Xian Defen 洗德芬
Sui Sin Far 水仙花
Sun Yat-sen/Sun Zhongshan 孫中山
Sze Tai/Shi Di 施娣
Tai Yuk Ching/Dai Yuqing 戴玉清
Taiping 太平
Tang Caichang 唐才常
Tang Paohuang/Tang Baohuang 唐保璜
Tong A-chick/Tang Azhi 唐阿植
Tong Shao-yi/ Tang Shaoyi 唐紹儀
Tongren hui 同仁會
tongshengzi 通生子
tongzhong 同種, 通種
Tongzhong shuo 通種說
Tsai Ting Kan/Cai Tinggan 蔡廷幹
Wang Jingwei 汪精衛
Wang Tao 王韜
Wang Zhaojun 王昭君
wangben 忘本
wangguo 忘國

Wanmu caotang yigao waibian 萬木草堂遺稿外編
Wong Chin Foo/Wang Qingfu 王清福
Wong Kam-fuk/Huang Jinfu 黃金福
Wu Jingchao 吳景超
Wu Tingfang 伍廷芳
Wu Zideng 吳子登
Xiangbao 湘報
Xiangxue xinbao 湘學新報
xianhui 賢慧
Xie Hui 謝暉
Xing Long 行龍
Xiongnu 匈奴
Xu Ke 徐珂
Yan Phou Lee/Li Enfu 李恩富
Yang Fang 楊坊
yanqi zuguo 厭棄祖國
Yi Nai 易鼐
Yige Meiguoren jiayu yige Zhongguoren de zishu 一個美國人嫁與一個中國人
  的自述
Yiming xiaozhuan 佚名小傳
Yiyu xiantan 譯餘閒談
Yu Geng 裕庚
Yuan Shikai 袁世凱
Yung Kwai/Rong Kui 容揆
Yung Wing/Rong Hong 容閎
zajiao 雜交
zazhong 雜種
Zhang Binglin 章炳麟
Zhang Jingsheng 張競生
Zhang Lianjue 張蓮覺
Zhongguo liumei xuesheng yuebao 中國留美學生月報
Zhongguo renmin 中國人民
Zhongguo titan de bada hunxue er 中國體壇的八大混血兒
Zhongguo yi yiruo weiqiang shuo 中國宜以弱為強說
Zhongguoren 中國人
Zhonghua minzu 中華民族
Zhongwai ribao 中外日報
Zhou Guanghu 周光瑚
Zhou Jianren 周建人
Zhou Yingtong 周映彤
Zongli yamen 總理衙門
Zou Rong 鄒容
Zou Taofen 鄒韜奮
zuguo 祖國

Selected Bibliography

Alabaster, C. G. "Some Observations on Race Mixture in Hong-Kong." *Eugenics Review* 11 (1920): 247–48.

Anbinder, Tyler. *Five Points: The Nineteenth-Century New York City Neighborhood That Invented Tap Dance, Stole Elections and Became the World's Most Notorious Slum.* New York: Free Press, 2001.

Anderson, C. G. "Address to the Welfare League." In Eric Peter Ho, *The Welfare League (Tong Ren Hui): The Sixty Years: 1930–1990.* Hong Kong: Welfare League, 1990, 9–10.

Ang, Ien. *On Not Speaking Chinese: Living between Asia and the West.* New York: Routledge, 2001.

Ashcroft, Bill, et al., eds. *The Post-Colonial Studies Reader.* New York: Routledge, 1995.

Bald, Vivek. "Overlapping Diasporas, Multiracial Lives: South Asian Muslims in U.S. Communities of Color, 1880–1950." *Souls: A Critical Journal of Black Politics, Culture, and Society* 8.4 (2006): 3–18.

Barlow, Tani E., ed. *Formations of Colonial Modernity in East Asia.* Durham, NC: Duke University Press, 1997.

Beck, Louis J. *New York's Chinatown: An Historical Presentation of Its People and Places.* New York: Bohemia Publishing Company, 1898.

Bhabha, Homi K. *The Location of Culture.* New York: Routledge, 1994.

Birchall, Diana. *Onoto Watanna: The Story of Winnifred Eaton.* Chicago: University of Illinois Press, 2001.

Broca, Paul. *On the Phenomena of Hybridity in the Genus Homo,* ed. Charles Carter Blake. Publications of the Anthropological Society of London. London: Longman, Green, Longman, & Roberts, 1864.

Brown, Melissa J. *Is Taiwan Chinese? The Impact of Culture, Power, and Migration on Changing Identities.* Berkeley: University of California Press, 2004.

———. "On Becoming Chinese." In *Negotiating Ethnicities in China and Taiwan,* ed. Melissa J. Brown. Berkeley: Institute of East Asian Studies and University of California Berkeley, Center for Chinese Studies, 1996, 37–74.

Carroll, John M. *A Concise History of Hong Kong.* Lanham, MD: Rowman & Littlefield, 2007.

———. *Edge of Empires: Chinese Elites and British Colonials in Hong Kong.* Cambridge, MA: Harvard University Press, 2005.

Chamberlin, J. Edward, and Sander L. Gilman. *Degeneration: The Dark Side of Progress.* New York: Columbia University Press, 1985.

Chan, Sucheng. *Asian Americans: An Interpretive History.* Boston: Twayne, 1991.

Chang, Kornel. "Enforcing Transnational White Solidarity: Asian Migration and the Formation of the US-Canadian Boundary." *American Quarterly* 60.3 (September 2008): 671–96.

Chao, Thomas Ming-Heng. *Shadow Shapes: Memoirs of a Chinese Student in America.* Peking: T. M. C., 1928.

Chen, Jerome. *China and the West: Society and Culture, 1815–1937.* Bloomington: Indiana University Press, 1979.

Cheng, Irene. *Clara Ho Tung: A Hong Kong Lady, Her Family and Her Times.* Hong Kong: Chinese University of Hong Kong, 1976.

———. *Intercultural Reminiscences.* Hong Kong: Hong Kong Baptist University, 1997.

Chow, Kai-wing. "Narrating Nation, Race, and National Culture: Imagining the Hanzu Identity in Modern China." In *Constructing Nationhood in Modern East Asia,* ed. Kai-wing Chow, Kevin M. Doak, and Poshek Fu. Ann Arbor: University of Michigan Press, 2001, 47–84.

Chow, Rey, ed. *Modern Chinese Literary and Cultural Studies in the Age of Theory: Reimagining a Field.* Durham, NC: Duke University Press, 2001.

Chun, Allen. "Fuck Chineseness: On the Ambiguities of Ethnicity as Culture as Identity." *boundary 2,* 23.2 (1996): 111–38.

Chung, Yuehtsen Juliette. *Struggle for National Survival: Eugenics in Sino-Japanese Contexts, 1896–1945.* New York: Routledge, 2002.

Cooper, Eleanor, and William Liu. *Grace in China: An American Woman beyond the Great Wall, 1934–1974.* Montgomery, AL: Black Belt Press, 1999.

Cott, Nancy F. "Marriage and Women's Citizenship in the United States, 1830–1934." *American Historical Review* 103.5 (December 1998): 1440–74.

Crossley, Pamela Kyle. *A Translucent Mirror: History and Identity in Qing Imperial Ideology.* Berkeley: University of California Press, 1999.

DaCosta, Kimberly McClain. *Making Multiracials: State, Family, and Market in the Redrawing of the Color Line.* Stanford, CA: Stanford University Press, 2007.

Darwin, Charles. *The Descent of Man, and Selection in Relation to Sex.* New York: Appleton, 1898.

Denison, Thomas S. *Patsy O'Wang: An Irish Farce with a Chinese Mix-up.* Chicago: Denison, 1895.

Dikötter, Frank. *The Discourse of Race in Modern China.* Stanford, CA: Stanford University Press, 1992.

Dong Lin, ed. *Zhongguo guojifa* [Chinese nationality law]. Chongqing: Guomin tushu chubanshe, 1943.

Dover, Cedric. *Half-Caste*. London: Martin Secker & Warburg, 1937.

Drachsler, Julius. *Intermarriage in New York City: A Statistical Study of the Amalgamation of European Peoples*. New York: Columbia University, 1921.

Du Bois, W. E. B. *The Souls of Black Folk*. New York: Knopf, 1993.

Duara, Prasenjit. *Rescuing History from the Nation: Questioning Narratives of Modern China*. Chicago: University of Chicago Press, 1995.

Dye, Bob. *Merchant Prince of the Sandalwood Mountains: Afong and the Chinese in Hawaii*. Honolulu: University of Hawaii Press, 1997.

Eaton, Edith Maude (Sui Sin Far). "Half-Chinese Children: Those of American Mothers and Chinese Fathers." *Montréal Daily Star*, April 20, 1895, reprinted in *Mrs. Spring Fragrance and Other Writings*, ed. Amy Ling and Annette White-Parks. Urbana: University of Illinois Press, 1995, 187–91.

———. "Her Chinese Husband." *Independent* 69 (August 18, 1910), 358–61.

———. "Leaves from the Mental Portfolio of an Eurasian." *Independent* 66 (January 21, 1909), 125–32.

———. *Mrs. Spring Fragrance and Other Writings*, ed. Amy Ling and Annette White-Parks. Urbana: University of Illinois Press, 1995.

———. "The Persecution and Oppression of Me." *Independent* 71 (August 24, 1911), 421–26.

———. "Sui Sin Far, the Half Chinese Writer, Tells of Her Career." *Boston Globe*, May 5, 1912.

Ebrey, Patricia. "Surnames and Han Chinese Identity." In Melissa J. Brown, ed., *Negotiating Ethnicities in China and Taiwan*. Berkeley: Institute of East Asian Studies and University of California Berkeley, Center for Chinese Studies, 1996, 11–36.

Espiritu, Yen Le. "Possibilities of a Multiracial Asian America." In *The Sum of Our Parts: Mixed-Heritage Asian Americans*, ed. Teresa Williams-León and Cynthia L. Nakashima. Philadelphia: Temple University Press, 2001, 25–34.

Farrer, James. "From 'Passports' to 'Joint Ventures': Intermarriage between Chinese Nationals and Western Expatriates Residing in Shanghai." *Asian Studies Review* 32 (March 2008): 7–29.

Ferens, Dominika. *Edith and Winnifred Eaton: Chinatown Missions and Japanese Romances*. Chicago: University of Illinois Press, 2002.

Fogel, Joshua A., and Peter Zarrow, eds. *Imagining the People: Chinese Intellectuals and the Concept of Citizenship, 1890–1920*. Armonk, NY: M. E. Sharpe, 1997.

Fowler, David H. *Northern Attitudes towards Interracial Marriage: Legislation and Public Opinion in the Middle Atlantic and the States of the Old Northwest, 1780–1930*. New York: Garland, 1987.

Franking, Cecile M. *From Ink and Sandalwood*. Warrensburg, MO: Mid-America Press, 1998.

Franking, Holly. *Mae Franking's My Chinese Marriage: An Annotated Edition*. Austin: University of Texas Press, 1991.

Furedi, Frank. *The Silent War: Imperialism and the Changing Perception of Race*. New Brunswick, NJ: Rutgers University Press, 1998.

Gaunt, Mary. *A Broken Journey, Wanderings from the Hoang-Ho to the Island of Saghalien and the Upper Reaches of the Amur River.* Philadelphia: J. B. Lippincott, 1919.

Ghosh, Durba. *Sex and the Family in Colonial India: The Making of Empire.* New York: Cambridge University Press, 2006.

Gilfoyle, Timothy. *A Pickpocket's Tale: The Underworld of Nineteenth-Century New York.* New York: Norton, 2006.

———. "Staging the Criminal: *In the Tenderloin,* Freak Drama and the Criminal Celebrity." *Prospects: An Annual of American Cultural Studies* 30 (2005): 285–307.

Gittins, Jean. *Eastern Windows—Western Skies.* Hong Kong: South China Morning Post, 1969.

Goodman, Bryna. "Semi-Colonialism, Transnational Networks and News Flows in Early Republican Shanghai." *China Review* 4.1 (2004): 55–88.

Gulick, Sidney L. *Mixing the Races In Hawaii: A Study of the Coming Neo-Hawaiian American Race.* Honolulu: Hawaiian Board Book Rooms, 1937.

Hahn, Emily. *China to Me.* Garden City, NY: Doubleday, Doran & Company, 1944.

Hall, Peter. *In the Web.* Birkenhead: Appin Press, 2012 (first edition 1992).

Hamrin, Carol Lee, and Stacy Bieler, eds. *Salt and Light, vol. 2: More Lives of Faith That Shaped Modern China.* Eugene, OR: Wipf & Stock, 2010.

Han Suyin. *Birdless Summer: China, Autobiography, History.* New York: G. P. Putnam's Sons, 1968.

———. *The Crippled Tree: China, Autobiography, History.* New York: G. P. Putnam's Sons, 1965.

———. *A Mortal Flower: China, Autobiography, History.* New York: G. P. Putnam's Sons, 1965.

———. *My House Has Two Doors: China, Autobiography, History.* New York: G. P. Putnam's Sons, 1980.

———. *Phoenix Harvest: China: Autobiography, History.* Reading, UK: Triad Panther, 1985.

Haney López, Ian. *White by Law: The Legal Construction of Race.* New York: New York University Press, 1996.

Hao, Yen-p'ing. "The Compradors." In *The Thistle and the Jade: A Celebration of 150 Years of Jardine, Matheson and Company,* ed. Maggie Keswick. London: Octopus Books, 1982, 85–102.

Harrell, Stevan, ed. *Cultural Encounters on China's Ethnic Frontiers.* Seattle: University of Washington Press, 1995.

Hayter-Menzies, Grant. *Imperial Masquerade: The Legend of Princess Der Ling.* Hong Kong: Hong Kong University Press, 2008.

He Zhang Lianjue. *Mingshan youji* [Travelogues of famous mountains]. Hong Kong: Donglianjue yuan, 1934.

Ho, Eric Peter. *Times of Change: A Memoir of Hong Kong's Governance, 1950–1991.* Leiden: Brill, 2005.

———. *Tracing My Children's Lineage.* Hong Kong: University of Hong Kong, 2010.

————. *The Welfare League (Tong Ren Hui): The Sixty Years: 1930–1990.* Hong Kong: Welfare League, 1990.

Hopkins, Timothy. *The Kelloggs in the Old World and the New.* San Francisco: Sunset Press and Photo Engraving, 1903.

Huang Zunxian. *Renjinglu shicao jianzhu* [Poems from the hut in the human realm, annotated]. Shanghai: Shanghai guji chubanshe, 1981.

Hu-DeHart, Evelyn. "From Area Studies to Ethnic Studies: The Study of the Chinese Diaspora in Latin America." In *Asian Americans: Comparative and Global Perspectives*, ed. Shirley Hune et al. Pullman: Washington State University Press, 1991, 5–16.

Hu-DeHart, Evelyn, ed. *Across the Pacific: Asian Americans and Globalization.* Philadelphia: Temple University Press, 1999.

Huie Kin. *Reminiscences.* Peiping: San Yu Press, 1932.

Ifekwunigwe, Jayne O., ed *"Mixed Race" Studies: A Reader.* New York: Routledge, 2004.

Jayawardena, Kumari. *Erasure of the Euro-Asian: Recovering Early Radicalism and Feminism in South Asia.* Colombo, Sri Lanka: Social Scientists' Association, 2007.

Ji Hong. "Meiguo yimin kuazhongzu hunyin de lishi he xiankuang yanjiu" [Research on the history and contemporary situation of interracial marriage among immigrant Americans]. *Zhongguo zhengfa daxue xuebao* [*Journal of China University of Political Science and Law*] no. 3 (2008): 55–62.

Jian, Esther H. *British Girl, Chinese Wife.* Beijing: New World Press, 1985.

Jian, Esther H., Bodun Jian, and Junyu Zhang. *Yige Yingguo funü zai Zhongguo* [An Englishwoman in China]. Beijing: Huaxia chubanshe, 1997.

Kang Wenpei. *Kang Nanhai (Youwei) xiansheng nianpu xubian* [A supplement to a chronological biography of Mr. Kang Nanhai (Youwei)]. Taipei: Wenhai chubanshe, 1972.

Kang Youwei. *Datong shu* [*One World treatise*]. Beijing: Guji chubanshe, 1956.

————. *Kang Nanhai ziding nianpu* [Kang Nanhai's chronological autobiography]. Taipei: Wenhai Chubanshe, 1966.

————. *Wanmu caotang yigao waibian* [A collection of miscellaneous essays from the grass-roof house among ten-thousand trees]. Taipei: Chengwen chubanshe, 1978.

Karl, Rebecca E. *Staging the World: Chinese Nationalism at the Turn of the Twentieth Century.* Durham, NC: Duke University Press, 2002.

Karthikeyan, Hrishi, and Gabriel Chin. "Preserving Racial Identity: Population Patterns and the Application of Anti-Miscegenation Statutes to Asian Americans, 1910–1950." *Asian Law Journal* 9 (2002): 1–40.

Knox, Robert. *The Races of Men: A Philosophical Enquiry into the Influence of Race over the Destinies of Nations.* London: Henry Renshaw, 1862.

Kuhn, Philip A. *Chinese among Others: Emigration in Modern Times.* Lanham, MD: Rowman & Littlefield, 2008.

Kuno, Emma Fong. "My Oriental Husbands." *San Francisco Bulletin*, May 25-June 19, 1922.

LaFargue, Thomas E. *China's First Hundred: Educational Mission Students in the United States, 1872–1881*. Pullman: State College of Washington, 1942.

Lam, Tong. *A Passion for Facts: Social Surveys and the Construction of the Chinese Nation-State, 1900–1949*. Berkeley: University of California Press, 2011.

Lamson, Herbert Day. *The American Community in Shanghai*. PhD dissertation. Harvard University, 1935.

———. "The Eurasian in Shanghai." *American Journal of Sociology* 41.5 (1936): 642–48.

———. "Sino-American Miscegenation in Shanghai." *Social Forces* 14.4 (May 1936): 573-81.

———. *Social Pathology in China: A Sourcebook for the Study of Problems of Livelihood, Health, and the Family*. Shanghai: Commercial Press, 1934.

Lee, Robert G. *Orientals: Asian Americans in Popular Culture*. Philadelphia: Temple University Press, 1999.

Lee, Vicky. *Being Eurasian: Memories across Racial Divides*. Hong Kong: Hong Kong University Press, 2004.

Lethbridge, Henry. "Caste, Class, and Race in Hong Kong before the Japanese Occupation." In *Hong Kong: Stability and Change: A Collection of Essays*. New York: Oxford University Press, 1978, 163–88.

Li Mo. *Bainian jiating bianqian* [One hundred years of change in the family]. Nanjing: Jiangsu meishu chubanshe, 2000.

Liang Qichao. "Xindalu youji jielu" [Selected memoir of travels in the new world] in *Yinbingshi wenji* [Collected writings from an ice-drinker's studio]. Shanghai: Zhonghua shuju, 1926.

Lim, Shirley Geok-lin. "Immigration and Diaspora." In *An Interethnic Companion to Asian American Literature*, ed. King-Kok Cheung. New York: Cambridge University Press, 1997, 289–311.

———. "Sibling Hybridities: The Case of Edith Eaton/Sui Sin Far and Winnifred Eaton/Onoto Watanna." *Life Writing* 4.1 (2007): 81–99.

Lin Man-houng. "Overseas Chinese Merchants and Multiple Nationality: A Means for Reducing Commercial Risk (1895–1935)." *Modern Asian Studies* 35.4 (2001): 985–1009.

Lin Xi. "Wo suo zhidao de Han Suyin" [The Han Suyin I know]. *Dangdai wentan [Contemporary literature]* 9 (1982): 26–27.

Lin Zixun. *Zhongguo liuxue jiaoyu shi: yibasiqi zhi yijiuqiwu* [History of Chinese overseas education: 1847–1975]. Taipei: Huagang chuban, 1976.

Ling, Amy. "Yan Phou Lee on the Asian American Frontier." In *Re/Collecting Early Asian America*, ed. Josephine Lee, Imogene L. Lim, and Yuko Matsukawa. Philadelphia: Temple University Press, 2002, 273–87.

Liu, Frances Tse, Terese Tse Bartholomew, and Frances McDonald. *Ho Kom-Tong: A Man for All Seasons*. Hong Kong: Compradore House, 2003.

Lombroso, Cesare. *Criminal Man*, trans. Mary Gibson and Nicole Hahn Rafter. Durham, NC: Duke University Press, 2006.

Lou Tseng-Tsiang. *Souvenirs et Pensées*. Bruges: Desclée de Brouwer, 1945.

Louie, Andrea. *Chineseness across Borders: Renegotiating Chinese Identities in China and the United States*. Durham, NC: Duke University Press, 2004.

Lowe, Lisa. "Heterogeneity, Hybridity, Multiplicity: Marking Asian American Difference." *Diaspora* 1.1 (1991): 24–44.

Lowe, Pardee. "The Good Life in Chinatown." *Asia* (February 1937), 127–31.

———. "Mixed Marriage." *Asia* (January 1937), 7–10.

Lui, Mary Ting Yi. *The Chinatown Trunk Mystery: Murder, Miscegenation, and Other Dangerous Encounters In Turn-of-the-Century New York City.* Princeton, NJ: Princeton University Press, 2005.

Mao Haijian. *Cong jiawu dao wuxu: Kang Youwei "woshi" jianzhu* [From 1894 to 1898: an annotated edition of Kang Youwei's "my history"]. Beijing: Sanlian shudian, 2009.

McClellan, Roland Guy. *The Golden State: A History of the Region West of the Rocky Mountains.* Philadelphia: William Flint and Co., 1876.

McKeown, Adam. *Chinese Migrant Networks and Cultural Change: Peru, Chicago, Hawaii, 1900–1936.* Chicago: University of Chicago Press, 2001.

Moss, Frank. *The American Metropolis: Knickerbocker Days to the Present Time, New York City Life in All Its Various Phases,* vol. 3. New York: P.F. Collier, 1897.

Moss, Peter. *Bye-Bye Blackbird: An Anglo-Indian Memoir.* New York: iUniverse, 2004.

Mullaney, Thomas, et al., eds. *Critical Han Studies: The History, Representation, and Identity of China's Majority.* Berkeley: University of California Press, 2012.

Ngai, Mae. *Impossible Subjects: Illegal Aliens and the Making of Modern America.* Princeton, NJ: Princeton University Press, 2004.

———.*The Lucky Ones: One Family and the Extraordinary Invention of Chinese America.* New York: Houghton Mifflin Harcourt, 2010.

Niu Chuangping. *Jindai Zhongwai tiaoyue xuanxi* [Selection and analysis of contemporary Chinese-foreign treaties]. Beijing: Zhongguo fazhi chubanshe, 1998.

Norr, William. *Stories of Chinatown: Sketches from Life in the Chinese Colony of Mott, Pell and Doyers Streets.* New York: William Norr,1892.

Norris, Frank. *Frank Norris of "The Wave": Stories & Sketches from the San Francisco Weekly, 1893 to 1897.* San Francisco: Westgate Press, 1931.

"On Mixed Marriage." *China Critic* 3.9 (February1930): 196–97.

Ong, Aihwa. *Flexible Citizenship: The Cultural Logics of Transnationality.* Durham, NC: Duke University Press, 1999.

Palumbo-Liu, David. *Asian/American: Historical Crossings of a Racial Frontier.* Stanford, CA: Stanford University Press, 1999.

Park, Robert E. "Race Relations and Certain Frontiers." In *Race and Culture Contacts,* ed. E.B. Reuter. New York: McGraw-Hill, 1934, 57–85.

Parker, David, and Miri Song. *Rethinking Mixed Race.* London and Sterling, VA: Pluto Press, 2001.

Peggy Pascoe. *What Comes Naturally: Miscegenation Law and the Making of Race in America.* New York: Oxford University Press, 2009.

Perdue, Peter C. "Erasing the Empire, Re-racing the Nation: Racialism and Culturalism in Imperial China." In *Imperial Formations,* ed. Ann Laura Stoler, Carole McGranahan, and Peter C. Perdue. Santa Fe, NM: School for Advanced Research Press, 2007, 141–69.

Phelps, William Lyons. "Chinese Students in America." *Chinese Students' Monthly* 6:8 (June 10, 1911): 705–9.

Pomfret, David. "Raising Eurasia: Race, Class, and Age in French and British Colonies." *Comparative Studies in Society and History* 51.2 (2009): 314–43.

Pratt, Mary Louise. *Imperial Eyes: Travel Writing and Transculturation*. New York: Routledge, 1992.

Pritchard, J. C. *Researches into the Physical History of Mankind*. 4th ed., vol. 1. London: Sherwood, Gilbert, and Piper, 1851.

Qiu Jian. "Tade gen yongyuan zai Zhongguo—fang yingji nüzuojia Han Suyin nüshi" [Her roots remain always in China—interviewing British female author Ms. Han Suyin]. *Juece yu xinxi* [*Policy and news*] 2 (2000): 25–26.

Reuter, Edward Byron. "The Hybrid as a Sociological Type." *Publications of the American Sociological Society* 19 (1925): 59–68.

———. *The Mulatto in the United States: Including a Study of the Role of Mixed-Blood Races throughout the World*. New York: Negro Universities Press, 1969.

———. *Race Mixture: Studies in Intermarriage and Miscegenation*. New York: Whittlesey House, McGraw-Hill, 1931.

Rhoads, Edward J. M. *Stepping Forth into the World: The Chinese Educational Mission to the United States, 1872–81*. Hong Kong: Hong Kong University Press, 2011.

Root, Maria P. P., ed. *The Multiracial Experience: Racial Borders as the New Frontier*. Thousand Oaks, CA: Sage, 1996.

———. *Racially Mixed People in America*. Newbury Park, CA: Sage, 1992.

Ropp, Steven Masami. "Do Multiracial Subjects Really Challenge Race?: Mixed-Race Asians in the United States and the Caribbean." *Amerasia* 23.1 (1997): 1–17.

Rowe, William. *China's Last Empire: The Great Qing*. Cambridge, MA: Belknap Press of Harvard University Press, 2009.

Saada, Emmanuelle. *Empire's Children: Race, Filiation, and Citizenship in the French Colonies*. Chicago: University of Chicago Press, 2012.

Sakamoto, Hiroko. "The Cult of 'Love and Eugenics' in May Fourth Movement Discourse." *positions: east asia cultures critiques* 12.2 (2004): 329–76.

Schwartz, Shepard. "Mate-Selection among New York City's Chinese Males, 1931–38." *American Journal of Sociology* 56.6 (May 1951): 562–68.

See, Lisa. "The Funeral Banquet." In *Half-and-Half: Writers on Growing up Biracial and Bicultural*, ed. Claudine Chiawei O'Hearn. New York: Pantheon, 1998, 125–38.

———. *On Gold Mountain: The One-Hundred-Year Odyssey of My Chinese-American Family*. New York: Vintage, 1995.

Shah, Nayan. *Stranger Intimacy: Contesting Race, Sexuality, and the Law in the North American West*. Berkeley: University of California Press, 2011.

Shangguan Tianyi. "Zajiao hunxue zhen neng gailiang Zhongguo renzhong?" [Can mixed-blood hybrids *really* improve the Chinese race?]. *Duowei zhoukan* [*chinesenewsweek.com*], August 24, 2001. www.chinesenewsweek.com/65/Commentary/4870.html.

Sharfstein, Daniel J. "Crossing the Color Line: Racial Migration and the One-Drop Rule, 1600–1860." *Minnesota Law Review* 91 (2007): 592–656.

Shu Xincheng. *Jindai zhongguo liuxue shi* [History of modern Chinese overseas education]. Shanghai: Shanghai shudian, 1989.

Sinn, Elizabeth. *Power and Charity: The Early History of the Tung Wah Hospital, Hong Kong.* New York: Oxford University Press, 1989.

———. "Xin Xi Guxiang: A Study of Regional Associations as a Bonding Mechanism in the Chinese Diaspora. The Hong Kong Experience." *Modern Asian Studies* 31 (1997): 375–97.

Smith, Carl T. "Abandoned into Prosperity: Women on the Fringe of Expatriate Society." In *Merchants' Daughters: Women, Commerce, and Regional Culture in South China,* ed. Helen F. Siu. Hong Kong: Hong Kong University Press, 2010, 129–42.

———. *Chinese Christians: Elites, Middlemen, and the Church in Hong Kong.* Hong Kong: Hong Kong University Press, 2005.

———. "Ng Akew, One of Hong Kong's 'Protected' Women." *Chung Chi Bulletin* 46 (June 1969): 13–17.

———. "Protected Women in 19th-Century Hong Kong." In *Women and Chinese Patriarchy: Submission, Servitude and Escape,* ed. Maria Jaschok and Suzanne Miers. Hong Kong: Hong Kong University Press, 1994, 221–37.

Smith, Richard J., John K. Fairbank, and Katherine F. Bruner, eds. *Entering China's Service: Robert Hart's Journals, 1854–1863.* Cambridge, MA: Harvard University, Council on East Asian Studies, 1986.

———. *Robert Hart and China's Early Modernization: His Journals, 1863–1866.* Cambridge, MA: Harvard University, Council on East Asian Studies, 1991.

Sokolsky, George. "My Mixed Marriage: A Jewish-Chinese Union." *Atlantic Monthly,* August 1933, 137–46.

Sollors, Werner. *Beyond Ethnicity: Consent and Descent in American Culture.* New York: Oxford University Press, 1986.

———. "The Bluish Tinge in the Halfmoon; or, Fingernails as a Racial Sign." In *Neither Black nor White yet Both: Thematic Explorations of Interracial Literature.* New York: Oxford University Press, 1997, 142-61.

Sollors, Werner, ed. *Interracialism: Black-White Intermarriage in American History, Literature, and Law.* New York: Oxford University Press, 2000.

Spickard, Paul. "The Subject Is Mixed Race: The Boom in Biracial Biography." In *Rethinking "Mixed Race,"* ed. David Parker and Miri Song. London and Sterling, VA: Pluto Press, 2001, 76–98.

———. "What Must I Be? Asian Americans and the Question of Multiethnic Identity." *Amerasia* 23.1 (1997): 43–60.

———. "Who Is an Asian? Who Is a Pacific Islander? Monoracialism, Multiracial People, and Asian American Communities." In *The Sum of Our Parts: Mixed-Heritage Asian Americans,* ed. Teresa Williams-León and Cynthia L. Nakashima. Philadelphia: Temple University Press, 2001, 13–24.

Stepan, Nancy. *The Hour of Eugenics: Race, Gender, and Nation in Latin America.* Ithaca, NY: Cornell University Press, 1991.

———. *The Idea of Race in Science: Great Britain, 1800–1960.* New York: Macmillan, 1982.

Stokes, Gwenneth, and John P. Stokes. *Queen's College: Its History 1862–1987.* Hong Kong: Queen's College Old Boys' Association, 1987.

Stoler, Ann Laura. *Carnal Knowledge and Imperial Power: Race and the Intimate in Colonial Rule.* Berkeley: University of California Press, 2002.

———. "Rethinking Colonial Categories: European Communities and the Boundaries of Rule." *Comparative Studies in Society and History* 31 (1989): 134–61.

———. "Sexual Affronts and Racial Frontiers: European Identities and the Cultural Politics of Exclusion in Colonial Southeast Asia." In *Tensions of Empire: Colonial Cultures in a Bourgeois World,* ed. Frederick Cooper and Ann Laura Stoler. Berkeley: University of California Press, 1997, 198–237.

Stonequist, Everett V. *The Marginal Man: A Study in Personality and Culture Conflict.* New York: Russell & Russell, 1961.

Survey of Race Relations Records. Stanford, CA: Hoover Institution Archives, 1924–27.

Symons, Catherine Joyce. *Looking at the Stars: Memoirs of Catherine Joyce Symons.* Hong Kong: Pegasus, 1996.

Tang Caichang. *Tang Caichang ji* [Collected works of Tang Caichang]. Beijing: Zhonghua shuju, 1980.

Taylor, Thomas Griffith. *Environment and Race: A Study of the Evolution, Migration, Settlement and Status of the Races of Man.* London: Oxford University Press, 1927.

Tchen, John Kuo Wei. *New York before Chinatown: Orientalism and the Shaping of American Culture, 1776–1882.* Baltimore: Johns Hopkins University Press, 1999.

Thompson, Laurence G. *Ta T'ung Shu: The One World Philosophy of K'ang Yu-Wei.* London: George Allen and Unwin, 1958.

Trumbull, J.H. *The Memorial History of Hartford County, Connecticut, 1633–1884.* Boston: E.L. Osgood, 1886.

Tsu, Jing. *Failure, Nationalism, and Literature: The Making of Modern Chinese Identity, 1895–1937.* Stanford, CA: Stanford University Press, 2005.

Tu, Wei-ming, ed. *The Living Tree: The Changing Meaning of Being Chinese Today.* Stanford, CA: Stanford University Press, 1994.

Vogt, Carl. *Lectures on Man: His Place in Creation, and in the History of the Earth.* London: Longman, Green, Longman, and Roberts, 1864.

Volpp, Leti. "Divesting Citizenship: On Asian American History and the Loss of Citizenship through Marriage." *UCLA Law Review* 52 (2005): 405–83.

Wallace, Kenneth E., and Cedric Dover. *The Eurasian Problem, Constructively Approached.* Calcutta: Thacker, Spink and Co., 1930.

Wang Huanchen. *Liuxue jiaoyu: Zhongguo liuxue jiaoyu shiliao* [Overseas education: Historical sources relating to Chinese overseas education]. Taipei: Guoli bianyiguan, 1980.

Wang Huiqin. "Huajia yanzhong de Han Suyin" [Han Suyin in the artist's eyes]. *Yishu jie* [*Art world*] Z3 (1994): 20–21.

Wang Qisheng. *Zhongguo liuxuesheng de lishi guiji, 1872–1947* [The historical trace of Chinese students abroad, 1872–1947]. Wuhan: Hubei jiaoyu chubanshe, 1992.

Wang Xingyuan. "Han Suyin de Zhongguo qingjie" [Han Suyin's obsession with China]. *Zhongzhou tongzhan* [*The United Front of Henan*] 12 (1997): 40.

Wang Yanwei, ed. *Qingji waijiao shiliao* [Historical sources relating to the foreign relations of the Qing dynasty], vol. 1. Taipei: Wenhai chubanshe, 1963.

Wang, Ling-chi. "The Structure of Dual Domination: Toward a Paradigm for the Study of the Chinese Diaspora in the U.S." *Amerasia* 21.1–2 (1995): 149–69.

Wang, Ling-chi, and Wang Gungwu, eds. *The Chinese Diaspora: Selected Essays*. Singapore: Times Academic Press, 1998.

Wang, Wendy. "The Rise of Intermarriage: Rates, Characteristics Vary by Race and Gender." Pew Research Center for Social and Demographic Trends. Washington, DC: Pew Research Center, February 16, 2012.

Watson, James L. *Emigration and the Chinese Lineage: The Mans in Hong Kong and London*. Berkeley: University of California Press, 1975.

White, Robin M. "Hong Kong, Nationality and the British Empire: Historical Doubts and Confusions on the Status of the Inhabitants." *Hong Kong Law Journal* 19 (1989): 10–41.

White-Parks, Annette. *Sui Sin Far/Edith Maude Eaton: A Literary Biography*. Chicago: University of Illinois Press, 1995.

Williams-León, Teresa and Cynthia L. Nakashima, eds. *The Sum of Our Parts: Mixed-Heritage Asian Americans*. Philadelphia: Temple University Press, 2001.

Wong Chin Foo. "The Chinese in New York." *Cosmopolitan* 5 (August 1888): 297–311.

Wong, Josephine Lai-kuen. "The Eurasian Way of Being a Chinese Woman: Lady Clara Ho Tung and Buddhism in Prewar Hong Kong." In *Merchants' Daughters: Women, Commerce, and Regional Culture in South China*, ed. Helen F. Siu. Hong Kong: Hong Kong University Press, 2010, 143–64.

Wong, K. Scott. "The Transformation of Culture: Three Chinese Views of America." *American Quarterly* 48:2 (June 1996): 201–32.

Wong, Sau-ling. "Denationalization Reconsidered: Asian American Cultural Criticism at a Theoretical Crossroads." *Amerasia* 21:1 and 2 (1995): 1–28.

Wu Jingchao (Ching-Chao Wu). *Chinatowns: A Study of Symbiosis and Assimilation*. PhD dissertation. University of Chicago, 1928.

———. *Chinese Immigration in the Pacific Area*. MA thesis. University of Chicago, 1926.

———. "Zhong Mei tonghun de yanjiu" [Researches on Sino-American intermarriage]. In *Shenghuo wenxuan* [Selections from *Life*]. Shanghai: Shenghuo shudian, 1933.

Wu, Tingfang. *America, Through the Spectacles of an Oriental Diplomat*. New York: Stokes, 1914.

———. *Wu Tingfang ji* [Collected works of Wu Tingfang]. Beijing: Zhonghua shuju, 1993, 405–14.

Wu, William Franking. *The Yellow Peril: Chinese Americans in American Fiction, 1850–1940*. Hamden, CT: Archon, 1982.

Wu, William Q. *Monsoon Season: An Autobiography*. Las Vegas: UniStar, 1996.

Xing Long. "Qingmo minchu hunyin shenghuozhong de xinchao" [New trends in marriage during the late Qing and early Republican era]. *Jindaishi yanjiu* [*Contemporary historical studies*] 3.63 (May 1991): 168–83.

Xiong Yuezhi. "Interracial Marriage and Half-Breed in Modern Shanghai." *Journal of Shanghai University* [*Social Sciences*] 17.4 (2010): 17–26.

Xu Ke. *Qingbai leichao* [A classified compendium of Qing anecdotes]. Shanghai: Shangwu, 1928.

Ye Junjian. "Zhongguo shi ta ganqing jituo de suozai—ji zhuming yingji zuojia Han Suyin" [China is the foundation of her emotional sustenance—on the famous British author Han Suyin]. *Yanhuang chunqiu [Yanhuang spring and autumn]* 7 (1994): 56-59.

Yeo, Florence. *My Memories.* Speldhurst, Kent, UK: Words & Images, 1994.

Yi Nai. "Zhongguo yi yiruo weiqiang shuo" [China should take its weakness for strength]. *Xiangbao leicuan* [Classified compilation of articles from the *Xiangbao*], vol. 1. Taipei: Taiwan datong shuju, 1968, 18–24.

Young, Robert J.C. *Colonial Desire: Hybridity in Theory, Culture, and Race.* New York: Routledge, 1995.

Yu, Henry. *Thinking Orientals: Migration, Contact, and Exoticism in Modern America.* New York: Oxford University Press, 2001.

Yung Wing. *My Life in China and America.* New York: H. Holt and Co., 1909.

Yung, Bartlett G. "'Drumming' Revolutionary China." *The World's Work* (March and April, 1914): 533–39, 690–98.

———. "The Water Supply of Greater Shanghai." *Journal of the Association of Chinese and American Engineers* 11 (1930): 31–37.

Zarrow, Peter Gue. "Introduction: Citizenship in China and the West." In *Imagining the People: Chinese Intellectuals and the Concept of Citizenship, 1890–1920,* ed. Peter Gue Zarrow and Joshua A. Fogel. Armonk, NY: M.E. Sharpe, 1997, 3–38.

Zhang Jingsheng. *Zhang Jingsheng wenji* [Collected writings of Zhang Jingsheng]. Guangzhou: Guangzhou chubanshe, 1998.

Zhang Zhiben and Lin Jidong, eds. *Zuixin liufa quanshu* [The newest complete book of six legal codes]. Taipei: Da Zhongguo tushu gongsi, 1987.

Zheng Hongtai and Wong Siu-lun. *Hejia nüzi: sandai funü chuanqi* [The women of the Ho family: the remarkable story of three generations of women]. Hong Kong: Joint Publishing Company, 2010.

———. *Xianggang dalao: He Dong* [The grand old man of Hong Kong: Ho Tung]. Hong Kong: Joint Publishing Company, 2007.

———. *Xianggang jiangjun: He Shili* [A Hong Kong general: He Shili]. Hong Kong: Joint Publishing Company, 2008.

Zhu Jiongqiang. "Zai Ruishi fang Han Suyin" [Interviewing Han Suyin in Switzerland]. *Wenhua jiaoliu [Cultural exchange]* 6 (2003): 12–13.

Zou Taofen. *Yige Meiguoren jiayu yige Zhongguoren de zishu* [The memoir of an American woman who married a Chinese man]. Taipei: Longwen chubanshe, 1994.

———. *Yiyu xiantan* [Idle talk following translation]. Shanghai: Xuelin chubanshe, 2000.

Zou Taofen and Han Song. *Shenghuo zhoukan duzhe xinxiang waiji* [Letters to the editor of *Life Weekly* magazine, vols. 1 and 2]. Shanghai: Shenghuo shudian, 1933.

Index

Abesser, P., 234

Afong (Chen Fang), 42, 101, 104

Afong, Henrietta, 103

Afong, Toney (Chen Xiru), 101, 158, 288n92

Afong girls, 103–4

Alabaster, C. G., 198, 232, 240

Alarm Bells (Jingshizhong), 49–50

Alexander, James McKinney, 42

amalgamation: and Chinese immigration, 34–36, 97; and glorification of the Eurasian, 131, 256, 257; and "inferior races," 119, 129–30; promoted by Chinese intellectuals, 50, 119, 119–22, 122–23, 124–25, 130–31; as a response to Western imperialism, 113–14, 124–25, 130; in theories of racial mixing and assimilation, 10, 95–96, 99–100, 142. *See also* interracial marriage; hybridity; miscegenation

Amerasians, 5, 264n9

American Asiatic Association, 72–73

"American race," 33

American wives in China, 65–67; Wilder's report on, 66, 75, 276n84. *See also* Franking, Mae (Mae Watkins); See, Ticie Pruett (Letticie Pruett)

ancestor worship, 202, 204, 236

Anderson, Catherine (Hung Wan Chi), 205*fig.*, 227

Anderson, C. G. (Carl) (Hung Iu-chi): and Anti-Mui Tsai Society, 229, 243; birth

and education of, 224, 226; call for Eurasian unity and the Welfare League, 20, 222–23, 229–31, 234–35, 237, 242–43, 245; and Chinese surnames, 231, 233–34; marriage of, 227–29; during the Pacific War, 249

Anderson, Charles Graham Overbeck (Hung Kwok-chi), 226

Anderson, Donald, 225

Anderson, Henry Graham (Hung Kam Ning), 224, 225, 234

Anderson, John Graham, 224

Anderson, Joseph Overbeck (Hung Kwok-leung), 226, 227

Anderson, Joyce. *See* Symons, Joyce Anderson

Anderson, William Graham (Hung Kwok-wah), 226

Ang, Ien, xvii, 214

Ann Arbor Times, 60–61

anti-Chinese movement, 35–36. *See also* Chinese exclusion laws

anti-Christian sentiment, 49–50

anti-miscegenation laws: affecting Chinese, 32, 36, 60, 269n26; role in racializing Asian immigrants, 13; struck down in 1967, 251. *See also* miscegenation

Anti-Mui Tsai Society, 229, 243

Aomen tusheng (Macanese), 265n13

Appo, George Washington: autobiographical sketches of, 169, 175–76; birth of, 92–93;

Lightning Source UK Ltd.
Milton Keynes UK
UKHW032136190922
409103UK00003B/367